BJ

Intonation and Its Uses

INTONATION AND ITS USES

MELODY IN GRAMMAR AND DISCOURSE

Dwight Bolinger

Edward Arnold
A division of Hodder & Stoughton
LONDON   MELBOURNE   AUCKLAND

Typeset in 10 on 12 pt Palatino by G&S Typesetters, Austin, Texas. Printed
and bound in the United States of America for Edward Arnold, the educational, academic and medical publishing division of Hodder and Stoughton
Limited, 41 Bedford Square, London WC1B 3DQ by Braun-Brumfield, Ann
Arbor, Michigan.

To the memory of L.

And all that was.

Preface

This book is a companion to *Intonation and Its Parts* (Bolinger 1986) but it is not a sequel in the sense that familiarity with the earlier book is indispensable for understanding the main content of the later one. Such familiarity is helpful, but a good portion of the first volume was taken up with explaining elementary matters that can be gleaned, if needed by the present reader, from other sources. And much of the rest of that volume was devoted to describing and justifying the intonational shapes whose meanings, once the shapes are identified, are more or less self-evident. Furthermore the graphic system of representation makes fewest demands on the reader. Add to this the careful specification of context—as has been the aim here throughout—and the intonation much of the time comes clear without elaboration; that is, how what is to be said is said under those circumstances.

This frees us to focus on the flesh and take the skeleton for granted. We go from the outlines of the patterns to how they reveal themselves in society and what they do in communication. There is a dimension of variation: differences among speakers relate to age, sex, occupation, and above all to location in social and physical space. Variation is a test for the working principle that intonation, in however veiled a manner, is always a reflection of internal states. Do women use more "tentative" intonations because they are more unsure of themselves? Are some societies "more affable" or "more inhibited" than others? Are children "more spontaneous" than adults? If so, what appear to be arbitrary differences between one group or speaker and another may have deep roots in human psychology.

As for the work that intonation does as an instrument of communication, the leading question is how far conventionalization goes. Does intonation cease to be an expressive medium and become a symbolic one, disengaging itself completely from its ties to emotion? We know that at least some of the arbitrary uses of tone in tone languages took their origins from associations that were originally expressive. This is a resource always open to children, who may substitute an intonation for a distinction that is later transferred to something in morphology or syntax. An example was the "low pitch for negation" strategy recorded (*Intonation and Its Parts*, p. 389) for two child subjects. But such cases are transitory in English. The fundamental iconic nature of intonation reasserts itself, and—at least in the cases so far studied and set forth in Parts II and III here—the contrasts are better understood as manifestations of feeling than as formal signals in the domain of grammar and logic.

My thanks are due to many more people than there is space to mention, and I hope that my citations from their works may serve as recognition of my indebtedness to them. Six in particular have helped me not only by their published writings but in fairly extensive correspondence, which I pray I have not abused in these pages: Isamu Abe, Alan Cruttenden, Anne Cutler, Laurenţia Dascǎlu, Ines Loi Corvetto, and László Varga.

As with the volume that preceded this one, my gratitude must again be expressed to "my" editors at Stanford University Press, Karen Brown Davison and Shirley Taylor, for their proof of the finest professionalism, which consists in caring about, as well as for, the rough pages entrusted to them.

D.B.

Contents

PART III. INTONATION AND GRAMMAR: BELOW THE CLAUSE

PART IV. INTONATION AND LOGIC

Intonation and Its Uses

Introduction: The Universality of Affect—and a Review of Symbols

In *Intonation and Its Parts* (Bolinger 1986), intonation was described as a nonarbitrary, sound-symbolic system with intimate ties to facial expression and bodily gesture, and conveying, underneath it all, emotions and attitudes. The role of convention was not ignored: if human beings did not adapt their means of communication to the accidents of history and culture, those parts of it that respond to feelings would be the same everywhere, and we know that they are not. But interlanguage resemblances of sound and meaning are so far-reaching and so persistent in the face of the relative arbitrariness and unintelligibility of the words and structures of a language that one does not "know," that there must be a common basis somewhere. The present volume carries on with this assumption and undertakes to show that even when it interacts with such highly conventionalized areas as morphology and syntax, intonation manages to do what it does by continuing to be what it is, primarily a symptom of how we feel about what we say, or how we feel *when* we say.

Of late there has been growing support for the sort of universal code that we have been more or less taking for granted in the realm of prosody, particularly intonation. We had a foretaste in Ohala's (1983) "universal frequency code" whereby high pitches depict smallness, nearness, nonaggression, supplication, uncertainty, and attitudes generally associated with defenselessness, whereas low tones convey various forms of dominance, power, confidence, and finality. There is also evidence that moving in the *direction* of high or low suggests the effect of the terminal—thus a very high pitch serving as a springboard for a very low one is weighted on the low side (Ohala 1984: 4). What Morton (1986) calls "expressive sound symbolism" pervades much of animate nature. The Carolina wren "escapes from a hawk and appeases a mate, using relatively high pitched and tonal signals; it chases an intruder and rasps, growls, and grades chirts into low, harsh forms."

On another front there have come some neurological indications of the fundamental affectivity, as against grammaticality, of intonation. B. Shapiro and Danly (1985) tested right- and left-brain-damaged patients, along with control subjects, using a reading task on which the speakers were told to express 'statement,' 'question,' 'happiness,' and 'sadness.' It was hypothesized that if the question-statement opposition is grammatical rather than affective, it should not suffer from right-brain damage, whereas the happiness-sadness contrast should be more or less obliterated, obeying the generally accepted localization of affect in the right hemisphere. The results showed no significant difference—patients suffering from anterior and central right-hemispheric damage had "flat speech" on both dimensions, question-versus-statement and happy-versus-sad. (Posterior damage gave results that are not relevant here.) This accords with our predictions, that question versus statement as far as intonation is concerned is an affective matter (curiosity versus confidence etc.), not a "propositional" (grammatical) one.

Similar results were obtained for accent in another study (Weintraub et al. 1981). Right-hemisphere-damaged subjects had difficulty discriminating sentences with different locations of accent. This accords with our idea that accent is for power or interest—both affective.[1]

Showing the primacy of affect calls for proving that claims of some form of unmotivated dependency relationship are false or in need of modification. That has been the main agenda for this book. Among the older claims is the supposed dependency relation between intonation and questions: a "question intonation" is said to mark a syntactic type quite apart from attitudes of curiosity or suspense. One more recent claim has to do with a supposed "intonation of factuality," another tries to rescue "contrast" as a phenomenon distinct from other manifestations of emphasis. The connections between intonation and the rest of our communicative system that these notions are based on are real enough; the error consists in a failure to see that intonation, far from being an arbitrary component of some higher unit, is a reagent that produces the observed effects through its own inherent meanings. Most of the chapters that follow are case studies of such intersections between intonation and some aspect of syntax, morphology, or logic. Naturally, new claims continue to come over the horizon, and one must continually start over, in hopes that evidence for the autonomy of intonation will eventually reach critical mass.

It is not as if intonation and other parts of prosody (length, rhythm, intensity) offered no clue at all to the development of those parts of the audible signal that have acquired more or less fixed and arbitrary uses. We constantly poach the forest of wild meanings in order to im-

prove the strain of domestic ones. And by "we" one should understand "children, especially." Take the prosodic feature of LENGTH. A
family drives by a fairground where a circus is spread out, and one of
the passengers, a twelve-year-old, cries, "Look at the c-i-r-c-u-s!"—
lengthening the word (as she explains later) to make it last as long as
the car is still passing by. That same child might be one of those who,
when younger, found a way to pluralize nouns not by adding a plural
suffix (-s, -es) but by stretching them horizontally (length) and ver-
tically (pitch)—two beautifully iconic ways of expressing 'more' (well
preserved in adult speech in informal ways—try saying *He sighed about
it* as fast as you can comfortably say *He lied about it*). (See Camarata
1988.) This is a grammatical *potential* for intonation: added length =
plurality. But as long as bigger size is expressed by bigger sounds
(and the sound for four things is bigger than the sound for two), the
wild has not yet become tame, and the distinction is prosodic rather
than grammatical. A bigger thing produces a bigger feeling.

A few terms, and some symbols, will benefit from a quick review.
First, the distinction between INTONATION and ACCENT. *Intonation* is
the inclusive term, referring to all uses of fundamental pitch that reflect inner states. (It might be clearer to put this negatively: all uses
that are not associated with the arbitrary tone of a tone language like
Chinese or Mazatec.) *Accent* is intonation at the service of emphasis.
In the shapes of the profiles it makes certain syllables stand out in
varying degrees above others, revealing to our hearer how important
the words containing them are to us, and revealing also, by the buildup
of accents, how important the whole message is.

PROFILE A is an intonational configuration whose distinguishing feature is an abrupt fall *in* or *from* the syllable that is made to stand out by
the fall, the syllable marked with the accent in the following diagrams:

```
             hó                    pós          Just i
I want to go              It's im        sib       má
           me.                       le.        gine!
```

PROFILE B is marked by a jump up *to* the syllable that is made to
stand out by the jump, with any following unaccented syllables usually continuing with a gradual rise but often staying level or even falling slightly:

```
       that the best you can do?     that the best you can do?
Is                                Is
```

```
       that the best you can do?
Is
```

PROFILE C is the opposite of Profile A: it is marked by *down to* rather than *down from*:

```
It won't                           Does it
        bíte you.                          bíte?

Just
     léave it to
                Béaver.
```

PROFILE CA is low-high-low. The accented syllable may cover the entire movement, as in the emphatic pronunciation of *Yes!*,

```
      e
Yé
    es!
```

or only the start of the movement, as in

```
       ri              ly                    e
It's           It's              It's      v
     tér ble!       lóve                  ló l
                        y!                    y!
```

(Vowel letters are sometimes doubled to show the movement graphically.)

PROFILE AC is the same as A but with a rise or sustention after the fall:

```
   cáre                          mé        Not
Be                Don't look at            yó
     ful with it.                   ee!        uu!
```

PROFILE CB is to B what CA is to A, but limited to low-high-slither—instead of a continuous rise after the upward jump, the tail goes down very slightly:

```
          you do it.
I won't
          lét
```

It can also be compared to CA with the slither replacing the abrupt fall. The CB profile is rare in American English and Southern British, but is fairly common in other dialects and languages.

The accent marks are used in two ways. Over a word, the mark signifies that the syllable to which it is attached is accented, as in the examples above. But over the letter symbol for a profile, the acute accent marks which of two or more pitches is higher and the grave which one is lower. So the two contours

```
                  próm            héld
    héld                                        próm
I         him to his     isₑ.     I      him to his     isₑ.
```

are represented by A + Á and Á + A respectively, and

```
                        ó                 fóught them
    fóught them                                        ó
We                           We
              f_f.                              f_f.
```

are represented by B + Á and B + À.

Part I

VARIATION

1. Age and Sex

If intonation is a common fund of possibilities that each language both shares with all other languages and yet conventionalizes in its own way, *within* languages there are differences that depend on upbringing, social class, age, sex, and even, in the case of trained speakers, personal choice. Unfortunately, the differences have not been very well documented. Most descriptions lump everything together as "voice quality" or "tone of voice," and deal with intonation only impressionistically.

Nevertheless, one generalization seems to be true of English and probably of most other languages: that the intonational configurations of which speakers avail themselves are the same for everyone, and that the differences are in frequency and modulation. An exception to this is probably "speaking like a child," at a stage before the vocal apparatus has matured and the intonational repertory has been fully acquired.

For adults, it is more a matter of conscious or unconscious choice, of favoring some patterns over others and of preferences in how to perform them, the latter being the domain of gradient differences: prolonging an accent, leveling off instead of going higher or lower, realizing a drop within a syllable rather than after it, and so on. Variations of this sort help us to tell not only who is speaking but something about the class, age, sex, occupation, physical build, and home area of the speaker.

The sources of variation lie somewhere between two classic extremes, biology and socialization. Age lies close to the biological extreme. In the crudest sense, children sound like children because with their smaller vocal tract the frequencies and resonances differ from those of adults. Class and home area, on the other hand, reflect the influence of society; there is no genetic program for sounding aristocratic or Southern.

As for occupation, it is not only at the social end of the scale but also to some degree at a different level. Whereas the other factors are either already in place, genetically, or are acquired for the most part unconsciously, occupational differences result from conscious choice, and at their most distinctive are restricted to occupational transactions. The New Zealand auctioneer, for example, uses a high level drone in describing the items put up for bid, then switches to an A profile in which the accent comes out as a shout and the tail is level (tonal ending) for the bidding, and winds up with an end tune in the shape of a B + C contour with level C (stylized) tail as a warning that a deal is about to be struck (Kuiper and Haggo 1984). Street vendors in Japan have distinctive styles for the particular merchandise they hawk—the flower vendor uses a lyrical chant, the spice vendor twists his lips to suggest the flavor of his wares, a ladder salesman hops up in a melodic succession to suggest the rungs of his ladders, and, at one time, the sandal-mender announced himself in a doleful monotone (Abe 1979). As Abe points out, using the "Fantasy on London Street Cries" by the seventeenth-century British composer Orlando Gibbons as an example, such convergences of song and speech are a part of all ages and climes. It is something of a stretch, however, to call these cases *intonation* in a linguistic sense. Rather they are a hybrid of language and music. In the more sedate professions, to the extent that, for example, talking *as* a lawyer contributes to talking *like* a lawyer when speaking in a nonprofessional setting, we can say that one's speech is a clue to one's occupation. But little is known of this.

Variation from region to region is dialectal; it shades off into variation between language and language and may involve not only differences in how the common stock of patterns is modified but differences in how it is constituted. This will be dealt with in the next chapter.

There is yet another form of variation that would occupy us if the "higher" levels of language were our concern rather than prosody. In its distinctive sounds, lexicon, and syntax, Modern English differs from Old English much as it differs from Modern German. Variation between $time_1$ and $time_2$ is as important as variation between $place_1$ and $place_2$. Unfortunately, the written record, the only solid evidence we have of times past, tells us even less about prosody than about distinctive sounds; these at least were recorded in symbols that can be compared. But aside from the skimpy evidence of not always consistent word spacing[1] and punctuation, there is little to tell us about pauses and less to tell us about tunes. As for accent, something may eventually be learned by studying word order (in a "free" language such as Latin, especially) and the way it reflects highlighting for importance (focus).

For now, we concentrate on age and sex, the varieties that bear the deepest imprint of our biological heritage.

Age

Though our grasp of historical development in the larger sense is weak, more and more is being learned about time$_1$ and time$_2$ where children are concerned, history writ small with its biological beginnings and its social endings.

The infant cry is the earliest form of vocalization and it seems to be the same around the world. A twenty-year project by a team of physicians at the University of Helsinki established the universality of pain and hunger cries.[2] The cry is an attention-getter, an alarm signal necessary for survival (see Lieberman 1967). It has a typical rise-fall shape, which is later conventionalized as the most common of the intonation contours in the languages of the world.

But there is more to the nature side of the nature-nurture sequence than just that initial push from pain and hunger cries. Infants are programmed to interact with their mothers in a communicative scheme that precedes language and serves as an organizing base for it. And though it seems strange to think of adults as similarly programmed (since it involves a set of latent behaviors that are not activated, except in play, before the childbearing years), adults, and especially mothers, appear to be motivated in a complementary way toward their infants. Intonation is the main auditory channel at this stage, and it is important to look at how it develops in children not only because they are a population with a manner of speech that needs to be described but because it is the foundation of all that comes later. The intonation that passes between mother and infant is intonation writ large. As Fernald (1984) describes them, the contours are magnified, sharply delineated, repeated, preserved intact when transposed from key to key, and associated with transparent needs and impulses of parent and child—ideal conditions for study. And what we find is that although the requirements of adult language will weigh upon them, those childish shapes remain, usually compressed and often put to strange use, but with the same affective meanings that imbued them from the start. We will recognize that the reassuring nuance of low pitch is no coincidence when we note how mothers use low pitch to soothe an excited infant; and that the resemblances between languages are no coincidence either, if all this starts with genetic endowment.

At the same time, the endowment does not spring full blown from the womb. There is a sequence, and we must try to determine why some things come before others. And there are other changes from outside, as children acquire such complex noises as words and come to associate them with particular pitches. And there is manipulation: children may do certain things by genetic design, but they are clever enough to observe the effects on others and eventually do them deliberately. And they are expert mimics.

If intonation is affective to begin with and does not shed its affectivity even when conventionalized, one can surmise what things will come first. The universal shape of the cry associates it with the rise and fall of subglottal pressure on the one hand and of nervous tension on the other. This is the classic shape of Profile A: there is a peak at which the voice is most keyed up, and then trails off. And if the infant prolongs the peak there is still a high pitch associated with high excitement. It is sufficient to cut the configuration in half—that is, to stop phonation in the middle—in order to get a simpler, rising profile. Rise and rise-fall are the basic patterns wired into the child's own nervous system and vocal apparatus.

This leaves two main adult uses of fundamental pitch that one could expect might be delayed. The first is the ultimately nonaffective and arbitrary development of phonemic tone. A study of the phonology of a Mandarin Chinese infant, "M," shows that the development of the tones does indeed come later (Clumeck 1977). M was almost two years old before he made the first clear distinction of tones. Initially, from a little over a year to slightly less than a year and a half, his vowels were unpredictable but his fundamental frequency responded to his affective state. Non-falling pitches were used if M "wanted something or was eager to have something, or if he was having difficulty in doing something and needed someone else's help. . . . Falling pitches . . . were used to accompany an action that M had just performed, also if he had found or discovered something, or if he was simply content" (p. 46). For example, "While trying to attach toy train cars together, M was unsure of himself and asked for help, uttering [ẽʔẽʔẽʔ:] with a high pitch. When the train cars were attached, he said [iː] very contentedly and with high falling pitch" (p. 46). The identical behavior was observed by the author of this book in his own daughter, whose home language was English.

At the next stage (1;5 to 1;10) M invented three or four words with more or less fixed pitches, one of which, at high or rising pitch, was used "to express worry or anxiety or to get another person to act on something" (p. 47), the others to point out objects. One could say that there was now a sort of lexical tone, though it was still consistent with the earlier affective use. This stage merged with the next one, which was associated with the invented word *nono* meaning something like 'this thing,' given a falling pitch as M flipped through the pages of a catalog looking at various "this things," but on three occasions given a rising or high level pitch as he looked at an adult as if to ask *What is this?* The same use of falls for pointing out and rises for asking has been observed in English, American, and Thai children (p. 48). At the next stage, M began to assign a particular pitch to all his words, on the hypothesis, apparently, that words do "have" pitch, but there was no distinction among tones: every adult word being imitated was given a high tone (p. 49). At 1;11 the first distinctive use of tone appeared.

A similar sequence—first, innately programmed actions and only later deliberate conversational signals—has been observed in gesture, for example in the movement of the eyebrows (Ekman 1979). The emotional signals—for example, raising the eyebrows in real surprise—are universal, "if differences due to display rules and elicitors are taken into account" (p. 193). "They occur before language and before the emergence of symbolic processes." The emblems, or conversational signals, are learned, and come later. Charles Darwin "noted that the Dyaks of Borneo show affirmation with brow raise and negation with the lowering and drawing together of the brows, 'with a peculiar look from the eyes' " (Ekman, p. 189).

The tonal use of pitch might be thought of as "unnatural." It does not correspond to the child's initial genetic program (though the capacity for it may be programmed for later use) and therefore is delayed. A second candidate for delay is those uses of pitch that might be called anti-natural, a behavior of pitch that actually goes against the genetic program. We are in a speculative area here and the evidence is very slight, but what there is seems to be fairly persuasive. The natural direction for raised tension is raised pitch. Our voice goes up when we are aroused by fear, anger, excitement, or intense interest. The last of these, interest, is the criterion that can be used for the most widespread use of pitch in marking the important part of utterances once language has been sufficiently established for individual words to receive accents. But not all the accents used by adult speakers are up. In fact, reverse accents go in the opposite direction: they are "held down." It hardly seems likely that Profile C, for example, would ever precede A or B. And that is apparently the case. In a study of two infants, Galligan (1987) found that one of them did not begin using the falling-rising tone to any great extent in utterances that he directed to his mother until the fourth period of the study, when he was approaching a year and a half in age; and there were none at all in the first period, 0;10.8 to 0;11.7, though during that same time there were a good many instances of pitch *rise* directed to the mother. A tape recording of a Scottish boy at sixteen months showed no reverse accents, though there were plenty of high-pitched ones. At a little over four years the "held-down" patterns were represented by at least CA, and by a little over five there was an abundance of C's and AC's. Cruttenden (1982: 10) quotes Miller and Ervin (1964: 30) as noting that the children they studied were using fall-rise freely by 2;2, and adds that his own children were using it "relatively early for emphatic contrast, e.g. *That not ˅yours.*" In their study of five children aged 2;2 to 3;9, Allen et al. (1977) found that pitch obtrusions were mostly up.

But why should there be a delay here if, as Fernald and Simon (1984) point out,[3] mothers from the start use salient low pitches to soothe and comfort their infants? An example is the German *jaaaa* employed "to soothe restless infants," whose shape as revealed by the tracings (p. 107) is clearly a C profile with prolonged low-pitched accent and high tail. The answer would seem to be that the child is limited at first to his own reactions; it is not his place to comfort anyone, and the "up" of excitement is the earliest manifestation of pitch contrast, which is automatically transferred, when words enter the picture, to meanings that are exciting, hence are accented *up*. The realization that pitch can be obtruded down for certain purposes as well as up comes later, though not too much later, given the abundant modeling by adults and the imitative skills of the infant.

Another anti-natural phenomenon is the decoupling of pitch from intensity and length. Usually they go together: an accent is marked primarily by pitch, but duration and intensity tend to increase at the same time when the pitch direction is up. In a study of French two-year-olds (Allen 1983) it was found that they regularly coupled higher pitch with increased intensity. This is something that they are forced to unlearn later, since adult French requires that raised pitch at the end of the utterance must be accompanied by *lower* intensity.

The genetic program for intonation is no bar—even in children whose adult language will be English or French or some other language without phonemic tone—to the child's developing at some point its own temporary scheme of lexicalized or grammaticized tonal meanings, like M's up *nono*(?) and down *nono*(.). This is the great path of *linguistic* as opposed to gestural-affective development that eventually gives the child a mental library of thousands of contrasts based on formant frequencies and sequences of distinctive sounds, and accidental contrasts of pitch are easily caught up in it, even though the language may be one that does not permit them and they must ultimately be unlearned. An example is pitch as a sign of negation, of which there are at least three cases on record. Two are reported by Weeks (1982: 160–61). One of the two children involved, Leslie, used a steadily falling pitch for negation, which differed from her usual terminal fall on just the last syllable of the utterance. It is easy to see how Leslie might have reached the conclusion that this feature, more salient to her ear than the presence of some unaccented negative particle, was what carried the negative idea. (Compare the way we distinguish *can* from *can't*, more by the reduced vowel in *I c'n do it* than by the barely distinguishable *-t* of *can't*.) The reason is that adult speech tends to use lower pitches in negative statements, perhaps because negation is so often a form of contradiction and high pitch might seem rude. Thus in response to *I wonder if she means it*, a high (rude or surprised?) rise on *doesn't* is less likely than a similar (but enthusiastic?) rise on *does*:

```
     do
                          does
She                   She
    es.                       n't.
```

It is possible here to have uniform downmotion with the negative response,

```
She
   doesn't.
```

which is most unlikely with *She does*.

Weeks's other child, Jennifer, used rising pitch for negation, but the examples cited (p. 163) look like angry rejections, where the emotion, at least initially, could be the first step toward grammaticization.

When can we expect that a child will attain full command of the intonational resources of his language? Perhaps never. Learning continues indefinitely. In tests conducted with ten-year-olds, Cruttenden (1985) discovered that they were still unable to discriminate some of the more "local" or context-limited intonational meanings even though their grasp of the broader functions was adequate. The tests were administered to adults as well as to children, and involved such test items as

    (1) She might have `told me. ('indignation')
    (2) She `might have ,told me. ('doubt')

In this particular case the adults did well with (1), less well with (2), and the children did poorly on both. A similar test by Iannucci and Dodd (1980) involved pairs like

(3) Áll the rabbits aren't in their cages.

(4) Áll the rabbits aren't in their cages.

Subjects were shown sketches pointing up the distinction to be made, in this case a picture of rabbits, some caged and some uncaged for (3), and none caged for (4). With (4), all the subjects did well. With (3), the adult subjects scored 96 percent but the children even by age seven were still managing only 58 percent and those of kindergarten age scored only 38 percent. It appears that the children have not learned the knack of using intonation to "patch up" the misleading position of the negative so as to make *not-are* signify 'not-all.'

But how can we be sure that the children's failure is due to intonational immaturity? Let's imagine that the children in the (3)–(4) test find nothing unusual in a plaintive rather than a matter-of-fact intonation. The AC profile is often used in that way, though adults may tend to take it more as 'reservation.' Using exactly the same intonation as (3), we can have

(3') Áll the rabbits are out of their cages.

which is clearly the sense of (4), but spoken in a whiny tone; and the same can apply to (3) itself. In fact, this is true even without the whine if the AC is motivated in some other way, say by a condition: *If all the rabbits aren't in their cages, then somebody must have stolen the lot of them.* So the intonation proves nothing. The 4 percent of adults who got the "wrong" answer raises the suspicion that the children are sensitive to something that the adults have learned to overlook. But the most important point is that in order to prove that the children are *intonationally* deficient, we must use tests that are not loaded against them along some other dimension. All that (3) does, intonationally, is set up a contrast involving the lexical items on which the accent falls: *all* versus *some* or *none* in this naturally closed set of three quantifiers. To be intonationally deficient the child would need to have the same trouble getting the meaning of

Christopher
    likes   it!

when it suggests that maybe the other children don't. *All* versus *some* and *none* is on the same footing, intonationally, as *Christopher* versus *Paul* and *Dolores*.

A similar but more subtle problem plagues (1) and (2). Here the children are expected to react to a difference between two senses of *might*. To assess the effect of intonation, that other obstacle, the contrast between a "root" sense and an "epistemic" sense of the modal verb, needs to be tested separately: Do the children at this stage know the difference between (1') and (2')?—

> (1') It was possible-for-her to tell me (she had the power to tell me but did not exercise it).

> (2') It was possible for-her-to-tell-me (her telling me was within the realm of possibility but I don't remember whether the possibility was realized).

In addition, the fact that not even the adults did especially well with (2) tells us that the root sense is normal there too: once again the intonation is potentially plaintive, and one can complain plaintively as well as indignantly, and children—just as with (3)—could be more susceptible to that suggestion. To cap all this confusion, the sense appropriate to (2) is also appropriate to (1) in a context like *I know she didn't write me about it but she míght have tóld me (for all I know)*.[4]

The question that remains is whether the children's failure to take an intonation with which they may be perfectly familiar and apply it in a situation filled with miscues really constitutes an intonational failure. If the adults' skill consists, even partly, in having some form of lexicon-like storage in which construction and intonation and collocation are welded more or less firmly and are available for retrieval whole, then the children probably still have some learning to do. On the other hand, if the adults' skill is inferential—given the broader meaning of the intonation one can deduce the meaning of the gestalt in terms of what makes sense in the context—then the children may already have a fully developed awareness of the intonation, but they lack the experience of the world—maybe they have not met enough situations of injured huffiness such as would lead to the root modal in (1)—that makes the right deduction possible. Very likely Cruttenden is right, and learning continues, but in relation to a configuration of language—intonation, lexicon, syntax, gesture—much more complex than the simplistic grammatical contrasts suggested by the experiments and the conclusions drawn from them.

Another test conducted by Cruttenden (1974) makes a better case for a locutionary-intonational complex that is probably learned and stored whole, though it is easily reconstructable inferentially. The situation is so restricted and frequent—reports on football scores—that remembering the whole formula would be communicatively more efficient. Here is how he describes it in Cruttenden (1982):

As is well known, the reading of results involving two teams can often be done in such a way that the result can be anticipated before the score of the second team is actually read, e.g. ˋLiverpool two / ˋBirmingham . . . (the 'draw intonation'—hence the second score is also two). In my experiment boys aged 7 through 9 (almost all of whom were football fanatics) were asked to guess the second score when it was left out. At least 50% of boys aged 9 showed nothing approaching complete competence.

Cruttenden is quick to recognize that the intonational pattern is one that is "more generally used throughout the language," and in fact it is not unambiguous even here, because one could have the same in a context like

> Glasgow ʹsix, Edinburgh ˋtwo;
> Liverpool ʹfour, ˋBirmingham two.

In both cases the repeated *two* is 'nothing new.' The children may lack either the general principle or the stereotype.

Getting back to the earlier stages, we find that uncertainty also plagues the attempts to mark the line between emotional and purposive or grammatical intonation. There is general agreement that children do have what Pye (1983: 601) calls a "built-in tie between intonation and affective state." But sooner or later a child will make the connection between what comes out automatically as a result of some emotion or sensation, and its effect on others—and contrive to play it for what it is worth. (Otherwise there would be no cranky babies using attention-getting cries in order to get attention.) This may come about by role-playing or it may have some glimmering of intellectual choice and logical deduction; even as adults we may simulate the affect that brings forth the intonation rather than choose the intonation directly. In any case, the communicator is doing something intentionally.

Here is how Galligan (1987: 11) puts the question:

Towards the end of period two (1;1.2) there was some indication that Sebastian used rising tones purposely to get a response from mother. Partly because of mother's high responsiveness, purposive use of rising tones could not be definitely demonstrated until Sebastian was 1;3.10. At that age he repeated his utterance with pronounced rising tone if mother failed to respond fully to his initial rising utterance. On the other hand, mother consistently responded to rising utterances from the very first observation when Sebastian was 0;9.25, as if he wanted a response from her. It may be that mother's interpretation was correct and that Sebastian purposely used rising tones from a very early age to gain responses from her. The difficulty, of course, is the objective establishment of purposive use.

Here Galligan interprets the repetition with pronounced rising tone as guaranteeing that the transition to purposive use has been accomplished. While the fact of REPETITION certainly seems to prove something of the kind, the increment of pitch that goes along with it is not demonstrably purposive. The mother has not responded as expected, the child is thwarted, and the higher pitch may signify no more than impatience. And if we attribute *any* rise to the presence of wants unsatisfied—curiosity is as much an affect as contentment—purposiveness is indeed hard to establish.

On the other hand, Sebastian's later increasing use of falling-rising tones in utterances addressed to his mother—from 1;4.17 on—is a better indicator of purposive behavior, for the reasons noted above. It is surely a learned intonation, and, as Galligan states (p. 10), its appearance "adds weight to the argument that Sebastian was purposely using rising tones to ask questions."[5] Galligan's other subject, Leslie, also produced a falling-rising example, at 1;2.15—again a likely indication that she was intentionally seeking a response. At 1;6 Leslie was repeatedly using fall-rise to ask whether a particular piece belonged at a particular place on a shape board (p. 14).

Galligan defines the grammatical use of intonation as the "combination of the same word with two different intonations" resulting in "different grammatical structures being assigned to the utterance" (p. 15). Though with the two children there were occasional manifestations at an earlier stage, the real onset was at about seventeen months. An earlier example on Sebastian's part was the use of the word *brush* with rising tone to ask if he could brush the doll's hair after touching it. Previously *brush* had occurred with level tone as a label of the object.

Clearly there is a step forward here, but is it a grammaticization of intonation? Have rising and level intonation been freed from the words to which they were previously fixed, to be henceforth attachable at will for a grammatical meaning, or has the word been liberated from its naming function and endowed with the additional status of verb, which can be asked about just as the object was asked about? The *grammatical* change here is what is usually referred to as "zero derivation." If Sebastian proceeded to convert nouns to verbs by keeping nouns level and putting a rise on the verb, that would be a grammaticization of intonation. But no evidence is offered for that. A rise continues to be used in those contexts about which the child is unsettled: prompts for identification, demands for goods, requests for permission, reassurance about correctness, and so on. If an old word with an old meaning that was attached to its appropriate intonation develops a new meaning that is appropriate to a different intonation, the new meaning will be attached to that intonation. The intonation means just what it meant before.

Galligan was trapped, as so many have been before her, by the linguists' fixation on questioning as a logical process rather than an affective one involving curiosity and suspense. She regards questions and statements as different *structures* because their "distinct intonations . . . indicate a meaning distinction *equivalent to* one made by the grammar of the language" (p. 1; emphasis supplied). This is no more justified than to call the exclamatory crescendo of *It's big!* grammatical because it is equivalent to the exclamatory syntax of *How big it is!* (where no crescendo is required). So long as a rising pitch conveys unfinished business—curiosity, pleading, suspense, however one wishes to characterize the affect—it cannot, with any assurance, be termed grammatical.

The empirical facts of course remain the same. What previously was a bond between a word and a pitch—a sort of lexical tone—is dissolved, and words contract new relationships with pitch and syntax. In this respect Galligan proves her thesis: intonation is already free of lexical bondage at the one-word stage, before "other indications of structure" come on the scene (p. 21). And if we want to *define* grammaticization as the point where a locutionary form "has a different meaning" according to what intonation it carries, that too is justifiable provided we recognize that constancy of affect and *degree* of conventionalization are factors of meaning. "A much broader conceptualization of meaning is necessary," says Fernald (1984: 24), "one that can accommodate affective associations, intentions, and motivations, as well as referential functions."

We come now to the accentual side of pitch, which poses its own set of problems. Since accent is relative, it is difficult to determine what if any significance it has before the two-word period—an intensifying function, perhaps, as children show heightened degrees of arousal about particular names of things or actions or qualities by exaggerating the prosody—length, volume, and pitch. This is usually abetted by adults, who present interesting things with the same interesting prosody—Fernald and Simon (1984: 108–9) found mothers using expanded contours 59 percent of the time when addressing their babies, but only 6 percent of the time when addressing other adults.

By the two-word period the stage is set for showing relative degrees of salience: what the child feels most keenly about is what will get the indicators of excitement, especially pitch. The result is that children quite early are able to pronounce "sentences" with normal patterns of accent. "Children operate with an appreciation of what is new . . . and stress accordingly" (Wieman 1975: 13). Primitively, arousal is the key, as it is elsewhere in the variations of pitch: "stress [= accent] is derived from intonation ontogenetically as well as historically," Pye concludes (1983: 601) in his study of Mayan children.

The essentially affective nature of early accent is supported by the research of Cutler and Swinney (1987), who found that younger children (around five or less) were able to produce utterances with natural-sounding accent patterns, but had greater difficulty than older children (around six or more) in interpreting utterances with those same patterns when produced by others. In reaction-time experiments the younger children did just as well, or poorly, with misplaced accents as with correctly placed ones. This seems strange—since we expect comprehension to precede production, not the reverse—until we consider that the child at that earlier stage is putting accents on what is most interesting and most exciting, a subjective reaction that involves no necessary intention, though some imitation may be involved in the way the feeling is expressed, given the mother's exaggerations. How to *use* prosodic information takes a little more figuring out.

At the same time, even the placement of accents can be disrupted if the child does not get proper feedback in the long run. This seems indicated by a study of children with normal hearing whose parents were deaf (Schiff and Ventry, 1976). The commonest single fault was in defective accent and intonation. Of eight children, six had problems with articulation and three with fluency (p. 353).

Sex

The biological differences between the sexes have come about by natural selection probably as a form of size-sound symbolism (see Bolinger 1986: 218–19). A higher pitch is associated with a smaller sound-producing object, one that is not a threat to the members of the same or other species and is therefore entitled to claim protection. This is literally the case with children, and to some extent it is the case also with women. Roughly speaking, the largest members of the group are male, and their voices have the lowest pitch. But this is not a sufficient differentiation, and in addition to his size the male also advertises his role of potential aggressor by means of a vocal mechanism that exaggerates the low frequencies: the boy's voice "changes" at puberty, as part of the overall reproductive cycle that also includes a spurt in growth and the onset of sexual potency. Though women's voices, like men's, reflect the difference in body size, they do not undergo the sex-specific change that lowers the pitch of their male counterparts'.

As if the biological polarization were not enough, both sexes cultivate the differences. Usually it is by exaggerating them—women enhance the "feminine" quality of their speech by exploiting the higher registers, though some female speakers do the opposite in order to sound more authoritative. Male speakers in many societies adopt a macho style by overusing the lower range of pitches. In Norway, at the Technical College of the University of Trondheim, "male students . . . adopt creaky voice during their period of study. Creaky voice becomes for them not just a feature marking the end of utterances as it is for many, but a permanent or semipermanent voice quality feature" (Foldvik 1981: 230). In Spanish, Peninsular males use creaky voice more than Mexican males do (Olsen 1975). The male stereotype is enhanced by the fact that creaky voice is often associated with authority: "qualities of know-how, factualness, expertise, reliability," and, in Edinburgh English, it is also associated with higher social class (Foldvik, pp. 230, 228).

There are other ways besides adopting a different register (with men it is creak, with women it is falsetto) that men can use to "try to talk as if they are bigger than they actually are" and women "as if they are smaller" (Sachs 1975: 154). One device is changing the formant structure of the vowels by altering the articulation, say by protruding the lips somewhat, to make the voice "deeper," or spreading the lips for the opposite effect. That some such skill has been acquired by children well before puberty is suggested by the fact that in one test when boys and girls of equal height and weight were compared, the boys produced vowels with markedly lower formants (Sachs, p. 156). Very young children already may tend to use lower-pitched vocalizations with fathers than with mothers (Lieberman 1967: 45).

So much for range, with male and female distinguished by low and high respectively, and each more or less constrained to make the difference larger than it would be if left merely to anatomy. What about pattern? Are certain profiles or contours preferred by one sex or the other? It is not likely that we shall find patterns exclusive to men or to women, but it is not hard—knowing what we know about the meanings of the contours—to imagine that women and men might have distinct preferences. If women have been more "subdued," would they tend to use subdued intonations, Profile C in particular, more than men do?

Hints on this point come from Edelsky (1979), in an experiment that asked men and women to say where they were born and what their favorite color was. The only sex-differentiated result that came out better than chance involved Profile C: "When questions to which only the addressees knew the answers were posed in an anonymous, impersonal speech event [this describes the experimental setup], addressees used one of four intonation patterns in their answers. Of these the falling terminal contour was used most frequently. The sex of both the subject and of the experimenter had only one effect on the pattern produced—a more frequent use of a rise-fall-rise contour when women responded to a female experimenter" (p. 27). (The example, 9 on p. 22, shows "rise-fall-rise" to be Profile C.) When subjects were asked to mark their impression of this contour on semantic-differential scales, "each sex heard its own sex as being more submissive, more incompetent, and less aggressive" (p. 26). It would have been interesting to know whether the experimenters in framing their requests themselves used a C profile, which is the normal thing in accosting questions and might have tended to prompt a C in the replies. What we need at this point is an experiment in which the sexes are tested for their intonation of wh questions, where A and C profiles have about equal chances of occurring and where authoritativeness versus submission provides a transparent contrast.

Edelsky's negative results (except for the difference just noted) in actual performance became positive in the *perceived* performance: though both male and female speakers used terminal rises and falls in roughly the same proportions, listeners nevertheless judged the rises to be more feminine and the falls to be more masculine. This of course may reflect expectations based on a wider range of utterances than the statement responses in this experiment. Fónagy (1969) in tests of Hungarian intonation found (p. 38) that wh questions "with a final rise were more frequent in women's pronunciation," adding that "the final rise gives the sentence a feminine nuance, the falling melody is felt to be more masculine."

The most incisive claims about male-female differences are those made by Brend (1975). Her observations about individual contours are probably in the main correct, as is her generalization that "most men have only three contrastive levels of intonation, while many women, at least, have four" (p. 86)—if we translate this simply to mean that the male range is more compressed than the female.[6] The actual configurations described by Brend are freely used by both men and women, and her diagrams of forms assigned to women alone differ only in their wider range, particularly in the feature of register: "Men . . . very rarely, if ever, use the highest level of pitch that women use" (p. 86), an obvious reference to falsetto. Where Brend claims that one or the other sex uses a particular pattern exclusively, it is likely that too much is being attributed to the contours as such. The contrast resides (apart from register and a female tendency to swoopiness) as much in the locutions as in the profile. Thus "the varying 'implication nonfinal' pattern in *I know he has gone*" with AC or CAC on *gone* tends "to be found solely in women's speech" (p. 86). But it depends on what the "implication" is. To give a note of warning, as in *He'd better try*, the shape is normal enough in male speech. An utterance such as *Oh, that's awful!* is already biased as feminine regardless of intonation. McConnell-Ginet (1983) properly emphasizes sex-influenced *variants* of general patterns rather than exclusive use of particular patterns by one sex or the other. The most important variants come under the general notion of "dynamism": female intonation tends to be wider in range, to use a greater variety of patterns, and to include a larger number of shifts within a given time span, than male intonation. McConnell-Ginet quotes Barrie Thorne to the effect that "there is evidence from male pathology that it's not some 'even keel' [that accounts for the male tendency to monotone] but a bottling up or repression" (p. 78). This is confirmed by M. Key (1975: 72) reporting an informal experiment: "A student of mine listened to children in the third, fourth, and fifth grades retell a story. The girls spoke with very expressive intonation, and the boys toned down the intonational features, even to the point of monotony, 'playing it cool.'"

McConnell-Ginet makes the important observation that there may be a connection between the female tendency to use sharply delineated contours and the traditional female role of dealing with young children "who are not yet socialized to attend reliably to verbal signals" (p. 83). We recall the "expanded contours" described by Fernald (1984), above.

To sum up, female speakers probably tend, more than men do, to (1) use a wider range including falsetto, (2) use inconclusive—i.e., rising terminal—endings, (3) favor reverse accents, and (4) increase the number of accents, hence profiles, in a given stretch of speech. Men tend to do the opposite, to which we can add to (1) that they are more apt to drop into the *lower* register change, namely creak.

Testing in all these areas has barely begun and many questions remain. What happens with yes-no questions—do men more often use terminal falls? Do women use more interior rises at pause points to allow the hearer to signal that he is paying attention? (This is frequent in U.S. Southern speech—see below, pp. 37–38.) At junctures between clauses, do the sexes differ in their preference for Profile B, Profile C, or Profile AC? Are women more inclined to use CA profiles where men would use A?—e.g.

female?   male?

```
      e                     Nev
Nev
                                e
    r!                          r !
```

How general is the supposed female preference for rising rather than
falling intonation? Lakoff (1973*b*) points out that women more than
men will turn a statement into a question; e.g., asked when dinner
will be served they will say *Six o'clock?*, implying 'Is that OK with
you?' Does this preference for a B over an A profile extend to *variants*
of the profiles? For example, do women prefer an A profile that is
risen to rather than fallen to?—

```
    female?                      male?

       should                Why
                                 should
Why
           I?                           I?
```

or a rising tail on a B profile rather than a falling one, as Brend implies?—e.g.

```
    female?                      male?

              im?                    know him?
             h
Do you know              Do you
```

Answers to these questions would go a long way toward establishing a feminine style, and would serve as a starting point for cross-
linguistic comparisons.

2. Dialect and Language

From one standpoint, the attention given to English in this book hardly justifies the promise of its title. From another, it is justified by the need to probe deeply into one language if all the subtle connections are to be traced.

Nevertheless, if there is truth in what we have assumed at every step—that intonation is the same, in spite of superficial differences, no matter where we find it, because of its ties to human physiology—then we must make at least a sampling of other languages to draw support from the likenesses and to try to explain the differences. There is no room for an exhaustive survey, but that is not a fatal defect because if two languages are highly similar in their main features and the link to emotion and gesture has been demonstrated for one, a similar link can be assumed for the other. It is hardly plausible, if questions of a particular type are characterized by a particular intonation because of the attitude they convey, that questions of the same type characterized by the same intonation in another language will be the way they are by chance or for some unrelated reason.

Most writers on individual languages who devote space to intonation incorporate their remarks in the general discussion of phonology, under the impression, inherited from a long tradition, that intonation is equally arbitrary in its connection with other parts or levels of language. Though no one any longer confuses tone and intonation—it is clearly understood that tone belongs in the system of phonemes (and tones in fact have in some cases been *derived* from phonemes)—the tonemic model influenced many to think that intonation ought to have similar ties to grammar, particularly syntax. And ties there are, though the problem is whether they are direct or inferred. It is the rare analyst who after describing a system that resembles English or some other previously analyzed language in every important respect actually points out the fact and asks why. The missing link is the one to gesture. No one doubts that there are characteristics of human movement, especially facial expression, that are specialized around certain meanings. Eventually we should have studies that assign intonation not primarily to grammar but to pragmatics. But meanwhile we have to make do with descriptions that try to establish the grammatical connection directly rather than to trace it through a layer of affect, attitude, and emotion.

Yet without some assumption of commonality, a comparison of languages would be little more than a collection of curiosities or coincidences. The commonality could be the universal structure of the human vocal apparatus. That—or a common origin about which we can do little more than speculate—is probably the basis for the widespread similarities among the distinctive sounds in all parts of the world. Languages with no plausible claim to common origin often have highly similar sound systems. The same must be true, up to a point, with fundamental pitch, which is constrained to go up, or down, or stay level, wherever it is found in human speech. But there is a difference. Whereas the rule is for words built up from the distinctive sounds not to suggest, by their structure, the meaning they convey, that degree of arbitrariness is not the rule in uses of fundamental pitch.

Again, tone languages are the exception, and traces are to be found elsewhere that resemble the arbitrariness of tone. A notable case is that of the "accent" languages of Scandinavia, such as Norwegian, which has a comparatively small number of word pairs distinguished only by not having the same "pitch accent," for example *bønder* 'farmers' and *bønner* 'peas' or 'prayers,' identical in pronunciation except for that feature (Fretheim 1984: 1). English makes a similar distinction in a few word pairs by stress alone, for example *mísfìt* 'a poor fit' and *mísfìt* 'social outcast,' but this distinction, though clear enough when the word is accented, tends to disappear when accent is removed. At the same time, English has some partially stereotyped uses of pitch that are reminiscent of tone languages (see Bolinger 1986: chap. 1), for example

(1) I⠀⠀⠀⠀⠀⠀⠀⠀⠀⠀⠀⠀⠀⠀⠀⠀⠀⠀se

se^e·⠀⠀⠀⠀⠀⠀⠀⠀(2) I⠀⠀⠀⠀⠀⠀⠀⠀⠀⠀e·

appropriate to 'I acquiesce' and 'I take exception' respectively. But these are not systematic and their meanings can be traced to other, broader tendencies. At the same time, such cases tell us something about how at least some tone languages may have evolved, with more diffuse intonational meanings specialized into more precise tonal ones.

So the arbitrary and the motivated or iconic are found everywhere mixed in varying degrees. Which we emphasize is partly a matter of taste and partly a matter of interpretation. After an incisive summary of differences in form and use of intonation, Gibbon (1981: 71) concludes that they "are not basically attitudinal at all but relatively conventional and arbitrary." The key word here is *relatively*. Suppose we have two communities one of which uses cleft constructions three-fourths of the time (*It was Jóhn who did it*) and the other uses a more straightforward syntax (*Jóhn did it*). This does not signify that the semantic difference between the two constructions has given way to a mere dialectal difference; both communities use both constructions— the difference is one of proportion, though striking enough to brand one community as "cleft speakers" and the other as "noncleft speakers." We must take account of differences, and of the confusion they sometimes cause, but at the same time it is best to consider the possibility that they stem not from underlying semantic distinctions but from the fact that not all communities share the same display rules. A false smile is still a smile.

There is arbitrariness in intonation, but it probably does not run very deep. It can easily happen that a "foreign" intonation (one that a native speaker might not be apt to use on a given occasion) may occur in the speech of a bilingual person and not even be noticed by those who speak the language natively (McCormack 1984). It is better to think of shifting zones of density in a generally smooth flow of traffic. (For conventionalization versus arbitrariness, a useful reference is Fónagy 1971–72.)

In what follows we shall be looking for both similarities and differences,[1] with a sharp eye to differences that may be only apparent. A logical place to start is with English itself, which like all other widely used languages has variants by region, sex, class, occupation, and other allegiances. The regional differences take first place, not only because they have been more generally studied but also because they are most like language-to-language differences. American English or Australian English thus compares with British English in roughly the same way that English as a whole compares with German.

British and American English

The thorough investigation of British-American differences is a task for the future; so far, we have only the occasional shrewd observation by an attentive listener, the practical comparisons in teaching manuals, and a few detailed probes into particular subtopics. Following are the differences most likely to strike the ear. Unless otherwise stated, British is represented by the Southern British variety—"Received Pronunciation" or RP—described by Jones (1956), and the American is what might be called the Network Standard.

1. Squares (American) versus swoops (British), with a wide range for the latter. Shakhbagova (1982: 51) notes that the way American intonologists have schematized intonation reflects pretty faithfully the angular turns of American English, and she illustrates with diagrams from an American textbook:

(3) <u>The situation is in</u>|to|<u>erable.</u>

(4) <u>Will you</u>|read it to me?

2. A greater proportion of high initial pitches for both questions and statements in British (compare Malone 1926 and Jones 1956: §§1041, 1042, 1057). The high initial pitches lead to more frequent and more extended falls (Watanabe 1978). Here is an example adapted from Jones (p. 294):

(5) Have
$$\text{y}_{\text{o}}{}_{\text{u}}\ _{\text{been}}\ \text{the}^{\text{re?}}$$

The swooping AC profile contrasts with the typical American angular upmotion with Profile B:

$$\text{you been the}^{\text{re?}}$$
(6) Have

3. A greater proportion of terminal rises in British. The rises may be the tails of C profiles or they may incorporate B profiles starting from a low pitch—there are more of the latter than there are in American, which gives British intonation a stronger lift at the end:

(7) Can you
$$^{\text{spare me}}\ _{\text{this}}\ \text{num}^{\text{ber?}} \qquad \text{(B+C+B)}$$

(8) Can you
$$^{\text{spare me this}}\ _{\text{num}}\text{ber?} \qquad \text{(B+C+C)}$$

The main accent in (7) is the final upmoving B; the C of (8) is normal in both varieties. The American preference may be for no accent at all; in (9) and (10) the word *rain* is understood from the real or implied question *When did it begin to rain?*

```
        hardly left the  ho
(9) We had                u
                           s
                            e
                              when it began to  rain·
```

```
        hardly left the ho
(10) We had              u
                          s
                           e
                             when it began to rain.
```

In (10), which is the American preference, *rain* is unaccented. Similarly with a parenthesis at the end of a sentence, which American English tends to play down completely, as in (12):

```
                  doctor every
(11) He had to have the        d
                                a
                                 y, he was so ill·
```

```
                        doc   every
(12) He had to have the    tor     d
                                    a
                                     y, he was so ill.
```

The same terminal B's are found where American English would prefer AC's for greater contrast. Thus in a sentence like *He's happy if he gets enough beer* (Malone 1926) the British speaker will tend to put a simple rise on *beer* whereas the American is more likely to use a rise-fall-rise, which gives the sentence a kind of but-not-otherwise ring. (See Bolinger 1986: 182 for the AC profile versus the B on a wider stage.)

4. A greater tendency in American English to use terminal C profiles only when the speaker is truly involved; this leads to starting the contour (normally B + C) at a higher pitch. British English makes more routine use of the C and starts out in a more relaxed manner. Sentences (13), (15), and (17) are examples of British contours from Coustenoble and Armstrong (1934: 46–47) matched with the less routine American alternatives, (14), (16), and (18):

```
      think she'll
(13) I            manage it.
```

```
(14) I think she'll
                   manage it.
```

```
         needn't get ex
(15) You              cited.
```

```
(16) You needn't get ex
                       cited.
```

(17) It won't
      bite you.

(18) It won't
      bite you.

5. A greater preference in British for A profiles in which the greater part of the downmotion occurs in the accented syllable and in the first following unaccented one if any. American English favors spreading it farther if there are more syllables following. The effect is to give the British style a more assured and positive ring. (See Bolinger 1986: 143–46 for the two forms of A.) The following British examples (from Watanabe 1977) show beginning and ending frequencies for each syllable plus the center frequency for the accented syllable:

(19) Nobody turned up.

310–340–290 150–150 120–110 140–110 110–100

(20) She should have been here ages ago.

220–240–200 135–95 95–80 100–80

The American values would tend to be more gradual. Coustenoble and Armstrong (pp. 175–78) associate this rapid drop with a pattern they call "contrast prominence," with the shape

(21) I'm delighted
      to see you.

Whether limited to the accented syllable or not, falls are more frequent and decisive in British English; the speaker gives the impression (to an American) of not merely reacting to the situation but controlling it. Here are some comparisons made by Shakhbagova (1982: 53–56):

American	British
(22) Then you've been married twice?	Then you've been married twice?
(23) You're feeling better.	You're feeling better.

```
                      se                           couldn't be
(24) He couldn't be                        He            s
                   e                                       e
                    n.                                      n.
```

A similar abrupt drop is common in British English before the accent
in a C profile, where American English is more apt to use a gradual
fall. The upmoving syllables *come in De-* in the British-style

```
                      come in De
(25) Can you
                           cember?
```

would tend to glide down in the American version.

On the whole, the impression the American gets from this variety
of British pronunciation is one of greater involvement (higher initial
pitches, wider intervals) and deference (more rising terminals), to the
point of exaggeration or affectation. Maria Schubiger, a longtime ob-
server of British intonation, notes an increase (from about 1934 to
about 1959) in the proportion of terminal rises (C or B profiles) in wh
questions, which she says "expresses greater regardfulness, a more
sympathetic attitude towards the interlocutor" (1959: 6). Jones is in
the same vein when he points out (1956: 294) that a command such as

```
(26) Come
          o
           n.
```

is normal addressed to a dog, but

```
(27) Come
          o
           n.
```

would be preferred for a person. This degree of solicitude is found
less in American English, where it may suggest that the speaker is
protesting too much, exerting himself to mask the opposite feeling.

Scottish English

Turning now to other dialect areas in the broad family of English,
we find in Scotland a comparatively low number—according to one
study of Edinburgh English (Kenworthy 1978) about a fourth—of
yes-no questions that have a terminal rise. Proportionately more have
a non-low fall after a high rise, for example

```
                       dif
                          ference?
                  ke a
(28) Does it make
```

This kind of tonal ending for questions is found in a great many languages (e.g. Russian, Sardinian—see below). To the Scottish ear it probably conveys less curiosity than a terminal rise, but it is nevertheless used in situations where the American speaker would favor the rise. G. Brown et al. (1980: 187–90) consider the two shapes to be in free variation and lump them together as "not low." With a deeper fall, according to Kenworthy (p. 273), the speaker is probably less ignorant of the facts. In at least one Scottish dialect, however, length is a factor: the farther the question is extended after the peak, the lower the tail goes (McClure 1980: 216).

As we might expect, those question types that in American English would tend to shift from terminal fall to terminal rise, or from a less pronounced rise to a more pronounced one, will show the same direction of shift in Scottish intonation. For example, the reclamatory question

(29) He'll be ar^{riv}ing $_{w}$h^{e}n?

'Tell me again when he will be arriving,' becomes, when spoken with astonishment,

(30) He'll be ar^{riv}ing $_{w}$h$^{en?}$

with only a very slight tendency to turn down at the end (McClure p. 210).

We thus have a situation that is predictable given a theory of gradience: Scottish intonation has the universal opposition between rise and fall, but the favored positions are farther toward the "fall" side than in American English. On the other hand, the more ceremonious C profile can be heard in Scottish as well as in Southern British and American English, e.g. in an invitation like

(31) Would you care for a sand$^{wich?}$

As far as wh questions are concerned, the Scottish variety is more like the American than the Southern British, in its tendency toward more nearly even peaks instead of disproportionately high initial pitches:

(32) How did you man age?

There is likely to be a tonal ending, not so low as in Southern British, and, unlike the usual thing in American English, a weak syllable before the final accent may carry the highest pitch of the last profile, as with the *a-* of *again* in (G. Brown et al., p. 185)

(33) Why are you do
                   ing
                       it all over
                                   again?

Anglo-Irish English

Other areas of Britain besides Scotland of course have their own typical characteristics. In part of the north of England we find a variety called Scouse, defined by Knowles (1984: 226) as "the dialect of Liverpool and Merseyside which arose in the nineteenth century as the result of large scale immigration from Ireland . . . and which remains an interesting hybrid of West Lancashire speech and Anglo-Irish." It has a number of characteristics that distinguish it from Southern British, whether in terms of restrictions or of mere tendencies. One is a preference for tails that remain relatively level, either high or low. Alan Cruttenden describes (pers. comm.) the high variety as "rise, plateau, slither"; unless the tail is fairly long, the terminal fall is so slight as to be barely detectable. So we find the following (adapted from Knowles, p. 239):

            l kinds of people go to it.
(34) it's l
           a

In our scheme of things this would be a CB profile with sagging tail. Similarly an example supplied by Cruttenden:

            ble album.
(35) It's a
        dou

The solution adopted by Knowles is that the level or sagging tail is essentially the same as the falling tail of Southern British, i.e., that it "counts" as a fall. And this makes the profile equivalent to CA, as in

            ble
(36) It's a
        dou   album.

But since the Scouse speaker is apparently free to use intonations like (36) also, and they are, according to Cruttenden, "more emphatic," it

remains to be decided whether the difference is due only to a gradation within a single profile or to there being two distinct profiles, with
some all-or-none shift from one to the other. Though American English scarcely favors CB, it does have all these possibilities.

The tendency toward a level tail that is low-pitched can be seen in
cases like (37), adapted from Knowles (p. 236):

(37) As we came round the corner of Commercial Road, —→
     a lady stepped off the side in front of the van —→
     and my husband swerved to avoid her...

The pitch on *Road, van,* and *-void her* gives a tonal ending for each
phrase but without the terminal rise that Southern British prefers.
Here it makes good sense to recognize a basic equivalence between
the terminal level and a terminal rise, with dialectal or situational
preferences. Either is quite normal in American English. (Has American English intonation perhaps been loosened up by its multifarious
background?)

A glance at the Anglo-Irish that gave rise to Scouse will help to explain some of the peculiarities just noted. The remarks to follow are
based on a conversation with a speaker from Belfast recorded by Eric
Jarman, and also in part on Jarman and Cruttenden (1976).

What immediately strikes the ear is that this speaker not once, in
the course of more than an hour's speaking, uses a terminal fall that
reaches below mid-level, and even this is infrequent. Almost all utterances, statements as well as questions, end either in a rise or in a
plateau (level or downtilted), the latter being the more usual. To the
American ear the effect is like constantly inserting 'y' know?' to suggest that what the speaker is saying is no big deal.

Adding to this impression is the fact that about three-fourths of the
accents are reverse accents (C or CB profiles by our reckoning), the A
profiles being reserved for special emphasis. The C or CB profiles at
the end of the utterance contribute to the offhand effect, and probably
help to account for the high terminals—after a reverse accent there is
no way to go but up. When the speaker does use a series of A profiles,
all but the ones that carry special emphasis are low-pitched, which
subdues things further, and the series tends to end with one or more
reverse accents rather than with A.

An emphatic A is generally followed by a C, as in

(38) Noth
     ing out stand ing.

(39) But I can't see really any ad$_{van}$tages in it.

But it may be followed by an A, though the A as just noted is apt in turn to be followed by a C. In (40) the contour is A + A + C + A, the final A having the typical plateau or slither as its tail:

(40) I quite like the i^{de}a of these $_{smal}$ler $^{cinemas.}$

By our reckoning, it would be just as practical to call the final A here a B with sagging tail. For the non-native ear it suggests the same lack of completion.

Yes-no questions level off to a plateau or a slither. If there are too few syllables to constitute a plateau, the question may sound like any ordinary one in American English:

(41) In $_{Lon}$$^{don?}$ (42) In our tests?

but with more syllables, the plateau or slither tends to declare itself:

(43) Did you see it?   (44) Have you seen the t$_{est}$?

and this may be true even with only one syllable, as in the surprised

(45) Did you not?

(Conceivably the profile in example 45 is equivalent to the high-pitched AC in American English that is common in surprised but somewhat incurious questions, e.g. *You did?* If so, the Irish simply omits the final slight rise of the tilde shape.)

A more fully planned question may take the shape that is common in Southern British, with its final C profile:

(46) Have ^{you} been to the uni$_{versity}$ $_{theater?}$

This too might develop its own slither if extended, e.g., by adding *these days*. Compare the plateau in

(47) This is in $_{Man}$chester is it?

There are too few wh questions in the text to make a generalization, but the C profile seems to be favored:

(48) Who   it?
        was

Jarman and Cruttenden illustrate the slither here:

(49) How on earth will you start about   alyzing all this stuff?
                                   an

The reclamatory question has the expected continuous rise:

(50) How many times did you say she wrote?

What remains to be settled is whether these differences reflect an unconscious attitudinal stance of some kind, or are purely mechanical—or are conventionalized somewhere between. The setting is that of a casual conversation. A broader affective range would tell us more.

In a wider sense, even a dialect apparently so deviant in its use of rises as Belfast English nevertheless conforms to the universal tendency to go down at the end, since rises at that point do not go as high as earlier rises (Cruttenden, pers. comm.).

Immigration from Belfast to the west of Scotland has led to a variety in and around Glasgow that resembles that of Scouse. Caroline Macafee (1983) points out the tendency toward C profiles at the end of statements, with resulting rising terminals, and summarizes as follows (p. 37):

Glasgow is intermediate between Edinburgh and Belfast (as described by Cruttenden, 1981), in that the local intonation pattern has both falls [A profiles] and low rises (from reversed peaks [= C profiles]) as the unmarked terminal of contour units, with the latter perhaps predominating for many speakers in casual styles. All three cities, however, share the prevailing use in English of a high rising terminal as a marked intonation, expressing "open" meanings.

The universal opposition of higher versus lower is thus maintained: a conclusive utterance may go up at the end, but an inconclusive one goes up more.

Southern U.S. English

Among varieties of English in the United States, there are characteristic differences especially between North and South. A trait that is associated with Southern speakers is the frequency of rising pitches in statements, both internally and at the end. Marvin Ching (1982: 96) quotes a passage from Terry Southern in which a female baton twirler at the University of Mississippi describes the problems with her costume:

> (51) Yessuh, I do. . . . Why, back home near Macon . . . Macon, Georgia? At Robert E. Lee High? . . . we've got these outfits with *tassels*! And a little red-and-gold skirt? . . . that, you know, sort of *flares out*? Well, now they're awful pretty, and of course they're *short* and everything, but I declare those tassels and that little skirt get in my way!

The importance of Ching's study is that it assigns a communicative purpose to what might otherwise be taken as a mechanical trait of a certain variety of English. Not all the junctures in statements are filled with rising pitches, even in Southern speech; and a similar though more sparing use of rising pitches is found in most varieties of American English. The problem then is to decide why they are used when the speaker obviously has a choice. The reason is pretty clearly a desire for feedback—something to reassure the speaker that the hearer is paying attention, that the proper level of interest is being maintained, that the message is getting across. What distinguishes the Southern speaker would then seem to be not the statistical frequency of rising pitches, but a greater desire for feedback and no inhibitions about showing it. The same trait has been noted for Australian English (Cruttenden, pers. comm.).[2]

In the discussion so far, the emphasis has been on differences. English is English. Resemblances are expected and hold less interest. When we turn to comparing languages rather than dialects our expectations change: Dutch is not "the same" as English, and we are conditioned to imagine that the intonation systems of the two languages are going to differ as much as anything else. This would mean that imposing Dutch intonation contours on an English utterance would be just as apt to make it unintelligible as imposing Dutch inflections on English verbs. Yet that does not happen. Such an experiment was actually performed (de Pijper 1983: 84) and the Dutch contours worked surprisingly well.

So it seems fair to set our sights on resemblances. If these shine through in spite of those other differences that make it hard or impossible to understand the intellectual-propositional content of a "foreign" utterance, then intonation would appear to be rather different from other aspects of phonology.

Unfortunately the cross-language comparisons of intonation are too few and too limited in detail to make it possible to do more than take a sampling in fairly general terms. There is only one intonational contrast—the one between questions and nonquestions—that has been examined in enough languages to permit a generalization that probably holds universally. In a series of studies covering 269 languages— Hermann (1942), Ultan (1969), and Bolinger (1978)—it was found that the average pitch in questions is higher than the average pitch in nonquestions. The favored means for achieving that high pitch is by a rise at the end, but the actual higher pitches may occur elsewhere, especially in an overall raising of the entire pattern. English has both possibilities. When saying something like *He got the maximum then* if the context is *They gave him five years.—He got the maximum then?—Yes,* the overall pitch will be higher than in *What did he get at the end of the first trial?—He got the maximum then. But later the appeals court reduced it,* even though the contour in both cases is identical. (There is nothing hard and fast about this. The "statement" could be higher if the speaker wants to convey surprise.)

Different languages play the averages differently. English favors the terminal rise, though not by a very wide margin, and the choice is connected with many variables (a study of upper-class Canadians— Séguinot 1979: 137—showed that males used the terminal rise only 53 percent of the time, while females did so 93 percent of the time); Swedish favors an overall higher pitch. An experiment by Hadding and Studdert-Kennedy (1964) presented artificially imposed intonation patterns to Swedish and American listeners who were told to judge them as questions or as statements. The Swedes tended to judge on the basis of overall pitch, the Americans on the basis of the terminal rise or its absence. If this were truly a *linguistic* difference, one would expect the result of the "wrong" choice to be an ambiguity or at worst something un-Swedish or un-English. But the overlap is so wide that the differences, such as they are, invite a nonlinguistic explanation: that the display rules in Swedish culture call for a little more reserve in the expression of curiosity. (We recall that for the Scottish speaker, whose yes-no question tends to have a terminal fall, the terminal rise is "more curious.")

But the important thing is that we are able to say that languages the world over tend to associate questions with higher pitch. If questions were a linguistic category rather than an attitudinal one, and high versus low pitch were the means of discriminating them, the choice of one or the other should be arbitrary and probably random from language to language.

Interesting as this universal tendency in questions may be, it is loose and rather vague, and it would be nice if we could discover cross-language similarities beyond the level of chance that reveal a finer attention to detail. There are many such, but our misfortune is that too few comparisons of more than two languages at a time have been made—even of these not a large number—and the evidence is scanty. (Some examples of one-to-one comparisons: Hungarian and English, Varga 1975; Japanese and English, Abe 1955; Swedish and Chinese, Gårding 1984; English and Serbo-Croatian, Browne and Nakić 1975. A more ambitious but still unfortunately sketchy account is Bolinger 1978.) Until more wide-ranging comparisons become available, we are limited to bits and pieces such as those in the remaining sections of this chapter.

One encouraging fact is that a careful look at specific intonations in English and what motivates them leads to hypotheses that can be spot-checked. If these hold up in random cases, and there are enough cases, then some sort of regularity must underlie the phenomena. One such area for testing is again that of questions. The Hermann-Ultan-Bolinger generalization is vague partly because it does not discriminate among subtypes of questions. On the basis of English—and anticipating a bit from Chapter 5—we can make the following predictions:

1. Yes-no questions will tend to rise at the end.
   (*Going somewhere?*)
2. Wh questions will tend to go down at the end.
   (*Who called?*)
3. Alternative questions will go down at the end.
   (*Is she coming or going?*)
4. Complementary questions will go up at the end.
   (*Your name? Your place of birth?*)
5. Reprise questions will go up at the end.
   (*What was that you just said? Am I coming?*)

The first prediction is the weakest, but the others are widely borne out. Cumulatively they overwhelm any idea that these intonations are basically arbitrary, especially since one can find solid discourse reasons for their being the way they are. A wh question is not purely a question—it assumes a fact to be true: *When did you stop beating your mother-in-law?* With an alternative question the speaker offers two or more choices, and the last one needs to be signaled as 'This is the end of my series,' so it goes down for the same reason that other "finished" utterances go down. A complementary question derives its very questionness from the fact that it is something unfinished—a proposed subject, for example, to which the hearer is to supply a predicate. And a reprise question is usually some form of repair—the speaker needs an immediate response in order to proceed, and tension builds accordingly.

Russian

In Russian there is a shape that resembles the one just described for Scottish English and for Scouse, a sort of Profile B except that it may contain a falling portion at the end as well as the more familiar continuous rise. The terminal fall makes it resemble CA, but the rise is the dominant part, and functionally the profile does much the same work as B in English. Like B it is used for questions, for continuations, and for statements of the obvious. For this last, compare

$$\text{(52) Because I } {}^{\text{had}} {}^{\text{to}^{\cdot}}$$

in answer to *Why did you do it?* Keijsper (1983: 127) here speaks of "the obviousness to everyone of some fact," quoting from Šustikova (1970). As in English, this counterpart of the B is not specifically interrogative. "Russian does not have a question intonation in a linguistic sense" (Keijsper, p. 127), but the B is encountered most frequently in yes-no questions (Odé 1986: 423).

Keijsper notes (pp. 122–23) another contrast that is strikingly like the one in English between an A profile approached from above (fall) and one approached from below (rise-fall).[3] The intonations are the same as in English, and the implications likewise. Say an adult has decided to read a story to a child. The child picks the story "Sneguročka," and the adult says *Sneguročka* with rise-fall. Then the adult starts reading, first announcing the title with simple fall,

(53) Snegu
    ${}^{\text{r}}{}_{\text{o}}{}^{\text{č}}{}_{\text{k}}{}_{\text{a.}}$

This would be the normal thing in English also, and the switch would cause the same effect in English: if on taking the book from the child's hands before starting to read the adult were to use the fall, it would suggest 'I would have known that you would choose *Sneguročka*, you always do'; and if the rise-fall were to be used to start the reading, it would suggest 'listen, what a surprise, here is *Sneguročka*.' The best way to appreciate this same contrast in English is with the formula that starts most bedtime stories and uses the simple fall:

(54) Once upon a time there was a little boy named Alex
                                                 ${}_{\text{ander.}}$

A rise-fall on *Alexander* would be unusual. (See below, p. 146.)

A third point of similarity is the occurrence in Russian of something closely akin to the use of a C profile in accosting questions in English (see Bolinger 1948). There is the same tendency to put the accent at the lowest pitch, as pointed out by Thore Pettersson (pers. comm.). An English example is

```
            this the way to
(55) Is
                   Elm street?
```

In Odé's material this profile occurs five times, twice on wh questions, where it carries the terminal accent (p. 424). Profile C, of course, is extremely common with this function in English.[4]

German

As might be expected from the historical connections, German and English are highly similar, and there is no need to go into details. But one point is of special interest because it has to do with the "functional load" of intonation. Even though the intonational means for conveying something may be available (and the means will tend to fit the meaning), the speaker does not have to use them: an intonation may suggest a question, but a change in word order can do so more definitely, and beginning the utterance with *I wonder if* will do the same. So it is to be expected that in any particular case where one language exploits the possibilities of intonation, another may use a change in syntax, a particle of some kind, or whatever.

An instance of this is the "modal particles" in German: words like *doch, eben, etwa, mal, aber, ja*, etc. In two influential articles (1965, 1980) Schubiger compares the use of the particles in German with the rise-fall intonation in English, which she describes as "an emotional variant of the fall" (1980: 279). It is, in fact, simply the A profile with a marked upglide. It may be at a relatively low pitch, as in

```
(56) What are you
                   P
                 u
             to here!
```

which German would render by *Was machen Sie da eigentlich?* with the particle *eigentlich* (1980: 289); or it may be at a relatively high pitch, as in

(57) s$^{o^{o^n}}$

er, if you can manage it.

answering the question *How soon do you want them? By Tuesday?*, which German renders using *noch*: *Noch früher, wenn du es einrichten kannst.* In this example we can see the very same shifting from one means to another within one language, because we have our own particle *even*, and when we use it we can play down the intonation somewhat, though we are almost as apt to retain it, perhaps focused on *even* itself:

(58) Even

     soon$_{e_{r}...}$

(59) E$^{e^{even}}$ soon$_{e_{r}...}$

How intonation waits ready in the background, regardless of the usual way of doing things, can be seen in the fact that German too can use it instead of the particles: "Attempts to convey the full content [of the message] without use of the particle result in substitution of gesture complexes or unusual intonation patterns" (Arndt 1960: 332).

Nor is English without its own array of particles, though they have only begun to be studied as a class. *Even* has been mentioned. Another instance is *well* (see Chapter 11), which can express a degree of tentativeness that may also be conveyed by a terminal rise. In response to *Is your paper done?* one may say either (60) or (61),

(60) Well,

         n$_{o.}$

(61) N^o

         $_{o^{o.}}$

to both of which the speaker will add something like *but I expect to have it ready by tomorrow.*

Dutch

The intonation of Dutch is a rich source of examples, thanks to the comparative work done by Gussenhoven (1983, 1985, 1987; see this volume, Chapter 14) and by de Pijper (1983). The intonation of Dutch is extremely close to that of English, down to much fine detail. But there are some apparent differences. Like German, Dutch has modal particles, and what Schubiger noted of German and English is also true of Dutch and English—intonation may do for one what a particle does for the other. In response to *Darling, we could never have made it* Gussenhoven's example 125 (1983) is appropriate,

(62) Oh, but we cóuld have!
(63) Ach, we hadden het wél kunnen halen.

where (62) puts a rise-fall on the auxiliary and Dutch inserts the particle *wel*. A small search, however, reveals the same particle in English, given a slight change in syntax:

(64) Oh, but we might wéll have!

The difference between the two languages may not be one of intonation at all but rather one of syntax, with the intonation in both languages striving to circumvent some fossilized construction. In the pair

(65) He has cycled for hóurs!
(66) Hij heeft uren gefíetst! (Gussenhoven 1983, ex. 66)

it looks as if English requires the main accent on *hours* whereas Dutch requires it on the equivalent of *cycled*. But if the syntax is adjusted slightly, English can have the same arrangement of accents as Dutch:

(67) The hours he's cýcled!

Actually both *hours* and *cycled* in English and their equivalents in Dutch are accented in either order, and the impression that the one in final position is "the" accented item is a reflection of climax.

Both English and Dutch can accent function words in utterances that are meant to rectify some preconception (counterpresuppositional utterances—see below, p. 366). For example, in response to *You're not bending back far enough!* one may say

(68) We can't bend back any farther thán this!

(69) We kunnen u niet verder tegemoet komen dán we dat al hebben gedaan! (Gussenhoven 1983, ex. 121)

'. . . than what we already have done.'

Apart from what is and what is not accented, there are also striking resemblances in the accent profiles. In the experiments of de Pijper (1983), Dutch intonation rules were applied to produce English configurations; they worked surprisingly well, from the standpoint of British English (pp. 84, 92). And since one of the main differences is in the wider range and number of movements in British English, which is lacking in Dutch, and American English differs from British in the same way, the resemblance between the two languages is even closer if Dutch is compared with American English.

Sardinian

A step farther away from English are the Romance languages, of which we will take a brief look at four: Sardinian, standard Italian, Romanian, and Spanish.

The remarks here are on Campidanese Sardinian, and follow notes kindly supplied by Ines Loi Corvetto. She distinguishes three tones, falling, rising, and level. The falling tone is essentially Profile A without initial rise, and has the same functions of statement, command, and the like. The level tone has the usual connective functions of a B profile. The rising tone is found on wh questions as well as yes-no (the syllables underlined are accented and correspond to the lines in the diagram):

(70) <u>Buffas</u> <u>bi</u>nu? 'Do you drink wine?'

(71) <u>Poi</u>ta te<u>le</u>fonara? 'Why does he telephone?'

The shape is that of CB but the function seems to be that of C, a reverse accent used for deference in asking a question, so that the nearest equivalent in American English would be

(72) D'you drink wi^{n}e?   (73) Why do$_e$s he telephone?

From a comparative standpoint the intonation in (70) and (71) is the most interesting because it is a further instance of the widespread interchangeability between a straight rise and a rise plus slither (as in Scots, Irish, and Russian above). The difference here between Sardinian and standard Italian is like the one noted above between Scouse and Southern British, or the one between the Russian spoken in Russia and the Russian of Russians who have lived abroad extensively and picked up a straight rise in place of their rise-plus-downtilt, as noted by Leed (1965: 72). In standard Italian there is the shape

(74) k$_w$a^n do?   'When?'

which is matched by Sardinian

(75) k^a^{n}du?

starting at a higher pitch. (The drop to -*du* may be slight or wide, with differences of attitude.)

The more obvious changes of mood can be seen in what happens when an utterance becomes ironic; (76), (77), and (78) all attach to the words *Bellu zɛzi*:

(76)   ╱.   ╱.
                   'Are you handsome?'

(77)   ╱.   ╲.
                   'You are handsome!' (pleased statement)

(78)   ╲.   ─.
               ('If you behave in that stupid way)
               you are nice (I don't think)!'

For (78), compare the English

(79) You're be_{au}_{ti}_{ful!}

with the same ironic meaning.

The most striking item in Loi Corvetto's inventory—offered as typically Sardinian—is (80) with its warning, set to the words *Kast*ja de *no* an*dai* a(m) *mari, la!* 'And see you don't go to the beach, la!':

(80)   ─ ·. ─.─. ╲.

The final syllable *la!* is "a sort of time-filling sound with a menacing tone." The speaker of American English is invited to imagine a Southern States speaker saying

(81) And ^{mind you don't go near the be_{ach, y'}} hear!

Italian

A glance at standard Italian ("educated Florentine") is revealing in what it shows about cross-dialectal differences sometimes being greater than cross-linguistic ones. As described by D'Eugenio (1976),[5] Italian is closer in some respects to American English than British English is. Most notably this has to do with the British tendency to maintain high pitches with abrupt falls, where Italian and American English use a more or less gradual descent (pp. 66–68). This is found with B + A contours,

Southern British   American and Italian

(82) I can't beli^{e}v$_e$ it!   (83) I can't ^{b}e$_{li}$^{e}v$_e$ it!

and also in B + C contours:

Southern British   American and Italian

(84) Is it so sur$_{si}$ng? pri   (85) Is it so sur pri$_s$^{i}ng?

The C profiles, favored for questions in Italian, have the same implications of restraint as in English: 'more polite,' 'personal involvement,' 'courteous elicitation.'

Romanian

Romanian is like Italian in its use of C profiles for questions, most strikingly when the main accent is emphasized, e.g.

(86) Cu$_{mi}$ne? = With me$\nearrow$?

(Dascălu 1979: 37–39). And Romanian is another of the languages that end a yes-no question with a fall when the phonetic conditions are right: the fall occurs unless the last word is accented on its final syllable or bears the main accent; in the latter case there is a continuous rise at the end (pp. 36–37). As in English, wh questions normally end in a fall, but—again as in English—echo questions and "reminder questions" are an exception. As in English, the echo tends to have a concave B profile with a terminal rise, the reminder a convex B profile with a downtilt:

(87) What was it you just said? (echo)

(88) Now what was I going to say? (reminder)

(Dascălu 1980). The reminder is spoken in a sort of musing way.

Another feature of Romanian intonation is the shape of parenthetical expressions (Dascălu 1974). For an English speaker, everything is familiar:

1. The parenthesis has, over all, a lower pitch.
2. The return to the main part of the utterance, i.e. the end of the parenthesis, tends to have a rise, but not a very high one. This ac-

cords with "declination"—the main part was already going down, so
there is less distance to climb in order to reach it.

3. The pitch range of the parenthesis is narrower than the overall
range.

4. The speed of utterance of the parenthesis is faster—as if the
speaker were under pressure to get back to the main business.

5. The speaker makes room for the parenthesis by widening the
overall range.

Spanish

In Spanish we find again the same basic accentual and intonational
shapes as in English. There is a stronger tendency toward lowering
the accents in the course of an utterance (Kvavik 1974: 355), so that
statements sound a bit more authoritative, and one profile, AC, is
rarely if ever encountered on a single syllable as so often happens in
English—e.g.

```
                        me
(89) Don't look  at
                    e e !
```

(The same restriction on AC is found in a number of European
languages.)

As in English, the profiles that fall and then rise with accent at a low
pitch (C, and B immediately following a trough) "are a civilized way
of asserting one's opinions without seeming abrupt or opinionated"
(Kvavik 1984: 180–81).

Spanish has the same emotive fronting that we find in English (cf.
Silva-Corvalán 1983: 133–37), as in

```
        thousand dol
(90) A
            lars it cost me!
```

Its geographical spread means that Spanish also has many dialectal
individualities, at least one of which, the "Speedy González" stereotype of Mexican Spanish, is familiar because it has been extended to
the English used by Chicanos (Penfield 1984). Contributing to it is the
Mexican tendency, when producing level tails at utterance end, to
pitch them relatively higher than they are in Castilian Spanish (Kvavik 1976: 412) or in American English, plus the tendency to use upward glides on accented syllables.

Chinese

There are obvious problems in trying to bring tone languages into the picture, because of the complicated overlap between intonation and phonemic tone. But it is wrong to exclude them on the theory that tone languages and intonation languages are separate and distinct classes. Abramson and Svastikula (1983: 144) say of tone languages that "Anyone with experience in speaking such a language . . . knows very well that the communicative use of sentence intonation seems to be as free as in non-tone languages." The trick is to unscramble the overlapping pitch variations in a running text. Since the early 1950's (see Samarin 1952), a great deal of progress has been made in separating the strands.

Chinese is the obvious example, and according to Gårding et al. (1983) it reveals some significant broad-scale similarities to the systems we have been looking at. I paraphrase their summary: a statement has a global fall over the final phrase, a question has a global rise; focus (main accent) is manifested by an upward obtrusion for high and rising tones, a downward for falling and dipping tones (these are the four phonemic tones); nonfocused material has a narrowed range, with what follows the focal accent narrowed more than what goes before; there is a change of direction when a new clause starts. The authors see these features as well-nigh universal (p. 59), and in Chinese the effect of the phonemic tones does not overpower them. In fact, in only one case as exemplified by Gårding's research (1985: 35) does a tonal pattern—the Chinese low tone—seem to perturb the global tendencies: in a succession of low tones, a local upturn at the end, rather than a general rise, signals 'question.' Among other similarities to nontonal languages is the tendency to have "much more fundamental frequency movement [before focus] than after focus" (p. 25)—the latter is what we see in the general flattening of contours after the main accent.

Xiao-nan Shen (1986) notes the following for Mandarin Chinese:

1. A tendency to rise at the beginning of the utterance, which affects all except the falling tone whose shape forces it to fall (p. 49).

2. Questions are marked by overall higher level, not specifically by terminal rise, although the tones that inherently rise rise higher in questions than in statements (p. 33). Wh and alternative questions are lowered toward the end almost the same as statements, but are higher to begin with and higher at the highest peak (p. 22).

3. Accent is manifested by widening the pitch range and by length-

ening; "rising tones rise higher and falling tones drift lower" (p. 53). The phonemic tones are more sharply distinctive.

4. In sentence-final syllables, the level (= high) tone "goes slightly downward with a falling terminal and upward with a rising terminal. The rising tone rises higher under a rising ending and lower under a falling ending. The falling tone drops deeper with a falling terminal and less deeply with a rising terminal" (p. 59).

It appears that tone does not afflict intonation with any fatal handicap. But in one case there may perhaps be real interference. If, as claimed by Gårding et al. above, a falling or a dipping tone is lowered for the mere fact of focus, then it would be difficult to use that lowering for a particular kind of focus, one signifying 'restraint,' which characterizes Profile C. At least one native speaker (Bingkun Hu of Fudan University) tried without success to produce this reverse accent.

Japanese

One of the most detailed comparisons we have is that of Isamu Abe (1955), comparing English and Japanese. Abe notes the following similarities:

1. Colorless statements fall.
2. Nonfinality is conveyed by a rise. This is found in declarative sentences used as questions and in tentative expressions like *Tabun* 'Probably.'
3. Straightforward commands fall, but commands may rise for courtesy.
4. Medial rising or raised pitch may denote something to come or may be a demand for attention.
5. Wh questions normally fall, but may use a C-type profile for courtesy or a terminal rise to call for repetition (reclamatory question).

Japanese is not as elaborately tonal as Chinese, but tone and intonation are accommodated in similar ways. For example, *ame* 'candy' has a rising tone, in contrast to *ame* 'rain.' Imposing a falling intonation on *ame* 'candy' results in an approximately level pitch—the 'fall' is there, but in disguise.

Polish

In a study of Polish questions (Petecka 1985) it was found that both major classes of questions, yes-no (whether in statement form or containing a particle marking it as a question) and wh, tended to rise at the end, yes-no going up farther than wh. The yes-no questions

mostly had C profiles: the main accent was at the lowest pitch. The
wh questions frequently had the main accent at the highest pitch—
presumably, with the final rise, this comes out as an AC profile. All
the statements in the test had the main accent at the highest pitch,
and a terminal fall. Except for the AC profile in wh questions, these
shapes are perfectly normal in American English (in English the AC is
normal enough in echo questions—see Bolinger 1986: 322—but tends
to be a bit too insistent for original questions). Other research on Polish questions cited in Petecka (p. 152) suggests that a terminal fall in
wh questions may also be normal.

So far, we have looked superficially at a variety of languages only
two of which are outside the family of Indo-European. For a somewhat closer inspection it will be useful to pick a couple of examples
from outside that family. Though it is always possible that diffusion
has been at work—intonation is probably at least as infectious as any
other part of language when speakers from different cultures come in
contact—there is a better chance of finding resemblances and differences that are due to the nature of intonation and not to borrowing, if
we compare languages of truly diverse origins. Our examples will be
Syrian Arabic, from the family of Semitic languages, and Hungarian,
a Finno-Ugric language, both at a respectable evolutionary distance
from English. The analysis of Syrian Arabic is by Ines Loi Corvetto
and that of Hungarian by László Varga.

Syrian Arabic

Loi Corvetto (1983) identifies three main profiles, which she labels
FALLING, RISING, and LEVEL. The first seems identical to our Profile A.
Its accented syllable is marked by an abrupt fall, and the preceding
unaccented syllables may approach the start of the fall from slightly
above or slightly below, with a tendency in either case to move uniformly up or down toward that position. Two typical diagrams are

(91)   ⌐\   arabii (p. 71)

(92)   )   alaⱩimin 'to the right' (p. 78)

Arabic apparently requires that the fall be carried out on the accented
syllable, without the variant that is possible in English, where the
drop may occur not on the accented syllable itself but in the interval
between that syllable and the following unaccented syllable (Bolinger
1986: 143–46). Of the two possibilities in English,

(93) He's a   so

            1

            dier.

(94) He's a   sol

                dier.

Arabic thus admits only the first. Loi Corvetto points out (pers. comm.) that (94) is a PHONETIC possibility when the accented syllable ends in a voiceless consonant, and this tends to be true in English as well, where we would say

(95) hop

        scotch

normally with no drop on the abrupt syllable *hop-*. But English has the option of lengthening that syllable, and the difference between a level accented syllable and a falling one then becomes apparent, with the semantic consequences noted in Bolinger (1986: 143–45).

The interpretations that Loi Corvetto gives the falling profile fit perfectly with those appropriate for Profile A. It signifies 'semantic completeness' (p. 108), and is used in assertions (whether or not grammatically complete), commands, exclamations, and certain types of greetings (p. 83).

The "rising" profile, which might be expected to match Profile B, actually seems closer to CB, as it requires a low-pitched onset for the accented syllable followed by a rise throughout that syllable, and with succeeding unaccented syllables on a downtilt:

(96)   `minal dʒaᵃmiˁah? 'from the university?' (p. 85)

(97)   kaifa haaluka? 'how are you?' (p. 86)

As these examples suggest, the profile is suited for wh as well as yes-no questions, and in this freedom with questions we see a resemblance to the English C profile, as it differs from C only in the direction of the tail. It very likely represents the same inhibition of the accent—as a courtesy device in questions—that is the case with C. In fact, Loi Corvetto's one-syllable examples, e.g. *man?* 'who?' and *laa?* 'no?' (pp. 84–85), are faithful reproductions of C, with no falling tail, which suggests that the terminal downtilt may be a further tempering device, not resorted to in one-syllable questions because of the *emotive* abruptness rather than because of mere length. In any case, it appears that CB and C can be conflated. The double inhibition of CB can be appreciated in an English question using the identical shape, e.g.

(98) Is it   i^s^e^to^ be so insistent?

        w

(99) What's the $\underset{r}{\overset{ason \; for \; this \; behavior?}{e}}$

Loi Corvetto's examples of the rising profile are all questions (wh and yes-no), and her definition of the profile's function seems to limit it to questions: "The chief function of this [profile] . . . is to indicate that the utterance is not complete, but unlike the level profile . . . the information is expected to be provided not by the same speaker but by the hearer" (p. 92).

The level profile has two variants, STEADY and UNDULATING. "In the sentence *huwa mataar kabiir* 'it's a big airport' " (p. 93),

(100) $\cdot \overline{} \cdot \overline{} \cdot \searrow$ (101) $\cdot \sim \cdot \sim \cdot \searrow$

(100) is "typical of a normal assertion, addressed for example to a person accustomed to traveling, while [101] reproduces the expression of someone who has slight acquaintance with travel" (p. 94). The level profile is used chiefly "to draw the hearer's attention to the information that is about to be given" (p. 98). What appears to characterize both variants is the relatively high-pitched tail, the 'more to come' implication of which is of course predictable. What is less clear is whether both variants are truly a single profile. The steady variant is a fair match for the English Profile B with downtilted tail (or a B carried out fully on the accented syllable and followed by a dropback), but the undulating variety looks more like a high-pitched AC—the diagrams show a tilde shape. From the English standpoint there would be nothing strange in having two such shapes—even if not the same profile— both used for 'incompleteness.' Both B and AC are normal to mark the dependency of subordinate clauses:

(102)   If he $\underset{}{\overset{co^{mes,}}{}} \underset{ me.}{^{ca}l_1}$

(103)   If he $\underset{}{\overset{c e^{s}}{ om}} \underset{ me.}{^{ca}l_1}$

—the AC in (103) has an emphasis and potential contrastivity that the B lacks. One can infer a similar difference in Arabic, from Loi Corvetto's description: "The initial phase of the level profile [undulating variant] can be likened to that of a partially emphatic falling profile, but is distinguished from the latter by the characteristic of the shallow fall plus the following slight rise" (p. 101); in other words, an A-rise, or AC. If configurations are truly contrastive, then we would expect a difference here, however much it may be diminished by the flattening of the AC. Loi Corvetto is, however, skeptical of any real contrast between the steady and the undulating varieties (pers. comm.).

That the steady variant is a form of B profile seems to be indicated by its status in female speech, which, for emphasis, may replace the level with a rise or rise-fall, as in (p. 97)

(104) ⌐·· ⌐· ⌐⌐, haðihi ħadiiqa dʒamiila 'This is a beautiful garden*

It is apparent that the accented syllables here are rising from the start, which differentiates them from the true "rising" profile in which the accented syllable is dropped *to*, as in examples (96) and (97). It appears that the pitch marking is that of B, whether the profile is in its "steady" form or its "female" form. The rise of the latter is of course a sort of augmentation, and Loi Corvetto's description implies a feminine tendency toward freer emotional display. Compare the English

(105) I've ne·ver been so embarrassed all my li
                                    in   fe!

—B + B + A, with a shape like that of (104).

One cannot tell from the description what freedom there may be to break away from the supposed grammatical restrictions attached to the profiles. Can a fall be used to ask a question if context and gesture permit? Can a rise (that is, the apparent CB labeled 'rise') be used for nonquestions, e.g. for something matching (105) except that CB replaces B,

(106) I've ver been so embarrassed...
           e
          n

and can the undulating profile be developed into a clearly marked AC with low-dipping drop after the early high? Even without answers to these questions the similarity between the two languages is remarkable, including certain rather small details such as perfunctory leave-takings (p. 105):

(107)   ·⌐,·⌐⌐   alaikums-salaam

(108) See you to mor row!
                      r

where both languages use the tilde-shaped AC (or "undulating level"). The chief difference seems to be the tendency to downtilt high-pitched unaccented syllables, where English has the option of moving higher, most striking in the case of yes-no questions.

It would help to know how native speakers react to the typical mistakes that foreign learners make. Do we sound excessively keyed up when we attempt to speak Arabic? Do they sound overly assured when they attempt to speak English?

Hungarian

Unless otherwise noted, references here are to Varga (1983), and unattributed observations are based on private correspondence with him. All the Hungarian examples are his.

A comparison of Hungarian and English shows both accentual and melodic resemblances. Accents of power may fall on alternate syllables (p. 120), as in

```
(109)  Mit          nál    U
          csi               is    mit
             jak   ram                  nál
                         ten     csi
                                    jak!
```

'What shall I do, Lord God, what shall I do?' Compare

```
(110) What      earth    I     do
          on           am   to
                            o!
```

There is also an emotional backshift, as in English, on an initial intensifier (Varga 1975: 35–36; see also Bolinger 1986: 83):

```
        aw                      Bor
(111) It's              (112)

        fully dull!          zasztoan unalmas!
```

Accents of interest fall as expected. In answer to *What did she do?* one may say

```
      sár
(113) A          in
        ga    get vasalta.
```

'The yellow shirt she-ironed,' with both 'yellow' and 'shirt' new to context, and accented. But to *What yellow thing did she iron?* one would say

```
              in
(114) A sárga
                get vasalt
                          a.
```

with *sárga* 'yellow' unaccented. (One also has the choice, as in English, of accenting *sárga* as if it were new.) Similarly, to answer *What are the children doing?*, one may have a contour identical to that of English:

```
                  ját               kert
(115) A gyerekek                           b
                       szanak a             e
                                             n.
```

```
                    play              gar
(116) The children are                   d
                          ing in the      e
                                           n.
```

with accents on the newly introduced *playing* and *garden* and with *the children* level (but optionally accented). On the other hand, to answer *Why can't we go into the garden?* one would say

```
               gye
                   rekek  ját
(117) Mert a                  szanak a kertben.
```

```
                   chil
                       dren are  play
(118) Because the                    ing in the garden.
```

The newly introduced *children* and *playing* are accented, but *garden*, being repeated, is not. The similarities go beyond the location of the accents; there is also a kinship in the profiles. In (115) and (116) the optional accent (not illustrated) on *gyerekek* and *children* would produce a B profile, normal for an accent on an item that is old in the context but appears as the theme; whereas in (117) and (118) the new-to-context *gyerekek* and *children* are given A profiles. (These MELODIC correspondences will be returned to in a moment.) If the subject is of such overpowering interest as to outweigh the verb, then the verb need not be accented at all even though it may mention something new to the context. This again is as in English, tying accent to relative interest, not directly to information. Suppose that instead of *children* we have the totally unexpected *ambassadors* playing in the garden. The answer to *Why can't we go into the garden* would then be

```
                        nagy
(119) Mert néhány
                        követ játszik a kertben.
```

(120) Because some am^{bas}
             sadors are playing in the garden.

As in English, the accents have wider and narrower ranges corresponding to the degrees of interest and power. If instead of *The children are playing in the garden* we have *The children are fighting in the garden*, the contour may remain the same but the intervals will tend to increase.

On the melodic side the parallels are extensive. Differences seem to reside more in the choice of profiles for particular purposes than in their shape. The FALLING tone corresponds to Profile A and is typical of ordinary statements, wh questions, and requests (pp. 126–29). The FALLING-RISING tone corresponds to Profile AC. The terminal rise leaves matters "open" as in English—for example, a continuation with *but* might be implied:

(121) Zár
     va van.

'It's closed' (but it will open soon) (p. 127). The RISING tone corresponds to Profile B in its most frequent manifestation, that of a simple rise, and—exactly as in English—its most consistent independent use is to mark complementary questions. This shape is, apart from gesture, almost the only way to tell that an utterance such as

(122) Your name?

is a question and not a command (see below, pp. 137–38). It also marks the end of an internal clause, as with *on to it* in

(123) If you hold on to it you'll double your profits.

The DESCENDING (downtilted) tone corresponds to Profile B with a descending tail and like B with that shape it is found in exclamations such as

(124) The way did they it was sim ply unbe lievable!

As in English, a headshake, to express wonderment and ineffability, would be a normal gestural accompaniment here. As both are non-falling (and correspond to two modes of B in English), it is not surprising that the rising tone and the descending tone can both serve, in a case like (123), to mark the end of a clause.

With the "stylized fall," Hungarian and English are practically identical in both form (terraced levels with the last well above creak) and meaning. It is used for calling someone (*John-ny!*), for playful boasts (*Got-cha!*, *You lose!*, *I told you!*), and for warnings (*Care-ful!*). (See Varga 1988.) The most striking difference is in the profile used for ordinary yes-no questions. When these are short, it is not unusual for English to use a manifestation of the profile that is identical to Hungarian (p. 124):

$$\text{(125) Ist}\ {}^{\overset{\text{v}}{\text{a}}}_{\text{n}_?} \qquad\qquad \text{(126) Ste}\ {}^{\overset{\text{ph}}{\text{e}}}_{\text{n}_?}$$

This looks to be a CA profile, not common on yes-no questions in English—it is the rule in Hungarian—but possible. But if the profile is to be called CA, allowance must be made for a freer distribution of unaccented syllables than is generally the case in English. The English CA typically leaps up from the accented syllable to the following, unaccented syllable, and then jumps immediately down, with any further unaccented syllables trailing after, as in

$$\text{(127) You're}\ {}^{\text{der}}_{\text{fon}}\ {}_{\text{of them now}_?}$$

Only if the utterance is highly charged is one apt to hear

$$\text{(128) You're}\ \overset{\text{der of them}}{\underset{\text{n}_{\text{ow}_?}}{\text{fon}}}$$

with additional syllables to the left of the peak. But this is the common shape in Hungarian (*Nap-* is the accented syllable):

$$\text{(129) Napbarnított}\ {}_{\text{volt}_?}$$

'Was he suntanned?' (p. 137). From the standpoint of pattern, then, the Hungarian could be called CA, but from the standpoint of usage the Hungarian pattern must be compared to B in English:

$$\text{(130) Was he}\ {}^{\text{suntanned}^?}$$

If this same steady rise is used on (129), a monolingual speaker of Hungarian will probably misunderstand it.

Another striking difference is in the shape of statement CONTOURS. This does not affect the shape of the profiles, but their relative height. In American English, question-answering statements tend to have their highest pitch on the final A; in Hungarian the tangent to the peaks goes down. A visitor from Hungary quickly notices the way Hungarian Americans tend to adopt the terminal high pitch from the English that they hear and use. (See Kontra and Gósy 1987.)

Whether or not it can be identified as Profile C (Varga associates [132] and [133] with [121], i.e. regards them as more like AC), at least the "held down" effect of the fall between two higher pitches gives the connotation of restraint and reassurance. Thus the more usual shape of a wh question such as

(131) Mit
        láttá$_1$?

'What did you see?' can be changed to

(132) Mit
        láttá^1?

to suggest greater curiosity and intimacy. And to reassure a child one may say

(133) Nem
        fog fáj$^{ni.}$

'It won't hurt.'

Other uses of the tones correspond in fairly obvious ways with the profiles in English. In alternative questions the norm is for the non-final constituent to have a terminal rise, as in English:

(134) Ad^{tál} vizet a virágoknak, vagy ^{n}$_e$ m adtál vizet a virágoknak?

(135) Did $^{you give}$ water to the flowers, or ^{d}$_i$ dn't you →

        give water to the flowers?

Since the constituents of an alternative question are best analyzed as a series of yes-no questions, we thus have, in this instance, a yes-no question (the first constituent) with a simple rise. But it is also a portion of an utterance that is incomplete, and we saw earlier that both Hungarian and English mark such nonterminal clauses with B pro-

files. This gives us a clue as to how to regard the profile that is the usual one with complete yes-no questions in Hungarian: the speaker goes up continuously, as with English B, but then drops on the last syllable, as if to say 'I'm through asking.' This also fits with the use of B in Hungarian (as well as English) complementary questions: they are by definition incomplete—the hearer is expected to finish them.
The AC profile, e.g.

```
            ott
(136) De             van?
           hon
```

'But he is at home (I hope)?' (p. 127) assigns the same interpretation to the tone as would be normal in the English

```
            is      ho              is      home
(137) But he            me?  =  But he
            at                      at          I hope?
```

Finally, the rising-falling tone of Hungarian yes-no questions, though not the norm for English, does parallel English in that both languages use their typical yes-no pattern on repeated questions as well (p. 128), e.g. the ordinary wh

```
(138) Mek                 (139) How
         kora?                      big is it?
```

becomes the repeated

```
         ko
(140) Mek                 (141) How big is it (did you ask)?
        ra?
```

Varga distinguishes between grammatical contrasts and attitudinal ones, contrary to our practice here, but even with that distinction the parallels are not obscured. An informal nondemanding wh question can, as in English, use a simple rise (p. 121):

```
(142) És mekkora?         (143) And how big is it?
```

Toba Batak

As each new description becomes available, one is continuously struck by the similarities with what has gone before. As a last example here, take a glance at Toba Batak, a Western Malayo-Polynesian language (Emmory 1984). Its pitch accents are formed in the same way as those of English, its commands have the same downward slope, and its yes-no questions share with 'incompletion' in general a favoring of terminal rise.

Impressions and Misimpressions

A question whose answer may shed light on both the degree of arbitrariness and the iconism of intonation is "How do speakers of different dialects or languages sound to one another?" It might seem beside the point to ask this question of those who speak mutually unintelligible languages, but hearers do form impressions of intonation and other prosodic and paralinguistic elements of communication, and our tendency to retain these mostly unconscious elements when we try to learn a new language provides a direct test of compatibility.

Edwin T. Hall, Jr. (1955) tells us what is apt to happen when an American tackles Chinese: "In the U.S. we raise our voices not only when we are angry but also when we want to emphasize a point, when we are more than a certain distance from another person, when we are concluding a meeting, and so on. But to the Chinese, for instance, overloudness of the voice is most characteristically associated with anger and loss of self-control."

In the comparison of varieties of English we noted the American's feeling that the speaker of Southern British is overstating the case, is "pretentious and manneristic" to quote Shakhbagova (1982), who also notes that Southern British speakers form their own impressions of Americans ("monotonous," "dispassionate") and of speakers of other British varieties as well. Alan Cruttenden reports (pers. comm.) that on first being thrown into the company of Liverpudlians he concluded that with their high-plus-slither they were being perpetually sarcastic, and it took some time for him to realize that this was their ordinary friendly tone. Elizabeth Uldall, the American phonetician who took up residence in Scotland, reported that "a very characteristic tune in and around Edinburgh is one which sounds distinctly plaintive to me, as it ends on a level mid pitch, but I am assured that it is not in the least plaintive as used here!" (Abe 1955: 389). An example is

```
                        your
(144) Come and                tea!
                 get
```

C.-J. Bailey (1983: 16n, 17) offers the following contrast among four dialects of English:

```
              Is  your
England:              mother  feeling  all
                                           rig ht?
```

```
             Is
Ireland:
                 your mother feeling all rig^ht?
```

```
                                             rig^ht?
                                       all
                              feel^ing
Northern           moth^er
states:
           Is your
```

```
                 your mother feeling all rig^ht?
Southern
states:      Is
```

Bailey describes the impression that each of these creates on an outsider: the English is condescending, the Irish is insultingly incredulous, the Northern is repetitive (echo question), and the Southern is unaccountably surprised.

Transplanted intonations can cause problems when native speakers misapprehend them. Spanish-speakers are apt to use, in answer to a question, the intonation that is better suited in English to a command; English-speakers are accustomed in such cases to hearing a double hump (A + Á), low-to-high:

```
     Spanish pattern            American English pattern

(145) My name's                                    Jo
                       (146) My ^na^me's
            Jo^h_n.                                   ^h_n.
```

In an interview, the native speaker of Spanish may sound rudely assured when speaking English. (See Kvavik 1988 for Spanish commandlike declaratives.) Gumperz et al. (1979) describe clashes of this sort, for example between East Asian and Southern British speakers of English. Someone from India goes to a bank in London to make a deposit and says to the teller

```
          cuse                               mon^e
(147) Ex      m^e, I want to deposit s^om^e
                                               y.
```

This gets the speaker off on the wrong foot, mainly because the CA profile on *money* seems to be emphasizing the obvious and doing it in a way that "an English person associates with pushiness." The steeply falling tail in Indic English, says Bailey (1983: 11), "creates a strange over-emphasis for the ear of other speakers of English." In place of (147) the English person would say

(148) I want to deposit some $^mon_{ey},$ $_ple^{ase}.$

with a low-pitched A profile on *money*. When the teller hands the Indian a form to fill out, the Indian says

(149) N$_{o.}$ This is the $^{wr}o^n_g$ one.

where the English person would say

(150) Oh no. This is the wrong $^on_{e.}$

Here the problem is both intonational and grammatical. The rising pitch on *This is the* suggests impatience on the Indian's part, and the high pitch on *wrong* does the same, plus the fact that *wrong* is emphasized, making the statement sound like an accusation. The English person plays the game more cagily, shifting the accent to *one*, though if he were to express himself with the antonym and say

(151) Oh no. This isn't the $^{ri}g^{h}t$ one.

he could make the same grammatical choice as the Indian, accenting the adjective rather than *one*, and suffer no ill consequences. In fact, by shifting the accent back a syllable from the end, he makes the statement actually sound less accusatory. This example illustrates the interplay of word choice, grammatical structure, and intonation that a speaker must keep in balance if he is to function according to the norms of the social group.

The prosodic features of Indian English that make it different from British or American probably stem from Hindi and other languages of North India (Gumperz 1982: 121), and suggest how readily such features can be grafted on to the grammar of a different language—and also the dangers inherent in the misinterpretation of those subtle cues to the uncodified rules of discourse that make continuity possible in our behavior toward one another. But the important point is that the interpretations are not random, as would be the case, across languages, if intonation were completely arbitrary. We may make wrong guesses, but we do not make wild guesses.

One could multiply these examples if the purpose were to assemble a list of curiosities, but our sample is large enough to show the nature of differences from language to language. Almost without exception, when hearers report their impression of intonations other than their own, they do so in emotive or attitudinal terms. Though misunderstanding is often the result, the confused interlocutors rarely complain directly of misunderstanding as they might with a mispronounced word ("She didn't say that right") or a jumbled grammatical construction ("He isn't saying that the right way"). The hearer reacts not so much to the utterance as to the speaker, who sounds snippy, or ingratiating, or condescending, or crabby, or cold, or cordial, or reserved, or pushy. Unfamiliarity with the conventions strips the intonation to its emotive core, and, at the other extreme, familiarity dulls one to the affective front that we all put up. Here, dialectal conventionalization is no different from idiolectal conventionalization. There are people whose preferred or habitual ways of expressing themselves, including their intonation, mark them among their fellows as cheerful, gloomy, frivolous, or overconfident, and we do not hesitate to characterize them in those terms even though, if we asked them, the victims of the characterization would protest that they did not *mean* to sound that way. (Our shock on first hearing our own voice played back from a recording reveals how deaf we can be to the way *we* are.) So the emotive stance, as revealed by the intonation and in other ways, is *there*, whether for an individual or for a whole culture, and the fact that it passes unnoticed or is given a different name is no denial of its existence.

Ivan Fónagy (1982: 83) warns against supposing "that a vocal gesture, or any other gesture, is really devoid of sense, deprived of its content by virtue of being systematically repeated," hence passing unnoticed. "It is more plausible to believe that the constant repetition reflects the continuing presence of an unsettled conflict. Signals that are permanently in evidence end up by no longer attracting attention. Thus it is possible to disguise a mental content by displaying it uninterruptedly."

But when speakers are stirred, and the display rules of their culture are weakened or suspended, those conventionalized differences that are so invisible to us and so manifest to others tend to level out. Speaking of American and British English, Shakhbagova writes (1982: 64), "In elevated, or animated, or highly emotional speech . . . one and the same emotion may be expressed by similar prosodic characteristics and be adequately perceived by hearers irrespective of their belonging to GA [American] or RP [Southern British] variety of English."

Part II

INTONATION AND GRAMMAR: CLAUSES AND ABOVE

3. Crosscurrents

Intonation and grammar are pragmatically but not linguistically interdependent. Neither can be used to define the other in any strict sense, but both cooperate in giving communicators a fix on their meaning. The relative independence of the two streams is the main theme in the chapters that follow, and is now accepted doctrine among most intonologists, after a long period in which linguists who came to intonation from grammar tried to fit it to grammatical structure. Typical of the current view is the generalization of Jassem and Gibbon (1980: 8) that "phonological structure is independent of grammar."[1] Even those who have worked most successfully to show a high degree of structure in matters of rhythm, with attendant correspondences at lower levels of syntax (word and phrase),[2] pull back from making similar claims for larger units. Selkirk (1980: 21) will go only so far as to say that "perhaps even syntax" may influence how many phonological phrases may comprise an intonation pattern. This is quite apart from the more inclusive problem of how supposedly syntactic categories such as question and statement are reflected in intonation. Here, the difficulty of pinning down particular meanings, whether grammatical or prosodic—and therefore of correlating the two—is emphasized by 't Hart (1984: 198): "There are at least ten times as many 'meanings'— or rather implications, or interpretative possibilities—as there are different intonation patterns, so that at least a given pattern must correspond to a set of implications instead of to only one."

The notion of a defining relationship between intonation and grammar rests on the assumption that there is such a thing as a neutral, emotion-free intonation. Obviously anger, enthusiasm, or panic will cause distortions that scarcely reflect such logico-grammatical categories as focus or parenthesis. So it is commonplace among the more traditional intonation experiments to have speakers instructed to speak "in as natural, relaxed, and unemotional a fashion as possible" (Abramson and Svastikula 1983: 145), which is supposed to lay bare "the strictly linguistic functions of prosody" (Vaissière 1983: 53). Unfortunately, instructions to freeze out all emotion are like saying to a subject, "Hold your hands at your side and wipe all expression from your face." Such "unemotional" gesture is interpreted in the context of all the other gestures that might be performed, and gets not a neutral but a negative interpretation—indifference, boredom, or whatever. If there is neutral speech, it is speech in which emotion has been not eliminated but tamed. As Classe observed many years ago (1939: 36), "Since all speech must needs be affective in so far as it is necessarily concomitant with some state of mind, there is no such thing as emotionally neutral speech; it is merely a matter of degree." One of our tenets will be that speakers "use emotive strategies for logical and grammatical purposes" (Bolinger 1986: 244). We therefore take the contribution that intonation makes to grammar and discourse as we find it, emotion and all, and will not appeal to the notion of neutral, colorless speech. (The notion of MARKEDNESS, however, will be invoked here and there, in the sense that some intonations are more usual for some purposes.)

Clues from Reading

However small the *direct* contribution of intonation to grammar, the indirect contribution to the pragmatics of communication is heavy. In a study of prose and poetry presented to listeners in two ways, one with normal intonation and the other in a monotone, it was found that monotone produced a loss of intelligibility (Glasgow 1952).

More serious than the lack of intonation is the choice of the wrong intonation. That rarely happens in normal speech, since our intonation reflects the way we feel about what we say; as G. Brown et al. (1980: 136) put it, "The overriding use of intonation is to allow the speaker to give notice of how he views the topic under discussion." But problems arise when we read aloud (and, subvocally, when we read to ourselves). The ordinary printed page is intonationally deprived, and since everything we say has to have a tune attached, when none is provided we invent—often with strange results. There is a sort of "reading stereotype" (Bolinger 1986: 77)—a tendency for readers to apply, mechanically, the pattern that assigns a major A profile to the last content word. A person coming upon a gravestone with the epitaph

> I told the doctor
> that I was sick.

is tempted to recite

```
                        si
I  told  the  doctor that  I was
                              ck.
```

—an A + A + A + A contour with peak on *sick*, which makes little sense. But if the epitaph is read as A + B,

```
   told
I      the                 sick!
         doctor that I was
```

the joke comes clear: I told him so and I was right and my being here proves it. One who misreads the line from Robert Frost's "The Death of the Hired Man," defining *home* as

> the place where when you have to go there,
> They have to take you in.

will, by a shift of emphasis from *in* to *take*, make home appear to be a repugnant place. The letter-writer who wrote a thank-you note to an invited speaker saying

> Now that I have you two, I shall have to get two more competent speakers.

was trapped by the radical difference between putting an A on *more* with no accent on *competent speakers* (the sense intended) and putting A's on both *competent* and *speakers*. Mark Twain's definition of a classic as *something everybody wants to have read and nobody wants to read* is unambiguous with *have* unaccented and in its reduced form ([həv] or [əv]) but ambiguous otherwise (perfect tense versus cause-to-be-read). The reader who comes across a passage like the following,

> To my anxious American eye it looks even worse: it looks as if America's "fight against Communism" is really a struggle to save face, not to lose prestige.[3]

is tempted to assign an AC profile to *prestige* ('it is x, it is not y'), instead of the intended apposition (*to save face = not to lose prestige*) with its final A.

Punctuation is often of little or no use:

> The house has not been painted since Grainger bought it, in 1921. Neither he nor his wife, who writes poetry, paints, and occasionally writes songs, is particularly aware of the physical attributes of any place in which they live.[4]

—this invites an A on *paints* with the reading that neither one paints, and the reader must then go back and revise, keeping the pitch a bit

higher on *poetry* and giving *paints* an AC (or a B). But writers aware of
the problem sometimes provide a hint:

> We met frequently at the laundromat. "And where do you live?" I
> asked one evening while we were waiting out the cycles. "I *live*
> here," sighed the man. "But I have my meals and sleep in a bun-
> galow a couple of blocks up the street with my wife and four
> children."[5]

The italics are a warning to put a strong AC on *live*, but the reader
must still improvise by putting an equally strong A on *here*, if the
quotation is to be understood.

Word Meanings Affected

Reading errors tell us how important intonation is, but they form
no logical class—anything, from a simple mispronunciation to a misplaced pause or a wrong choice of profile, can create confusion. We
need to look more closely at the ways and places in which intonation
combines with words and grammar to convey a meaning or an intent.

In some respects the intersection seems almost lexical—individual
words and phrases take on different senses when different intonations
are imposed. Function words are especially affected. The word *only*,
for example, has the meaning 'but' as well as the meaning 'no more
than.' The distinction is pretty reliably cued by accent, the 'but' sense
usually being the unaccented one. This ambiguity caused trouble in
the reading of the following passage, where either interpretation
makes sense:

> The sciences . . . form one of the ways in which man seeks to gain
> understanding. . . . They are, then, proper materials for the hu-
> manist. . . . Physics and biology surely provide basic stuff for the
> critical mind of the humanist, as do literature and music. Only
> science . . . is . . . out of bounds for him.[6]

The phrase *only science* can be handled in either of two ways:

$$\text{only}\ {}^{\text{sci}}\ {}_{\text{en}}{}^{\text{c}}{}^{\text{e}} \qquad\qquad {}^{\text{only}}\ \text{sci}\ {}_{\text{en}}{}_{\text{c}}{}_{\text{e}}$$

The first yields 'but then,' the second 'science is the only thing.'

The word *once* functions now as a temporal adverb ('on one occasion'), now as a conjunction introducing a subordinate clause ('if, as
soon as, when'). Since subordinate clauses are more apt to have in-

conclusive terminals, an AC profile terminating such a clause is more apt to cue 'when,' an A 'on one occasion':

> He showed a peculiar knowledge of the mountain flowers. Once he
>   went out of the way to pick one . . .[7]

The word *so* following a verb and unaccented tends to signify 'thus,' but to signify 'the truth' if accented in that position:

```
                 e?          said
Did they  com        -- He       so.  (said thus, said they did)


All those things you said             so
                           just  weren't
                                      o.
```

A number of pronouns, too, are partially distinguished by accent— *one, some,* and *any* are among them. *I háve one* with unaccented *one* probably signifies 'I have a token of that which has already been iden- tified'; *I have óne* signifies 'I do not have two (three, etc.).' Though not lexical at the outset, such accentual and intonational contrasts some- times become lexical as the internal structure of the word is affected. *I have one egg* retains *one* as long as the numerical value remains upper- most, but as the word is routinized into an indefinite it loses the ac- cent and is deformed to the present indefinite article *an: I have an egg.* And now, even when reaccented (*I said I had án egg, not síx eggs*), the form remains *an.*

Some expressions divide themselves between "content" uses on the one hand and "function" (or otherwise colorless) uses on the other. When this happens, it is natural for the content use to be the one most often accented, and therefore cued by accent. The verb *be- come* has the content sense of 'to befit' as well as the merely copulative sense of 'come to be.' A common mispronunciation of the Eugene O'Neill title is

```
Mour
    ning becomes Elec
                    tra.
```

implying the nonsense 'Mourning turns into Electra' (the misreader takes *becomes* to stand for the more frequent of the two senses of the verb, lulled by the fact that titles are often arbitrary anyway); it should be[8]

```
            comes
Mour
    ning be
            Electra.
```

Similarly with the noun *variety*, meaning 'variedness' as well as 'kind' or 'sort,' the latter being relatively empty, hence less apt to be accented:

```
                                        fo
That
      variety is  no  longer to be

                              und.
```

—'that kind.' If this signified 'that degree of variedness,' *variety* could easily carry the highest pitch.

More or less lexicalized phrases may be affected in the same way. The phrase *in time* has the two meanings 'eventually' and 'opportunely.' The first, referring to what is probably going to happen anyway, is not apt to be signaled by high pitch; the second, referring to a contingency, may suggest an emergency, and then is apt to be highlighted:

> They couldn't get her to the hóspital in tíme to sáve her.

The phrase *nothing but* may signify 'only, just,' which is relatively colorless; or the *nothing* of the phrase may deny existence, and then is apt to be accented. So, depending on whether *nothing but* is unaccented or is given a high-pitched B profile, the following is standard English for 'I want to feed him something besides fish' or substandard 'Fish is all I want to feed him':

> I don't want to feed him nothing but fish.

A similar split can be seen in *more or less*. A survey included the question *Has your attitude become more or less isolationist?*; 20 percent of those reading it understood *more-or-less* in the colorless sense of 'somewhat.'[9] This error could not have occurred had the question been spoken. (We see here one of the ways in which writing has to compensate for lack of intonation: the composers of the test should have used the wording *more isolationist or less isolationist*.)

There is no real difference between these quasi-lexical contrasts and grammatical contrasts conveyed in the same manner. The formula adjective + *as* + x + *be* carries the contradictory meanings 'because of' and 'in spite of,' depending on the intonation:

```
Strong                        fraid
          as he  is, I'm a

                              of him.
Strong as he
                  I'm not afra
          i                    id
           s,                     of him.
```

The intonation is not designed to do this; it happens by accident. What the intonation does is distinguish between something 'not new' in the first example ('knowing how strong he is'—the *is* is assumed, not asserted) and something 'new' or newly asserted ('declare him to be very strong—it makes no difference') in the second. The second is a manifestation of the 'even' sense (see pp. 177–79). New versus old also distinguishes an appositive from what is ambiguously either appositive or vocative in the following:

```
        great ma
He's a           po
            n, Na  leon.

        great ma
He's a
            n, Napoleon.
```

(For vocatives, see Bolinger 1986: 268–70.)

It can also happen that an intonational difference may radically alter the circumstances of use of a given expression without actually promoting a lexical split—the meaning remains the same but is so sensitive to the intonation that it becomes "too much" for a particular context. This happens with the expression *all right*. As Jones (1956: §1069) points out, *all right* is generally pronounced with a rising terminal, and when it is not, "it may have the effect of a threat." More precisely, when *all right* is given an A or an AC profile (an AC, of course, has a terminal rise, so it is the assertiveness of the A part that seems to be crucial), it is grudging or defiant. Part of the semantic properties of *all right*, which basically refer to acquiescence or approval, is a kind of hedge, which is softened with a C profile but intensified with an A. (Gesture—raised eyebrows and a nod—can also soften it, suggesting that the speaker is agreeably surprised.) So it is difficult to respond to *I want you to help me* with

All right. I'll be along in a moment.

using an A profile, though the unhedged *OK, sure thing*, or *you bet* serve perfectly well with the A. In this context a C—or a B—is normal. Similarly, if A is used to respond to *How was the concert?*, it readily suggests 'I defy those who say the opposite.' And when argumentative, *all right* with A suggests unwilling concession, and is unlikely in the context

All right, I see that now.

where *OK* is normal, but fits well in

All right, but you didn't tell me that.

The effects described here are all the more pronounced when *all* is given a separate A profile lower in pitch,

$$A^1 \quad r^{i^g}$$
$$\quad 1$$
$$\qquad {}^{h}_{t.}$$

and are somewhat muted when *all* has a B at higher pitch,

$$All$$
$$\quad ri$$
$$\qquad {}^{g}{}^{h}_{t.}$$

The main reason for not regarding these quasi-lexical variations as truly lexical is that they are incidental to the main business of intonation, which is to convey affect. Content words are more important than function words as a rule, and we highlight them for that reason, not in order to distinguish them from homophonous function words. Intonation does not systematically distinguish a *once₁* from a *once₂*, but it marks the inconclusiveness of a subordinate clause and offers the lexical distinction as a bonus. And so on.

Intonation works blindly even when a bifurcation becomes fully lexicalized. The history of such pairs as *human-humane, urban-urbane,* and *divers-diverse* shows intonation acting to preserve an older stress pattern that suits one of the members of the pair better than the other. The sense of *humane, urbane,* and *diverse* is more descriptive than classificatory; it is colorful and highly intensifiable (we are more apt to say *How urbane!* than *How urban!*), and it favors a climactic accent that eventually freezes into a terminal stress, resisting the mechanical process that backshifted the stress in the companion forms *human, urban,* and *divers* (along with the bulk of the English lexicon).

Pragmatic vs. "Literal" Meaning

The looseness of the tie with lexicon and grammar is also manifested in the attachment of the intonation to the pragmatic rather than the literal meaning of an expression. When the attachment has resulted or is resulting in a new lexical meaning (derived from the pragmatic one), there may be no difference between this correlation and the ones just noted by which intonation helps to create bifurcations. For example, *good-bye* may be a genuine farewell, or it may be used as a form of dismissal, 'that's the last of.' Someone going on a diet might say

```
Good-bye
        sug
           ar.
```

with a B + À contour and with the accent on *good-bye* shifted to the first syllable, following the rhythm rule for the separation of accents (see Bolinger 1986: 60–63). But the same person, literally bidding farewell to his sweetheart whom he addresses as *Sugar*, would say

```
        bye,
Good-
        sugar.
```

using an A + C (or AC, depending on whether *Sugar* is regarded as a separate profile or a tail) and keeping the normal stress on *good-býe* (which suggests that *Sugar* is *not* accented, for otherwise the stress on *good-bye* would tend to backshift). The first sense, the pragmatic one signifying dismissal, uses the same intonation as would be used with *No more sugar!*

Similarly, the formula *I wouldn't if I were you*, which literally puts *I* in contrast with *you* and would be expected to take the shape

```
I
                        yo
    wouldn't if I were
                          uu.
```

instead is given the same intonation as *You shouldn't, you know*, in keeping with its use as advice or warning (Bolinger 1986: 79–80):

```
    would
I
     n't if I were you.
                   yo
```

The pragmatic reason for choosing the distinctive intonation may not be obvious at first glance. Take the literal and the figurative senses of *Is that so*, the first to ask a question and the second to express disbelief, the latter with the intonation

```
    tha-a-at
Is
        so!
```

The same intonation is also encountered on less stereotyped expressions of skepticism such as *Is thát a fact, Well dó tell, You dón't say, Áre you indeed*. It takes its ironic overtones from an exaggerated use of a B + À contour, one of whose possible implications is 'wonderment'

(Bolinger 1986: 286); the speaker overdoes it as a way of suggesting the opposite (he knows that his hearer knows that he can't be so worked up about the matter that he must ponder it heavily). A frank B + Á might be ironic too, but could just as easily be genuine, and a B + B,

$$\text{Is} \quad \text{that} \quad \text{so}^?$$

would almost necessarily express true feeling.

Such is the autonomy of intonation that it may directly contradict what the verbal content of an expression seems to require. Someone is worried about how long a job will take, and the speaker says,

Don't   It won't take a

    worry.   minute.

The second sentence here means 'It won't take even a minute,' which ought to confer a high pitch on *minute* (see p. 178). But the speaker wants to *reassure*, and makes the correct choice of two B + C contours accordingly.

Perseveration

A further indication of the loose tie between intonation and grammar is the perseveration of intonation, its tendency to spread beyond the verbal material to which it most immediately attaches. Given the attitudinal basis of intonation, this is to be expected: the speaker has adopted a mood, and if it is a dominant one, it may not be easy to switch off when other verbal material, to which it is less appropriate, comes along. The following was overheard from a salesperson:

    you want to show this lady

Do   the birthday cards?   They're ⟶

in that box there in the corner.

The intonation of the preceding question affects the following statement. The same happened in the following:

              these,

Do you want to carry   and I'll put ⟶

                bag?

the other things in the

The intonation may even carry over to the speaker's next turn, as in the following, spoken by a parent to a child:

Do you want to ^tell her^ that the ^bus driver^ ⟶

has already called the ^bus?^

The child then asks, *What do you mean, Daddy?*, and the parent replies,

that it's ^already time to^ ^go?^

A falling terminal for an appendage of this sort would be perfectly normal, of course.

It might seem as if perseveration could be explained as a purely mechanical IMITATION.[10] But this would not explain why it is powerful enough to blank out the usual intonation cued by the verbal material. And the idea that what is continuing is a MOOD is supported by cases where the same mood is maintained by a different intonation. Here is an attested example:

```
                  do
What were you
               ing                          left?
                   there, after all the others had
```

The speaker presents his demand with the usual falling pitch, but it is also a question, so he prolongs it with a rise. We do this regularly with vocatives:[11]

```
                  do
What were you
               ing            John?
                   there,
```

If we look on pitch as a reflection of the speaker's mood (even allowing that he may manipulate it by *adopting* a change in mood—"method acting"), then nothing that happens in the broader movement of pitch can be regarded as accidental or as purely mechanical.

Mismatches and Adjustments

Mismatches of the *I wouldn't do it if I were you* type are common enough, where a new meaning imposes its own intonation. But the phenomenon is more pervasive and extemporaneous than a focus on such stereotypes would lead one to believe. The following is an attested example of a ghost sentence—one that is carved intonationally out of a larger sentence:[12]

Rath_{er} than ^{ou}r going ^{the}re for   ^{Christ}mas,   I'd ^{much} rather ⟶

have _eth^m [pause] come ^{here} at ^{New}Year[']s.

The speaker has two things in mind: 'I'd rather have *them'* (they as our guests, not we as theirs) and 'I'd prefer the visit at New Year's.' The AC profile with its pause signals a double function for *have* (ordinary transitive in 'have a guest,' causative in *have . . . come*) and for *them* (object of *have*, subject of *come*).

Similar examples in French are cited by Barbizet et al. (1979). In one, the speaker produces *Ce n'est pas comme cela* as if it were an independent exclamation as far as the intonation is concerned, yet his syntactic plan is to go on and produce the postposed subject of a cleft sentence. He does this first by adding *que*, required by the rule for cleft sentences, and then correcting it to *qu'* as required by what follows:

> Ce n'est pas comme cela! . . . que . . . qu'un programme d'économies peut-être fait.

This kind of intonational remolding of syntax is most evident in running discourse with its constant false starts, corrections, introductions and reintroductions, floor-holding and floor-yielding, upplaying and downplaying. Intonation and syntax make their separate contributions to conversational interaction. There is where they come together, not in a higher or more properly *linguistic* domain.

The extemporaneous nature of the connection with grammar can be seen in a kind of twofold elasticity: text to tune and tune to text. In order to display a given prominence or a given tune, the speaker may increase the length of a locution by adding words and rearranging if necessary (see Bolinger 1986: 85–86 for examples). Suppose the speaker in making an affirmation wants to be both positive and upbeat. He can do this with total informality by using the interjection *uh-huh* (see below, pp. 287–89) with a drawled downglide on *uh* for the positive part and an upglide on the *huh* for the upbeat part, A + B. But suppose he wants to verbalize the positiveness by saying *yes* instead of *uh-huh*. He can't simply adjust *yes* to the A + B by lengthening the word—its unitary nature would force a unification of the con-

:our to a single profile, AC, with unwanted implications of tenta-
:iveness. So he utters a positive-sounding A on *yes* and adds *uh-huh*
with an upbeat B:

Ye
$\qquad$ huh•
  s, uh–

—the separate A and B are the given and the syntax is adjustable, in-
:luding reversible (*uh-huh, yes,* with B + A).

Attempts at Grammatical Explanation

The looseness of the tie becomes most evident when we try to express rules of correspondence that are truly based on grammatical
principles. Where connections have been established, they have generally turned out to be approximations rather than rules, e.g. the notorious "questions go up at the end" (see Chapter 5). Intonational descriptions, many of them otherwise sound, are strewn with failures of
this sort; the temptation has been almost irresistible to take some
pragmatic function of intonation and turn it into a grammatical one.
Later chapters will deal with a number of such attempts. For a sample
here, take the carefully designed instrumental study by Cooper and
Sorensen (1981) on "declination," the tendency of utterances to drift
down in pitch as they move toward the end. The study proposes a
"topline rule" supported by experiments that show a more or less
regular decline regardless of how long the utterance is or what material may be interpolated. Where the problems arise is in the attempts
to explain irregularities and exceptions. The example sentences include the following:

> The *cat* in the *garage* ran *swiftly underneath* the *car.*
> *Days pass quickly* in the *middle* of *winter.*

Among the findings was the fact that *swiftly* and *pass* tended to be
higher in pitch than the rule predicted. For *swiftly,* the authors theo-
rize that this happens because, being an adverb, it tends to be focused
and therefore is more likely to be accented. This of course signifies a
connection between intonation and a grammatical category, that of
adverb. But if adverbs as such tend to rise in pitch, why was *quickly*
not similarly affected in the second sentence? We have to look at the
extemporaneous treatment of the adverb *swiftly,* which in the first
sentence describes an event, not a platitude like the one expressed in
the second sentence, and also at the inherent colorfulness of that particular adverb; the circumstances decree that *swiftly* shall be highlighted, not because it is an adverb but because of what it means and

does in that utterance. As for the higher-than-predicted pitch on *pass,* the authors look at the syntax: *pass* comes directly after *days,* and the topline rule lacks the time needed to show its effects. That may be true, but we have already noted that this sentence is a platitude, the sort of utterance that is ideal for a B + À contour (see Bolinger 1986: 280, 282–84). Even a sentence with enough added syllables to allow for a drop would still tend to keep that B lilt, with no early drop in pitch: *Days intervene one by one in the course of our lives.* What keeps the pitch high on *pass* is the speaker's mood in expressing a truism and not an event.

4. Demarcation

Probably the most indispensable syntactic use of prosody is to divide discourse into segments and to establish an informal hierarchy of beginnings and endings whereby major constituents can be distinguished from minor. It is necessary to speak of prosody in general here rather than of intonation separately, because pause and rate are as important as pitch. Usually the three work together. Where pitch drops, rate slows, and silence ensues, it is pretty safe to assume that the speaker has come to the end of something, and the deeper the fall, the slower the rate, and the longer the pause, the higher up on the scale of separations the particular separation is.[1] No one of the factors is definitive: we see many instances of falls that are not for a syntactic break but for "separate attention" (e.g., sounding authoritative by way of speaking "with finality," Bolinger 1986: 294–95); speakers may slow their rate for a variety of reasons (fatigue, to help the hearer grasp what is being said, to emphasize); and pauses may signify that the speaker has forgotten what he wants to say. Taken together, the three prosodic cues can be counted on so long as nonprosodic cues cooperate (such other cues include syntax—there are places in sentence structures where pauses can be expected—and gesture). But intonation is probably the most important cue: "A child (or an adult) learning a language is likely to find intonation a more reliable guide to syntactic structure than pauses—for which . . . the determinants are many and various" (Studdert-Kennedy 1983: 204).

Beginnings are important too, but mostly in conjunction with endings. This does not refer to absolute beginnings: the first person to speak is first by reason of making any verbal signal at all. But most beginnings, including absolute ones, are at a relatively high pitch: the speaker commands attention (and commands themselves are typically high initially—see below, p. 146). The reader can experiment by reading this paragraph aloud; in a rough sort of way, each sentence will tend to start at a pitch higher than the immediately preceding one, as if to declare its independence from what has gone before. The combination of pitch drop for finality and pitch rise for a new beginning is a double cue for separation, in addition to pause and quickened rate, but the latter are less predictable.

The demarcative function of prosody is probably universal, in the sense that all languages use intonation, rate, and pause to mark divisions, and use them in highly similar ways, though proportions differ. Here is a description of demarcative intonations in Cayuvava (a language spoken in Bolivia), which in broad outlines could as readily be a description of English and other Western European languages:

1. A fall and trail-off after the final strong accent, indicating that the speaker intends no further utterance.

2. A maintenance of the level of the final accent, indicating an intention to continue immediately.

3. A similar level with a sharp rise on the last syllable, indicating a question.[2]

Intonation performs both a direct and an indirect service to this sort of chunking. Directly, an extreme transition in pitch, either up or down but especially down, is a clue to a break. The middle things in discourse tend to hold to middle pitches. This is not a definitive clue—extreme transitions may be accentual or may reflect some extreme of feeling such as anger or enthusiasm—but it is a helpful one. Indirectly, intonation contours, to the extent that they have more or less predictable outlines, will generally coincide with segments of discourse that are unitary on other grounds as well. In the latter, indirect, sense, intonation assists chunking in the same way that syntax does: we can predict that *Johnny took a bath* may well represent a unit of discourse at some level, because we can recognize the pattern of subject and predicate; similarly

```
           care
         be        ful!
Better
```

with its familiar B + ÁC warning is a recognized intonation pattern and likewise represents a unit of discourse. It is the predictability of such patterns, intonational and syntactic, that allows loquacious speakers to run on without pause and still produce utterances in which the boundaries are recognizable.

One type of separation should be mentioned in order to be dismissed: the division between words, shown by spacing on the printed page. Such divisions are real enough and are registered in various ways, chiefly by the simple fact that we recognize the word shapes of our language—this is like the indirect contribution of recognized syntactic and intonational patterns just mentioned. But word division is not registered as such by the prosody, in English.[3] What *is* registered, in slow, emphatic speech, is word accent, and since accents potentially come one per word, a slowed-down, fist-thumping version of a sentence like *Whý shóuld ánybody resórt to víolence?* does have a sort of prosodically marked word division, though the borders are indistinct. But in normal speech all that one can predict is that an accent will correspond to a word stress, and if the word is left unaccented, it is lost in the stream. If people's resorting to violence has already been under discussion and a speaker asks *But réally, why SHÓULD anybody resort to violence?* there is no prosodic separation into individual words (unless one grants prosodic status to the feeble hints contained in full versus reduced syllables) after the word *should*.

The hierarchy of breaks—major versus minor separations between one clause and another—is in some cases fairly well cued by intonation even in the absence of pause (Bolinger 1986: 212). If two separations are both marked by B profiles, the one with the higher tail will be the major one, enabling us to tell the difference between

    (1) If you néed me when you gét there, cáll me. (B + Ь́ + A)
    (2) If you néed me, when you gét there cáll me. (Ь́ + B + A)

—the comma corresponds to the higher rise. The same is true of two successive AC profiles, the major break (comma) coinciding with the AC that has the higher peak (before the fall-rise). But when AC and B are used together in that order, the AC tends to mark the major break regardless of the height of the B, so that

```
                              get there
        need
If you            when you            call      (AC+B+A)
          m e                              me.
```

will correspond to (2) even though the AC is lower in pitch than the B. When the order is reversed, B + AC, relative height again takes effect but only to the extent of evening the score: a lower B will come across as (1), but a higher B, the shape

```
            need  m e
If you            when you   get       call
                          there
                                   me.
```

can be taken either way. This whole question—including the role of A profiles—needs further study and testing.

These are large-scale subdivisions, in which profiles are exaggerated to provide easily recognized "terminals." But on a smaller scale intonation cooperates with rate and pause to help mark the finer grain of constituent structure. It does not do this in a way that is easy to formalize. Its inefficiency in marking something quoted, for example, is such that the speaker often resorts to saying *quote . . . unquote* or to gesturing with the middle and index fingers of both hands to represent a pair of quotation marks. Improvisations are frequent. The speaker who, to describe a spelling error, said

> I wrote the word *cues*, which is c-u-e-s, c-u-s-e.

quite deliberately extended the pause at the second comma and pronounced the *s* preceding the comma on an exaggerated AC profile, realizing that the succession of spelled letters would otherwise be confusing. Someone reading the following aloud,

> The normal course will have one to three hour-examinations per term and a three-hour examination at the end of each term.[4]

will feel a need to put a pause after the first *three* and resume on *hour* with an abrupt upskip and also possibly a glottal stop plus head and hand gestures, to avoid the suggestion of *three-hour* as a constituent at that point.

The rate-and-break marking of constituents is iconic: the speaker puts together things that belong together and keeps apart things that belong apart. The rest of this chapter discusses some of the more familiar cases.

Coordinate vs. Hierarchic Modifiers

When two prenominal modifiers modify a noun independently of each other, they tend to be separated by a break, generally marked with a comma in writing:

> Edith Staines talked in a loud, determined voice.

Besides the slowed rate, there is a profile separation, with *loud* on a B (or possible AC) profile and *determined* on a B (less likely AC) with a lower tail: as with clauses, the higher pitch marks the major break—*determined* "belongs with" *voice*, but *loud* does not "belong with" *determined*—it reaches out to *voice*. On the other hand, in

> She was lecturing on the early Italian immigrants.

no slowing interrupts the succession in the noun phrase, and both adjectives, barring some special emphasis, have B profiles with tails at approximately equal heights. *Italian* is an immediate constituent of *immigrants*, and *early* is an immediate constituent of *Italian immigrants*.

Here as elsewhere in its connections with grammar, the prosody behaves like a standby device: handy when needed, but ignored or more or less faded out when not. The extent to which the prosody is negotiable may be seen in the trouble that is often caused when speakers fail to take precautions. The following phrase from a radio report,

> . . . guarded by weak, old levees.

was heard as *guarded by week-old levees*. The error made sense, and the monosyllabic adjectives gave too little room for intonational maneuver (this would probably not happen with *twenty foot-high poles* versus *twenty-foot-high poles*, given the extra syllables). At normal conversational speed the following is several ways ambiguous:

> Some sophisticated persons don't believe this.

'Some out of all those people who are sophisticated,' 'some persons who by the way are sophisticated persons' (inference: 'and prove themselves so by not believing this'), 'a group of sophisticated persons whom I know' (referential indefinite, most likely with *s'm* for *some*). The second reading interpolates *sophisticated* and might be punctuated *Some, sophisticated, persons*, suggesting the elaborate prosody that is required if the speaker's intent is not otherwise clear: AC profiles on both *some* and *sophisticated* with the lower trough on *-ca-*, and *persons* with a C (because it is an "empty word"; otherwise again AC, for instance if *professionals* replaced *persons*), plus a marked slowing after each adjective.

Speakers regularly ignore the demarcative signals with certain adjectives that behave like hypocoristic, diminutive, augmentative, etc. affixes. *Big, little,* and *old* are examples: *a nice old house, a great big bear, a cute little baby* (contrast *a pleasant, turn-of-the-century house; a huge, towering bear; a darling, wee baby*). But combinations of restrictive adjectives require more care. A speaker is apt to be dissatisfied with an awkward coupling and resort to paraphrase, as in the following:

> The frame is OK, but do you have another, smaller canvas—I mean another canvas that's smaller?

These adjective combinations are an aspect of the larger question of PARENTHESIS, and will be further discussed in Chapter 7.

Other Phrasal Divisions

Similar to the adjective-adjective-noun problem is the adverb-adjective-noun problem, where the adverb modifies the adjective but is homophonous with another adjective. Question: is the adverb-adjective sequence chunked in a detectable way? The speaker of the following,

Are there sorority houses in all-girls schools?

realized the ambiguity as soon as the sentence was uttered, and repeated it, emphasizing *all-girls*—to no avail, since the ambiguity remained, except that the hearer was on notice and could double-check the context or ask for a paraphrase. A similar ambiguity is found in *She picked the brightest-colored one*. The prosody *can* make the distinction, but does so in the course of other business. If the speaker says

```
        brightest
the
              col
                 o
                  r
                   ed
                       one.
```

with the familiar B + À contour, the main effect is the highlighting of *brightest*—one could almost say *the brightest one: colored* is more or less redundant. But incidentally the B + À tends to be a synthesizing contour (see Bolinger 1986: 280–84); and that suggests the hyphenation of *brightest-colored*. But with a B + Á contour,

```
              col
the brightest
                 o
                  r
                   ed
                       one.
```

the speaker may be answering a question (*Which one did she pick?*) and B + Á is the most typical contour for that purpose, but it also highlights *colored* and favors the interpretation 'the brightest of the colored ones,' that is, *colored* is taken as contrastive.

Noun phrases of course are not the only ones with problems. The verb phrase in the sentence *I didn't want to run after that* is ambiguous as between intransitive *run* plus temporal *after*, and transitive (phrasal verb) *run after*. The intonation is a potential help in that a temporal phrase such as *after that* (like *now*, *then*, *tomorrow*) is more often than not unaccented, whereas both elements of *run after* are likely to be accented. So we have the probable shapes, respectively *after that* and *run after*,

```
           run
I did n't want to                          (A+A)
                      after that.
```

```
                  ru   af
I did n't want to    n   t er that.        (A+A+A)
```

But with presupposition or contrast, either could go the other way. The same possibility of disambiguation through accent is present in the sentence *They don't live right here. Here* is apt to be unaccented, but intensified *right here* is apt to be accented—so with unaccented *here* we have the likelihood of *live right* (virtuously), and with accented *here* the likelihood of 'dwell' (*right here*). But there is no way to make the distinction secure short of exaggerating the rhythmic connection of *live-right* or *right-here*.

Verb phrases with infinitives are frequently ambiguous as between complement and purpose: *Now he has all the wine that he wants to drink* can refer to all the wine that he cares to drink or all the wine for drinking that he wants. Adjusting the rate so as to clump *wine-that-he-wants* or *wants-to-drink* helps to clear this up. A verb phrase with complement adjective may create an ambiguity with a noun phrase in which the adjective is a premodifier, as in *Have you noticed how young John looks?*—this can be 'John looks how young' or 'young John looks how.' The first interpretation gains a slight advantage if *John* is given a dropback to make it clear that *looks* is on a separate B profile. Otherwise (and even then) only an exaggeration of the rate is of much help. The prosody is only one of many cues that give us a fix on our meaning.

Numerical Sequences

Like the letters of the *cues* example above, a string of numbers (or other arbitrary symbols) offers no syntactic sign of how the items are grouped. A counting series then can be grouped by inserting a pitch change (up or down) or a pause or both, dividing the string into rhythmic or arrhythmic segments: *one-two, three-four-five, six-seven-eight-nine,* etc. In the following, only by adjusting the rate can the confusion be cleared up to some degree:

> The sports section was initially pared down from four to six pages
> in the New York edition to a single page in the national.[5]

The adjustment is to speed up *four-to-six*. But the result is still unsatisfactory and shows how ad hoc the prosodic remedy is—a careful editing would have changed *from four to six* to *from between four and six*, or, more drastically, would have revised the passage completely: *The sports section, initially four to six pages long in the New York edition, was pared down to* . . . Such verbal and prosodic trade-offs are frequent.

Where the distinctions are intonational, numerical sequences exhibit the same traits as were noted earlier in connection with *the brightest-colored one.* Suppose one asks *What's your new address?* and receives the reply

Twenty Seventh Street.

Is this to be interpreted as *27th Street* or as *20 Seventh Street*? Without exaggerating, changing the rate is no help. But if *twenty* is highlighted on a B + À,

```
Twenty
       Sev
          e
           n
            t
             h   Street.
```

it gains a slight advantage as *20 Seventh Street.* And if *twenty* is downplayed, as in

```
          sev
Twenty-      e
              n
               t
                h   Street.
```

the word *twenty* can more easily be heard as unaccented rather than as B-accented, leaving *twenty-séventh* with only the accent on *-seventh*, which is normal for a compound; so this favors *27th Street.*

To what extent is this distinction based on the choice of an accent pattern and the incidental effect of an intonation pattern? It seems likely that the compound status of the second configuration simply reflects the stress pattern of compounds and is chosen for that reason. But in the first configuration the distinction is more fragile; there can be a variety of reasons for using a B + À contour. If the person answering the question has difficulty remembering his new address, and it suddenly comes back to him, he may say, brightly,

```
I                  Twenty-
  remember                                          two-o-
                        sev            number
              w!          e   n                        t
           no             n  t                          h
                           th  Street--                  r
                                                          ee.
```

Or the speaker may be in the mood to say *Twenty-seventh Street, if it's any of your business,* giving the same B + À profile for speaker-dominance.[6]

Discontinuous Constituents

Constituents that are grammatically immediate—that belong together by virtue of their grammatical connection—are often separated to make the discourse meaning of a sentence clearer.[7] Grammatically, the adverb *slowly* in *Slowly they crept in* modifies the verb, *creep-in-slowly*, but is separated from it by the subject *they*. The speaker wants to convey the feeling that the whole scene is in slow motion, and disrupts the grammar to accomplish it. The intonation tells us that something special is happening—a B + À contour is used, with descending B tail, and *slowly* is drawled:

```
S-l-o-w-l-y they crept
                      i
                       n.
```

The intonational dramatization puts the hearer on notice that something may have happened to the grammar.

Such instances with adverbs are frequent, and especially troublesome if the adverb is a function word. The favorite example with the pop grammarians is "misplaced *only*" (Bolinger 1986: 144). They argue that *He only wanted to help* would have to be construed as *only-wanted* rather than as *only . . . to help*, and one should therefore say *He wanted only to help*. But since *only* and *help* are the important words, they will be highlighted accentually, and that is enough to link them.

The word *yet* is a more subtle case. In a sentence such as

We're a long way from being out of the woods yet.

if *yet* is totally unaccented, it is probably an immediate constituent of *being out of the woods*, and the same is true if *yet* carries an AC profile. But if it carries an A, it is almost certainly an immediate constituent of the main verb *are*: 'We are still a long way from being out of the woods.' Profile A is the most assertive profile, and *yet* has become the most important word in that sentence, a warning not to take things for granted—things being the whole content of the sentence, focused on the temporal aspect of the verb. *Still* would be highlighted in the same way.

But the main problem of constituency where adverbs are concerned is not one of immediacy versus nonimmediacy but which of two immediate constituents claims the adverb. An ambiguity such as that in

They relay constantly updated news like what you just heard.

where the hearer may be caught between *relay-constantly* and *constantly-updated*, can be managed by change of rate and pause-plus-fall.

A more delicate problem is posed by the so-called sentence adverbs, which are immediate constituents of everything else in the sentence and accordingly stand next to it,

> Clearly, they had won.
> They had won, clearly.

or inside it:

> They clearly had won.
> They had clearly won.

The same adverbs often function as manner adverbs and tend to follow their verb immediately (*He spoke clearly*). The two kinds of adverbs are fairly well distinguished by the prosody, above all in the position where they compete most strongly, at the end. So *He died happily* and *He died, happily*, with their B + A (or A + A) in the one and A + C in the other, leave little room for doubt in most contexts.

All the same, the contextual dependence is heavy and the prosodic distinction is not guaranteed. To answer *Did he lĩve happily?* one can reply

```
            di                              di
       he                         / but he
  No,/                       No,/
          e                            e
           d  happily.                  d  happily.
```

with A and A + C (or AC) respectively—in both cases *happily* is a manner adverb. The identical responses can be used to answer *What ever happened to John?*, where *happily* is a sentence adverb: it can be replaced with *I'm happy to say* with the same intonation. (The comma, in writing, is less ambiguous than the intonation; we would probably not punctuate the manner adverb with a comma, but at normal speed that would not affect the intonation; it would take an exaggerated pause before the adverb to compel—virtually—the sentence-adverb interpretation.) The intonation that almost guarantees a manner interpretation is a separate A profile for the adverb (an AC would still be ambiguous). But even an A is amenable to the sentence-adverb interpretation, if the speaker is very emphatic; this could be clearly marked by gesture, lengthening of the accented syllable, etc.—compare *happily* with *thank God!*, which would be synonymous in such a context:

```
     di     ha-a-                   di         Go
  He                             He
                pi                         thank
              l                      ed,       d!
     ed,       y!
```

What all this means is what has been reiterated before: the intonation helps out with distinctions in the course of other business. What those low-pitched endings really signify is 'this is not worth getting worked up about.' That in turn is suitable for all sorts of obiter dicta— asides, parentheses, vocatives, ascriptions, mild oaths. The sentence adverb is normally an obiter dictum, a side comment, not of the essence. So it prefers a typically inconspicuous intonation—and is thereby "disambiguated" from an adverb that is central to the utterance. As Schubiger (1958: 90) points out, "There is no direct relation between sentence structure and tonetic stress," but, "as certain elements of the sentence are intrinsically weightier than others, tonetic stress incidentally becomes a means of grammatical differentiation, though of strictly limited range." Where a distinction is secure, it is apt to result from a convergence of cues which together are so strong as to preclude ambiguity. For example, a sentence-adverb interpretation of

```
        nev
He                    clear          (A+AC)
        er
         speaks,       1ʸ˙
```

is almost impossible; the emphasis of the AC and the strong suggestion of 'manner' in the word *clearly* itself rule it out. But *obviously* in that position would be ambiguous: 'It's quite obvious that he never speaks' and 'He never speaks in an obvious manner.'

The prosody serves other adverbials besides simple adverbs, for example, participles:

Escaping, prisoner caught.
Escaping prisoner caught.

The first would most likely carry an AC profile, which would be unusual in the second unless for pronounced contrast—the interpretation 'caught while escaping' is more likely than 'the escaping one, not the other one.' Infinitives similarly:

She was foolish to say that.
She was foolish, to say that.

In the first, her folly begins and ends with her saying that; in the second, her folly in other matters is inferred from her present foolish act ('She had to be foolish in order to say that')—*to say that* becomes a sentence adverbial. With B + A the first sense comes through almost unambiguously; with AC + A there is a bare possibility of the second, and with A + A the possibilities are about equally divided. A similar pair, ambiguous as between the senses 'in order to be sure' and 'of course,' is

> I tried it out to be sure.
> I tried it out, to be sure.

A similar case is prepositional phrases used adverbially. Ordinarily there is no way to distinguish the two senses of

> I received a letter from Mary.

—the prosody does not tell us whether this is 'I received from Mary' or 'a letter that was from Mary'; since most of the time it makes no practical difference, it is possible that we process the general sense and are unaware of any ambiguity. But once again if a SENTENCE adverbial is involved, prosody is important. The following, spoken by a radio announcer,[8] is punctuated as it was said, and illustrates one of the ways in which written punctuation goes astray:

> Like a lot of people you're probably asking, "What can I do?"

The announcer was probably reading from notes, and carefully put a pause at the comma before the quotation, where no pause is needed, and neglected to put one after *people* (along with a likely AC profile on *a lot of people*) where it is needed to make the sentence adverbial clear. Without it, the hearer may have to revise the false assumption that *you're probably asking* is an adjective clause (*people whom you are probably asking*).

In all these instances the main contribution of prosody is to distinguish what is loosely connected from what is tightly connected. A sentence adverbial is a sort of appendage, and is marked off accordingly—the speaker *feels* the separateness, and supplies an iconic separation. (See Chapter 7 for adverbials as cases of parenthesis in dependent clauses.)

Ellipsis

"Grammatically complete" sentences, as conceived by grammarians, may be unduly repetitious, and such sentences are usually pared down. For example, *John saw Jennifer and June* is, supposedly, a reduction of *John saw Jennifer and John saw June*. From a practical standpoint, whether it is or not depends in part on whether John saw Jennifer and June together or separately—at separate places or on separate occasions. The complete form would be most unlikely if he saw them in each other's company, but the pared-down form is completely ambiguous as far as just the words are concerned. The prosody, however, can help to tell them apart—and it does it in the same iconic way as the superfluous words *and John saw*, by putting in a SEPARATION to denote the separate actions.[9] We can separate with words, and we can separate with pause-and-profile. *I want to wait and to see* is like *I want to wait, and see; I want to wait and see* joins *wait-and-see* into a single process, verbally and prosodically. This, of course, involves a question of constituency, since the *to* of the last example belongs with *wait-and-see* as a unit. It is false to assume that there has been any ellipsis at all, but the word order does not show it; the prosody does.

The prosodic separation is mostly by pause, but intonation accompanies it and may take over. If we say any of the following,

John saw Jen^{nifer} and Ju$_{ne}$.   (B+A)

John saw Jen ni^{fer} and Ju n$_e$.   (AC+A)

John saw Jen ni$_{f_{er}}$ and Ju n$_e$.   (A+A)

the separation provided by the tails of the initial profiles is a hint that the coordinated elements may be separate. Nevertheless, one could add *together* to each sentence without producing a contradiction. The intonations could have a purpose totally unrelated to actual coupling—the first, for example, to 'leave it up to the hearer,' a sort of flip reply which could be appropriately followed by *if it's any of your business*; the second is more positive—it could suggest 'don't give me any argument.' With the third it is difficult to rule out separation completely—Jennifer and June may be together, but the speaker is thinking of them separately.

The one intonation that gives a fairly good signal of togetherness is B + A with minimal change in pitch between profiles, that is, with the start of the A as if part of the B tail, as in

John saw Jen^{nifer} and ^{Ju} n$_e$.

But again, this is 'togetherness' in whatever sense, including the togetherness of huddled speech; no actual contradiction results from replacing *and* with *and then*.

The clearest test of togetherness is with lexical conjuncts. Someone visiting William and Mary College would say

```
            William and Ma
We visited
                    ry.
```

a B + A with the A starting about the same pitch as the B. It would
take a considerable emotive overload to justify either a rising B tail
with lower pitch on A or an initial AC. As for A + A, it would be virtually impossible, unless addressed in exasperation to a very dense
person. In one of its forms, B + A does "synthesize."

Coordinate adjectives incur the same kind of ambiguity, though the
syntax is better able to cope with it. The following—with singular
nouns—are unambiguous, because the article provides the separation where needed:

> a red, white, and blue flag
> a red, a white, and a blue flag

But the plural is ambiguous in writing:

> red, white, and blue flags

(To avert the ambiguity syntactically, a determiner can be inserted:
some red, some white, and some blue flags.) More than elsewhere, however, the comma here is misleading. In speech the ambiguity tends to
disappear. With level B profiles and a fast rate, we take the adjectives
to modify the noun as a group. The reasons for coupling are various.
The more familiar the combination, the faster it tends to go—*red-
white-and-blue* is practically a compound. The closer the adjectives are
semantically, likewise: *quick and easy solutions*. The whole matter of
constituency where coupled adjectives are concerned, however, involves considerations that have little or nothing to do with prosody.
There is, for instance, a difference between concrete and abstract or
unique nouns. We can say either member of the following pairs

> a happy and a well-adjusted childhood
> a happy and well-adjusted childhood
> an humble and a contrite heart
> an humble and contrite heart

but we do not—except in the unlikely event of there being two chick-
ens—have a choice in

> *a young and a tender chicken
> a young and tender chicken

With abstractions and unique nouns, separation answers to style:
whether prosodic or syntactic or both, separation makes the expression more dramatic, as in the following with a succession of A profiles

and—optionally for still greater separation—a succession of indefinite articles, all modifying the unique noun *earth*:

> There they were, Adam and Eve, stranded on a rocky, (a) watery, (a) windy, (a) volcanic, and (an) alien earth.

A final problem is the uncertainty we often feel, especially when writing and having to decide whether to insert a comma, about the first of two adjectives not separated by *and* that are part of the same noun phrase. Is it a discontinuous constituent of the noun, as in the earlier example *guarded by weak, old levees*, or is it an immediate constituent of the noun plus the second adjective, hence continuous, as in *early Italian immigrants*? In the case of *a miserly rich man*, the second adjective with its noun is a virtual compound, modified as a unit by *miserly*: rich men are a *class* in our society. It would sound rather strange to say *a rich miserly man*, or even *a rich, miserly man*. But what about *a miserly wealthy man*? The second adjective is still more of a classifier and the first more of a describer, but the comma—and the prosodic separation—would be less out of place. The distinction is a gradient one.[10]

In other forms of ellipsis the question of coupling is less in evidence but there are more complex problems of constituency. Usually, as in the following examples of "gapping," no difficulties arise (the ( ) marks where some element has been dropped):

> I didn't hear whether they had arrested ( ) or only pursued the suspect.

> I gave Mary the calculator and ( ) John the typewriter.

Or their interpretation may depend on our rejecting some farfetched interpretation of the utterance:

> Sue baked a cake yesterday and Sally ( ) today. (Greenbaum and Meyer 1982: 144)

But in the following,

Un^{less} our so^{ci}ety falls ( )   or is   a   ^{blown} pa^rt, we shall...

the intonation is essential for showing that *apart* belongs as much with *falls* as with *blown*. Two features are required: the B profile on *falls* and the C on *apart*: the first for the implied incompleteness and the second for the suggested repetition—*falls* "looks forward" to *apart*, and *apart* "looks back" to where *apart* would have been had it appeared alongside *falls*. The sentence is still ambiguous, but is less so than if an AC were on *falls*; an A on *apart* would practically guarantee that that word is not to be taken with *falls* but only with *blown*.

In the next example it is the customary intonation of the type of sentence that makes the difference:

> I'm not in the philosophical part of the book yet, so ( ) reserve judgment.

This is ambiguous as between 'and therefore I reserve judgment' and '(you) reserve judgment' (imperative). Normally the imperative would have a high-pitched B on *-serve* and a fall thereafter, whereas the statement would have a lower overall pitch with a slight peak on *judg-*. Obviously, this is a prime example of prosodic disambiguation in the course of ordinary prosodic business; its nonce relationship to the demarcative function is seen in the fact that the sentence is still to some degree ambiguous.

Finally, there are ambiguities that are cleared up by accent alone. The following is ambiguous in writing:

> The bills were not discussed in the Senate, though they were ( ) in the House.

The auxiliary *were*, next to the "deletion site," picks up the accent. In the full form of the verb (*were discussed*), *were* could be unaccented; but not to accent it here would make it refer to location. Auxiliaries in general are affected, including *be* before an adjective:

> It's embarrassed me, as it hás ( ) her. (versus *it's her)
> She's happier here than she ís ( ) at home. (versus *she's at home)

If the relationship between prosody and constituency is as informal as it appears to be, it should not be difficult for prosody to go against expectations and create new constituent relationships or wipe out old ones. There is evidence for both possibilities. In recent years a novel sort of annunciatory phrase containing the verb *be* has arisen, probably starting from some such "pseudocleft" sentence as *What it is is that x*, blended with something like *The point is that x*, yielding a double *is* there as in the first sentence: *The point is is that x*. Normally sentences divide between subject and predicate: *The books / are on the table*. But in a sentence beginning *The point is that*, the *that* clause is what states the content of the utterance, and *the point is* comes to be felt as a sort of conjunction, with a shift of accent to the verb. So we get the constituent arrangement *The point is, that* with an AC on *is* and a pause following. The proof of this division is in the further syntactic outcome. The traditional subject-predicate division is strong enough for the predicate to maintain its hold on the verb, which is then reduplicated, on the model of *what it is is*. Some attested examples showing subsequent developments, from radio broadcasts in the San Francisco area:

> The thing of it is is . . .
> There's one thing that struck me is that . . .
> It just seems to me is that . . .
> One of them is of course is that . . .
> The reason is, Chad, is because . . .[11]

The same annunciatory constituent can be found with simple noun predicates. Thus either of the following may be heard:

> Their decision, was death by hanging.
> Their decision was, death by hanging.

The latter is more dramatic, with its likely AC on *was*.

If the predicate is a description (adjective) rather than an identification (noun), then nothing is being announced and the division, if any, will be subject-predicate. So the prosody of the sentence

> The point is capital.

will tend to differ depending on whether *capital* means 'funds' or 'of prime importance': in the first case *is* has its full form and may be accented; in the second, *is* runs the prosodic gamut, and may even be reduced: *The point's capital.*

Instances of the overriding of constituent relationships by prosody are commonplace. The prosody creates its own macro-constituent answering to a mood or a passion. The following utterance consists of two full sentences and was spoken without a break on a C + B + B + A contour (accents as marked):

The following,[12] again two complete sentences, was spoken as if it consisted of two connected clauses with no pause between; the speaker connects them in his mind because of the causal relationship between them—he is not "through" with his idea at the end of the first sentence:

5. Questions

It has been emphasized repeatedly in this book that no intonation is an infallible clue to any sentence type: any intonation that can occur with a statement, a command, or an exclamation can also occur with a question.[1] Nevertheless there are some interesting correlations. They cannot be covered exhaustively; since we are not dealing with categories *of* anything, but only with encounters among prosody, syntax, gesture, and context, all of which are variable, the forms of interaction are practically infinite. Intonation especially affects the other variables in subtle ways because of its gradience, and also because it, along with gesture, conveys the speaker's feelings most directly, and indirectly the speaker's intentions—and these override the import assigned to a syntactic arrangement almost as often as they support it. For example, if something is in question form but is intended as an order, it may have an intonation appropriate to a command, as in the B + À

```
                    hand me that
                              chis
(1) Would  you
                               el?
```

A minister announcing from the pulpit, *Shall we all join together in singing Hymn No. 57?*[2] uses the same B + À. Contrariwise, something in imperative form intended as a question will have an intonation more often encountered with questions; e.g. the B + B

```
            me that again?     =
(2) Give                          What  did you just say?
```

And a question given in lieu of an answer will probably have the intonation that an answer in statement form would have, e.g. in answer to *Why did you do it?* the repeated B + Á

(3) Why do you sup^{po}ₛₑ? Because I ^{had}ₜₒ.

All the same, something can be said about the predominance of terminal rises if all forms of questions are lumped together. A Wierzbicka-style analysis of the term QUESTION would probably include components like the following:[3]

> I want to know something
> I assume that you know it
> I say: I want you to say something that would cause me to know it
> I say this because I want you to do it
> I know that you don't have to do it

The final component here is what distinguishes a question from a command such as *Tell me X*. It puts the speaker in the position of SUPPLIANT, and the intonation tends to reflect a corresponding mood: rising terminus, lack of assurance.[4]

Yes-No Questions

Roughly, the rising terminus in yes-no questions corresponds to Profile B. (In wh questions it is more apt to be C.) One form of yes-no question, using the question tag *eh?*, invariably has a contour ending in B, usually A + B:

(4) He's ^{com}ᵢₙg, e^{h?}

(Other such tags may or may not have the rise. In *He's coming, is he?* the *is he?* may rise or may just extend the fall on *-ing*.)

But how little dependence there need be on intonation can be seen in what happens when other clues are available. Consider volitional verbs used in the present progressive, second person:

(5) You're saying that I picked up the wrong one.
(6) You're wondering why I'm here.
(7) You're opening a new branch office.

Any of these, even when spoken at a relatively low pitch and with a terminal fall, is likely to be a question, simply because it is a bit unusual to tell another person what he is doing of his own volition; for such an utterance to be appropriate, it is usually something brought up for confirmation—a tagged *eh?* would be a natural addition. (An act assumed to be done unawares is a different matter, e.g. *You're spoiling our fun.*) The power of *you* to cue a question regardless of intonation and grammatical form is corroborated by Geluykens (1987: 489), whose subjects identified "statements" containing *you* as questions more than half the time.

Though yes-no questions are commonly associated with a rising terminal, what partial restrictions there are depend on overall contours more than on terminals. To test the limits, two points can be raised: (1) Are there contours that are more or less restricted to yes-no questions, even though the majority of such questions are found on contours that are more ambivalent? (2) Are there contours that are rarely or never encountered with yes-no questions?

These are empirical matters that can be settled only by a census of actual utterances. Lacking such a census, the best we can do is play some hunches. The answer to the first point is probably no, though it is possible that one or more contours have no use, say, 90 percent of the time, for anything but yes-no questions. This may well be the case with a B + B contour that is terraced upward (see Bolinger 1986: 229, 309). An utterance such as

```
                         why?
              tell you
(8) Did they
```

is of course syntactically a question, but

```
                    why(?)
            told you
(9) They
```

is almost as likely to be a question. As a statement it would call for a context like this:

> (10) I can't understand them. They did that without the slightest provocation.—Well? They told you why. What more did you expect?

The same intonation is found on commands that carry a hint of warning (*Just leave it alone*) and on objections (*That's easy to say*), and this suggests why it is likely to occur with questions. What most distinguishes the contour is its terminal level at a relatively high pitch—a rise in that position is more usual, for both questions and nonquestions, and is quite hospitable to nonquestions, as the level is not. A question may need to be CURBED—the speaker may want to restrain a display of concern or arousal. A nonquestion is less apt to encounter such a motive for reducing the upmotion; the hearer is less involved in it—no answer is called for—and the speaker can let go.

For a contour that would be somewhat unusual with yes-no questions, at least in American English, we can look at B + AC. Though a sort of "demanding question" can be found on this contour (see Bolinger 1986: 322), it is the 'demand' rather than the 'question' that seems to be conveyed and that accords with other uses of the same contour—in fact, this effect is found with wh as well as with yes-no questions:

(11) Did they show any ap ti tude?

(12) How do we get out of here?

The one place where B + AC is almost routinely used is with echo questions. We can imagine (11) or (12) spoken by someone who is repeating a question from the interlocutor, and implying 'Was it really necessary to ask that?'

Looking at somewhat more complex contours, we find one that seems to be almost impossible with yes-no questions, though wh questions give no trouble. Take first an utterance that is intended as a nonquestion:

(13) They were actually forced to dig their own graves.

—A + C + À with the last A lower-pitched and leveling off at the end well above creak. There is some such implication as 'this is a cause of wonderment,' largely from the suspense of the arrested fall at the end. It is virtually impossible to construe this utterance as a question, though with a fall to creak it might come through as a question asked for verification: 'Can this astonishing fact be true?' And if the issue is forced by substituting a yes-no question that is marked syntactically by inversion, the result is practically incoherent: *Were they actually forced to dig their own graves? Equally unacceptable:

(14) *Would they really object at all?

(15) *Would n't anybody have any money?

—though perhaps (14) would be barely possible as a rhetorical question. Either (14) or (15) would become more nearly normal with a terminal fall to creak; (15) would need some such interpretation as 'Aha, I have it now: it *is* the case, is it not, that nobody would have any money?' A wh question such as

(16) What
      do you sup   they meant by that?
             pose

is normal as a question that a speaker might address to himself—in wonderment—as much as to someone else. It, too, is improved if the terminal fall goes all the way. And all these examples become more likely with a final Á rather than À.

Much more testing would be required, but it appears that something is happening on this contour that goes against the mood that speakers are normally in when they ask yes-no questions. Perhaps the half-fall at the end is neither curious enough for an original question nor assertive enough for a statement brought up for confirmation; and the upmotion with downmotion on either side of it is too controlled. Whatever the explanation, there is no reason to suppose that this restriction is some arbitrary grammatical fact rather than the indisposition, for asking questions, of the underlying affective meaning of the contour.

In between the most-used and the least-used intonations, we find the full array of contours employed with yes-no questions. They differ from the most-used contours in that the latter, at least by inference, do *ask* in their own right: a rising terminal with its meaning of incompletion is germane to the fundamental incompleteness of questions. Other contours attach their own meanings, which may have nothing to do with asking. And of course at the opposite extreme we find utterances that rely on context or gesture if they are to be interpreted as questions at all—neither their intonation nor their syntax gives a clue:

    (17) You'll like dinner tonight. — We're going to have fried prawns
    [looks pleased]. — No, another favorite of yours: beans and chili.

The question here could have been introduced with *Let me guess* (and it could be argued that it is a guess rather than a question, though no such category is generally recognized). A questioning gesture (eyebrows raised) would be a normal addition.

The intonation of (17) is meant to have steady downmotion from a high initial B (B` + À), and can just as readily occur with a syntactic question. The meaning of 'that settles it' can be seen in the appropriate following context:

```
     gonna have
(18) Are we        be
                     a              a          I'm going  →
                    n        Because if we    re,
                     s?

somewhere el
             s
              e.
```

The CA profile similarly does not ask in its own right, but readily accommodates gestures and syntax appropriate to yes-no questions, e.g. the B' + CA contour in

```
       they intend making a       a
(19) So
                       fuss
                            bout it do they?
```

The C profile is common with yes-no questions in such contours as B + C, A + C, and CB + C, and carries its usual downplaying nuances, for 'courtesy,' 'restraint,' 'reassurance,' etc.:

```
            like to
(20) Would you         some?              (B'+C)
                    try
```

```
        this the way to the
(21) Is                    sta tion?       (B'+C)
                       bus
```

```
        can't
(22) But       you                         (A+C)
                  see?
```

```
      n't we better
(23) Had            first?                 (CB+C)
                call
```

Apart from individual contours, is there some general statement that one can make about the intonation of questions that will distinguish them from nonquestions and will be valid for all languages? From all available descriptions, it appears that the one distinctive trait is HIGHER PITCH, either throughout or, especially, toward the end. Though the rising terminal seems to be most widely used (and even where less used, may come through as 'more surprised,' hence 'more curious'), it is by no means universal. As we saw in Chapter 2 (p. 39),

104   *Intonation and Grammar: Clauses and Above*

some languages, including Swedish and even some dialects of English, favor high pitches overall rather than the terminal rise.

An intonation that ends relatively high but sounds rather strange to the ear of the American or Southern British speaker is a kind of CB profile, especially in longer questions with one or more syllables trailing after the main accent. Shorter questions—those *ending* in the accent—are more apt to have a terminal rise, but in the longer ones the unaccented syllables at the end form a plateau or trail downward. It is the routine use rather than the contour itself that strikes the American ear, since American speakers do use it occasionally, especially in a sort of resigned rhetorical question:

(24) Could ^{ything} have been more useless?
an

This general pattern seems to be quite widespread—see above, pp. 41 and 45. It is found (competing with rising terminals) in Hausa, which marks questions with intonation only, according to Lindau (1984), who argues that the downward trailing terminal reflects the general tendency to drop at the end and has nothing particular to do with questions. Other languages and dialects with similar patterns are Syrian Arabic (Loi Corvetto 1983), Campidanese Sardinian (Loi Corvetto, pers. comm.), Romanian (Dascălu 1975), Serbo-Croatian (Browne and Nakić 1975), and Russian (Leed 1965). It is also strikingly present in Anglo-Irish (Knowles 1984; see above, pp. 36–37, for the English spoken in Belfast and northern Britain). It is obvious that "high pitch for questions" includes high sustentions as well as high rises. In fact, American English freely uses a level terminus that is appreciably above creak:

(25) Is ^{it} true?

—reflecting a mood midway between the doleful and the thoughtful: the lower (but not lowest) pitch at the end says 'no excitement,' but still, appropriately for questions, leaves matters up in the air.

British English generally, but probably Midlands and northward (including Scotland) especially, makes heavier use of terminal fall than American English does. In the Masterpiece Theater production of D. H. Lawrence's *Sons and Lovers* the Nottinghamshire girl Miriam asks

(26) Will you ^{bring} me some ^{more} of your ^{sketch}_{es?}

—A + A + Á with fall to creak. A terminal ÀC is also common, as in

```
              like some
(27) Would you          t  a?
                         e
```

—with the typical high-pitched B and lower ÀC. Even in American English the case for the terminal rise has probably been overstated, both in terms of frequency and in terms of significance. Fries (1964) and Cohen (1972) have found that terminal falls are at least as frequent as rises. One can get a sense of the contribution of high pitch at the end, without the addition of terminal rise, by looking at utterances that are declarative in form but are intended as questions. Speakers often preface what they regard as a question (as shown by the use of the question mark) with the verb *wonder*:[5]

```
                                         stri
(28) I wonder if they're planning to go out on
                                              k
                                               e?
```

With this intonation—highest peak at end—a hearer would probably feel constrained to answer. But with the highest peak at the beginning,

```
     wonder
                  planning          out    stri
(29) I    if they're         to go      on
                                              k
                                               e?
```

the speaker is apt to be musing to himself—he might go on with *that would explain the way they've been behaving lately*. Similarly, in responding to another person's unclear explanation of something, e.g. 'Why Jones wasn't more insistent on having x,' it would be a bit incongruous to say

```
(30) O
         he doesn't ne
      h,              e
                       d
                        it?
```

but (31) would be normal:

```
                  need
(31) O   he doesn't
      h,
                   i
                    t?
```

—'*that's* what you mean!' To clinch this as a question one can add *then* at creak, extending the tail; but it is not essential.

We saw earlier that when B + A or A + A contours are used as answers to questions, they are apt to have the highest peak at the end. Both questioner and respondent APPEAL: the one for an answer to be given, the other for it to be accepted. Both ends of the question-answer exchange favor a rise toward the end but not necessarily a rising pitch as terminus. The generalized higher pitch is not so much a marker of questions and answers as a symptom of the tension a speaker is under when engaging in an informational exchange. The symptom is then to some degree conventionalized as 'appeal.' The role of falsetto here was treated in the discussion of register (see Bolinger 1986: 216–21), for example the reply to the question *Do you punish him?*:

```
                to.

             have
(32) When I
```

with *to* at falsetto, interpretable as 'I appeal to your understanding.'

Questioning as mood regardless of syntax can be seen in the ways in which intonation "spreads." A speaker preparing to ask a question will often put the "questioning" intonation on a preceding or following "statement," as in the following excerpt from a conversation recorded by Tannen (1984: 82):

(33) I read The French Lieutenant's Woman? Have you read that?

(Punctuation here represents intonation.)

Wh Questions

Typical shapes

Wh questions have their own partial restrictions, not identical to those of yes-no questions. The B + AC contour, for example, though not highly frequent, is found more often than with yes-no because of the generally more demanding nature of wh questions:

```
                  do
        what did you
(34) So
                    with it?
```

The restriction most often noted (applying only to ORIGINAL wh questions—see below, pp. 135–40, for questions that repeat) and which makes them most unlike yes-no questions, is the comparative unusualness of contours ending in B. To respond to *The club held a meeting yesterday* with the B + B

(35) And how many were there?

would sound unexpectedly tense, perhaps making the speaker out to be highly perturbed over some serious consequence of the number present. This intonation is usually found only with a reclamatory question, e.g. someone says *Ten people were there* and you fail to understand clearly and ask for a repetition:

(36) How many (did you say) were there?

But, as we have just seen, if the reason for being keyed up is powerful enough, the wh here need not be reclamatory.

Otherwise, the whole array seems to be open to wh questions:

(37) A+A   So   whére   did you   pút   it?

(38) CA+A   Whére   did   you   pút   it?

(39) A+C   Whére   did you   pút   it?

(40) CA+C   Whére   did   you   pút   it?

(41) B+A   Whére did you   pút   it?

(42) B+C   Whére did you   pút   it?

(43) C+C   So   whére did you   pút   it?

(44) CA+CA   But
```
                   would                      a
              why          dó  thing like
                      he                    that?
```

(45) A+B   Where
```
              did you  pút it?
```

And so on, plus, if we wish, reversing the peak heights in (37) and (38) and the troughs in (43)—the latter, with the second trough higher, would become much more threatening.

The comparatively infrequent CB profile is not unusual in questions where the speaker feels to some degree inhibited or reticent—for example, in accosting questions. These favor an initial profile with a downtilting tail (CB has such a tail by definition), so that initial CB's and downtilted B's are frequent. The holding-down of the accented syllable in the CB contributes to the overall restrained effect. The question is addressed to a stranger:

(46) CB+A   How do you get to
```
                              Elm
                                 Street from here?
```

(47) B+A   How do you get to
```
                           Elm
                              Street from here?
```

The more inhibited (46) is more likely than (47), especially given the rather positive note of the A. But gestural and other factors will affect the balance. On the other hand, in

(48) CB+C   How do you get to
```
                       Elm Street from here?
```

(49) B+C   How do you get to
```
                       Elm Street from here?
```

the chances are about equal. The toning down of the C is so strong that whether or not there is an initial toning down is hardly noticed.

Intersections with grammar

The intersections of question intonation with grammar and discourse are a virtually unexplored domain, which we can address only with a sampling to prove that there is a domain to explore. Take the question of "key" as it affects the position of a wh question in a discourse. An initial wh question is apt to have a B᾽ + À:

(50) He   Geor   ^{What did you tell Jo}
      y,   ge!   bn yesterday?

(Discourse-initial statements have the same tendency; see below, pp. 146–47.) Later in the conversation, B + Á is more likely:

(51) And   what did you tell ^{Ma}
                                    _{ry?}

If in place of this B + Á one were to hear a B᾽ + À as in the first instance,

(52) And   ^{what did you tell} Ma
                                   _{ry?}

it would sound as if the speaker were about to accuse his hearer of something, or perhaps as if he were keyed up trying to remember what it was that the other had said (if the other obliges with an explanation, the speaker might then say *Oh yes, I remember now*).

Or, on the grammatical side, take what happens when the interrogative word is governed by a preposition. In such cases the speaker may have the option of blunting the otherwise sharp high-pitched initial position of the interrogative word by putting the preposition in front of it. The more formal syntax contributes a degree of reserve that may obviate the need for restraint (reverse accents) on the intonational side. Thus, using the latter device, the rather accusatory

(53) ^{When do you expect to have it}
                                 fin
                                   _{ished?}

is softened by replacing the final A profile with a C:

(54) ^{When do you expect to have it}
                                 _{finished?}

But putting the preposition in front may give (53) the desired amount of reserve without further change:

(55) By what time do you expect to have it fin ished?

Similarly *Whose money are they buying it with?* versus *With whose money are they buying it?*, *Who was it written by?* versus *By whom was it written?*, etc.

The most radical alteration of the syntax of wh questions comes about by putting the interrogative after the verb. This device is not apt to be used for asking a question out of the blue. One may accost a stranger with *When is the next bus due?* but hardly with *The next bus is due when?* (it might get by on a B' + C contour). Mostly there needs to be a close tie with what precedes, with everything up to the interrogative word constituting the theme and the interrogative word itself the rheme. Usually the question does one of three things. (1) It repeats and questions some part of what has just been said, e.g. a reclamatory (see below, p. 138) such as the response to *He drove the screw with a hammer*:

(56) He drove it with what?

Or (2) it calls for supplying something that the interlocutor has omitted, e.g., in response to *She was buying— she was buying— . . .* :

(57) She was buying what?

Or (3) it extends the interlocutor's utterance with a coordinate clause, as in response to *I begged them to get me out of there*:

(58) And they took you whe re?

or with a qualifying expression of some kind, as in response to *I was just snooping around*:

(59) Looking for wha t?

or to *She got a present*:

(60) From who o?

As the diagrams suggest, the usual terminal is a fall, though (56), the reclamatory question, almost requires a rise, whether the rise of the B profile as shown, or the rise of a C:

```
        drove it with
(61) He
                 t?
            wha
```

Rises may appear elsewhere, with affective overtones. To say

```
              where?
         took you
(62) And they
```

in place of (58) may suggest unfinished business—for example, a lawyer cross-examining a witness whose answer has already been rehearsed may routinely use this B + B.

Wh questions are commonly stripped down to just the interrogative word, alone or accompanied by only a case-forming preposition (or, less frequently, gerund). When this happens, if the interrogative word comes first, as in

(63) I'm going to the party. — Who with?

the implication is the same as in the full form *Who are you going with?* But if it comes last, as in

(64) I'm going to the party. — With who(m)?

the implication is probably not *With whom are you going?* but *You are going with whom?* This simply reflects the theme-rheme dynamics of the full form, preserved in the intonational structure: what precedes the interrogative word assumes the role of theme. Compare also

(65) We were just sitting around. — What doing? (Doing what?)

The form with the interrogative word first is the more curious, the more likely to express a new thought. This accords with what was noted above about questions out of the blue. It tends to adopt the higher key as well:

```
         do
(66) What                          (67) Doing  wha
         in                                       t?
           g?
```

Much more could be said about what contours are appropriate for what purposes. Predictably, a classroom question such as *When did Columbus discover America?* would tend to have B' + À (see E. Fuchs

1935: 11–12)—the speaker is not interested in the information. The same with a question one asks oneself, e.g. *What shall I do now?* (p. 7). Wh and other questions used as reprises are treated below.

Complementary Questions

Complementary questions are the same as wh questions if the class is defined by the form of the answer. Grammarians have been inconsistent in their criteria for classifying questions. With yes-no, the definition is usually in terms of the answer: both syntactically marked *Did they go?* and syntactically unmarked *They went?* are classed as yes-no. But only those questions that contain one of the interrogative words (*who, whom, whose, which, what, where, whither, when, why,* and *how*) have been allowed as wh questions. To classify in terms of answers, we would have to combine (68) with (69) and (70) with (71):

> (68) The Prime Minister resigned. — For what reason? (Why?)
> — He had lost the support of his cabinet.
>
> (69) The Prime Minister resigned. — The reason being? — He had lost the support of his cabinet.
>
> (70) She is only fifteen. — So what? — She's too young for the job.
>
> (71) She is only fifteen. — So? — She's too young for the job.

As the examples show, what the wh question accomplishes with the blank-filling wh word, the complementary question accomplishes with the unfilled blank, leaving the hearer to infer what should go there. It offers unlimited ways of soliciting an informational answer without using a wh question or a direct order or request (*Tell me . . . , I want to know . . . , Make a guess . . .*). Some are more or less stereotyped. The *what if* question has a counterpart in *suppose, supposing,* and *if,* and *but if*:

> (72) Your duty is to accept service on a jury. — What if (and if, suppose) I don't want to?

What then? is often added to explicate a *suppose* question, and the same is true of other means of expressing a condition on something already mentioned that may raise a question about it—it averts ambiguity with yes-no:

> (73) I don't think this will work out with only ten. — Add two more? (What then?) — That will solve the problem.
>
> (74) I don't know about the prospects for a good crop this year. — With good weather? (What then?) — Well, that's the gamble.

The same happens with *What about* in complementary questions that propose a topic:

(75) My friends are all invited. — And John? (What about hím?) — I
guess I forgot that one.

Complementary questions require a thorough investigation on the grammatical side before we can say what intonational restrictions there may be, but given the backup from gesture it is probably true that any intonation that serves with other questions may be employed with complementary ones. Without gesture, a rising terminal is the usual thing. Thus *Your name* with terminal fall and a straight face is apt to be taken as a command, 'Tell me your name'; with raised eyebrows and/or a terminal rise, it is a question: 'What is your name?'

Alternative Questions

Alternative questions have been singled out as a class as much because of their intonation as for any other reason. Yet in this respect they do not differ (except in cohesion) from a series of yes-no questions that the speaker considers to exhaust the possibilities, as we see in

(76) Is it g^{ood}, ba^{d}, or $in^{dif}{}_{fe}{}_{re}{}_{nt}$?

(77) Is it g^{ood}? (No.) Is it b^{ad}? (No.) Is it in $^{dif}{}_{fe}{}_{re}{}_{nt}$ then?

Each of the nonfinal alternatives has the expected B profile and the last one has an A because the speaker is "through."

As with other question types, profiles other than B can readily be found with alternative questions, though the contour . . . (B +)B + A is most typical. In the Stenström corpus (Stenström 1984: 211) the rise plus fall was more than three times as frequent as the fall plus fall (A + A).[6] The . . . (B +)B + A is so compelling that it may bias a question toward alternative even if intended as yes-no. The following, recorded from a television program,[7]

(78) Is it either the motion $^{picture\ or\ the}$ →
$_{legitimate\ the}$
$_{ater\ that\ you\ are\ connected\ with?}$

was taken by the person addressed as an alternative question even though the word *either* makes nonsense of such an interpretation.

As before, other contours add their own nuances. An AC + A is more demanding—in (79) the speaker perhaps implies 'Make up your mind!':

(79) Are you $_{i}n^{g}$ ^{com} or staying ^{ho} $_{m}e?$

A terminal B may have the same effect, but is extremely keyed up. The speaker starts with *For God's sake make up your mind!* and continues

(80) Are you $^{com}i^{ng}$ or staying $_{h}^{ome!}$

Without this degree of tension one is not apt to encounter a terminal B in an alternative question. Someone asking *Would you like coffee or tea?* with B + B is most likely seeking a yes or no answer, not a choice, though this shape is sometimes met with in blends: a stewardess on an airplane might use it to elicit a reply like *Yes, thank you, I would— coffee, please.* Another example of a tense question using a terminal B is (81), put by an examining counsel to a witness who has been giving evasive answers:

(81) Were you there or $n^{ot?}$ I'd like a direct $^{answer\ please.}$

Notice how the demanding B + B "spreads" to the following statement.

If C's replace the B's, and even if a C also replaces the final A, the result is quite ambiguous as between yes-no and alternative:

(82) Is it re^{d} or ^{blu} $_{e?}$ (83) Is it re^{d} ^{or} $blu^{e?}$

What the intonation conveys here is affect, regardless of the type of question. The speaker might add *I've already asked you six times!*— the C's suggest impatience under tight control. B + A is equally ambiguous (and insistent, without the restraint).

In short, no intonation seems to exclude alternative questions. We have, as always, a conjunction of phenomena, which facilitate alternativeness to varying degrees. One not mentioned up to this point is rate. When two or more alternatives are closely linked, as they tend to be in a yes-no question using *or*, the linkage is apt to be cued in part by a faster rate. So if

(84) Is it ^red or
                  blu
                    e?

is pronounced *red-or-blue*, the yes-no interpretation is somewhat
reinforced, whereas if there is an appreciable pause after *red*, the alternative interpretation is almost guaranteed.

Tag Questions

Types using tags

Tag questions[8] are hybrids, part statement (as a rule) and part question. The term is generally restricted to utterances that contain a statement which is then immediately questioned by repeating the auxiliary
verb (or substituting *do* if no other auxiliary appears in the statement)
plus the appropriate pronoun:

(85) You've seen him, have you?
(86) I'll just have to spank you, won't I?
(87) They can't really offer more, can they?
(88) It's too late, isn't it?
(89) She bought the place, did she?

As the examples show, the stem (main part) and the tag do not have
to have the same polarity—one may be positive and the other negative.

The use of the auxiliary verb in this way is a typically English device. More usual generally is the device of tagging some element that
may be little more than an intonation-carrier. English shares this
possibility:

(90) It's too late, hunh?
(91) She bought the place, eh?
(92) They're coming tomorrow, no?

There are other ways of qualifying a statement in the direction of
questioning it, some of which are closely related, semantically, to
tags. In a sense, when we say *Did they find it?* in place of *They found it?*
we are "adding" the same element that is tagged in *Find it, did they?*
The same goes for another form of tag that will be looked at briefly
later. When we say *I suppose he's coming* we are most likely seeking
confirmation—the verb *suppose* is stereotyped in that function, and it
is readily tagged: *He's coming, I suppose?*

Tag questions using the auxiliary verbs are mostly a subtype of yes-
no, and will be so treated here, though there is the possibility of tagging both alternative and wh questions. The former are mostly limited to alternative questions containing only two alternatives, tagged

in the middle: *You'd like it in hard cover, would you, or will paperback serve?* The intonations are probably limited to those with a rising terminal on the tag, that is, one would find

(93) You'll go
<pre>
                 will
(93) You'll go   prod
             ingly won't you, or must I
                                                   you →

      all the way?
</pre>

with a C profile on the tag, but would not find, except as an afterthought (in which the speaker converts a yes-no into an alternative), something like

<pre>
             cra
(94) He's   (A+A, A+A)
              is   on
      zy,   n't he, or is it   ly put o n?
</pre>

Tagged wh questions are usually reclamatory, e.g.

(95) Henry went to Milwaukee. — Where did he go did he? (was it?)

(The *was it* tells us that tagged reclamatory questions readily shift to the cleft construction in the tag—a sort of hybrid, in this case based on *Where was it that he went, was it?*)[9]

Polarity, same and reverse

The intonation of tagged yes-no questions predictably adjusts itself to the nature of the tag, same-polarity and reverse-polarity. Reverse polarity is conducive, that is, it implies that the speaker expects agreement. Same-polarity is intensive. For example, the questions

(96) You like him, don't you?
(97) You don't like him, do you?

expect *yes* and *no* respectively, whereas

(98) You like him, do you?
(99) You don't like him, don't you?

only intensify whatever implication is already present in the stem.

The intonation of both types reinforces or attenuates their inherent qualities. The customary reinforcing intonations have, in fact, been partially lexicalized onto the carrier syllables *eh* and (in American English) *hunh*, the former representing a B profile, the latter an A:

(100) You like him, eh? = You like him, do you?[10]
(101) You like him, hunh? (A + A) = You like him, don't you?

The adoption of *hunh* in this role dates from about 1950. (See below, p. 265.) With both *eh?* and *hunh?* the stem ends in an A or CA profile; that is, we do not say things like

(102) *You like him, eh?

which are normal with *do you?* This reflects the meaning of *eh?* and *hunh?* questions: the speaker is comparatively confident that the statement in the stem is a fact. Though *do you?* may serve the same purpose when it has the same intonation, its possibilities are wider.

With a reverse-polarity question on an A + À contour the expected answer is almost a certainty—the speaker may not even pause for it:

(103) You like him don't you? I knew it all along.

The contours with a rising terminal are less apt to be satisfied without a response—this applies to A + C,[11] A + B, B + B, and C + B, e.g. B + B in the context

(104) I won't marry him. — Why not? You like him, don't you?

You like him don't you?

The intonation in each instance plays its customary role. The terminal fall of the A + A closes the matter—though this is a question, it has the lowest degree of curiosity. The rising terminal of the other contours leaves the matter up in the air. In addition, the C of the A + C is deferential—the matter is courteously left open for a denial even though confirmation is expected. But with B + B the rising terminal is not deferential—the effect of the rise would be there even without the tag:

(105) Why not? You like him. What could be more natural?

The rising pitch here is a reaction to a real or supposed rejection; the speaker would be surprised if what he assumes were not true; so B + B turns out to be more insistent than A + C. The difference can be seen by comparing contexts. A + C requires no assumed rejection; it may come in sequence with the speaker's own idea:

(106) I think you ought to marry him. You (do) like him, don't you?
That's the main thing.

B + B would not be appropriate here; no contrary viewpoint ('I won't marry him') has been expressed that needs to be combated. (An A + B is barely possible.)

One restriction that we find in the intonation of tag questions has to do with relative height in A + A contours. Whereas both AC + À and AC + Á are acceptable, A + À is but A + Á is not:

```
            like                                              don't
                    don't                        like
(107) You                          (108) *You
            him,                                        him,
                    ᵧoᵤ?                                        ᵧoᵤ?
```

The reason probably is that the strong appeal of the high pitch on the tag does not sort well with the quiet confidence of the preceding A. (With a pause between the profiles, that is, with the Á no longer tagged but an independent utterance, the sequence is possible, as we can see by adding *now* to the tail.) That same confidence is not present in AC, and AC + Á is normal.

The restriction on same-polarity tags is even stronger, affecting not only A + Á, which becomes impossible even when stem and tag are separated,

```
            did                                              Did
        saw                                          saw
(109) *You                          (110) *You
            her,    ᵧoᵤ?                                 her.    ᵧoᵤ?
```

but also A + À, which, while not impossible, is rather hard to motivate. Someone saying

```
        saw
                    did
(111) You
            her,    ᵧoᵤ?
```

might be responding reflectively and critically to the interlocutor's having said (or suggested) *I saw her*—the mood can be seen in the appropriateness of adding *hm*:

(112) You saw her, did you? Hm. That puts a different face on the matter.

Probably the best case for A + À with same-polarity tag can be made for questions with elliptical stems, e.g.

```
        wi                          see  a
              will          we'll
(113) Oh you          Well              bout  tha
        11,      you?                         t.
```

Corpus studies suggest that A + A examples with same-polarity tags are rare (Nässlin 1984: 139; none were found in her count—pers. comm.).

Though C + C is possible regardless of relative height of the trough, the situation is similar. Given a lower second trough,

```
            him
(114) You
       like        you?
           don't
```

the cohesion is tight—there is even some doubt as to the appropriateness of calling the contour C + C rather than simple CAC, since *You like him?* with the same import and with *him* executing the entire high-low-high after *like*, is normal. The *don't you* can hardly be regarded as an independent sentence (try tagging it with *now*). But if the second trough is higher,

```
                    you?
            him
(115) You          don't
       like
```

the *don't you* may readily be split off—*now* can be added (*don't you now?*) and a pause can be inserted after *him*. These possibilities raise the whole question of fusion between the two parts of a tagged question. Are they one sentence or two?[12] The problem of "one" or "two" is an even livelier issue where tagged commands are concerned (see below, pp. 165–67).

There is also a restriction on B + A (whether À or Á) which applies to both same-polarity and reverse-polarity tags:

```
                 do (don't)
         know it
(116) *You
                      you?
```

```
          it
     know    do (don't)
(117) *You
                      you?
```

This seems to be a case of contrary intentions. The B is too unsettled for a tag that suggests that things *are* settled, and the contentiousness that justifies the B + B is absent.

With C in the stem, almost anything goes (except that the tag may not be AC—but this seems to be a general restriction on the tag; see below).[13] So we find C + A, C + C, and C + B:

(118) You
                  don't
      know ^{it}
               $y_{ou?}$

(119) You
          know ^{it} don't $y^{ou?}$

(120) You
               don't $y^{ou?}$
      know i^t

The same is true of AC in the stem, e.g. AC + C:

         know
(121) You
         i^t don't $y^{ou?}$

Examples (118)–(121) all have reverse polarity. The same possibilities exist for both C and AC in the stem with same-polarity tags except that the tag may not be A; so C + C, C + B, AC + C, and AC + B are all right, but not C + A or AC + A. We have seen the acceptable C + C in (114) and (115); (122) is an unacceptable C + A:

(122) *You
              do
      know ^{it}
            $y_{ou?}$

The contour B + C appears to be out of bounds for both reverse-polarity and same-polarity tags. Testing this requires a word with a string of unstressed syllables following the stress:

          $nece^{ssary}$
(123) *It's un
                is $^{it?}$ (is$^{n't}$ $^{it?}$)

If the pitch is allowed to drop on *-ary* the result is CA + C, which is normal:[14]

           ce^s
        ne sa_{ry}
(124) It's un   isn't $^{it?}$

The restriction on B + C is not surprising—B and C are the extremes of playing up and playing down. But this and other similar restrictions raise the problem of why such contours should be normal elsewhere and not here—a B + C is perfectly normal in an utterance not involving a tag, e.g.

```
                    everybody for him
(125) It was
                            self.
```

The likeliest reason is the relative independence of the tag, and the ill-defined territory between one utterance (hence one contour) and two. Compare, for fused versus unfused contradictions, in this instance words rather than profiles:

> (126) Do you like it? — Yes and no.
> (127) Do you like it? — *Yes. No.

Aside from this restriction on B + C, same-polarity tags seem to be normal as part of any contour with a rising terminal (and on almost none with falling). Examples have been given for most, but A + B, B + B, and A + C need to be added:

```
        found                                       did you?

(128) You                                (129) You  found   it
                  did  you?
            it
```

```
        found

(130) You
                it    you?
                  did
```

The favoring of a rising terminal of course fits the intensifying function of the polarity tag. The speaker does not suggest the answer he expects. In Nässlin's corpus (p. 165), same-polarity questions more often elicit "real informative answers" than "mere agreements." They are basically more inquisitive, and the rising tag makes them more so by adding upmotion or increasing it.

It was mentioned above that the unlikelihood of C + AC was exceptional among contours containing C in the stem, which for the most part combine freely with tags that use other profiles. We can generalize: tags do not use an independent AC profile. This raises a question about tags as a class: to what extent are they accented at all? Since the A part of AC must represent an accent, and cannot, like the C, be confused with the upmoving *part* of an AC, perhaps the failure of AC to appear on tags indicates that tags are basically unaccented. The one clear exception is a reverse-polarity tag using an A profile, which shows its accented nature not only by the other markers of accent besides pitch that it can readily carry (extra length, extra intensity, emphatic movement of the head) but also by the fact that it can occur independently of the stem and even be addressed to another person (see Bolinger 1986: 266), e.g.

(131) She's
      cra   Is
          ᶻy.   nᵗ
                          she (John)?

Tags on other profiles seem on the borderline of being mere extensions of the contours that would appear on the stem if no tag were present, and this impression is underscored by the readiness with which they may appear with reduced volume, length, etc. The ambiguity is notorious with a stem carrying AC, as we have noted a number of times. Someone asking (with a nod of the head)

(132) You
          like
              hiᵐ?

is already using a rising terminal to which a deaccented tag may be added without changing the mood:

(133) You
          like
              ʰiₘ don't yᵒᵘ?

The tag here might be heard as having a C profile of its own rather than being a tail to the AC. If the tag were on a potential B profile,

(134) You
          like
              ʰiₘ doⁿᵗ yᵒᵘ?

the ambiguity would be reduced somewhat in the direction of A + B, and indeed such a question does sound a bit more insistent. Another problem case is B + B. If the second B is not realized with a clear jump to the second accented syllable, the result is indistinguishable from a simple B with an unaccented tag as part of its tail. In these cases the tag assumes the status of such unaccented terminal elements as vocatives, certain sentence adverbs (e.g. *apparently, fortunately*), certain anaphoric pronouns and adverbs (*him, then*), etc. Same-polarity tags are more likely to be unaccented than reverse-polarity; they are mere intensifiers, not essential to the grammatical meaning of the utterance. This is especially noticeable when the tag forms part of the tail of an A; in that position it is unmistakably without accent:

(135) You ᵃ
          gree
              then do you?

Don't you would be possible here but much less likely.

Polarity	A + À	A + Á	B + A	C + A	AC + A	A + B	B + B
Reverse	+	−	−	+	+	+	+
Same	+*	−	−	−	−	+	+

Polarity	C + B	AC + B	A + C	B + C	C + C	AC + C
Reverse	+	+	+	−	+	+
Same	+	+	+	−	+	+

Table 1. Contours of Questions with Tags

*See remarks on p. 118, above.

The lack of accent of the tag on the tail of the A is corroborated by the fact that only in that situation is a reversal of polarity from negative to positive unambiguously equivalent to no reversal—a tag such as *do you* after a negative stem becomes equivalent to *don't you* and both are equivalent to *eh*:

(The *do* is a stronger assertion of the negative than *don't*—it has the effect of *You dislike it do you?*)[15] Rising tags are ambiguous as between true reversal and assertion, e.g. B + A + C,

A tag on its own independent A profile is unambiguously conducive, not intensive, when polarity is reversed.

Table 1 summarizes the likely and unlikely contours. The contours with initial CA are omitted on the assumption that they will have the same distribution as contours with initial A. Except for À vs. Á, diacritics are also omitted as they do not discriminate for acceptability.

Elliptical tag questions

All examples of tag questions up to this point have been with full declarative stems, except for the elliptical type *You will will you?* Two other elliptical types are important, one based on the full declarative, the other on a type not thus far examined, an instance of which is

(138) Is it hurting is it?

with an interrogative stem. This type of tag question, with inversion in the stem as well as the tag, is so insistent that it is almost certain to be spoken on a B contour. Its apparent redundancy and low frequency may tempt the analyst to regard it as a speaker's error. But the elliptical type based on it is too frequent and too clearly patterned to be considered a lapse.

The two elliptical types overlap in a case like

(139) Hurting is it?

One possible source is (138). The other is the corresponding declarative

(140) It is (It's) hurting is it?

The derivation is phonological, by apheresis.[16] The first two words of the full form, *is it* or *it is*, are dropped, and (139) is what remains. Call the (138) derivative Int(errogative), the (140) Decl(arative).

We can prove that (140) is the source for Decl (139) by observing that conducive reversal of polarity is normal, using an A + À contour:

(141) Hurting isn't it?

This obviously can be based on *It's hurting isn't it?* but not on *Is it hurting isn't it?*

And we can prove, in two ways, that (138) is the source for Int (139). For the first, we need an example that is not ambiguous like (139), and we find this in a form using the infinitive, for instance

(142) See them did she?

which would be based on the full *Did she see them did she?*—obviously not on

(143) Saw them did she?

although this would be a perfectly good Decl question. Now when we try to make the question conducive the result is ungrammatical:

(144) *See them didn't she?

The Decl, however, converts with ease:

(145) Saw them didn't she?

So Decl and Int are distinguished by the fact that Decl but not Int admits reversal of polarity for conduciveness.

The other proof is the possibility of retaining the subject in Int, regardless of the verb form. The subject can also of course be "retained" in Decl as well, but the effect of retaining it is simply to return to the full form: *Saw them didn't she?* becomes *She saw them didn't she?* What distinguishes Int is that unlike *she saw, she sees,* etc., there is no grammatical agreement between subject and verb, since the auxiliary, which does show agreement, has been dropped, that is,

> (146) Your leg hurting is it?
> (147) Mary see them did she?

come from *Is your leg hurting is it?* and *Did Mary see them did she?* respectively, with just the auxiliary peeled off. In other words, partial ellipsis is possible with Int; it is not possible with Decl, as there is no **Is hurting is it?*

Given that (146) and (147) are Int, with retained subjects, we can apply the polarity-reversal test:

> (148) *Your leg hurting isn't it?
> (149) *Mary see them didn't she?

This agrees with (144): Int does not allow reversal of polarity for conduciveness.

This also shows the basis for the ambiguity in (139). Without the subject and without conducive negation, (139) can be taken either way. Adding the subject forces the Int interpretation, adding conducive negation forces the Decl.

Although Decl *may* use a nonfinite form of the verb, as in (139) interpreted as Decl, Int *must* use such a form—if it uses a verb at all—since what has been dropped is precisely the form that indicates finiteness, the auxiliary. In addition to verbs there are three other lexical classes that can fill the same slot: adjective, noun, and locative adverb—all as predicates of *be*.[17] So we get the following array of Int subtypes, to which optional subjects have been added:

> (150) (You) going are you?
> (151) (Somebody) find it will they do you think?
> (152) (Your car) broken down had it?[18]
> (153) (That horse) sure to lose is it?
> (154) (Her friend) a lawyer is he?
> (155) (All the candidates) here are they?

Int is also commonly found without the tag, e.g.

> (156) Going?
> (157) Suffer from arthritis?
> (158) Sure to lose?

Such questions are of course heavily dependent on context for interpretation.[19]

Given their distinct sources, Int in a form like (138) that almost has to have a B profile, Decl in forms associated with possible reversal of polarity with its favoring of A profiles, it is obvious that the two elliptical question forms will carry on with these same preferences. This can be seen most clearly when the stem is an infinitive and the tag contains *does*, making the question unambiguously Int:

(159) Li^{ke} it does he?

(159) Li^ke   it does he?

The corresponding Decl is *Likes it does he?*, which may have the same intonation but more easily accepts downmotion. It is easy to become confused here because the infinitive is homophonous with plural finite forms, so that a sentence such as *Like it do you?* can be taken either way. When that happens, the hearer uses the intonation along with other clues to decide whether what he is hearing is Int or Decl. But since both can occur on a B profile, it may be that under those circumstances and perhaps others as well, we are simply deaf to the distinction.

All the same, whereas a B or a C profile in the stem may be ambiguous, an A or AC profile there points to Decl. If this is true, an unambiguously Int sentence should be unacceptable with A or AC, and such seems to be the case:

(160) *His ^{mother} spank ... him ^{does} she?

—a B or a C profile here would be normal, as would the same sentence with *spanks*. *Spanks* of course makes the sentence Decl.

Though both Int and Decl take their origins in grammatically complete forms, they have developed senses that set them apart from their sources. A Decl, for example, can be used to pose something as a hypothetical possibility, leading to comment:

(161) Pay ^{tax} es should I!   Like ^{hell} I will!

(162) Act the ^{foo} l will she?   Well we'll ^{have} to do something →   about th a^t!

The full forms *I should pay taxes* and *She will act the fool* would make these more like regular questions than hypotheses. The old discourse particle *forsooth* fits the hypothesis interpretation. The hypothesis represents a sort of inward debate, as when one responds to a suggested course of action with

>(163) Act the fool, eh? Well, I suppose I can if I must.

Nonauxiliary tags in nonquestion form

The regular auxiliary tags do not exhaust the possibilities of tagging, nor are questions the only things tagged. The language has a largely unexplored realm of sentence satellites, mostly adverbs and adverbial elements tagged and untagged, that reveal English to be as rich in "modal particles" as German, though perhaps less systematic. Some of these are treated in Chapter 10 on exclamations. Among the tagged ones are those italicized in the following:

>(164) I just do, *that's all.*
>(165) Oh, he'll tell you, *all right!*—count on that.
>(166) It's really good, *you know.*
>(167) They tried, *you see,* but it didn't work out.

These have characteristic intonations (mostly B or C, though the first can also be A + C).

Of principal interest here are the tagged adverbials that are not themselves questions—thus differing from the auxiliary tags—but have come to function as question-markers. They are formulas that disclose the speaker's confidence in what he is asserting: assessment of its truth or likelihood (*of course, I suppose*), authority for saying it (*you say, I understand, I infer*), etc. When that confidence is tentative or shaky, the speaker is probably angling for confirmation, and we interpret the utterance as a question—about the content of the stem, not the tag:

>(168) He's coming I suppose? — Yes he is. (*Yes you do.)
>(169) He's coming you say? — Yes he is. (*Yes I do.)[20]

The motive for *you say, you claim, you figure,* etc. as a question-marker is, of course, the fact that one does not usually put words into one's hearer's mouth unless to get confirmation.

Some of these tags are firmly enough stereotyped as question-markers for the utterance to have a terminal fall and still most likely be interpreted as a question:

>   com
>(170) He's
>   ing I suppose? (I hope, I gather)

A number of them are stereotyped for 'uncertainty' despite the literal meaning of the words, and that too makes for questioning. Examples include *no doubt, doubtless, naturally, surely,* and *I trust:*

(171) He's
com
        ᶦⁿᵍ no doubt?

Though *I suppose* and *I presume* are strongly formulaic for questions, *I guess* is not, though it too implies uncertainty. *I imagine, I'll bet,* and *of course* can easily go either way. Thus

(172) He
likes
     ᶦt I'll bet(?)

can be a question or a statement; gesture and context tell the difference.

It might be expected that expressions of this sort, which allow a question interpretation even given a final A profile with a deep fall, would have their interrogativeness enhanced by a rising terminal, but that is not clearly the case. It is true that something like

(173) He's
com
     ing I suppose(?)

seems a little higher on the scale of interrogativity, but a terminal rise may actually work against the question interpretation because of other motivations for the rise. The speaker of (173) might go on to say *But he's not doing it with much enthusiasm.* The rising pitch only implies 'something left unsaid, more to come.' Since the terminal fall does not invite that sort of inference, it may make a better question. Position is obviously a factor. If the speaker utters (173) and abruptly halts, the hearer will feel that it is up to him to carry on; hence, "this is a question." A question is "when the speaker intends one."

It is possible that one or more of these tags are invariably question-markers. I suspect that *I trust* is one, as used colloquially. On the other hand, *I know* is not a question clue at all. When given a terminal rise, as with the AC

(174) He's
com
     ing I know·

it does not ask for confirmation of the stem but rather reaffirms it, and implies uncertainty about something else: 'I can say as to that but not as to other matters.' And it is not an uncertainty that expects to be resolved by something the interlocutor may say—in other words, it is not a question. The same goes for *right enough*. It also goes for *true*, *yes*, and *to be sure*, except that now the tag is more apt to be given a separate profile:

(175) He's
       com

      in^g' to be su^{r}e·

—the fusion is less close than with *I know* and *right enough*, which have the option of the simple AC of (174) or the AC + C of (175).[21]

I suppose reveals its tagginess also in the fact that it is not apt to be used with an independent A profile; a case like

(176) He's
      com
              po
    ing I sup
            s$_e$.

is rather unusual, and the same goes for *I imagine, I guess, no doubt*, and *doubtless*. In fact, when we try to say *He's coming no doubt* with this A + À contour the impulse is to add *of it* (*He's coming, no doubt of it*), which yields an expression of certainty, not a question. Nor does a question result when ÀC replaces À, though now the utterances are perfectly normal:

(177) He's
      com
              po
    ing I sup
            s$_e$·

'but I don't know for sure.' Similarly *I imagine, I surmise, I guess, I assume*, etc. But now we have left the domain of tags; these expressions with ÀC have the literal sense of the verb: 'I guess (assume, etc.) but I don't *know*.' The literalness of the verb here makes a good test for *I trust*. Though literally it ought to be able to contrast with *know* the same as the other verbs, it is a little strange in the A + ÀC frame, which is to be expected if, as claimed above, it is a question-marker in its own right.

Not all the adverbials reject A + À utterances as questions. We can say

```
                com
(178) He's                 cou
            ing of   rse?
```

and intend a question by it (cued by raised eyebrows etc.). The same
goes for *naturally* and *surely*. As for *I know, true, right enough, I don't
doubt, yes,* and *to be sure,* they are all normal with A + À, but, as before, they do not yield questions—any uncertainty has to do with
some other matter. There is also a wide range of assertive adverbials
that are not attracted to 'uncertainty' in any sense and accordingly
accommodate the A + A (even A + Á as well as A + À) without difficulty, though they too have the option of being tagged without accent: *I guarantee, I assure you, you may be sure, it's quite clear, obviously,*
etc. They do not, of course, yield questions.

To sum up: there is a gradient range of adverbials, not themselves questions, which manifest varying degrees of stereotyping as
question-markers. Even though many of them are literal expressions
of certainty, it seems that by so much as bringing up the matter of
certainty they tend to pose a doubt about it, which favors 'question.'
This is not true of all such expressions and there is no apparent reason why some should develop an affinity to questionness and others
not, from the standpoint of their literal meaning: *definitely* is literally
no more 'certain' than *surely,* but *surely* makes a good question-
marker, *definitely* does not. The bifurcation of *surely* and *sure* is typical
of this development. *Sure* not only falls in the same class with *I know*
(affirming what is asserted in the stem and expressing uncertainty
about some other matter) but virtually requires the separate A profile
that is only an option with *I know*:

```
            com
(179) He's       su                              sa
         ing,       But  that's the most I can
         re.                                    y.
```

As with auxiliary tags, the typical adverbial tag is unaccented. If it
falls, it is the tail of an A. If it rises, it is on the tail, or extends the tail,
of a C or an AC, though the analysis here is affected by the ambiguities already noted in Bolinger (1986: 268–70), e.g. between AC and
A + C. Again as with auxiliary tags, an independent A profile is the
exception; an auxiliary tag may take it when conducive (*You knew that
didn't you?*) and an adverbial tag may take it with *of course* and one or
two other expressions. As for an independent AC, it returns the literal sense to the verb and is not a question-marker.

The element of arbitrariness in these restrictions is the fault of the lexicon, not of intonation, which plays its normal complementary role. *Sure* versus *surely* and *I trust* versus *I believe* are lexical anomalies (though if we knew their history we could probably explain the shifts); but the profiles function in their own sphere and maintain their identity. For example, the AC of *I suppose* in (177) leaves open to discussion the appropriateness of 'suppose' just as *I saw Jóhn* with AC leaves open the appropriateness of 'John.' Upness and downness have their general affective meaning, reacting with whatever lexical and grammatical material they occur with. If this cross-cutting material is absent, the intonation may still be able to go it alone. The simple utterance

```
         com
(180) He's
         in g·
```

with its AC profile, may be a question equivalent to (173) or a statement equivalent to (174). In both cases there is incompletion, but the reasons for it differ.

Nonauxiliary tags in question form: cohesion

Tags may take the form of nonauxiliary questions, and be attached to statements (*They have proof did you say?*) and questions (*Is this in use do you know?*). When attached to statements, the same possibilities are broached as with auxiliary tags, for example, same polarity for intensification, reverse polarity for conduciveness:

(181) He's coming do you think?
(182) He's coming don't you think?

—with the difference that in (182) the tag is not able to take an A profile; this is to say that only with the auxiliary tag (*He's coming isn't he?*) is the speaker able to express that high degree of confidence. But it can be achieved by combining these additional tags with auxiliary tags—even to the extent of tags on tags:

(183) They're coming aren't they you think don't you?

The intonational possibilities are equally complex. Thus in (183), although the stem carries the highest pitch, the pitch on *don't you* may reach almost as high even though the pitch on *you think* may remain on the same low level as *they*—the coaxing effect of *don't you* probably attaches to the utterance as a whole. On the other hand, if the sentence takes the shape

(184) They're coming aren't they don't you think?

the contour may be A + À with *they don't you think* the tail of the À, or A + À + B or A + C + B, the B having the same coaxing effect as before. This is an unexplored realm in which we are not equipped to enter, a limbo between sentence and discourse where syntactic cohesion shades off to loose collocation.

Cohesion comes in all degrees. Auxiliary tags seem to be more closely tied to the stem than the other tags, and yet the possibility of putting them on a separate A profile, or even addressing them to a different person, in the case of reverse-polarity tags, argues for a relatively loose degree of cohesion. They also rather freely allow the insertion of other material such as nonauxiliary tags, vocatives, etc., especially with reversal of polarity:

(185) You like it, I suppose, don't you?
(186) You're a real card, Jack old boy, aren't you?

Same-polarity auxiliary tags are more tightly connected:

(187) ?They'll manage, do you think, will they?
(188) They'll manage will they do you think?

The adverb *now* in one of its uses is a test for the relative independence of a tag. It is a prompter, signifying something like 'Mind you, put other considerations aside, don't give me any argument on this' (see below, pp. 291–92), and is a common way of prodding an answer favorable to the speaker's viewpoint whether attached at the beginning or at the end of a question:

(189) Now wasn't he a good fellow after all?
(190) He was a good fellow after all, now wasn't he?
(191) He was a good fellow after all, wasn't he now?

The attachment of *now* to the tag in (190) and (191) points to the tag as a relatively independent question; especially in (190), the speaker is free to pause. With the more cohesive same-polarity question, *now* is less apt to be attached to the tag, but it still may be used to urge not a favorable answer but a prompt one:

(192) You like it, now do you? (do you now?)

The insistence of *now* is reflected in the intonation. As we would predict, insistence is not very compatible with the restraint of the C profile, with the result that the tags in (190) and (192) are not apt to take a C. The B profile is fine, and the conducive (190) may also have A. When *now* comes at the end, the conducive (190) allows a C, but nonconducive (192) is not congenial.

Sex-related differences

Is there a difference between the sexes in the matter of who uses more tags? Lakoff (1973b) argued that women use them more than men, and that they are symptomatic of insecurity. (By the same token, rising terminals are more frequent.) Nässlin (1984: 166) found that there is in fact a difference, but it is in the elaboration that women tend to add after the tag rather than in the tag itself, which both sexes use equally. The women's utterances are more apt to be taken as needing an informative answer; men tend simply to agree with one another but a woman's tag question is apt to elicit an explanation or a dispute.

Reprise Questions

Reprise questions differ from original questions in that they involve a more or less verbatim repetition of what has been said. Here we have a functional rather than a formal classification of questions. The classification of original questions benefits from syntactic clues that to some extent distinguish yes-no, wh, alternative, and complementary questions. Reprise questions are not marked as such (except sometimes verbally, with *did you say?*, *you wanted to know?*, etc.), but they strongly favor Profile B. The subclasses include:

REFLEX QUESTIONS, which repeat a preceding nonquestion (in whole or in part) for confirmation:

John's coming. — (You say) John('s coming)? — Yes.

ECHO QUESTIONS, which repeat a question, for confirmation:

Are you coming? — (You ask) am I coming? — Yes. — Yes, I am.

DITTO QUESTIONS, which repeat, on request, the speaker's own question:

Are you coming? — What? — Are you coming?

RECLAMATORY QUESTIONS, which call for a repetition of something said by the interlocutor:

It's going on five. — What? (What did you say?) (It's going on what?)

QUOTED QUESTIONS, which are reported direct questions:

"Are you coming?" she asked.

Echo and reflex questions

These are a special case of yes-no questions, and accordingly they favor a B profile—all the more so since they are usually asked under pressure, which tends to compel the rising pitch. But to the extent that other considerations are mixed in with the plain desire for a re-statement, other profiles may be used. Disbelief mixed with surprise would favor a contour with a final C or AC. Expectation of some sort of conclusion would favor A, as would lack of real curiosity (here the questioning might be by way of gesture). Compare the surprise-curiosity of the B in (193) with the disbelief of the AC (or A + C) in (194), both focusing on the unexpectedness of its being John who knew:

(193) Jo^h_n knew that we were coming?

(194) J^o^hⁿ
        knew that we were
                         com_in^g?

And note the readiness to draw a conclusion when A is used (the ascription *you ask* is not essential, but specifies the question as echo):

(195) Are^{they}^{com}
               ing, you ask?

After the interlocutor says *yes*, the speaker goes on with *Well, I can explain about that.*

A modification of the reflex question, which might be called pseudo-reflex, occurs when the speaker puts words into the interlocutor's mouth, and questions them. The pseudo-reflex is an extension of the syntax of the original utterance, in the form of a modifier of some kind. The usual contours end in B or C (A and AC would tend to be sarcastic, suggesting something already known which the hearer has been too heedless to consider). So, in response to *We're going to have a good time* one might hear either (196) or (197), plus variations:

(196) With everybody ^{sick?}   (197) With ^{everybody}
                                                            sick?

Echo questions are of some formal interest in that when the echoed question is wh, the result is an apparent wh question which is actually yes-no:

(198) How did you get there? — How did I get there? — Yes, that's
what I said.

It is often claimed that the B typical of yes-no questions is what distinguishes these false wh questions from real ones, and indeed, roughly,
it does; but we have already seen that original wh questions can also
have B (see above, pp. 107–8). It is the weighting of the higher pitches
in general that favors echo over original: a B + C in the shape

(199) How do we get to

               street?

       Elm

is almost certainly echo; if original it would have to be either rudely
insistent or genuinely urgent—a normal accosting question such as
this might be would have CB + C:

(200) How do we get to

               street?

       Elm

(And yet [200] could still be an echo question—one asked in medi-
tative surprise: 'Well, now, that's an interesting question for you to
have posed.' As an accosting question it is "controlled" because of the
social situation—a question addressed to a stranger; as an echo question the speaker tones down his surprise. See Bolinger 1986: 246–52
for the "contradiction contour.") The same is true—with the same
two contours—of the yes-no question *Is this the way to Elm Street?*

The high pitch that favors echo and reflex may be on the accented
word of the A profile in a B + A + C contour. This means that B + Á
+ C strongly favors echo-reflex, B + À + C less strongly favors original; and the same difference affects B + ÁC versus B + ÀC:

         John

(201) How did   (probably echo)

         know we were

               there?

(202) How did John   (more likely original)

         know we were

               there?

      ea

(203) Is it   sy to   (204) Is it ea sy

         do?   to do?

(205) Go^{ing} $_{th?}$ nor   (206) Go^{ing} nor $_{th?}$

Though in (205) and (206) the higher accent on (205) would, on a gamble, assign it to reflex, it could easily be a very bright and cordial original question addressed as an invitation to a hitchhiker; in that mode it would sound a bit more British than American.

There is always some tendency to reword echo and reflex questions, but this does not alter the strong favoring of B profiles. Rewording may be quite optional, as in (207), which could just as well be expressed simply as *How did I get there?*:

> (207) How did you get there? — You want to know how I got there? — Yes.

Or the rewording may be more or less obligatory, as happens with complementary original questions, which are usually changed to the more explicit wh,

> (208) His reason being? — What was his reason? — Yes.

and also happens with yes-no original questions lacking interrogative syntax, which are apt to be made explicit either with auxiliary inversion or with an ascription, e.g.

> (209) They got there late? — Did they get there late? (You want to know if they got there late?) — Yes.

More interesting than the obvious echo questions as a test for the functions of intonation are what might be called concealed echo questions, where the speaker has to infer, from unduly indirect or maladroit or embarrassed probing by the interlocutor, what he is being asked. The echo question is then a mixture of inference ('This is what you are trying to find out') and question ('is it?'), and the pitch reflects the internal debate. If inferencing is uppermost, a B + A contour will probably be used; if questioning, a B + B, but now the terminal B is more apt to show impatience than questioning:

> (210) Do you . . . I mean does it seem to you that I . . . Well, do you really believe . . . — Am I blaming you? (Is that it?) — Yes.

Ditto questions

Ditto questions offer the speaker two main choices with a third choice in the background. The first is to repeat the same intonation as in the original question. The second is to treat the repetition as a nonquestion, implying 'What I said was . . .' The third is to act as if the listener were deaf or stupid, in which case the intonation may become a caricature, and almost any contour will do, in addition to increased volume.

The first choice by definition involves no change in the contour, though there is a tendency to raise all the pitches somewhat. The second choice tends to replace B profiles with A, since the utterance is now a statement, but that is not guaranteed, since impatient nonquestions readily use B. Yes-no questions are of course more drastically affected than wh questions by the B-to-A shift. But wh questions too may be altered, if the original question is on a B + À contour, by shifting to B + Á—the speaker is now *answering* a question, and the usual question-answering form has the higher A (see above, p. 59):

(211) How did you _{get}

        _{th}_{ere?} --   wh^{at?} --   (I said)   how did you ^{get}   _{th}_{ere?}

But the reverse seems to be a possibility as well, when the speaker makes the first choice, that is, *asks* the question a second time instead of answering: B + Á may go to B + À, but with overall pitch level raised. The reason for these shifts, in one direction as well as the other, may be partly an extraneous one: an aversion to parroting.

With the second choice there are various other possibilities depending on changes of syntax. The last example might be worded *I'd like to know how you got there*, in which case the "answering" type, B + Á, is most likely, though B + B is possible. If the less insistent verb *wonder* is used, the B is less likely: *I was wondering how you got there*. The nominally yes-no *Could you tell me how you got there?* increases the chances of B + B.

A dittoed alternative question has the same two possibilities as the wh question—the shift is from B + À to B + Á. But there is also the reverse: change is more likely than faithful reproduction.

Complementary questions, when original, have terminal B profiles more consistently than do any of the other types, and are most drastically altered when dittoed. More often than not, the repetition substitutes a wh question:

(212) His reason being? — What? — What's his reason?

(If a verbatim ditto imitates the original B, the speaker will probably find it necessary to add qualifiers: slowed pace, exaggerated pronunciation, shaking head—this is the "deaf or stupid" condition mentioned above.) Even if the wording remains the same, the intonation usually goes from B to A, and then the 'what I said was' statement is indistinguishable from the 'tell me' command:

(213) Your $na^{me?}$ -- What? -- Your $^{na}m_e$ (please).

Reclamatory questions

Reclamatory questions are intended to elicit repetitions. GENERAL RECLAMATORY QUESTIONS call for a complete repetition, and employ formulas like *What?*, *How's that?*, *What did you say?*, *Eh?*, *I beg your pardon?*, *Say that again?*, *Come again?*, *Run that past me again?* RESTRICTED RECLAMATORY QUESTIONS use any interrogative word, with or without additional (unaccented) context from the original utterance:

> (214) Campbell phoned me at 2 A.M. — Who (did)? — Campbell.

> (215) Campbell phoned me at 2 A.M. — When (did he phone you)? — At 2 A.M.

The intonation most often used is a simple B contour, but any contour with a terminal rise or sustention seems to be possible. This of course excludes A. The A is quite normal in an original wh question, and we see the contrast in

> (216) Marie brought you a present. — What? [A] — I can't tell. It's still in the box.

> (217) Marie brought you a present. — What? [B] — I said Marie brought you a present.

An A in (217) would be incongruous, and the same is even true of *What did you say?* (A terminal A, as in B' + À, would be normal in [217] after a pause, as a delayed reaction on the speaker's part: *What did you just say?*)

One rather unusual restriction is offered by the CAC profile: it is not apt to be encountered with one-syllable reclamatory questions. The problem is apparently the excessive emphasis of CAC by comparison with AC—the speaker is registering a degree of astonishment that is more appropriate with an echo question, one in which the very fact of the other speaker's having used a certain interrogative word inspires incredulity. So we may have, in response to *Why did you do it?*, the echo using CAC on *why*,

(218) Why⌒? Because I ^{had} to! Why do you sup^{po}s$_{e?}$

This would not do in a reclamatory question calling for a restatement of a reason, e.g. in

(219) I did it because they forced me to. — Why? — Because they forced me to.

—an AC expresses about as much astonishment as one is permitted here.

Longer reclamatory questions are permitted with rise-fall-rise, but rather than CAC the contour should probably be regarded as CA + C: the material at the trough is weighty enough to be marked as accented. Thus we may have the multi-word general reclamatory

```
          's                             did
(220) Hów        t?!      (221) Whát        you
          thá                                  sá y?
```

```
                  was
(222) Whát
              that  you  said?
```

although the single-word general reclamatory *What?!* would be most unusual with rise-fall-rise. For a restricted reclamatory question also using CA + C, take the response to *I went to New York by train, to Los Angeles by plane, and to Miami on horseback*:

```
           did
(223) Hów       you  get  to  Mi    i?!
                                  ám
```

Reclamatory questions comprise the great bulk of wh questions using uninverted order, that is, keeping the interrogative word where it would be in a declarative sentence (see above, p. 110): *He told you what?*, *They did it how?*, *She got there when?* The normal intonation is a simple B contour on the interrogative word, with everything else unaccented:

```
                        what in his sandwich?
(224) He told you to put
```

As before, a B + C is normal, and so—though exceptional—is B + AC:

```
          told you to put
(225) He
                           in his sandwich?
                     what
```

(226) He told you to do wha
                        $_{at}$?

but B + CAC is hardly interpretable:

(227) ?He told you to go wh^{e}
                          $_{r}$e^{e}?

Reclamatory questions are often used as a ploy to create the impression that the speaker has the knowledge he is supposed to have (and might be embarrassed at not having), and only needs to be reminded of it. In this case there is no actual prior utterance that needs to be repeated, only the supposition of one. For example, George has just spoken of his visit to Italy, and Ernest, fearing that George has already told him when the visit was, asks—probably adding some "up" gesture such as a raised hand—

(228) wh^{en} were you there (now)?

The cleft construction, with *it* referring to knowledge supposedly already specified, is common in such reminder reclamatories, as is also the B + C contour with tonal ending (a natural consequence of the pretended lower degree of curiosity):

(229) When was it you were
                      there?

By the same token, if a plain B is used, it will not rise as far as with reclamatories that call for an actual repetition.

Quoted questions

Quoted questions (see Bolinger 1946) are questions reported after the fact, usually by someone other than the original speaker, but using direct discourse:

(230) She came in, sniffed, and said, "Who's been smoking in here?"

(231) I'm sort of expecting Jack's next question. "Where did you put that line?" he shouts at me.

(232) "Are you ready?" the driver asked.

These are handled differently depending on whether the ascription precedes or follows the quotation. If it precedes (and if the reporter is faithful) the intonation of the quotation is the same as that of the original. If it follows, certain accommodations are made, and these are what interests us here.

Colloquial speech is very sparing with final ascriptions. Usually when speakers quote they put the ascription first; it is only in extremely vivid narrative that one is likely to find an unprompted final ascription, which is why (231) was put in the historical present.

On the other hand, prompted quotations are very common: most of them are read from a printed page—(232) is a typical example. Though oral reading is often distorted by bad habits (such as always interpreting a question mark as a rise in pitch, or always putting the main accent at the end of a sentence), we shall assume in what follows that the reader's imagination is faithful to the original.

The intonational peculiarity of quoted questions (of all direct quotation, in fact) is that a final ascription is normally continuous with the contour of the question and must be added without altering the mood. This is accomplished in either of two ways: by fitting the ascription onto the contour as part of the tail, or by resetting the tail.

The first procedure involves trimming somewhat the end portion of the quotation, to make room for the ascription. So with a B profile,

$$\text{(233) "Can't you} \quad \overset{\text{see?" they}}{} \quad \overset{\text{asked.}}{}$$

—here the rise that would have appeared on *see* is transferred to the ascription. Similarly with an A:

$$\text{(234) "What are you} \quad \overset{\text{do}}{} \\ \text{ing?" I inquired.}$$

Here the ascription continues the downmotion that would otherwise have been carried out fully on *-ing*. If the quotation ends with the accented syllable of the A, the entire downmotion may be carried out on the ascription; so we have two possible realizations:

$$\text{(235) "Who} \quad \overset{\text{wou}}{} \\ \text{ld?" he asked.} \qquad\qquad \text{(236) "Who} \quad \overset{\text{would?"}}{} \\ \text{he asked.}$$

In (236) the mood of the question proper would be destroyed if the ascription were dropped—the A profile would become B.

Resetting the tail affects contours that end in profiles with rising terminals. There is a dropback, and the upmotion resumes on the final verb. Resetting is apt to be found only when the terminal upglide has already attained a fairly high pitch, and is mainly to avoid crowding the high pitches. Examples of B, C, and AC:

```
                    ing?"
(237) "Are you comᶦⁿᵍ        she wanted to knoʷ·
```

```
(238) "Are
          they
              crimᶦⁿᵃˡˢ?"  he deᵐᵃⁿded·
```

```
                 ten
(239) "Was  it
         in        l?!"  I blurted ᵒᵘᵗ·  "It ⟶
             tionᵃ
                      wa
     most certainly
                    s!"
```

(*Out* is part of the phrasal verb *blurt out*.)

Though most ascriptions are handled in the manner just described, with the speaker not interposing himself so as to alter the mood, there are exceptions, with ambiguity as a possible result. Normally, as we have just seen, the terminal intonation represents the intention of the original speaker; the words of the ascription are foreign but the intonation is not. But it is possible for the speaker to impose his own "incompleteness" when he intends to go on. In (240) and (241) we see two possible ways of handling the ascription:

```
            the                            the
(240) "Who's                 (241) "Who's
          re?" he asked.              re?" he asked·
```

(240) is unmistakably intended to reproduce an A profile, and (241) is probably meant to do the same. The upmoving ascription is the speaker's own incompleteness—he plans to continue, perhaps with *Is it somebody I know?* But it is also possible that the original had AC, as would be the case with

```
                             No
         the
(242) Who's
         ᵣe youᵘ sayʸ?     ᵇodyₗ!
```

The quoted question here is an echo question as well, which the context helps to distinguish from an original question such as (241).

(Also, an original question using AC in a context such as *Who's there? Is it somebody I know?* would tend not to dip down so close to creak.)

Even when the ascription carries out the supposed intent of the original as far as general shape is concerned, one cannot be sure that *some* part of the movement is not infected by the speaker's own mood. When the reader produces (233), it is possible that the original ended with a lower rise, to which the reader has added because there is more to come.

Throughout, we have seen that intonation is autonomous. One can calculate probabilities, but there are no defining connections between intonation and question type. It is not a transcendent grammatical datum that echo questions almost always go up, if one considers that speakers tend to be more keyed up when they ask them.

6. Nonquestions

There is a rough correspondence between syntactic types such as IN-TERROGATIVE and speech acts such as QUESTIONING:

Type	Act	Example
interrogative	questioning	Is it good?
declarative	stating	It's good.
imperative	commanding	Be good!
exclamatory	exclaiming	How good it is!

But as we saw in the chapter on questions, the whole domain of speech acts is more complex than these simple correspondences suggest. There are wh questions and complementary questions as well as yes-no questions, and declaratives are used for questioning as well as for stating: *It's good?*, *You did?* Declaratives and interrogatives can be used to issue commands: *You'd better be good*, *How about behaving yourself for a change?* Anything that can be said can be exclaimed: *Wow, that player's good!* And the speech acts themselves are divisible almost infinitely into shades of courtesy, distance, reticence, control, domination, submission, acceptance, confidentiality, suspicion, reverence, surprise—a number of which have received detailed attention in the expanding field of Pragmatics, though the extent to which transitions from one mood to another are managed by intonation is not always given its due.

In this chapter we address declaratives and imperatives. Exclamations, even though in one small area they have a distinctive syntax (*How good it is!* vs. *How good is it?*), are typically so fragmentary (*Oh!*, *Blast!*, *Huh!*, *Naughty, naughty!*) that they will be left to Part III.

Declaratives

In their statement mode, declaratives have always been considered the basic sentence type: they more readily occur alone, they are more apt to conclude a discourse, their inflections and word order are less marked, they display the speaker more in control of the situation, and they do most of the serious business of communication, which is to inform (how many sentences so far in this chapter have been anything but statements?)—and this in turn makes them the primary object of truth-value logic. Their place in our work has accordingly been privileged from the beginning, with abundant examples, and not much needs to be added here.

Needless to say, a statement does not have to be syntactically complete. The answer *Too bad* serves equally with *That's too bad* as a response to *He lost the race*, and the intonation can be identical if the number of syllables provides a sufficient display. (The same goes for commands: *Down!* is equivalent to *Get down!*)

As with other sentence types, we have seen that statements as such place no limitations on the contour types that can occur with them. Though statements in most varieties of English and in most other languages usually end in a fall, that is no more a defining characteristic than is a terminal rise in questions. What counts is the speaker's intention, manifested in speech acts of warning, persuading, pontificating, pleading, hinting—all possible with declarative syntax, and all, in some general way, "informing." Take a situation that might produce something that could be called URGENT REQUEST. The speaker's general behavior betokens some obvious emergency that requires him to do what would ordinarily be considered rude: push his way through a crowd. He cries,

```
(1) Ple                hur                        by
  a
    s    I'm  in a    r    Will you  let me
     e!                y!                    y!
```

The hearers recognize the circumstances and make way, without resentment—the B + Á contours convey both the urgency and the plea. If the speaker were to substitute B + À, as in

```
        in a                let me
          hur                   by
(2) I'm              Will you
       r y!                     y!
```

the hearers might well take exception: the speaker shows himself "in control" by using the lower pitches, and does not have the excuse of being carried away by the urgency of his errand. He seems to be making a deliberate and presumptuous demand.

Given the complexity of all the interacting modes, the most we can do is single out a few of the major speech acts where the role of intonation in declarative statements (nonquestions, noncommands) is especially conspicuous. I select four: answers, pronouncements, observations, and warnings, corresponding roughly to . . . Á, . . . À, . . . C, and . . . AC respectively.

Answers and pronouncements

It was pointed out in the last chapter (p. 137) that answers to questions tend to have a shape that allies them to questions—highest pitch toward the end—whereas statements that come out of the blue tend to have the highest pitch toward the beginning. So if you ask *Where are you going?* I am more apt to say *I'm góing hóme* with B + Á. To use B + À might suggest an unfriendly continuation: *I'm góing hóme—I dón't líke you any more*; the B + À is repeated. (The B + Á could be used in the latter context, but would sound peevish rather than petulant or sulky.) On the other hand, if the speaker is not answering a question but making a pronouncement—announcing an intention in this case—then *I'm góing hóme, pléase excúse me* with the same B + À repeated would be quite appropriate, and if B + Á were used the speaker would appear to be under some strong compulsion. The question-answer favors B + Á because it is keyed up as an appeal for acceptance. The pronouncement favors B + À because it is keyed down to show the speaker in control, and furthermore the initial high pitch is itself annunciatory: 'Listen to what I am about to say.' The keying down is speaker-oriented, an intonation of fiat rather than appeal (Bolinger 1986: 60).

Pronouncements are intonationally indistinguishable from commands (see below), and for good reason: both put the speaker in control. As far as intonation is concerned, all the following are the same, and are commutable with some sort of command:

(3) I don't give a damn what
                    she thinks!

(4) The name you just called me is insult
                                    ing!

(5) What real dif
            ference does it make?

—paraphrasable with the following, using the same intonation:

(6) Let her think whatever she pleases.
(7) Don't you dare call me that!
(8) Don't bother me with it!

A MOOD of pronouncement can thus be carried by any major syntactic type, including questions, which can easily be veiled commands:

(9) Will you please make up your
mi
nd!

(10) Haven't you eaten just about e
no
ugh!

(11) Now
which one of you buggers is gonna come
ne
xt?

—with (11) followed by *Get a move on!* Some of these, like (9) or like *Why don't you just shut up!*, are formulaic; others, like (11), are not.

Observations

Statements with terminal rises tend to be viewed as somewhat unusual, though there are situations in which a fall would be inappropriate. The commonest of these involve observations, with Profile C. An instance from Bolinger (1986: 180) involved a pedestrian who was in the line of fire as a motorist passed him on a rainy day; the motorist slowed down so as not to plow through a puddle and make a splash. The pedestrian voiced his appreciation to a companion:

(12) That's
con
side
rate.

This points to something obvious, without intent to inform as would be the case with an A profile. Similarly, imagine two friends visiting an art gallery. They pause before a canvas and one says to the other

(13) That's
an interesting
pic
ture.

The C profile projects the requisite degree of casualness: the terminal rise leaves the field open for the speaker to carry on with an explanation of his opinion, or for the hearer to respond with something like *Yes, I agree.* A contour with a terminal Á or À would be less usual under the circumstances: the Á might suggest that there was reason to expect otherwise—the notorious contrastivity of Á—and the À would sound as if the speaker had reached a weighty conclusion: he is delivering his pronouncement.

Observations can come out of the blue, but occur when potential conversationalists have been interacting already for a time or are at least on an assumed familiar footing. One would not be apt to say, out of the blue and to a total stranger,

(14) Den
$$\text{ver's a}$$
$$\text{fun}^{\text{ny}} \text{ place.}$$

but it might readily be said out of the blue to one's momentary companion. The observation is "offered for comment," so to speak. To use an . . . A out of the blue for such a remark—one with no apparent connection to anything—would be very strange.

What appears to set the terminal C apart from the A as a conveyor of observations rather than fact-transmissions is not just the shape of the profile but also the overall direction of the accents. A contour with multiple C's can be made to resemble one with a terminal A if the C's are arranged on a downmoving tangent: the result is an impression of terminal downmotion in spite of the terminal rise (which continues to function in its own right for reassurance or whatever). So if one says either (15) or (16),

(15) That   (A+C)
$$\text{was a silly mis}$$
$$\text{ta}^{\text{ke}}.$$

(16) That   (A+C+ó)
$$\text{was a}$$
$$\text{sil}^{\text{ly}} \text{mis} \text{take.}$$

the effect is still that of an observation—the tangent to *sil-* and *-take* in (16) is rising. Neither would be very appropriate in agreeing with a speaker who has just said *You should have been more careful.* On the contrary,

(17) That   (A+C+Č)
$$\text{was a}$$
$$\text{silly mis}$$
$$\text{ta}^{\text{ke}}.$$

with a downmoving tangent to *sil- -take*, would not be very good as an observation but, with a prefaced *Yes*, would be quite all right for agreeing with the other's criticism. The speaker is saying, in effect, 'You're right, I was careless.'

Warnings

If any intonation can be said to verge on a specific speech act, it is AC in the sense of 'warning.' Warnings are as often imperative as declarative, and the combination of imperative and AC is especially potent in the contour B + ÁC:

```
                    wa
           of my
      out
(18) Keep          yy!
```

It is easy to speculate on how the segments work together to produce this effect: the rise of the B denotes arousal, the abrupt fall is assertive, and the terminal rise is suspensive—consequences will follow if the hearer does not take heed. The profile does not "mean" 'warning'—its meaning is a synthesis of those tensions and relaxations; but the synthesis is very useful in performing the speech act of warning. If we try to assign AC exclusively to warning, counterexamples come readily to mind. But they tend to be allied in sense to 'warning.' For example the simple AC in

```
       told
(19) I
       you soo.
```

coming after a failure to heed a warning, or the B + ÁC

```
                    my
          no skin off
(20) It's           nose.
```

as a disclaimer of responsibility: it's up to you (or someone else). The disclaimer idiom *Beats me* is virtually stereotyped on B + AC. Other disclaimers are frequent as well: *Don't blame me, I did my best, I wish I knew, It's up to you, It's your move.*

Predictably, the 'arousal' component of 'warning' can be tempered either by doing away with the upmotion of the B or by replacing ÁC with ÀC. In the following response to *He says he needs ten*,

```
                ni
         give him
(21) I can       ne.
```

the speaker implies 'but no more, he can take it or leave it'; but if B + ÁC is replaced with A + ÁC,

```
             ni
        give
(22) I can   him ne.
```

the foreclosure of alternatives gives way to a negotiable alternative. Changing B + ÁC to B + ÀC, on the other hand,

$$(23) \ \text{I can} \quad _{g}\text{ive}^{\ h\text{im}} \ \text{ni}$$
$$\quad\quad\quad\quad\quad\quad _{n}\text{e}^{\cdot}$$

tempers the foreclosure somewhat less. The speaker may be half willing to negotiate, or may just not want to spend time parleying.

Imperatives

We have already noted the association between downmotion and the sort of mood that goes with issuing a command—the speaker is in control, and is not subordinating himself to the hearer. We have also seen that commands with this intonation can come in a variety of shapes, of which the so-called imperative, the form that is identical to and probably simply *is* the infinitive of the verb (*Sit down, Come in, Let me see*), is only one manifestation. Others, using the same intonation, include *You may sit down, I'd like you to hand it over, Off with you, How about giving your seat to the lady?*, etc. The speech act of commanding is more beholden to the intonation than to the syntax.

The close tie between commands and downmotion can be seen in the intonation of commands using any of the various courtesy formulas that mitigate the presumption of ordering someone to do something. The most typical is *please*, but others include *kindly, do me the favor of, have the courtesy to,* and *be good enough to.* Testing with *please,* we find that when it is initial it is almost invariably a springboard for the downmotion of the rest of the command, as with B + A and B + C in the following:

$$(24) \ \text{Please hand me the } _{p}\text{li} \quad\quad\quad (\text{the} \quad\quad\quad \text{pliers})$$
$$\quad\quad\quad\quad\quad\quad\quad\quad _{e}\text{r}_{s.}$$

To say out of the blue,

$$(25) \ \text{Please hand me the } \quad^{p}\text{li}$$
$$\quad\quad\quad\quad\quad\quad\quad _{e}\text{r}_{s.}$$

would be puzzling, though it would do quite well as an answer to *What did you say?*

Other functions of the imperative

If commands may be performed with other things than imperatives, imperatives may perform other things than commands, and as those other things are distinct speech acts, the intonation changes accordingly. An imperative may give permission, and then takes an intonation appropriate to conveying assent. In the following, responding to *May I speak my mind freely?*, one could say *Of course* with the same contour:

```
          do                      cour
(26) Please              Of    s
          o.                        e.
```

Or it may—as part of an ongoing exchange—be a cordial invitation rather than an order:

```
       do                      fresh
(27) Sit       Let me bring you some re
        w                                 ment.
         n.
```

Or one may put a wh question in imperative form without altering the usual intonation for a wh question in that context—say in response to someone's unreasonable plan of action:

```
              why
(28) Please tell me
                  y.
```

—with the same intonation as for *But why?* (*Please* moves down from its normal perch.) Or take the contrast between a command and an answer, where both might occur in the same context:

(29) How can I get there? — Just fóllow mé.

With *me* higher than *follow*, this is as much an answer as a command: 'That's the way to get there.' It would be appropriate to add *that's how*. If *follow* is higher than *me* (but both are still accented), we have the downmotion typical of commands, and the response is more command than answer: the speaker is telling the hearer what to do, and might well add *Let's go!* and proceed to lead the way. These interpretations are not open-and-shut, but to take the utterances in the opposite sense implies a substantial change in mood. If the first were primarily a command, it would be an urgent one—the speaker is keyed up. (The reader can test this by adding, again, *Let's go!* with *go* higher than *let's*.) And if the second were primarily answer rather than command (try again adding *that's how*), the effect is self-assured. It is difficult to get this interpretation because the suggestion of 'command' is so strong; rewording as *Just by following me* makes the feat easier.

Another situation where the mood wavers, this time between command and question, is that of a response—in imperative form—that rejects a request. You have been asked *Please help me lift this* and you reply with either of the following:

(30) Do it your^{se}$_{\text{l}_{\text{f}}}$.   (31) Do your ^{own} ^{lifting}.

Though a rejection of this sort is inherently rude, it becomes unmitigatedly so with the shape

(32) Do $_{\text{it}}$ $_{\text{your}_{\text{s}}}$ $_{\text{e}_{\text{l}_{\text{f}}}}$.

with the peremptoriness of the continuous downmotion. The affinity of (30) and (31) to a question can be seen in the readiness with which they can take a wh tag:

(33) Do it your ^{self} $_{\text{why can't you?}}$ You're stron^{g}$^{\cdot}$

The tag is less appropriate with (32).

The long and short of it is that imperatives, like interrogatives, are open to all intonations because they are open to all effects of mood. If I wish to threaten imminent retribution, I may say, with a B profile,

(34) Put ^{it} $^{\text{do}^{\text{wn}}}$$^{!}$

If I wish to wheedle, I may say, with C plus rise,

(35) Put $_{\text{it}}$ $_{\text{do}^{\text{w}}}^{n}^{!}$

If I wish to suggest that I am bored with the whole thing, I may say with stylized C, i.e., tonal ending,

(36) Put it

       down!

If I wish to add finality to (34), I may say, with CA,

     o

(37) Put it ^{d} ^{w}n !

These in addition to the À and Á already noted:

(38) Put it

     ^{d}$_o$
       ^{w}n!

           (39) Put it ^{do}

                      ^{w}n!

The foregoing are all command-*like*, deontic, in the broad sense; but the imperative is also one of the ways of expressing 'condition':

    (40) Look across the field and you'll see a rabbit = if you look across . . .

Even here, downmotion produces something more like a command— a sort of dare or at least a warning:

(41) Do that and you're

                   de

                     ^{a}d!

Remove the downmotion and this becomes more like a plain condition:

(42) Do that and you're ^{de}

                    ^{a}d.

Tagged imperatives

Another point of similarity between commands and questions is the appending of tags to imperative forms, as in (33) above, but there are important differences in what kinds of tags there may be, in how close a link there is between the stem and the tag, and in what the overall function of the tag may be. The three points can be summarized:

1. A question tag embodies, centrally, an auxiliary verb, a personal pronoun, and, optionally, the negative *n't* (in very formal style, *not*):

    is he?   will she?   don't you?
    do they?   must I?   do you not?

Peripherally there are other types of question tags: *Is she happy do you think?* In the first case, imperatives are more restricted, in the second, not.

2. The attachment of the *will you* type of tag is looser with the imperative than is the case with questions. The disjuncture is wider and it is sometimes harder to tell whether the combination should be regarded as one sentence or as two or more.

3. In general, question tags reinforce questionness whereas imperative tags—the ones in question form—mitigate imperativeness. *It's OK?* becomes a more insistent question as *It's OK is it?* but *Help me* is softened by adding *would you?* Other tags may reinforce imperativeness, however: *Sit down, damn you!*

Attempts have been made to "derive" the tags on imperatives from the same sources as those that appear with questions, but they founder on the second of the factors named above. It has been claimed, for instance, that imperatives, as expressions of WILL, are derived from *will* sentences—since *You will go* may be used as a command and *You will go, will you?* has the same sort of tag as appears normally with questions, the form *Go, will you?* can be derived by first adding the auxiliary tag to *You will go* and then deleting everything up to the stem verb (Katz and Postal 1964: 74–79). But this proposal is unworkable, mainly because *will* is not the only tag possible, and imperative tags in general have a much more "added on" appearance than do question tags. If we try to interpret an affirmative tagged question as added on we get a sort of contradiction: *He likes you. Does he?* But the same with an imperative is normal. We not only may say *Help me. Will you?* but also *Help me. Can you?*, and we can proceed to multiply the loosely added taggable elements: *Help me. Can you? Will you?* Nässlin (1984) regards stem and tag as more or less independent sentences orbiting together (see below, pp. 426–27); tagged imperatives are the most convincing examples.

Of course this is not to say that

(43) Help me here, can you?

and

(44) Help me here. Can you?

have identical meanings. Any native speaker senses a difference: (43) has a modification of the command—one that mitigates its force. The response *I can but I won't* is more appropriate to (44) than to (43); the two parts are responded to separately. A *yes* answer to (43) includes an agreement to perform the act.

Tagged imperatives thus seem to represent a kind of syntactic blend in which one sentence is incorporated as a modification of another, facilitated by the family resemblance to a single sentence whose parts have been shifted around. *Help me, can you?* is both *Help me. Can you?* and *Can you help me?*, either of which can serve, pragmatically, as a command. This kind of blending opens up broader vistas of tagging than the narrow focus on *do you?*, *has he?*, and the like. The same process is evident in tagged statements like

(45) He's coming, I suppose.

which can be related to *I suppose he's coming* and *He's coming. I suppose.* The same kind of softening as with *can you?* is found with the tagged *I suppose*, which mitigates the confidence of the assertion *He's coming*, and yet is not as drastic as the independent *I suppose*, which would be given an AC profile (or possibly, more as an afterthought, a C or a B) and would not only soften the assertion but enfeeble it.

On the syntactic side there is a resemblance between tagged imperatives (the basic type *Help me, can you?*) and a form of tagged questions examined in Chapter 5 (pp. 123–27):

(46) Like it, do you?
(47) Got them, has he?
(48) Find out, would she?

These, exactly as with the imperative, may function independently of the tag:

(49) Like it?
(50) Got them?
(51) Find out?

—especially, but not necessarily, with an implied *you* subject. (Commands have less difficulty in this respect because *you* is almost always the implied subject.)

This is the point of closest convergence between *will* (*can, would,* etc.) questions and imperatives, since (46), (47), and (48) are exactly the same structure as *Help me over here, will you?* Without the tag, as in (49)–(51), and with added *please* to accentuate the similarity, we get

(52) Help me over here, please?
(53) Help me over here, please.

with uniformly rising intonation in the first making it almost unequivocally a question ('Will you help me over here, please?'—used as a command) and falling intonation in the second making it an imperative. (The intonation is no guarantee, however: the rise can be used on a very urgent and demanding imperative. To get this slant, adjust the facial gestures: lowered eyebrows for imperative, raised for question.)

Other forms of tagging interest us here as a release from the analysts' straitjacket that has confined tagged imperatives to the most obvious auxiliaries, *will* and *can*. A rough classification follows, with examples.[1]

I. Tags in yes-no question form
    1. Auxiliary tags

    > Let me help you, may I? (shall I?)[2]
    > Go right away, shouldn't you?
    > Wait a minute, can't you? What's the rush?
    > Step this way a moment, will you kindly?

    2. Fronting of unmarked infinitive complement

    > Do it now, hadn't you better?
    > Try making up with her, don't you think you should?

    3. Fronting of marked infinitive or subjunctive complement[3]

    > Take it up with them promptly, mightn't it be best?
    > Give him the benefit of the doubt, may I ask just this once?
    > Go along with them now, would you be willing?
    > Stay with this just a couple of days longer, would you consent?
    > Play up to him, haven't I told you these many moons?
    > Have a drink with me, would you like?
    > Turn it in before six, remember?
    > Give them a little encouragement, don't you want to?

    4. Fronting of complement not in construction with tagged main verb (delocutive or cognitive)

    > Take care of the whole thing at once, wouldn't you say?
    > Make the best of it, don't you think?
    > Don't contradict me again, do you understand? (savvy?, see?,
    >   capisce?, catch my drift?)
    > Just leave her alone, do I make myself clear?

    5. Fronting of underlying gerund

    > Let me try, do you mind? (= Do you mind letting me try?)
    > Handle this with the utmost tact, may I ask the favor?

II. Tags in wh question form

    > Do it yourself, why can't you?
    > Take the best, why shouldn't you?
    > Do it now, what do you say? (cf. What do you say you do it now?)

III. Tags in declarative form

1. Imperative as complement

Deliver them at once, I must ask (request, demand, urge, suggest, etc.)

Don't wait any longer, I tell you (I keep telling you). (for a command that is repeated)

Give me a bite, hint, hint.

Get there early, you'd better.

2. Imperative as subject

Do it now, is when I'd like you to.

Do it now, would be best.

Do it now, is my recommendation.

Do it now, makes the best sense.

IV. Tags in imperative form

Get there early, don't forget.

Have it finished by ten, remember.

Read it carefully, let me suggest.

Give them plenty of time, mind.

V. Conditional tags

Bring me both issues, if you don't mind. (cf. do you mind?)

Hand it over, if you would. (cf. would you?)

Let me help you, if I may. (cf. may I?)

Conditional tags show once more the pervasive resemblance to the syntax of questions: *Is he coming, may I ask?* = *Is he coming, if I may ask?*

This sampling by no means exhausts the variety of tags that may be found or invented—the patterns are highly productive, and run all the way from the firmly conventionalized *please* (an old optative main verb meaning 'may it please you'), which may be taken either as an imperative or as a question (*Help me, please?*), to complex subordinations like

(54) See the doctor is the best thing for you to do, won't you?

(55) Keep the secret one day longer, shouldn't you, don't you think, hint, hint?

It is not even necessary that the speaker take explicit responsibility for issuing the command—he may do it through a surrogate:

(56) Do it now, your friends are all saying, do it now.

Imperative tagging can be conceived, from a prototype standpoint, as a field in which *will you* is at the center, along with its inverted pronoun subject and its status as an auxiliary that does not take *to* with the infinitive, with *can* at a slight remove, other *to*-less auxiliaries (*may, shall*) a little farther out, and at progressively greater removes, tags that incorporate modifiers, that take the imperative as subject rather than as an implied complement, that embrace *to* infinitives, that expand to include more than one subclause not necessarily in question form, and that—as we shall see—need not even contain "words." The tag not only admits of a huge lexical variety but can have its own independent intonation. We show this, for example, in the punctuation of *remember*—with declaratives as well as imperatives—which can be a question or a command in its own right:

(57) I left it on the table, remember. (unaccented tail on B + AC contour)

(58) I left it on the table, remember? (B following B + A)

(59) Have it here early, remember.

(60) Have it here early, remember?

A final general point about tags is that many of them, particularly the shorter ones, may be inserted medially:

(61) Try, won't you, to curb that temper of yours.
(62) Have it finished, remember, by ten.

The tag that does this most freely is *please*, which is so firmly attached to its verb that split infinitives are not uncommon in some types of directive:

(63) I'd like you to please sit down.

The intonation shows the affinity—*please* has the same prominence as the verb—though incidentally this is not apt to happen in the form

(64) I'd like you, please, to sit down.

What this suggests is that *please* is being treated as initial, with *I'd like you to* as a kind of exterior deferential formula.

Please has other properties that entitle it to a separate look. First, it is, as Ross (1975: 238) points out, "a litmus for requests." This is not entirely true, as it appears now and then with a formal use of imperatives to grant permission (see example [26], above), perhaps a retention of its earlier sense 'may it please you':

(65) May I have some? — Please help yourself.
(66) I'd like you to see our latest catalog. — Please come in.

But the generalization is close enough, and serves both to exclude rough directives that are not requests,

(67) ?Please beat it.
(68) ?Please get your ass out of here.
(69) *Please go to hell.

and to embrace directives that are not imperatives, including questions:

(70) Who are yóu, please, if I may ask?
(71) May I please go?
(72) Would you please tell me what this is?
(73) I'd like you to please be quiet.

This includes instances of detached *please* whose interpretation depends on the context rather than on the utterance in which it appears:

(74) Please, you don't understand!
(75) Oh please, I didn't mean to forget!

The *please* is a request for exoneration or forgiveness, for something that is not mentioned in the sentence.

Second, as an independent utterance *please*, like a number of other particles likewise used independently (*oh, well, hm,* etc.), develops some almost stereotypic ties with intonation. A pronounced A profile is a strong request. A low-pitched A is apt to be ironic—the interlocutor has been guilty of mildly unacceptable behavior and *please* is a reminder to heed the proprieties. A C profile is likely to involve a repeated request—the interlocutor has already refused once, and the C wheedles; B similarly and more strongly, and AC still more strongly. An A with a minimizing downskip—the initial pitch is quite high but is scarcely more than a grace note, and the low pitch is sustained—is an entreaty, appealing to pity or sympathy. A level B at a fairly high pitch may suggest that the interlocutor owes this consideration—the speaker should not have to ask. These intonational ties are of course tendencies, not fixtures.

Third, *please* also has somewhat stereotyped roles in relation to its position. The tags in cases like

(76) I'd like you to stand here, will you?
(77) I'd like you to stand here, if you don't mind.

readily carry their own independent profiles, though they also may be tails to the last preceding profile. But *please* in that position,

(78) I'd like you to stand here, please.

is almost always a tail, and is condescendingly formulaic, sounding like an afterthought for the sake of minimal courtesy. Initial *please*, regardless of intonation (but on an independent profile) is quite the opposite. Medial *please*, as in

(79) I'd like you to please stand here.

is perfunctory but not condescending. Flexibility of position is one thing that distinguishes *please* from *kindly*, which must directly precede the verb it modifies:

(80) I asked him to kindly accompany me.

(81) *I asked him kindly to accompany me. (starred in the relevant—directive—sense)

Tagging and negation

In general, the tagging of a negative command is the same as the tagging of an affirmative one:

(82) Get there early, remember.
(83) Don't get there too early, remember.
(84) Just do it now, I'd rather you did.
(85) Just don't do it now, I'd rather you didn't.

Except for problems of negative concord, as in (85), and limitations on specific tags as in

(86) *Don't come in why don't you?

the match between affirmative and negative is straightforward. Negation is accomplished simply with *don't*.

But there is a different class of negation which imposes a fairly strong barrier against tagging and thus tells us something about the meaning of auxiliary tags (the *will you, can you* type) in general. It is widely used in formulas.

(87) Post no bills.
(88) Use no hooks.
(89) Have no fear.
(90) Leave no stone unturned.

(91) Make no mistake about it.
(92) Ask me no questions and I'll tell you no lies.

The usual negative is *no*, and the construction is still productive:

(93) Do no more for the moment.
(94) Speak to no one.
(95) Agree to negotiate, but make no promises.
(96) Buy nothing but the best.
(97) Vote for none of the foregoing.

Not also appears, as a modifier of something other than the verb (where it is now archaic: *Ask not what your country can do for you*):

(98) Believe not a word they say.

(99) Think not of yourselves alone.
(100) Take not one cent more than you have coming to you.

One difference is that this kind of negation is stylistically "elevated," as can be seen if we colloquialize (99); more than the negation has to be changed: *Don't just think of yourselves.* A more important difference is that this process of detaching the negation from the verb makes the command much more categorical than it is with the otherwise universal *don't.* Comparing (101) and (102),

(101) Fight to the death. Ask no quarter.
(102) Fight to the death. Don't ask any quarter.

we sense the near-trivialization of the injunction in (102).

The reason for the difference is the positive form of the verb. Instead of merely negating, the speaker affirms the negation. Negative imperatives share this trait with declaratives having the same contrast between *not any* (Neg . . . *any*) and *no* (Aff . . . *no*): "the affirmativeness of the verb is interpreted not factually but as a positive attitude—the speaker is more assured, more categorical" (Bolinger 1977b: 64). There is "a higher frequency of inclusive concepts (abstractions, mass nouns, plurals) and a lower frequency of singular, particular, concrete concepts," and also a greater frequency of formulaic expressions. Just as *I spoke to no one* is more categorically assertive than *I didn't speak to anyone*, so *Speak to no one* is more categorically mandatory than *Don't speak to anyone.*

The upshot is that *don't* and *do* share a usage that is partly concealed by the growing tendency of *don't* to generalize to all forms of sentential negation, as in the commonly heard *Let's don't* and the still childish *Will you don't snore please?*[4] The affirmative *do* shows the difference from *do*-less imperatives better than does the negative *don't*, but one can still observe the proportion: *Do take a vacation* is to *Take a vacation* as *Don't take a (any) vacation* is to *Take no vacation.* In other words, the imperative without *do* or *don't* is more categorical, with *do* or *don't* it is more persuasive.

This is reflected both in the likelihood of there being any tag at all, and in the nature and intonation of the tag. The categorical *Take no vacation* is not likely to be tagged with *will you?* or otherwise, and if we say *Do no more for the moment, will you?* the terminal rise is not apt to be high. On the other hand, *Don't take a vacation, will you?* presents no problems. The persuasiveness of *do* can be seen in its close affinity to the coaxing *won't you?*:

(103) Do sit down, won't you?

With a negative stem this is less clear, but we readily admit the *will* softened in another way, by tense:

(104) Don't turn around for a moment, would you?

Though he does not treat the Aff . . . *no* type of negation, Bouton (1982: 30) makes a distinction that is relevant here. He points out that unless the speaker is referring "to some action that is going on at the moment" a high-rising tag cannot be used on a negative stem. So *Don't talk, will you?* with a high terminal rise has to mean 'Stop talking,' not 'Refrain from talking in general (or at some future time).' This is not absolutely correct (see below, pp. 411–12), but it is a good approximation, and it strikes at the kind of action that the *no* type of negation cannot refer to. We do not say *Talk no longer* in order to stop someone from continuing to hold the floor (if we want to be that categorical with ongoing activity we incorporate the negative in the verb: *Stop talking*; as for *Say no more*, it refers to the message, not the words). *Eat no more of that!* would be interpreted as a dietary precaution rather than as an order to interrupt. On the other hand, *Don't talk* and *Don't eat any more of that* may well serve to check ongoing activity. Pulling someone up short in an ongoing activity is the very place where a categorical imperative might be rude, and also where one is most apt to use an urgent intonation. There is thus a gradient: *no* negation, infrequently tagged, and if tagged (a step up on the persuasive scale), accompanied by a low-pitched terminal; *don't* negation in a nonurgent situation, with low-pitched terminal; and *don't* negation with ongoing action, making a stronger appeal reflected in a higher-pitched terminal. The two forms of negation overlap pragmatically, but the formal contrast corresponds to a semantic distinction.

Another difference between *don't* and *no* negation is the tendency in the former to avoid repeating the negative in the tag:

(105) Don't buy anything but the best, will you?
(106) *Don't buy anything but the best, won't you?

This is no problem for *no* negation, since the verb is preserved in the affirmative and there is no true repetition:

(107) Buy nothing but the best, will you?
(108) Buy nothing but the best, won't you?

The restrictions here almost duplicate those in questions, where negation is concerned (compare *You'll buy nothing but the best, won't you?*, *?You won't buy anything but the best, won't you?*). This shows up additionally if we give the tags an A profile instead of a B: (105) and (108) are still good—the reversal of polarity makes the two very much like conducive questions (*You'll buy nothing but the best, won't you?*). But (107) becomes unacceptable; the same tends to happen with questions (see above, pp. 118–19).

Intonation of tags

More important, initially, than the choice of this or that type of tag, is the general question of whether the tag is accented, since that determines the possibility of one or more profiles in the tag, as against none. Unaccented tags are commonplace, here as well as in other tagged constructions, e.g. tagged questions:

```
               like
(109) So you                              (tagged to A profile)
            it do you?
```

```
(110) You                                 (tagged to C)
          be
       lieve  him don't you?
```

```
                y do you suppose?
(111) Will they be   read
                                          (tagged to B)
```

Or in tagged statements. Example (112) is dialectal but is included because it most closely matches the kind of auxiliary tags that are central to the system:

```
              self
(112) She helped her                      (tagged to A)
                  she did.
```

```
(113) You can decide                      (tagged to C)
                later you know.
```

```
                to you see.
(114) I never meant                       (tagged to B)
```

The unaccented tag, in fact, is characteristic of all such appended material, including extrapositions with cleft sentences,

> (115) It's yóu who must decide.

ascriptions,

(116) I can't hélp it, he said.

verbs of cognition,

(117) You're offénded I see.

and so on. In all these the rhematic accent comes early in the sentence, and the rest trails off. The same terminal A profile with low-pitched tag readily occurs with the imperative, usually as part of a B + A contour (B + À or B + Á):

(118) Sit dówn, won't you?
(119) Be quíet, can't you?
(120) Try agáin, why don't you?
(121) Just say nóthing, hadn't you better?

A tail on a B profile takes its usual upward course. Such commands are most natural in routines where the speaker is managing a group:

(122) Have your tickets ready will you?

(123) Step this way would you please?

The same goes for a stem having a C profile:

(124) Write your would you?
names

and for AC (generally in a B + ÀC contour):

(125) Take your seats would you?

It is difficult to generalize about tag intonation because once we look beyond the central auxiliaries *will* and *can* we find that the intonation may depend on the choice of tag. The person who says, with B + À,

(126) Be quiet, will you?

comes across as peremptory; the one who says, with B + À + B,

(127) Be qui
             e
              t, will you?

sounds insistent. On the other hand, *are you game?*, though roughly
synonymous with *would you?*, is not apt to be found as a low-pitched
tail—we sense the equivalence of

(128) Try a_{ga}
                in, would you?   (129) Try a_{ga}
                                                 in, are you game?

where both express a degree of eagerness, but whereas *are you game?*
virtually has to have a terminal rise, *would you?* may lie flat. The contrary case is *why don't you?*, which is probably an unaccented tail in all
cases, most often low level but sometimes rising. If it is accented, i.e.
in the shape (normal for a wh question)

             no   don't
(130) Go   Why

         w.   you?

the punctuation, even without pause, has to be as shown—the "tag"
is unfused and no longer a tag but an independent question.

Another instance of fixed intonation—which also illustrates the
growing end of tagging, since it is a fairly recent stereotype—is *all
right*, as in

                 anything I can d   call
(131) If there's   o for   just   right?
                                you   me all

As spoken,[5] this contained no trace of pause. The B profile on *right* is
required, reflecting the shape when *All right?* is an independent question—always with rising terminal and almost always with B; the tag
simply tightens the requirement. (With separation, a C is possible.)

A longer tag has greater freedom to reach out to something in the
broader context. In response to *When shall I do it?* the AC tag in

          now
                        like
(132) Do it
         (is when) I'd   you t_o

leaves an opening for the hearer to refuse: 'I have a preference, but I
won't insist on it.' The same is true of *would be awfully nice* with AC
on *nice*.

The converse is also true: intonation may be the best clue that something *can* be a tag, especially when the tagged material is relatively complex, as in (132)—it is reassuring to be able to utter (*is when*) *I'd like you to* as a low-pitched tail. Given this test, plus the close juncture (lack of pause) between stem and tail, we can safely admit, as tags, even fairly long stretches with accents of their own, such as the AC in (132) or something like

> (133) Do it right away is the best time.
> (134) Do it right away if you don't mind.

where in addition to the AC's on *time* and *mind* there can be A's on *best* and *don't* (provided their peaks are *lower* than those on the stem—see above, pp. 47–48 for accents within a parenthesis).

There are, of course, tags that do not accept the role of low-pitched tail—see (131) for *all right. Do you mind?* comes close to being another instance of this, especially if appended to a B + Á stem, though the B + Á can easily be accommodated if *do you mind?* is given its own B profile:

<pre>
                 have
(135) ?Let me
                      it do you mind?
</pre>

<pre>
                 have
(136) Let me   ind?
                                  m in
                      it, do you
</pre>

(The comma indicates the greater likelihood of a separation at that point.) On the other hand, if there is some *preparation* for that low terminal pitch, *do you mind?* more readily accepts it. This may come about by adding another tag such as *would you* ahead of *do you mind?* on the tail:

<pre>
                 have
(137) Let me
                      it would you do you mind?
</pre>

or by changing the stem to B + À so that lower pitches are already approaching the tag:

<pre>
(138) Let me
                 h
                  a v
                     e it do you mind?
</pre>

The "tagginess" of the tags in (136)–(138) has a further test in the inclination of the hearer to respond separately to the tag. A response such as *No I don't (mind), and I will* is more likely for (136) than for (138). A separate response is also more likely for some tags than for others, which is to say that tags can be graded for independence from the stem, e.g.

    (139) Let them know who's boss,
      (a) understand?
      (b) do you understand?
      (c) do I make myself clear?
      (d) and I hope I make myself clear?

(139a) with a low-pitched tail is not apt to be given a separate response, but if *understand* rises, the possibility increases; (139d) is unlikely to manifest a flat terminal level at all, and is correspondingly more apt to elicit something like *Yes, you do, and I will.* Our willingness to countenance this kind of telescoping, without protesting "Please, one thing at a time!," testifies to the mutual attraction of stem and tag even when a double answer is possible.

It is instructive to compare tagged questions in this same regard. In

    (140) Is he better have you heard?
    (141) Is he better have you found out yet?
    (142) Is he better would you be willing to say?

(142) is the one most likely to get a double answer, e.g. *Well, I'm a little reluctant to say it, but I guess he is.* (This example assumes a *yes* answer to the stem—it does not propound *whether* he is better but *that* he is better.) So it appears that there is the same freedom to tag and to accumulate tags:

    (143) Is it going to rain have they decided?
    (144) You're sure of that are you if you don't mind my asking?

But as we noted earlier (p. 154), with the auxiliary tags *will you?*, *can you?*, etc., the link is not as close in the imperative as in questions, and this shows up in a greater freedom to manipulate accent and intonation. With questions, the tag is routinely accented on the auxiliary verb or not at all. Instances of added accents are rare, and are probably confined to questions used as exclamations or demands:

    (145) It was a great game, wás ít nót!
    (146) It was a great game, wás ít éver!
    (147) I may sit down, máy Í pléase!

We note the change of syntax to accommodate the extra accent in (145).

Extra accents on the imperative are like those in (147), not surprisingly, since (147) is a demand:

(148) Do it promptly this time, wóuld yóu pléase!

And since the imperative permits not only personal pronoun subjects in the auxiliary-type tag but also indefinite subjects (see below, pp. 415–18), there is the added possibility of accenting those subjects:

(149) Help me, won't sómebody pléase!

Even the personal pronoun may be accented if used deictically:

(150) Step up on the platform, would yóu there, young man, please.

The possibilities of accenting the auxiliary on an A profile in connection with conducive negation (reversal of polarity, with negative tag) were illustrated with examples (105) and (108)—a kind of blending with questions of the same type.

The problem of whether a tag is accented or not is complicated by the notorious ambiguity between AC(+B) and A + B or A + C (Bolinger 1986: 268–73). The stem does not distinguish clearly between a terminal fall and a terminal rise. The difficulty is shared with all utterances containing appended material—ascriptions, for example, as in

(151) **Come** to

       morrow, she said.

Is the quoted utterance supposed to be on an A profile,

(152) **Come** to

       morrow.

or an AC

(153) **Come** to

       morrow.

with a rise at the end of the stem itself? In the latter case it could be argued that the ascription merely completes the upmotion at the end of the utterance as a whole and does not pick up an accent; but in the former it is hard to avoid assigning an independent Profile B. Exactly the same happens with an imperative in which *will you?* replaces *she said.*

That imperative tags can be regarded as accented even in the doubtful cases is pretty well demonstrated by the behavior of the "wordless" tags *hm?*, *huh?*, *hunh?*, *eh?*, which have other uses besides that of serving as tags to imperatives. As tags to questions, they may occur in the one environment guaranteed to be unaccented, the low-pitched level tail of an A profile:

(154) You like
      it eh?

As tags to imperatives they rarely occur except in potentially accented environments. *Hunh* is the most versatile, appearing not only in B profiles (where all can occur) but also in A, CA, and AC:

(155) Gimme a little ta
                     ste,   hunh?   (B profile)

(156) Make it e
             a   hu nh?   (AC profile)
              rlier next time,

Hunh closely resembles *please* in its capacity to wheedle, on these same profiles. So when we encounter an AC stem,

(157) Gimme a little t
                    aste,   hunh?

it is reasonable to assume that the tag is something more than a tail to the AC, and the overall contour is AC + B. The tag is a supplementary bit of prodding.

On the rare occasion when an *eh* or a *hunh* does appear as tail to an A profile,

(158) Sit over he
                re, hunh?

the effect is question-like—in fact, (158) is more invitation than command. Something like *Try to do better next time, hunh?* would hardly have that sort of low-pitched tag.

The "wordless" tags are the quintessential tags, for they are that and nothing more. Whereas something like *will you* may occur separately and independently, as we saw in the case of (43) and (44) above, with *Help me here, can you?* and *Help me here. Can you?*, no such separation as the latter can occur with *hunh?* It is never an afterthought. The least pause converts *hunh?* to a reclamatory question: 'What did you say?' (see below, p. 265).

Though this chapter (p. 154) rejected the transformational derivation of commands from questions, it is impossible not to sympathize with the effort, for resemblances are strewn everywhere. Commands and questions share not only tagging but specific tags, including the basic ones; both may be rendered conducive by reversed polarity; both may front the simple form of the verb and tag the auxiliary, that being the construction we call "imperative"; in some situations the overlap is such that we cannot be sure whether the utterance is question or command. Above all, the function of both is ultimately the same, to evoke a response—with only the difference that with questions the response is specified to be a speech act. A command can do that too—*Tell me what time it is* is as good as *What time is it?* And a question, though almost always answerable, is often incomplete without a physical response: *May I have the sugar, please?* Questions seem best viewed as a subdomain of commands.

7. Dependent Clauses and Other Dependencies

Though the preceding sections have dealt with independent clauses as if they could be clearly distinguished from dependent ones, the border is indistinct. First because, from a discourse point of view, two grammatically independent clauses may relate in the same way as the two parts of a sentence containing one independent and one dependent clause. This is the case with parataxis, where two independent clauses are set side by side:

(1) I couldn't wait. I didn't have time. = I couldn't wait because I didn't have time.

(2) There's plenty for all. Help yourself. = Since there's plenty for all, help yourself.

(3) Try it out. You'll see what I mean. = If you try it out you'll see what I mean.

It is also true of conversational dyads in which speakers contribute the parts of a larger unit:

(4) I couldn't wait. — (Because) you didn't have time, I suppose?
(5) You couldn't wait? — (No, because) I didn't have time.

We find (see Bolinger 1986: 261) that question-answer pairs are similar intonationally to longer sentences in which the theme corresponds to the "question" to which the sentence is addressed, and the rheme corresponds to the answer. The kinship is clearest in dialects that repeat the subject. The exchange

(6) (And) John? — He stayed behind.

is thus related to *John, he stayed behind*.

Second, because there are degrees of independence even among nominally dependent clauses, and degrees of dependence among nominally independent ones. *I looked at her and she smiled* has two independent clauses, but it fulfills much the same discourse function as *When I looked at her she smiled*, containing a dependent *when* clause. Both *whereas* and *though* introduce dependent clauses and they are roughly synonymous, but *though* clauses are more loosely tied and can be afterthoughtive and therefore relatively independent, which is not true of *whereas* clauses:

(7) The Republicans are concerned about that issue. Though the Democrats don't seem much worried about it. (The Democrats, though, don't seem much worried about it.)

(8) *The Republicans are concerned about that issue. Whereas the Democrats don't seem much worried about it. (*The Democrats, whereas, don't seem much worried about it.)

In point of independence, *though* is close to the coordinating conjunction *but*: *But the Democrats don't seem much worried about it*. (The almost total independence of *but* can be seen in its freedom to introduce an extraneous idea, such as *But let's talk about something else*.) *Although* also figures in this gradient (Schubiger 1958: 97).

Given this degree of uncertainty it should come as no surprise that on the one hand no strict correlation will be found between intonation and type of dependent clause, and on the other hand that intonation itself is a prime factor in conveying degrees of independence, as we can see with the roughly synonymous *now that* and *because*. Answering the question *Are you going to the party?* one may say *Yes, I'm going*, and continue with either of the following:

(9) now that I'm well aga^{in}

(10) be^{cause} I'm well a gain.

Because is more independent: it looks back to an explanation; *now that* looks forward to a consequence and is incomplete without it, and this is reflected in the inconclusive intonation (Bolinger 1984: 408).

Conditional Clauses

The most interesting class of dependent clause is the conditional, for much the same reasons that make questions the most interesting type of independent clause. In fact, conditions are like questions in many ways. *Are you coming?* and *If you are coming* both pose a hypothesis rather than a fact. *If* is the complementizer for indirect yes-no questions: *Did he do it?* → *I asked if he did it*. Auxiliary inversion can be used for conditions just as it is for questions:

(11) Had you been there before?

(12) Had you been there before, you would have known what the place was like.

But most important, exactly as with questions, intonation can be the main cue to the fact that a clause is meant to be conditional. This is because, as with questions, any major syntactic type can express a condition, and intonation may therefore make the difference:

(13) You crack a joke, he gets mad at you. (declarative)
(14) Do I crack a joke? He gets mad at me. (interrogative)
(15) Crack a joke, he gets mad at you. (imperative)

Although the interrogative type using *do-did* would normally be split into two parts nowadays, as in (14), formerly *do-did* could appear with an obviously dependent clause:

(16) There were some who would hold a higher rank . . . did they write for persons less given to the study of magazines and newspapers.[1]

The declarative type—(13) above—is especially frequent in Black English (Tarone 1973: 32–33).

As with questions, for these instances to be readily interpreted as conditional they need appropriate intonation or appropriate gesture—and these turn out to resemble pretty closely the intonation and gesture appropriate for questions. In fact, if the sentence *You want me, come and get me*[2] is pronounced

(17) You want me, come and get me.

it could as easily be punctuated *You want me? (Well, then) come and get me*. This suggests that B profiles are the most likely:

(18) Give him an inch, (and) he takes a mile.

(19) They pay up, (and) I don't sue.

(20) Make ^{waves,}

         (and) you ^{don't make} _{friends.}

The appropriate gestures here are raised eyebrows and outflared hands, exactly as with questions, though raised shoulders are apt to replace the head-nodding that is used to coax an answer to a question.

   Conditions such as these, without an explicit *if* or other conditional subordinator, are about as dependent on intonation as questions are. Various intonations will serve the purpose, though for obvious reasons an A profile is least likely. What it takes is something that will cue the hearer to expect an 'if-then' relationship, something to suggest that given A, B will follow. This can be done verbally, for example by adding an expression of minimization such as *no more than, just, all you do is*, etc.:

   (21) You no more than crack a joke, he gets mad at you.
   (22) Just crack a joke, he gets mad at you.

—or just the simple *and* at the head of the following clause, as in (18)–(20). With these verbal assists (as with expressions such as *I wonder, I'd like to know, I suppose*, etc. in questions), intonation is less needed and an unexaggerated A profile can be used:

(23) Just ^{crack a} ^{jo}
                    _{k_{e,}} he gets ^{mad} at _{yo_{u.}}

But intonation itself can minimize (Bolinger 1945), with an exaggerated downskip, in which case an A, now low-pitched, is again appropriate:

(24) You ^{crack a}
                         he gets ^{mad}
              jo   at
               k,   yo
               e,   u.

Here *crack a* tends to reach the top of the range: 'All you do is crack a joke and . . .' Or the accented syllable may itself be at the highest pitch, at or near falsetto, especially if gestures of minimization (raised shoulders, outflared hands for 'that's all, nothing concealed') are there to help out:

```
           jo
        crack a
(25) You
                 he gets  mad   at
              k
               e,              yo
                                  u.
```

With the profiles that have a terminal rise or a tonal ending there is no problem: 'more to come,' hence a 'then' consequence, is easy to infer. So for the C profiles in

```
(26) You       me,
                 come and
          want              ge
                              t
                                me.
```

```
(27) Make
            waves, you  cause hard
                             feel
                               i
                                n
                                 gs.
```

with accents on *want* and *waves*. Similarly AC profiles as in

```
(28) Give him     in
             an
                ch,        takes a mi
                    he
                               l
                                e.
```

But AC (and A likewise) is unlikely in a conditional clause that does not point to a consequence, one such as (17) above:

```
            want
(29) ?You              get
               come and
          m    e,
                      m
                       e.
```

This is probably related to the fact that AC is also unusual in yes-no questions (see above, p. 101). Adding *if* makes (29) normal.

Another way of cuing in the condition-consequence relationship is by deemphasizing the result clause: it is 'so unimportant that it is an automatic result.' So changing (13) once again we get

```
(30) You crack a  jo
               k
                e,
                   he gets mad at you.
```

With the result clause unaccented in this fashion, the conditional clause is intensified merely by its contrast and no further intensification, whether by word, intonation, or gesture, is required. But it is not excluded: *You so much as crack a joke . . .*

In all these cases, besides helping to cue the condition, the intonation is performing its other functions. The B profiles in (17)–(20) impart a flippant, no-skin-off-my-nose tone (see Bolinger 1986: 175). These conditions tend to be gnomic expressions similar to *Easy come, easy go; You pays your money, you takes your choice; Ask me no questions, I tell you no lies*. An AC profile in the same place would suggest more involvement on the speaker's part; he is not merely repeating a formula but is producing an assertion of his own; it shows concern, and is commonly associated with warnings. And there is, of course, the contrastivity that AC may convey. Compare the following:

(31) Call him
$^{\text{Christo}^{\text{pher}}}$ and he'll be sat
$_{\text{isfied.}}$

(32) Call him Chris
$_{\text{topher}}$ and he'll be sat$_{\text{isfied.}}$

(33) ?Call him
^{Christopher} and he'll be $_{\text{satisfied.}}$
Chris

(34) Call him
$_{\text{topher}}$ and he'll be $_{\text{satisfied.}}$

The B profile in (31) suggests 'That's all you need to do.' The AC in (32) suggests 'Call him that rather than anything else.' The final C profile in (34) with its terminal rise adds 'Can't be sure of any satisfaction otherwise' to the meaning of (32). But in (33) the B profile in the conditional clause with its lack of contrastivity does not sort with the 'but not otherwise' suggested by the final C with its terminal rise. To the extent that (33) is acceptable, it is probably by way of hearing the B as a CA with delayed fall (see Bolinger 1986: 157).

Our conditional sentences thus far have been mostly without *if*, to test the contribution of intonation to the successful identification of conditions. We have found much the same situation as with questions: there are no defining intonations, but there are facilitating ones, particularly B and AC profiles. What about conditions with explicit subordinators, *if* and its synonyms? The problem again is as with questions, which have their own explicit interrogative signals (auxiliary inversion, wh words, and some marginal items such as *I wonder* and *I suppose*). Among the other subordinators that can serve to pose a condition are *supposing, assuming, allowing, granted that, given that,* inversion of certain auxiliaries (*had I . . . , were I to . . . , could we but . . .*), and probably an indefinite number of other expressions that might be pressed into service, such as *on the premise that, taking as a point of departure the possibility that*. (*On condition that* is more likely in the 'proviso' than in the 'if' sense; *in case* introduces an element of forehandedness and purpose, something like *lest*.)[3]

The question is whether even with these explicit cues the intonation still contributes to the conditionality. As with an explicit interrogative, an explicit *if* clause will be conditional regardless of the intonation. With initial *if* (and with *and* deleted), the initial profile in the perplexing example (33) comes through acceptably as a delayed CA. And there is no need to resort to extremes, as in (24) and (25), to make the conditional intent clear. But the supporting intonations are still available, and since, as we saw, they perform other functions as well in conditional sentences, they are available when needed for those functions. The not-my-responsibility tone of a B is still present when *if* is used, as in

```
                  it,
         need         take
(35) If you                    it.
```

and the concern and involvement of the speaker are apparent in the AC of

```
             vo                              chil
(36) If you get a di        what becomes of the
                      ce,                        d
                    r                             r
                                                   en?
```

Also, certain of the subordinators—at an extreme, even *if* itself—are on the borderline between condition and concession, i.e. between plain *if* and *even if, even though*. Take an utterance like *Granted that he's a dimwit, he deserves (doesn't deserve) to be treated like one*. The affirmative verb is consonant with 'if,' the negative with 'even though,' and the same minimizing downskip that assisted the conditionality of (24) and (25) now assists the 'even' of the concessive interpretation:

(37) Grant

```
     ed that he's a dimwit,     he    does
                                         n't  →
            treat
  de serve  to be       ed like o
                                 n e!
```

The extremely high initial pitch would be out of place in the 'if' interpretation:

(38) Grant
           ed that he's a   dim^{wit,}
                                  he de^{serves to} ⟶

        treat
  be   ed like one.

The high pitch accords with what we know about 'even' in general. If we hear

                Chi

        emperor of
(39) The
                     na wouldn't have such gall!

we know that the meaning is 'even the emperor of China.' To achieve the 'even though' effect on *if* itself, the word would have to be spoken virtually in falsetto: *IF he's a dimwit . . .*

    The 'extreme' that facilitates the 'even if' interpretation can be achieved by verbal hyperbole, and then need not be present in the prosody. An utterance such as *He can jump off the Plaza Towers and he won't convince me* can be spoken in a narrowed range. Further in connection with range, there is a quasi-stereotype in which the *if* clause is at the end: *You couldn't do it if you tried, I wouldn't do it if I could*, involving just a few expressions such as these two—one would not encounter *You couldn't do it if you attempted* nor *I wouldn't help you if I felt like it* in this sense, though with explicit *even* the result is perfectly normal and the same intonation is retained:

        wouldn't do it if I
(40) I
                         co^{uld}.

        wouldn't help you if I
(41) ?I
                        f^{el}t like it.

        wouldn't help you even if I
(42) I
                            f^{el}t like it.

The typical configuration, with the downward leap, is encountered here, but when the expression without *even* is stereotyped in this sense, it no more needs an extreme prosodic treatment than does the one with *even*. On the other hand, if the clauses are reversed, the prosodic exaggeration is apt to be resorted to:

(43) If I

$$^{c}o_{uld}$$
     I wouldn't help you.

Just as it assists 'even if,' 'even though,' intonation also assists 'and if,' a form of complementary question to which the interlocutor is expected to supply the result clause as an answer:

             co
(44) And sup^{posing} nobody
                   $^{m}e_{s}$?

An appropriate reply would be *In that case we'll cancel the concert.* As with complementary questions in general, this one has a wh question paraphrase: *What if nobody comes?* Or the wh can be added as a tag to the complementary question: *And supposing nobody comes, what then?* There is also a paraphrase using the imperative of certain of the subordinators already mentioned: *Suppose (assume) nobody comes.* It might be argued that these are really commands, not questions, and bear the same relation to 'and if' complementary questions that

      na
(45) Your
        $^{m}e.$

Tell me your name' bears to

          na^{m}e?
(46) Your

Your name is . . . ?' (see above, p. 113). But the functional identity can be seen in the fact that *what then* makes as good a tag for *Suppose nobody comes* as for *And supposing nobody comes.*

The intonational relevance of all this is that 'and if' complementary questions tend to have terminal A profiles, as in (44), regardless of what subordinator—*what if, suppose,* etc.—they use. The B profile tends to be a bit demanding, and the AC more demanding still, as if the speaker is hanging on an immediate answer. An A or a B can be used rhetorically, as in

```
                          comes?
              nobody                    see what I
(47) And if              You                    me
                                                  an.
                                            ti
        whole thing would be a waste of
   The                                        me.
```

The speaker does not wait for an answer, which would hardly be the case with an AC here. But the AC would be normal if no question, rhetorical or other, were involved, as in

```
                 co
              nobody                                        ti
(48) And if                       whole thing would be a waste of
                    me   s, the                              me.
```

Little has been said thus far about the position of the conditional clause in a larger sentence, and most of the examples of such sentences have had the clause in initial position. That is the position where other conditional subordinators than *if*, including zero, more or less freely occur. Elsewhere—in the interior and at the end—*if* reigns almost supreme. In part this is because condition → consequence is the normal order of events, so that the most explicit subordinator is not needed where a condition can easily be inferred. Just an infinitive or a prepositional phrase may be sufficient:

(49) To get a better view, we'll have to climb up to the ledge.
(50) With enough money I can buy the car.

Though (49) is easily reversed using *if—We'll have to climb up to the ledge if we want a better view*—without that change the conditional sense is lost unless a rather elaborate prosody is resorted to. Other subordinators are less satisfactory than *if*. It would be odd to say *I'll buy the car supposing I have the money* (compare **I'll buy the car only supposing I have the money*).

Postposing the *if* clause responds to the thematic organization of the sentence. In *Supposing I have the money, I'll buy the car* we in effect answer the question *What will you do if you have the money?* But in *I'll buy the car if I have the money* we answer the question *In what circumstances will you buy the car?*

As with other postposed themes, the *if* clause can be postposed and remain thematic if set off by pause and given a terminal rise (a C, B, or AC profile). So we get

(51) I'll ^{buy} the ^{ca}
r, if I have the mon^{ey.}

with a B profile at the end. But if we say

(52) I'll ^{buy} the ^{car} if I ^{have} the ^{mon}_{ey.}

the *if* clause is rhematic, and the A profile virtually guarantees that interpretation, even if the speaker inserts a pause after *car*, which would suggest an afterthought in this contour. On the other hand, no accent at all on the *if* clause would equally guarantee the "postposed theme" interpretation:

(53) I'll ^{buy the ca}
r, if I have the money.

This too is in accord with general principles whereby the theme is likely to have been mentioned already and therefore needs no accent.

Intonation is a more reliable cue than pause in these interpretations, especially in comparatively routine expressions like

(54) Come ⁱⁿ
if you ^{wish.}

which tend to be spoken without pause. It is not merely the terminal rise here but the contour as a whole that counts. In this example the A profile on *in* implies new information, and *if you wish* can remain level (accentless) and still represent a postposed theme. But in

(55) Come ^{in if you}
_{wish.}

the B on *in if you* implies old information, and the C on *wish* is formally polite new information: we recognize this as a rather cool answer to *May I come in?*—the *come in* part is repeated.

The intonation of *if* clauses used as independent answers to questions reveals the fundamental up-in-the-airness of the hypothetical meaning. The favored profile is AC. For example, in answer to *Do you enjoy entering contests?* one may say

(56) If I see some chance of suc‑ceed‑ing.

A B profile would also be possible but with its greater incompleteness would be more in need of an explicit affirmative:

(57) If I see some chance of suc‑ceeding, yes.

An A profile in place of the AC in (56) would be harder to motivate and would probably need a gestural backup such as raised eyebrows. The underlying kinship with questions can be seen in the fact that the wh adverbs *when* and *where* behave like *if*, and could replace it in (56). On the other hand, if there is no "question" about it, the A profile is normal:

(58) When‑ever I see some chance of suc‑ceeding.

Similarly *wherever*, and possibly *always if* though AC here remains more likely. Other subordinators more readily accept A: they are less "hypothetical" than *if* (and *when*, *where*). There is a graded series in the following answers to *Are you going to pay them a return visit?*

> (59) If I get the chance.   AC
>   When I get the chance.   ↑
>   As soon as I get the chance. |
>   The moment I get the chance.   ↓
>   The first chance I get.   A

Other Adverbial Clauses

With dependent clauses of all types, including the conditional ones just examined, the chief *grammatical* role of intonation is that of cuing degrees of connectedness, to which we can assign the term NEXUS. Though conditional clauses are the prime example, in other types of clauses as well we find intonation filling in, so to speak, for some missing lexical subordinator. For example, *when* in

> (60) I sit there watching them. He turns his head, she turns hers; he raises an eyebrow, she raises one; he drums his fingers, she drums hers.

Or *whereas* in

(61) She looks right, he looks left; she smiles, he frowns; she clasps
her hand around her knee, he clasps his around his head.

The explicit subordinators are unnecessary because the synonymy or
antonymy of the terms for the actions tells us what the relationship is,
and the nexus is taken care of by the contour in which a B or an AC
profile leads to an A profile.

And again, as with conditional clauses, the intonation tends to reinforce the nexus even when the explicit subordinator is there. An example of grammaticized subordination is the *-ing* construction in the
following:

```
(62) Know              felt
        ing how they                made tracks fa
                        a      me,  I
                         bout                        s
                                                      t.
```

```
        made tracks fa
(63) I
                 s     know       felt
                  t,       ing how they  a
                                          bout me.
```

As (62) and (63) show, the same thematic reversal can take place as
with conditional clauses, the AC profile helping to preserve the dependency when the subordinate clause is moved to the end. But—as
with conditional clauses with explicit subordinators—we may readily
use an A profile on the *knowing* clause, and would then possibly offset
the conclusiveness with raised eyebrows and slight nods. There is a
triple message: the terminal fall says 'There was no uncertainty about
this action, I was perfectly aware of what was good for me,' the nod-
ding head reinforces the affirmation, and the raised eyebrows help
with the nexus:

```
        made tracks fa
(64) I
                        knowing how they f
                                          e
                   s                       lt  about me.
                    t,
```

The AC profile is probably the most frequent nexal intonation in
American English, though B and C are normal enough.[4] Examples
using the explicit subordinator *once*:

```
              cov                no keeping the scandal  →
(65) Once dis
                     d,  there was
                    e
                   r
                  e

     out of the
              pa
                pers.
```

(66) Once dis^{covered,...}   (67) Once dis_{covered,...}

Explicit subordinators vary in how close a nexus they impose, and intonation tends to follow suit. There is a gradient in the three subordinators *or*, *else*, and *otherwise* (with *else* tending to become *or else* colloquially). It could be argued that these connectors introduce independent rather than dependent clauses, and yet when we compare an *or* sentence with an *if* sentence we see how hard it is to draw the line:

(68) I had to stay behind or I would have missed the opportunity.
(69) If I hadn't stayed behind I would have missed the opportunity.

In (68) we can substitute (*or*) *else* and *otherwise*, in that order, with increasingly loose nexus. With *or*, Profile B at the end of the first clause has its best chance—the nexus is closest; with *otherwise*, Profile A—the nexus is loosest; but Profile AC works with all three, though best with *or* and (*or*) *else*. The punctuation reflects the nexus: no punctuation is needed with *or*, a comma is most likely before (*or*) *else*, and a semicolon would be favored with *otherwise*.

We earlier saw a similar gradient with *whereas*, *though*, and *but* (p. 172). A fourth term can be added: (*and*) *yet*. Amending *though* to *although*, to move it a little closer to *but*, we get the gradient *whereas*, *yet*, *although*, and *but*. *Whereas* invokes the tightest nexus. It calls for a fairly explicit adversative tie between the two clauses. Thus it would be odd to say ?*The place seemed crowded, whereas there was hardly anybody there*, but it is normal to say *The place seemed crowded, whereas in fact there was hardly anybody there* or *The place seemed crowded to us, whereas to everyone else it seemed as if there was hardly anybody there*: we have the explicitly counterbalanced *seemingly* versus *in fact* and *to us* versus *to everyone else*. The three others relate their clauses more loosely. So we have this scale of diminishing nexus:

(70) The place seemed crowded, whereas in fact there was etc.
                              (and) yet (in fact)
                              although (in fact)
                              but (in fact)

It is not a smooth gradient because other semantic elements are involved than mere adversativeness (for example, *yet* is apt to relate to something the speaker knows but is news to the hearer, whereas *although* is more apt to relate to what the hearer already knows and needs to be reminded of), but the intonation nevertheless reflects the nexus: the likelihood of Profile A increases down the scale, though never surpassing the likelihood of AC.

Parenthesis and Restriction

Nexus is critical to a type of clause not yet discussed, which is defined not by internal structure but by being "in some significant way external to the sentence" (Ziv 1985: 181). This is the PARENTHESIS. The definition by Nosek (1973: 100) is as good as any: "Parenthesis . . . is a dependent satellite part of the utterance, wedged into a non-compact primary (frame) utterance from which it differs. Parenthesis . . . expresses a secondary communication." By definition, the parenthesis interrupts the prosodic flow of the frame utterance, and this naturally has some peculiar and fairly predictable effects on intonation. There are additional effects if we follow Svensson (1976) and expand the definition to include elements that might be "wedged in" but are often tagged on at the end as well:

(71) The application, *as it turned out*, had been directed to the wrong post office.

(72) The application had been directed to the wrong post office, *as it turned out*.

We are naturally interested in parentheses not as they occur in writing (where they are rather more frequent) but as they occur in colloquial speech. Anything as awkward as the following, from a university bulletin, would be corrected in speech by restarting the sentence:

(73) The department has now asked, *since next year will be Kelley's third year*, the dean to appoint a "friendly outsider" to canvass . . . (Cornell University, 1973–74)

The intonation is more than a reflection of the fact that a given segment of discourse is a parenthesis; it is often the main cue differentiating it as such. Compare the final parenthesis of (72) with the ending of (75):

(74) The prizes were distributed—*and don't tell me otherwise*—as honestly as anyone could expect.

(75) The prizes were distributed as honestly as anyone could expect, *and don't tell me otherwise*.

Few would regard the latter case as parenthetical. There are also uncertain cases even when the supposedly parenthetical element is wedged in:

(76) *I rather imagine* your New York friends are going to be delayed.
(77) Your New York friends *I rather imagine* are going to be delayed.
(78) Your New York friends, *I rather imagine*, are going to be delayed.
(79) Your New York friends are going to be delayed, *I rather imagine*.

If the pitch level of (77) is kept the same as that of (76) we might prefer to say that we have a sentence in which there is no parenthesis but in which a movement transformation has occurred: the subject of the subordinate clause in (76) has been fronted in (77). Intonationally (76) and (77) are similar and so are (78) and (79).

The typical parenthesis has three prosodic characteristics: it is lower in pitch than the matrix sentence, it is set off by pause(s), and it has a rising terminal (B, C, or AC profile). In final position it may be accentless—a low terminal level. The pauses reflect the separation from the rest of the utterance, the lower pitch represents the incidentalness, and the terminal rise provides the linkup—the parenthesis is incomplete by itself. Within the parenthesis the normal accentual and intonational contrasts may be retained, but confined to a lowered range (Daneš 1960: 40). And the lowering may be compounded. Though there is a practical limit to recursion, we do find parentheses within parentheses:

> (80) When the opportunity comes, *and it will*, **I'll bet**, *sooner than you expect*, you've got to be ready to grab it.

Here *I'll bet* is inserted in *and it will sooner than you expect*, which in turn is inserted in the matrix sentence.

The characteristics of delimiting pause, lowered pitch, and terminal rise are what we expect to find in parentheses, but any one of the three can be suspended, and the suspension will often depend on the length and the syntactic makeup of the parenthesis. The shorter it is, the more easily the pause can be skipped, and that has resulted in some reinterpretations over the years. Compare the following:

> (81) She is, *undoubtedly*, affected by what she heard.
> (82) She's *undoubtedly* affected by what she heard.

The word *undoubtedly* is a sentence adverb and as such is illocutionary—it is "outside" the sentence proper, making a comment as to the truth of the statement: 'It is undoubtedly true that . . .' But (81) and (82) are not equivalent. In (82) the speed of utterance and consequent shrinking of the pause, plus the position of the adverb, have caused a partial shift of allegiance: *undoubtedly* now "belongs to" *affected* as much as to the frame sentence as a whole. To some degree it is an intensifier of *affected*. We can sense this more clearly by comparing it with some other adverbs of this class that have evolved more fully into intensifiers:

> (83) She is, *truly*, affected by what she heard.
> (84) She is *truly* affected by what she heard.

This is the history of *very* ('verily') and, more recently, of *really*. Actually, adverbs that comment parenthetically on the truth value of an utterance tend to fuse with the frame sentence anyway and then are no longer recognizable as parentheses. This is most apt to happen when the adverb gets into the position that would be occupied by *not*:

(85) She's affected, *no doubt*, by what she heard.
(86) She is, *no doubt*, affected by what she heard.
(87) She's *no doubt* affected by what she heard.

The prosody shows that (87) does not contain a parenthesis:

(88) *She's, *no doubt*, affected by what she heard.

One such adverb loses its identity completely: *rather*, in its fusion with the *'d* of *would* (or *had*). Compare:

(89) *Rather* ('instead'), I would stay home.
(90) I would, *rather*, stay home.
(91) I'd *rather* stay home.

The result is a compound verb. It is apparent in all these cases that with the loss of pause the intonational distinctiveness has been lost too. *I'd ráther stay hóme* takes on the same accent pattern as *I prefér to stay hóme*. And it is also apparent that although the distinctive pause end of the gradient is favored, any degree of pause is possible.

A lexical item that fits syntactically with the utterance as a whole is naturally a better candidate for fusion than is a syntactic outsider, such as an exclamation:

(92) Mine is, *unfortunately*, too old for the purpose.
(93) Mine's *unfortunately* too old for the purpose.
(94) Mine is, *alas*, too old for the purpose.
(95) *Mine's *alas* too old for the purpose.

The opposite of fusion is what happens to a normally weak word just before a parenthesis. In order to play down a parenthesis we may play up what precedes it. Sweet (1898: §1895) calls this "break stress." We note how the word *is* is made prominent in (81), (83), (86), (92), and (94), and *would* in (90).

A long parenthesis is apt to call for longer pauses to enable the speaker to collect his thoughts and the hearer to integrate what precedes the parenthesis with what follows—extra "processing time" is needed. So in

(96) The financial assistance (*you remember that some vague promise was made that the firm would get it*) was uh contingent on retrenchment in two departments.

the speaker is apt to come to a sudden halt before beginning the parenthesis, and to put a marked hold at the end of it, resuming the main sentence with a slow hesitation sound.

Relative pitch height, usually in the shape of lowered pitch for the parenthesis, also has its ups and downs. We would be in trouble if we had to depend on it absolutely. In the following badly written passage the slightly lowered pitch due to normal declination could be taken as parenthetic, leading to a ridiculous interpretation:

> (97) The abashed two were ordered to dress, handcuffed, and were led to waiting cars.[5]

By raising the AC profile on *handcuffed* we make a stab at suggesting 'This is part of the frame sentence,' as it was intended, but even that could be parenthetic—the speaker might be thinking 'Of all things, *handcuffed*—and expected to be able to dress!'

The fact is that the pitch level depends on the nature of the parenthesis. If it is a question its pitch may well go higher than that of the frame sentence:

> (98) I asked his pardon—*what else?*—but he wasn't disposed to forgive me.

Similarly with a parenthesis offered as a strong appeal or rebuttal:

> (99) I was trying, *of course*, to do all I was asked, but the man was simply being unreasonable.

Here the *of course* may take a high-pitched A profile rather than a low-pitched C; the high pitch on *course* underscores the speaker's willingness to go the extra mile. Rebuttal and protest are evident in

```
                       if
                                lo
(100) Tha                                            no consequence at
         a t,     you will al    o w,  is of                             a
                                                                          l
                                                                           l.
```

with the highest pitch on the *if* of the parenthesis.

If the speaker intends the parenthesis as an essential direction to the hearer to take the frame utterance in a particular way, that may be reflected in a higher pitch on the parenthesis. 'Don't overlook this' and 'Don't misunderstand me' warnings commonly behave this way:

> (101) No matter what your field of study, *whether in science or in liberal arts*, you must master the signals.[6]

> (102) John—*and all this is conjecture, remember*—probably had had a little over the mark when he proposed.

The parenthesis-within-a-parenthesis, *remember*, has a lowered pitch within the higher pitch of the primary parenthesis. For obvious reasons the parenthesis in

(103) I asked his pardon, *damn it!*, but he turned me away.

may go up.

Terminal rise may be criterial in the sort of distinction we saw in (76)–(79), between a fronted subject ("extraposition") and a genuine parenthesis. If we say

(104) Jo   kno   mon
    ʰn I   w has the
                   ᵉy.

with *know* ending above creak, the result is ambiguous as between

(105) John, *I know* (= I know it), has the money. (parenthesis)

(106) John I know has (= I know that John has) the money. (extraposition)

But if *know* ends at creak, the sense is almost unambiguously that of (106). This is a local effect, depending in part on the lexical makeup of the element in question—specifically, here, on the fact that *know* has a stereotyped intransitive use (105) as well as a regular transitive one; if the unambiguous *as you know* were used instead, creak would merely result in a more positive parenthesis, not an extraposition.

Local effects aside, what we find in general is that terminal rise may be reduced or suspended depending on degree of nexus, which in turn depends on discourse factors and to some degree on the point at which the insertion is made. This awaits careful study, but the favored insertion points cluster around the verb phrase and differ among themselves in nexus, as can be seen in cases like

(107) John *as you know* had wanted to consider the offer.

(108) John had *as you know* wanted to consider the offer.

(109) John had wanted, *as you know*, to consider the offer.

(110) ?John had wanted, *as you know*, time to consider the offer.

(111) John had wanted, *as you know*, a little time to consider the offer.

(112) John had wanted time, *as you know*, to consider the offer.

Though all these parentheses would probably have a terminal rise, those in (107) and (108) could be considerably flattened. The doubtfulness of (110) is due to the juxtaposing of two main accents—the rhythm is bad (see Bolinger 1986: 54–55, 61–62).

As you know might be termed a COMMENT, and that category probably subsumes the majority of parentheses. But there are (at least) two
other discourse types, REVISIONS and DECISIONS, with a tendency to
realize the intonation differently. Revisions use expressions such as *I
mean, perhaps I should say, correction, rather, no, that is,* etc., and because they are meant to deny one alternative and affirm another, they
favor A profiles:

> (113) The lift-off was at six—*no, earlier than that, around five-thirty*—
> on the morning of the 26th.

> (114) I was going to call your boss—*correction: your secretary*—be-
> fore you got in.

A revision may be posed rather than imposed, as in the following
from Nosek (1973: 104):

> (115) It is next to certain—*I am tempted to say certain*—that I can es-
> tablish that Althaus was killed by one of your men.

Revisions are metalinguistic repairs: the speaker makes a ceremony
of correcting himself. Most repairs are simply made, with only a
headshake to mark them; we would probably not regard such cases as
parentheses (e.g. *I prized—pried—open the door*).

Decisions are at the opposite extreme: instead of reaching back they
reach forward, and they are as a rule maximally suspensive. The
speaker is bidding for time while making up his mind, and the locution is apt to have the same level intonation as the hesitation sound
mm, which could appear (or be added) in the same place, as with
maybe in

> (116) They're going to pick—*maybe*—six of the best for the final run.

The final syllable of *maybe* is prolonged. Other fillers of this kind include *well, let's say, oh, how shall I say it, let me think a moment.* But if the
speaker is truly nonplussed and needs to take time out, a decided
break, with an A profile, is available. We note such a change when
now is added:

> (117) Joan was expected to bring—*let me see*—napkins, silverware,
> buns, and potato salad.

> (118) Joan was expected to bring—*now let me see*—napkins . . .

Comments are the largest category, embracing all that qualifies in
some way the intent or import of the frame sentence or some part of
it. They may refer to truth value (examples [119] and [120] are from
Nosek 1973):

> (119) But it's there all right, waiting to be—*yes*, verified.

(120) Even if it's true—*and I don't say it is*—you still sound pretty cheap saying it.

(121) A home of your own, *after all* (*when all's said and done*), is what counts the most.

They may comment on incidentalness, make comparisons, express degree, describe a protagonist, or convey anything else *about* what is being said that may enter the speaker's head:

(122) You, *by the way*, are the favorite candidate in that precinct.

(123) Emory, *unlike his father*, never seems to know where he's headed.

(124) A liberal education enhances—*more than most people realize*—the potential for advancement in specialized fields.

(125) When Mrs. Lacey comes into the shop—*and a pleasanter lady you'll never find*—she doesn't look a day over thirty. (Nosek)

All these would have terminal rises, and all but (122) would favor AC profiles. (Incidentalness—the *by the way* of [122]—is too unimportant to merit more than a C or a B, though *incidentally* itself might take AC if the speaker wants to suggest 'more than incidentally,' a deliberate understatement.)

The discussion thus far has concentrated on ADVERBIAL parentheses: the insertion is loosely attached to the frame sentence. But the question of parenthesis has been of more interest to grammarians in a different sphere, that of NOMINAL modification, especially as it has to do with the distinction between restrictive and nonrestrictive (parenthetical) adjective clauses. This is also the area where the contribution of prosody has been most widely recognized. Examples like the following, from Chisholm and Milic (1974: 427), are found in almost any grammar of English:

(126) The bus drivers *who now belong to a union* went on strike.
(127) The bus drivers, *who now belong to a union*, went on strike.

In (126) 'bus drivers' embraces more than those drivers who belong to a union, and the *who* clause narrows the group to just those who do. In (127) 'bus drivers' and 'who' are coextensive: the clause is not needed to tell us *which* bus drivers are referred to—it is a bit of extra information thrown in, hence parenthetical, even though connected syntactically by the relative pronoun *who*. And the prosody shows, by the close versus loose nexus (the latter represented by the commas), which of the two clauses is restrictive and which is parenthetical or nonrestrictive.

The subordinators mostly involved in the restrictive-nonrestrictive contrast are zero (*the man I saw*), that (*the man that I saw*), *who*(*m*) (*the man whom I saw*), *whose* (*the woman whose purse they stole*), and *which* (*the place from which they came*), but place (*where*) and time (*when*) subordinators are also found, as in these answers to *You do your jogging in the park?*

> (128) Yes, in the park *where the ground is level.*
> (129) Yes, in the park, *where the ground is level.*

—(129) implies that the entire park is level.

Nonrestrictive clauses resemble the earlier parentheses not only in prosody but also in function. Though for the most part they modify only nouns and noun phrases (and necessarily do so in the case of *who*, *whom*, and *whose*), a *which* clause may modify the entire frame sentence:

> (130) After staying awake for thirty-six hours, *which would have had me flat on my back,* Gary showed up for work as if he hadn't lost a minute's sleep.

The similarity here to other parentheses can be seen in

> (131) Flo kept grabbing double handfuls, *which I found disgusting.*
> (132) Flo kept grabbing double handfuls, *to my disgust.*
> (133) Flo kept grabbing double handfuls, *disgustingly.*

The similarity also works the other way—syntactically disconnected parentheses may refer to particular nouns, and this construction is often preferred colloquially:

> (134) Some friend of yours, whose name I didn't catch, left a package for you.
>
> (135) Some friend of yours—I didn't catch his name—left a package for you.

If we are to understand the role of intonation in this area of syntax, we must make certain that our dichotomy is the correct one. Is the dividing line truly between what is restrictive and what is not, or is it something that just happens to approximate restrictive versus nonrestrictive so closely as to fool grammarians, who are notoriously fond of logical formulations? The logic of restrictiveness is clear—it is the classical one of inclusion-exclusion shown in Figure 1. Our experience with intonation should warn us that if intonation responds to restrictiveness and nonrestrictiveness it will not be because it is linked in some formal way with such a logico-grammatical pair of categories but because those categories are associated with some discourse factor that triggers the intonational contrast directly.

Restrictive   Nonrestrictive

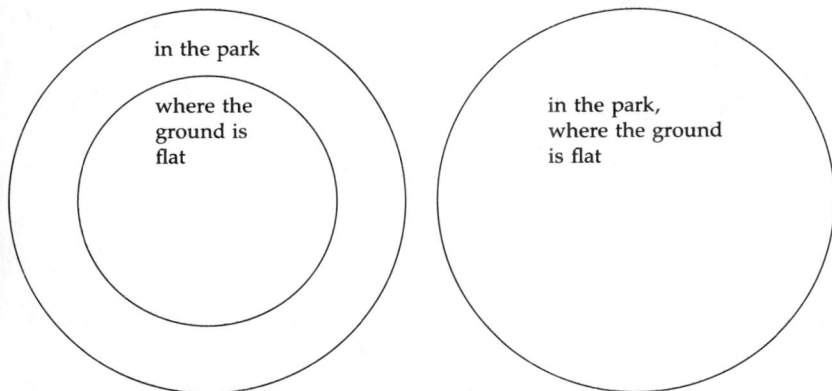

in the park

where the
ground is
flat

in the park,
where the ground
is flat

Fig. 1. Restrictiveness vs. nonrestrictiveness

We found several gradients in our treatment of other parentheses.
There is a gradient here too. First, prosodic separation does not necessarily signify nonrestriction:

(136) What man, *who is really a man,* would do a thing like that?
(137) What man *who is really a man* would do a thing like that?

The separation of the dependent clause is not because it is nonrestrictive—it is restrictive in both cases—but because in (136) the speaker
starts out with a noun that supposedly does not need qualification (*no
man would do that*), and then decides that it does. The dependent
clause is a restrictive afterthought, more or less equivalent to *if he is
really a man*. In (138) the afterthoughtiveness is explicit:

(138) The story I told you—*that you enjoyed so much, remember?*—
was one I made up for our daughter when she was six.

The speaker supplies the *that* clause as one means of identifying
which story is meant; it is therefore restrictive.

Second, some adjective clauses are not clearly restrictive or nonrestrictive:

(139) The indictment was against a certain Congressman from Alabama *who had been accused of influence-peddling.*

Is the *who* clause necessary here to distinguish this Congressman
from others not so accused, or has the person already been sufficiently identified by *a certain* and *from Alabama,* leaving the *who* clause
as just one more item in the narrative? A comma pause before *who*

would clinch the latter, but its absence is no proof either way. All we can tell is that the clause is not afterthoughtive. On the other hand, in a case like

(140) The tree limbs had formed a little archway *that I was able to push through.*

does the speaker have in mind a 'penetrable archway,' restrictive, or something like

(141) The tree limbs had formed a little archway, *and I was able to push through it.*

nonrestrictive? Restrictiveness or nonrestrictiveness here is simply irrelevant.

Discussions of restrictiveness usually make reference to a contrast between *that* or zero versus *which*, or between *that* or zero versus *who(m)*, as in

(142) The Steinway *that (which) was sold yesterday* went for almost ten thousand.

(143) The Steinway, *which (*that) was sold yesterday*, went for almost ten thousand.

(144) The hostages (*that, whom*) *they failed to rescue* were later ransomed.

(145) The hostages, *whom they failed to rescue*, were later ransomed.

This is to say that *which* and *who(m)* may be used in either restrictive or nonrestrictive clauses, but *that* and zero are limited to restrictive ones. And this of course is reflected in the prosody: *that* and zero will not be used with clauses that are set off parenthetically.

The claim is probably true as far as zero is concerned: if there is no explicit subordinator, a nonrestrictive clause will appear to be something other than an adjective clause:

(146) The machines *they failed to produce* brought them no revenue.

(147) The machines—*they failed to produce*—brought them no revenue.

(A parenthesis is normal without *that* with a change of syntax to an appositive construction: *The machines, the ones [that] they failed to produce, brought them no revenue.*) As for *that*, we have already seen, in (138), one example of a restrictive clause set off parenthetically as an afterthought. Compare

(148) I'm always thirsty. — You should drink water, *which quenches it best.*

(149) Which is the wine that I'm tasting now? — It's the older vintage, *that we tried yesterday.*

Though *which* might be used in (149), it is not colloquial. In fact, it is not colloquial in (148) either—we would prefer to say *You should drink water; that quenches it best,* or some other paraphrase. In any case, (149) is an instance of a nonrestrictive *that* clause set off parenthetically. It appears that neither limitation holds: *that* as well as the wh words can be used restrictively and nonrestrictively, and parenthesizing is not confined to nonrestrictives.

So it seems that something more than syntax is involved in the choice of subordinator—perhaps the subordinators themselves differ in meaning. We can learn something about this by observing the contexts in which they are not likely to occur. Quirk et al. (1972: 870) record

(150) *John is not the man *who he was.*
(151) *My typewriter is not the machine *which it was.*

Note also

(152) *He told me everything *which he knew.*

With (150)–(152) the choice is absolute. More finely balanced preferences are indicated in

(153) A formula *that obviously offers a great deal of promise* is the new antiviral preparation developed by Lilly.

(154) (?)A formula *that surprisingly offers a great deal . . .*

(155) A formula *that* as everybody knows *was favored to . . .*

(156) (?)A formula *that* as few people know *was favored to . . .*

If *which* is to be inserted in any of these, it will work best in (154) and (156).

These judgments point to the wh subordinators as in some sense the "marked" ones. As long as things run along routinely and the dependent clause does not introduce something unexpected, *that* or zero seems to be favored. But if something interrupts that routine flow, with new or extraneous information, then the wh is favored— and this goes for *where* and *when* too:

(157) The last place (?*where*) *she lived* was Greenwich Village.

(158) The place (*where*) *I would like best to live* is . . .

(159) The only time (?*when*) *I saw him* he was off work.

(160) The only time (*when*) *it would be convenient* would be on a weekend.

This accounts for the comparative infrequency of *which* in colloquial speech; more direct ways of handling the unexpected are favored, such as giving it an independent clause (the thirst-quencher example above). It also accounts for the preference for wh in nonrestrictive clauses, which bring in more or less extraneous information. And it accounts for the preference for *that* in restrictives, since if we need to call on some property of an entity to distinguish it from other entities in its category, we are usually compelled to appeal to a property that is known: unless my interlocutor already knows that I lost my wallet, it will do me no good to say *the wallet that I lost*. The effect of *obviously* and *surprisingly*, and of *as everybody knows* and *as few people know*, is predictable. The marked-unmarked opposition also accounts for the matching of subordinators and intonation in the following two completions of the sentence beginning *I wanted to get word to him as soon as possible* (Bolinger 1977b: 12–13):

                              else

(161) about someone

                        (that) I knew was available.

                                            vail
(162) about someone else who I knew was a
                                                  ^able.

The terminal level in (161) implies shared knowledge (availability has been under discussion). The final A profile in (162) implies information that the speaker *brings* to the scene; it is unexpected. It is not that *that* or zero must be used in the first and *who* in the second, but that these two are the likely choices and, when they are made, they help to convey routineness on the one hand and unexpectedness on the other.

A *that* in an uninterrupted sequence of clauses gives way to a *which* at a major break:

> (163) Listen with even half an ear and you can't fail to notice the many misaccentuations which, through affectation or ignorance, are perpetrated by advertisers and announcers.

Without the interrupting parenthesis, the normal thing here would be *misaccentuations that are perpetrated*. But such a parenthesis is rare in speech anyway, and we already have the marked situation—writing—where *which*es abound. If the adverbial modifier had been one more easily integrated into the syntax and therefore not felt as parenthetical, *that* would again be normal: *misaccentuations that day by day and in every way are perpetrated.*

In a sequence of two clauses modifying separate nominals, the tendency is to put the wh subordinator first if both wh and *that* are used:

(164) Judges' Cave—that's the place associated with the men *who were the judges that condemned Charles I to death.*

(165) An invertebrate *which has a jointed body that is usually protected by a shell* is known as an arthropod.

Presumably the higher modifying clause has a little more shock value than the lower one: *that* is subordinated to *which.*

This order is reversed when the subordinators modify the *same* nominal; *which* introduces the more remote of the two clauses, the one that the speaker has to work harder to connect up:

(166) How do you send *something that's on paper which shouldn't be folded?*

Both clauses are intended to modify *something.* If *which* and *that* are exchanged, *that shouldn't be folded* is virtually forced to modify *paper.* For the markedness of *who* as against *that,* consider

(167) I bet you don't know what a hype is. — A hype is a drug addict *who uses a hypodermic.*

(168) If a junkie is an ordinary drug addict, what's a hype? — A hype is a drug addict *that uses a hypodermic.*

The *that* points back to something already mentioned. The contrast shows up sharply in the associated use of the pronoun *one;* (169) relates to (167), (170) to (168):

(169) A hype is one *who uses a hypodermic.*
(170) A hype is one *that uses a hypodermic.*

In assigning marked functions to the wh words, English is true to its history. The language has adopted all three of the major strategies for connecting relative clauses to the main sentence: simple juxtaposition or zero (*the man I saw*), a demonstrative pronoun, *that* (*the man that I saw*), and the wh interrogatives (*the man whom I saw*). Since a demonstrative pronoun points to something already there, *that* is most comfortable with antecedents already known. But an interrogative "raises a question": if there is something unusual about the syntax or about the antecedent, then a wh word is available. Given a restrictive clause, i.e., one that is not unusual syntactically, one may resort to a wh as a reminder to the hearer to jog his memory, as in the following contrast:

(171) The books *that markers were stuck in*—you remember—belong on Shelf A.

(172) The books *in which markers were stuck*—you may have forgotten—belong on Shelf A. (Bolinger 1977d: 65)

On the other hand, given a nonrestrictive clause, i.e., one that is dragged in syntactically, one may nevertheless resort to *that* as a way of suggesting an antecedent that is highly familiar. The Quirk et al. example (1972: 872)

(173) I looked at Mary's sad face, *that I had once so passionately admired.*

has *that* not for the grammatical reason that *which* "might imply a too parenthetic relation" but because *which* would destroy the aura of familiarity that the author desires. One gets a caricature of this contrast by substituting the primitive values of *that* and *which*:

(174) I looked at Mary's sad face, that face I had once so passionately admired.

(175) I looked at Mary's sad face, which face I had once so passionately admired.

We have explored the question of restrictiveness sufficiently to be able to say that it is tangential to prosody. A restrictive clause may be parenthetical, though it usually is not; a nonrestrictive clause is usually parenthetical, but it does not have to be—the *who* clause in (162) is nonrestrictive and yet is spoken without pause. Similarly *that* is usually restrictive, but need not be, the wh words are free to be either restrictive or nonrestrictive, and neither type is confined to any particular kind of nexus. It is no wonder that the subjects in a listening test involving parenthetical expressions had their greatest difficulty in trying to make up their minds between restrictive and nonrestrictive clauses (Nemni 1981: 106).

Two marginally interesting facts have emerged. Adjective clauses without a subordinator cannot be parenthesized, and *that* clauses, with their affinity for the familiar, tend to employ less in the way of pitch excursion. We have seen the flat level in (161), and in the pair (171)–(172) the latter would favor greater tension and higher pitch.

The matter of restrictiveness does not stop with clauses employing the subordinators that have been identified thus far. There is a relatively new subordinator, *plus*, signifying 'in addition to which' and identifiable as such by the tendency to evoke a terminal rise in the preceding clause, which is less the case when *in addition* is used without *to which*:

(176) John is willing, plus he knows the country and its people.

(177) John is willing, In addition, he knows the country and its people.

Nor is the question of restrictiveness confined to the sorts of finite adjective clauses we have been considering. There is something very similar to restrictiveness-nonrestrictiveness in the 'motive' versus 'cause' contrast which partly distinguishes *because* from *since*. A motive is in tight nexus with the action it leads to, and when motive is evident, *since* is doubtful:

> (178) I went there because I wanted to.
> (179) *I went there since I wanted to.

If the *since* clause is parenthesized and the action is seen impersonally, then it may get by:

> (180) I went there, since I wanted to.
> (181) Since I wanted to, I went there.

But a better context for *since* is a fully impersonal one:

> (182) The pavement was wet, since it had just rained.

Because is optional here, but in (183) it is required if the subject is acting purposely:

> (183) I minced along because the pavement was wet.

There is also something resembling the restrictiveness-nonrestrictiveness contrast in phrases with *for to*, as pointed out by Ladd (1980: 94–95). In the pair

> (184) Helen left diréctions for George to follow.
> (185) Helen left directions for George to fóllow.

without a context to serve as guide, the hearer's best guess is that in (184) George is supposed to follow the directions, whereas in (185) he is being directed to perform the act of following. As Ladd notes, in (184) the *for to* phrase gives "merely supplementary information about the directions," but in (185) "it is restrictive, giving the hearer essential information which narrows the possible range of referents." In our terms, the accents here fall at the point of greatest interest. In (184) the speaker intends unaccented *follow* as more or less redundant in the light of *directions*—following is what directions are for. In (185) accented *follow* is the substance of the directions.

Though this is a good example of prosody helping to cue a meaning, it is not really a matter of restrictiveness as it is usually defined in relation to adjective clauses. If (184) is contrasted with *Helen left diréctions for George to deliver*, it is apparent that both sentences contain the equivalent of restrictive clauses: *Helen left diréctions that George was to follow, Helen left diréctions that George was to deliver*. And when (185) is similarly paraphrased, it turns out to be neither restrictive nor nonrestrictive as far as the grammar goes, but appositive:

(186) Helen left directions that (to wit, saying) George was to follow.

The appositive clause does give essential information about the directions (just as the appositive *John* gives essential information about *brother* in *my brother John*), but a restrictive clause should be expressible with *which*, and this one is not: *Helen left directions which George was to fóllow* is a paraphrase of (184) (with a shift of emphasis), not of (185). The subordinator for appositive clauses is *that*.[7] But grammatical subordination is a matter of definition, and appositives could be embraced.

Restrictiveness is an issue also in a narrower zone of syntax, that of adjectival and adverbial modification. The latter we have already had a partial view of, in parenthetical modification by sentence adverbs:

(187) The bell rang out clearly.
(188) Clearly, the bell rang out.
(189) The bell, clearly, rang out.

Versions (187) and (188) are virtually unambiguous, restrictive and nonrestrictive respectively. But (189) is not necessarily marked by the prosody: *clearly* is an adverb associated with truth value, and such adverbs, as we saw, can readily fuse with the following verb—the commas could be omitted. A better adverb to illustrate parenthesis would be *ominously*.

With adjectives, the prosody assists to some degree in distinguishing restrictive from nonrestrictive and coordination from subordination. The latter is the easier contrast to illustrate:

(190) She met a tall, handsome stranger, not a short, ugly acquaintance.

Given the specific contrasts, these adjectives should probably all be regarded as restrictive. What the pause and the probable high-pitched B profiles on *tall* and *short* tell us is that *tall* and *handsome*, and *short* and *ugly,* are coordinate modifiers at the same level: *a stranger tall and handsome, an acquaintance short and ugly.* Compare those with

(191) They gave us expert legal advice ≠ *advice expert and legal.

(192) We sat on a rickety wooden table ≠ *a table rickety and wooden.

Here the modifiers are not coordinate: the correct equivalents are *legal advice that was expert, a wooden table that was rickety.* There is not likely to be any pause, and if the adjectives are separately emphasized, the first one will probably be on an AC profile. The likely choices are

```
          rickety wooden
(193) a                    ta
                             b1
                               e.
```

```
          rick    wooden ta
(194) a
            e t^y          b1
                             e.
```

with *rickety* separately emphasized in (194). But since the first of the two adjectives in each of the paired coordinate examples of (190) can also have AC, the intonation is less informative than the degree of pause.

Another complication is that many adjective modifiers exhibit a high degree of fusion with each other and with their nouns: *good old John* has *good old* as a sort of stereotype, and the same can be said of *level head* in *a shrewd, level head.* Other examples: *nice little boy, great big dog, fond old man.* The sequence often depends on whether there is some degree of redundancy in one of the adjectives—if it has this property it tends to precede. So young beef is apt to be tender, and we say *tender young beef*; a throaty voice is almost by definition deep, so we say *a deep throaty voice.* Similarly *bold new step, soft clammy hands.* Though this is not *logical* subordination as in the case of *bad legal advice* (see below), it is a more fundamental subordination-for-importance: the semantically peripheral item occupies the peripheral position. Prosodic separation is optional: *tender, young beef; deep, throaty voice* (but not *bad, legal advice*). If the order is reversed, separation is almost mandatory: *young, tender beef; throaty, deep voice.*

Restrictiveness affects adjectives in a more fundamental way: it divides them into two classes. The first embraces those adjectives whose primary function is to identify, hence restrict: *legal advice, differential calculus, electrical energy* (the *-al* suffix is very frequent). When used for this primary purpose, such adjectives do not take degree modification (*a more differential calculus*, *the energy is very electrical*). The second class embraces adjectives that convey the qualities of things, that paint pictures on noun canvases. They may be used to restrict as well. When we say *They climbed the high mountains of Peru* we may have in mind that they did not bother to climb the low ones (*They climbed the mountains of Peru that were high*). Or we may have in mind that the mountains of Peru are reputedly all high (*They climbed the mountains of Peru, which are high*). The two meanings commonly differ in their intonation. The second, with purely descriptive *high*, tends to feature an initial B with downmoving tail:

```
         high mountains of Pe
(195) the                    r
                              u.
```

In place of this B + A contour, the first meaning tends to have A + A (or simple A on *high* if Peru has been under discussion):

```
         high                   ru
(196) the        mountains of Pe
                                  u.
```

By suggesting a purely descriptive intent, the initial B dramatizes the description:

```
        mighty wind
(197) A            swept down from the hills.
```

Other prosodic markers of dramatization are usually added, especially extra length—on *high* in (195) and on *wind* in (197). The B of course does not "mean" 'this is dramatic.' That follows, contextually, from the more fundamental sense of connectedness, redundancy, 'not separately important' (hence potentially important for other reasons). There may be quite other reasons than dramatization for something not to be separately important. If you ask me what sequence the chapters of a textbook should have, I may reply

```
         easy lessons should come fi
(198) The                            r
                                      st.
```

The context invites treating 'easy lessons' as something given. But if you want to dispute the fact, then 'easy' becomes separately important and you say

(199) The syllables are a waste of time.

When a restrictive and a descriptive adjective together modify a single noun, the descriptive adjective takes the peripheral position, as noted above: *bad legal advice, illegible alphabetic symbols, mysterious molecular forces*. There is no prosodic separation. When two restrictive adjectives modify a single noun, the more peripheral one takes the more peripheral position: *domestic political issues* speaks primarily of political issues; *political domestic issues* speaks primarily of domestic issues.

Cleft Sentences

A special case of clearly restrictive modification is the cleft sentence, with the form

(200) It's a cálendar that I need.

Related to this is the "pseudocleft"

(201) What I need is a cálendar.
(202) The thing I need is a cálendar.

The corresponding "simplex" sentence of course is the plain

(203) I need a cálendar.

Clefting adds a syntactic focus to the accentual focus that is already present in the simplex. It is generally used when the focus is in dispute:

(204) Who woke me with that phone call in the middle of the night?
— Máry did. — Nonsense! It was yóu who did! (It was yóu!)

Analyzing the syntax is not our concern here, but a closer look suggests that clefting is a single process and that cleft and pseudocleft are essentially the same. The context in which (200) is used requires that *it* have an antecedent. One may come into a room and announce *I need a cálendar*, but not *It's a cálendar that I need* (unless the speaker is presumed to have been talking to himself). But if the question of what is needed has already come up, then (200) is appropriate: *It (the thing) that I need is a cálendar → It (the thing) is a cálendar that I need. It that* is equivalent to *that which*, in turn equivalent to *what*: *That which I need is a cálendar, What I need is a cálendar*. The order is syntactically immaterial: *A cálendar is what (that which, the thing that) I need*. The independent function of *it*—its status as a referential pronoun and not a mere grammatical plug inserted when the word order is changed—can be shown in the other pronominal forms that can occupy the same position as *it*:

> (205) I thought they were rather nice pictures. I wonder why she didn't buy one of them.—Oh, those (they, it) were (was) calendars that she saw.

The prosody of cleft sentences is the same as that of the corresponding simplex sentences, with adjustments made for the different order of the items. In the following responses we see how simplex and cleft forms can be used in the same circumstances and with the same presuppositions (with the one major difference noted above, that the simplex can come out of the blue):

> (206) I saw Hénry yesterday.
>   (a) You saw Géorge (, didn't you?) (A)
>   (b) It was Géorge you saw. (A)
> (207) Máry bought the lámp.
>   (a) Géorge bought the lamp (, didn't he?) (A)
>   (b) It was Géorge who bought the lamp. (A)
>   (c) Mary bought the cháir (, didn't she?) (A)
>   (d) It was the cháir that Mary bought. (A)
> (208) Máry bought the lámp.
>   (a) Géorge bought the lámp, Máry bought the cháir. (Á + AC, AC + Á)
>   (b) It was Géorge who bought the lámp, what Máry bought was the cháir. (Á + AC, AC + Á)
>   (c) Máry bought the cháir, Géorge bought the lámp. (AC + Á, Á + AC)
>   (d) What Máry bought was the cháir; it was Géorge who bought the lámp. (AC + Á, Á + AC)
>   (e) It was the cháir that Máry bought; the one who bought the lámp was Géorge. (Á + AC, AC + Á)
> (209) Sómebody bought the lámp.
>   (a) Did Máry buy the lamp?
>   (b) Was it Máry who bought the lamp?
> (210) Mary went ahead and bought something for the house.
>   (a) Mary bought a lámp, did she?
>   (b) Mary bought a lámp, was it?

The same accents and the same profiles are available for the cleft sentences as for the simplexes. Old items (thematic) take AC, new items (rhematic) take A, regardless of order. Thus in (208) *Mary* and *lamp* have both been mentioned, but *George* and *chair* are new: in all five responses, *Mary* and *lamp* are on AC profiles, *George* and *chair* are on

A. In place of the AC—but with different implications—A, B, or zero could be used. Thus in (208c) since Mary has already been mentioned, *Mary* does not need to be accented at all; the purpose of the AC is to emphasize the theme: 'As for Mary, she bought the chair.' The A's can be replaced with AC's, with some such implication as 'Is this maybe what you had in mind?' Thus in (208a) an AC profile on *chair* suggests 'Were you perhaps confused about what she bought?— it was really the chair, you know.' This substitution is more difficult in the cleft construction. It works fine in the simplexes, e.g. (206a) spoken as

(211) You saw
$$\text{You saw } {}^{\text{Geo}}_{\text{r}\text{g}}{}^{\text{e}\cdot}$$

implies that the speaker is not denying that you saw someone, but denying only that that someone was Henry. But

(212) It was
$$\text{It was } {}^{\text{George}}_{\text{you}} {}_{\text{sa}\text{w}\cdot}$$

assigns the AC to the utterance as a whole, not just to *George*, giving it a potentially menacing tone.

So the AC profile helps to identify the theme, but does not guarantee it. If all the profiles are AC, as they could be in (208a), for example, we fall back on relative height: ÁC + AC, AC + ÁC—the higher AC is the rheme, the new item. Relative height is actually more crucial here than in the mix of AC's and A's: in place of (208a) as it stands, with terminal AC + Á, we could have AC + À. Final position gives that A the final word, outweighing the higher ÁC. The lowered pitch assigns 'confidence' to the utterance as a whole. It does not have that effect with AC, which is an unconfident intonation to begin with.

Clefting complicates the picture, as we see,[8] but does not alter the essentials.

Series

Most treatments of intonation have something to say about parallel items in sequence—"series intonation" (see Bolinger 1986: 154–55). We have already dealt with alternative questions, which are merely the interrogative manifestation of this type of contour. It makes no difference, intonationally, whether we say

(213) Are they
$$\text{Are they } \text{work}^{\text{ing,}} \; \text{play}^{\text{ing,}} \; \text{or } \text{loaf}_{\text{i}_{\text{n}_{\text{g?}}}}$$

or say, in answer to *What are they doing?*,

(214) One of three th_in_{gs:}   work^{ing,} play^{ing,}   or   loaf   _in_{g.}

The identical intonation can be used in both, and for the same reason: the sequence is "up in the air" until the last member of the series is reached, at which point it is complete. That is, the terminal fall will occur *if* the speaker is finished. If he is not, it won't, as in the following answer to the same question:

(215) Work^{ing,} play^{ing,}   loaf^{ing···} who   know   s?
   or

Series intonation resembles questions in certain broad tendencies from language to language. The favored pattern in Hungarian is identical to that of American English: B profiles with rising tails on all items except the last, which has an A profile (Varga 1975: 126–27). Russian, French, and German do the same (Navarro 1944: 86). Romanian is like English in that the rise in a member of the series resembles the rise in yes-no questions, but as that type of rise is not the same in Romanian as in English, the two languages differ in their series intonation as well (see above, p. 47). But if the members of the series are full sentences, then the terminal rise asserts itself and the series intonations are the same (Dascălu 1971). Peninsular Spanish favors the same sagging tail as Romanian except on the next-to-last member of the series, which takes a rise (Navarro, p. 86). American English readily does the same when the series is fairly long: it is as if the speaker were somewhat bored with the task of recalling what he wants to include, producing a sort of drawl, which livens up as the next-to-last item is reached and he knows that no further search is required:

(216) We had roast   duck,   and   cauliflower,   and mashed →
   po tatoes,   and   fruit   and ice   cre   _{am.}

Given any degree of arousal, such as might be occasioned by an abrupt question, the Spanish pattern becomes identical to the favored one in American English: rises on all items except the last (Navarro, p. 92). So all in all, it is fair to claim something very close to identity across a wide spectrum of languages.

What is probably more important as a general feature of series intonation is not the particular profile that is used on any one item (aside
from the last, which for obvious reasons is almost always an A) but
the repetition of the same profile. This is a cohesive device in discourse; Fox (1984: 129) calls it "coordinating intonation," marking successive elements as in some way equivalent. With a mere two-member
series we are not apt to find this imitation of one profile by another;
the opposition of nonfinal and final pattern then prevails:

(217) They came i^n and sat down.

But in a series of three members or more the nonfinal ones tend to
imitate:

(218) They came $i^{n,}$ looked a$round,$ and sat down.

This kind of series intonation is found over larger expanses of discourse, including series of whole sentences:

(219) They were late to school. They didn't do their homework.
They ganged up on the other kids. No won
der they were in trouble.

The same parallelism is exploited in the normally rising first member
of a string of B + A contours (see [60] and [61] above):

(220) In the first place, he was rude. In the second place, he →
was careless. And in the third place, he was drunk half the time.

In this piece the speaker has elected to signal the end of the series by
putting an AC on *third place* instead of the B that occurs on *first place*
and *second place*. It would be just as normal—and would add more
finality—to have AC's on all three members; or to use all B's for more
offhandedness. A sequence of AC + A, AC + A, B + A would also be

normal: the AC's would contribute their finality and the B, coming
just before the final group, would imply something like 'This goes on
and on, see?—no end to it.' There would be little to motivate the sequence AC + A, B + A, AC + A, however.

A series imitation may use all A's, for dramatic or authoritative
effect:

(221) There were pla n e s, and tan k s, and gu n s!

A drillmaster may bark a succession of A's:

(222) On tw thre fou e, o, e, r.

A series-final item tends to override the favored question-answering
contour, B + A with highest pitch on the A, as in the non-series answer to *When do they come?*—

(223) They come on Thurs da y.

and use instead a lowered final A:

(224) They come on Tuesday, Wednesday, and Thurs day.

A higher-pitched A at the end would be overly insistent, as if the
speaker were confronting opposition.

Contours in series have the usual possibilities of playing up unaccented syllables as a sign (or symptom) of greater tension. In the series contours, this is most apt to affect the conjunctions *or* and *and*:

(225) I don't know whether I'm going or coming or wha t!

(226) I see her fussing and arranging and worrying all day lo ng!

Normally *or* and *and* would drop back, as, in fact, the second *and* in (226) does.

   Though imitation as far as discourse is concerned is a cohesive device (and we may think of it as used "on purpose" to hold things together), it probably represents, more directly, a perseveration of the same attitude on the part of the speaker. This can be seen also in cases like the following:

(227) Knowing how much she ^{hated} ^{me,} was I to make ^{friends} ^{with} $^{her?}$

(228) I wasn't going to make ^{friends} ^{with} ^{her,} knowing how much she ^{hated} $^{me!}$

In (227) the initial clause refers to a fact, not a question, and yet it uses the same rising intonation as the question following; the speaker has already adopted an incredulous stance. The same goes for the indignation in (228): 'How could you suggest such a thing!'[9]

Part III

INTONATION AND GRAMMAR: BELOW THE CLAUSE

8. Accent and Morphology

The use of fundamental pitch in English, and in "intonation languages" in general, is highly motivated and iconic. Despite some degree of conventionalization, it is a response to feelings, an expression of moods, attitudes, and emotions.

Morphology—word forms and their components—stand almost at the opposite extreme. If we look upon words as tools for conveying meaning, we see that they are, by and large, almost completely unadapted to their purpose, and are therefore unlike most other tools that human beings make use of. A knife must be adapted to cutting and a spade to digging—spades are of little use as knives and knives are not efficient diggers—but the word *knife* could serve just as well as *spade* to name a spade, and the word *spade* could just as well be used to designate a knife (in fact, *spade* comes from the same source as the Spanish *espada* 'sword,' a glorified knife). In only one respect are the majority of words adapted to their purpose: each is sufficiently different in form from all the rest so that once their meanings are agreed upon, verbal transactions can take place. Rather than an ordinary tool, a word is a medium of exchange: the distinction between *knife* and *spade* is like the distinction between a five- and a ten-dollar bill.

If intonation is largely motivated and morphology is largely arbitrary, what do the two have to do with each other? Their paths cross at the point where accents are assigned. Although accenting for power offers the speaker almost complete freedom to put an accent on anything, normally speakers are more economical and reserve their highlighting for what they consider important, and when one continuous portion of an utterance is felt to function as a unit, it will usually be allotted a single accent, if it is accented at all. This is a practical matter: if everything is accented, nothing stands out, and particular emphasis is destroyed.

So we come to the question of how much material may fall under the sway of a single accent. The issue overlaps syntax as well as morphology, but morphology is the arbitrary end of the process and needs to be looked at first.

Accent, in its arbitrary guise, is like the arbitrary tone of a tone language: it can be used to distinguish words. Usually it operates alongside other factors: the verb *refúnd* differs from the noun *réfund* by the location of the stress; but it also differs in the quality of the vowel of the first syllable: reduced [ɨ] in the verb, full [i] in the noun. Here and there, for some but not all speakers, the difference may lie in just the location of the stress: *undertáking* 'enterprise,' *úndertaking* 'funeral business'; *interséction* 'act or process of mutually crossing,' *íntersection* 'crossroads'; *misfít* 'a poor fit,' *mísfit* 'a person not well adjusted to his environment.'

On the other hand, the purpose of applying an accent is rarely to distinguish one word from another. Accents are to highlight a word within the utterance or to lend power to the utterance as a whole. It is only the fact that most words have more than one syllable that makes the *location* of the accent on a particular syllable a possible distinction between one word and another, and its actual use solely for that purpose is probably limited to citation forms, for example *I said úndertaking, not undertáking*. Much of the time the contrast in accent is suspended, as in

```
      can't i^ma
 I
         gine such an undertaking.
```

where no accents occur after -*ma*-, and the last word could, except for the syntax, as easily be *úndertaking* as *undertáking*. Since accent is thus often not realized at all, we speak of the *potential* for it to be realized on a given syllable, rather than the actual realization, as the distinguishing feature, and for that purpose we use the term STRESS. Thus *úndertaking* is stressed on its first syllable, and also accented on that syllable *when* the speaker decides to accent it.

Stress is therefore not an intonational feature. But we cannot avoid investigating it where the scope of an accent is concerned, because the deaccenting that results in the ultimate stress pattern of many words obeys the same principles as the deaccenting that a speaker applies more or less freely whenever he chunks a string of material under a single accent. Nor can we avoid it in the opposite direction, that of the *extra* accents involved with accents of power. In cases of variable stress, the speaker is free to choose whichever variant suits his purpose of climax or anticlimax. The word *gangrene* has variable stress. If we are really shaken we are more apt to say *It's gángréne.* than *It's gángrene!*

The change of stress pattern is revealed in the process of word formation. We must therefore see how the movability of accent figures in the creation of new words.

Compounding

As institutions change, the word stock of a language must change to keep up. Sometimes the forms remain the same and the meanings are altered. *I don't buy that* 'I don't agree with that' is a relatively new sense of *buy*, arrived at by an obvious metaphor. Other times new forms are introduced, through coinage, borrowing, or inspired accident. UNESCO is a coinage, made up of the initial letters of *United Nations Educational, Scientific, and Cultural Organization* (this kind of coinage is an ACRONYM). *Serendipity* was coined by Horace Walpole after the fairy story "The Three Princes of Serendip." *Fifth Column* was borrowed from Spanish, a "loan translation" of *quinta columna*. *Blitzkrieg* and the shorter *blitz* came directly from German. The form *humane* is not merely an alternate of *human*; the accident of having two rival forms made them available for a distinction in meaning. *All shook up* is a similar accidental "bifurcation" alongside *shaken*—it separates the emotional meaning from the literal.

Intonation—in the form of accent—is involved in word creation on a large scale in just one area: that of compounding, specifically the process of drawing upon the existing stock of words to make combinations that function as unit words, often fusing their parts completely. Thus *aircraft* we recognize as *air + craft*—it is "transparent"; *daisy* we no longer recognize as *day's eye*—it has become "opaque." (A first "conceptual" step toward fusion is simply *writing* without space, as in *meadowlark* vs. *meadow mouse*.) Accent helps to mark the item as a unit by fixing the stress on a single syllable, usually on the first element of the compound. Elements following the first are thus deprived of the potential for accent that they formerly had—"compound stress" takes over from "phrasal stress":

Phrasal stress	becomes	Compound stress
Fífth Cólumn		Fífth Column
smáll tálk		smáll talk
bíll of fáre		bíll of fare
sécret sérvice		sécret service

We recognize in this loss of potential for an accent to the right the same phenomenon that was noted in Bolinger (1986: 350) where it was explained that within a unit word, full syllables to the left of the (main) stress are normally free to receive an extra accent (or even, under certain rhythmic conditions—e.g. *ábject póverty*—to get the *only* accent), whereas full syllables to the right are not. It is thus a guarantee of one-word status for there to be full syllables to the right of the accented syllable that are not permitted to receive an accent (except under rare conditions of climax). *Contribution* receives its main accent on the syllable *-bu-* and also may be given a secondary accent on its full first syllable *con-*; but *contributory* has but one place for an accent, the syllable *-trib-*; the next-to-last syllable, *-tor-*, even though full, is not accented because it is to the right. So when *flagpole* took the first step toward one-word status it lost its potential for accent on *pole*, becoming like *tadpole*, which had no such potential in the first place, in Modern English.

Accents are important in the formation of compounds, but the case can be overstated. Most compounds are recognizable as such regardless of stress: if our culture recognizes the entity, the name for it can take any shape, including any position for the stress. So a *bill of fare* is a bill of fare with one stress or with two. And some compounds— compounds, that is, defined semantically—retain the phrasal stress indefinitely. This is especially true of compounds formed of adjective plus noun:[1] *scárlet féver*, *shórt círcuit*, *sácredców*, *hélping hánd*, a *Déar Jóhn*, a *góod thíng* (*He's looking for a good thing*), *stáined gláss* (specialized in a way that *tinted glass* is not). The *Random House Dictionary* marks the two compounds *dúmb shéave* and *dúmb show* differently (the more "popular" form is the one that has undergone the shifting of the stress). A compound in which the elements continue to make their own separate contribution, even though the overall sense is quite specialized, is more apt to retain the phrasal stress. So we have a potential contrast in the following:

> They refused to yield the ríght of wáy.
> You'll find a pedestrian ríght of way a block or two north of here.

It would also be a form of overstatement to claim that when an element is no longer accented, it is because that element is now less important than the element that carries the stress. In English and in other languages of the Indo-Aryan family there has been for a long time a *mechanical* tendency to shift the stress to initial syllables (Emeneau 1956: 9).[2] Many compounds come to be stressed on the initial element simply because they are felt to be unitary. "The Ódd Cóuple" as name of a popular television program was soon being called "The Ódd Couple." When Frances Trollope wrote the following in 1836,[3]

> "Do we walk too fast for you, Lucy?" said Edward, pausing for a moment.

"You can take a shorter cut," she replied, "than that which leads by
our door."

the fact that *short* is compared (*shorter*) indicates that what we now call
a *shórt cut* (and write *shortcut*) was at that time potentially still a *shórt
cút*. For many if not most American speakers the mechanical backshift
has operated in words such as *óatmeal*, *bóy scout*, *méat loaf*, *Róbin Hood*,
ápple pie—all still with phrasal stress in Scotland. We can detect backshifting as an active process in the forms that speakers unconsciously
create:

> [Going to] the Hárvard dance. (sixteen-year-old)
>
> There are people who would rather put their héad in the sand.
> (Congresswoman Barbara Boxer, Nov. 20, 1983)
>
> I saw it at their ópen house. (television program)

All the same, in the majority of compounds there tends to be at
least *some* bleaching out of the final unaccented element. It is generally a word that is used to make a number of similar compounds, and
the initial element comes to stand out somewhat contrastively. The
process is therefore not entirely mechanical, and accent plays an indirect role in playing down the part that is less important. Here are examples of items having the same second element, some of which we
would recognize as compounds (the spelling may reflect this), others
possibly not:

> house: státehouse, cóurthouse, stórehouse, bírdhouse, whóre-
> house, dóghouse
>
> stalk: béanstalk, córnstalk, célery stalk
>
> hill: ánthill, dúnghill, mólehill
>
> heap: trásh heap, gárbage heap, júnk heap
>
> tree: élm tree, shóe tree, Chrístmas tree
>
> center: méssage center, shópping center, médical center
>
> announcement: néws announcement, wédding announcement
>
> foot: ténderfoot, clúbfoot, hótfoot, bárefoot
>
> matter: prínted matter, réading matter, gráy matter
>
> lag: tíme lag, jét lag
>
> shortage: hóusing shortage, fóod shortage, ammunítion shortage

Noting the frequency of these forms, one is prone to ask why compounding should be seen as a morphological (word-forming) rather
than a syntactic (phrase-forming) process—if the latter, it would obey
syntactic rules and there would be no point in drawing up lists of

compounds; the list would be infinite. Yet dictionaries do list the forms, and when we look more closely at the possibilities we see that in spite of an extensive overlap between morphology and syntax, the two need to be kept distinct. Speakers are not free to make up just any compound, nor entirely free to dissolve the ones already created. On the latter score, consider this sentence from a story by Henry Steele Commager (in *Jack and Jill*, Dec. 1957, p. 2):

> Christmas meant a Christmas tree, of course.

In a context like this, where Christmas has just been mentioned, it is possible to say *Christmas trée*; but it would be just as normal to keep the compound intact: *Chrístmas tree*. The more fused the compound, the harder it is to crack. So *June means June bugs* is not apt to have *June búgs*. And to say *roadblóck* in *As we were traveling along the road we came to a roadblock* is almost impossible.

As for the freedom to invent, it is circumscribed both semantically and formally. Semantically there needs to be some extant concept or entity in the culture, or at least within the frame of reference shared by the speakers (that would be the case with a nonce form such as *Hárvard dance*). For example, both of the following might describe the same event:

> He was arrested for beating his wife.
> He was arrested for wife-beating.

but not both of these:

> He was arrested for beating his aunt.
> *He was arrested for aunt-beating.

Wife-beating and child-beating are recognized problems in our society; aunt-beating and adult-beating are not.

The formal restriction decrees that not just any noun, for example, may figure in a noun compound, as would be the case if the formative process were a purely syntactic one. We have *chíld-beating* but not *off-spring-beating*, *lóve feast* but not *afféction feast*, *pléasure cruise* but not *enjóyment cruise*. To kill mice we may resort to *rat poison* but not to *mouse poison*. We may take a *séa voyage* but *ocean* calls for phrasal stress: *ócean vóyage*. Examples such as these prove that the first element as well as the second has its restrictions. For the openness of *sea* by comparison with *ocean* consider *séaweed, séasick, séascape, séa captain, séafarer, séa legs*. We can say *A séa wind moaned through the pines*, but the phrasal stress would almost be required in *An ócean wind moaned through the pines* (unless of course we had just been talking about the wind). The second element, as we saw above, tends to be a word that has taken on a sort of generic sense. This happens with *Frísby Street* as against *Frísby Láne*, where *street* is the generic term. A *sóft ball* is a *sóft báll* specialized among a variety of ball types. *Adhésive tape* is one of many kinds of tape. Similarly *Frénch horn, dárk lantern, ráwhide, hárdware, Gráham crackers,* the *hígh country*. There is a loose sort of stereotyping even when the second element is not noticeably bleached out. One may *construct* a building or *erect* a building, but whereas *buílding construction* is normal, **buílding erection* is not—anything that is normally built on a large scale can use *construction* as second element: *máll construction, hóuse construction, ármy base construction, búsiness office construction*. If the second element tilts toward the unusual, phrasal stress is generally required. So whereas we can have *báby snatcher, báby peddler,* or *báby seller, báby bóotlegger* would add a stress on the second element.

Enough examples have been cited to show that while length is not a DETERMINANT, the majority of words used for compounding, especially the more or less generic terms, tend to be short. This is not a completely independent factor, since shortness is already related to high frequency, but it points up the resemblance between compounds and derivatives, the latter using affixes like *-er* (*worker*), *-dom* (*kingdom*), *-ling* (*princeling*), etc., which are short and inconspicuous.

The literature on English compounding is extensive (the standard work is Marchand 1969), and the sampling in this chapter has left many questions untouched, among them the part-of-speech relationships and the transformational relationships or meanings: a *pipe fitter* is one who fits pipes, a *Cookie Monster* is a monster that is a cookie, *mad money* is money for when you are mad, a *talking machine* is a machine that talks, etc. Our chief concern has been to show the relationship between accent patterns and the fossilization of stress. The story of the compound is one of physical loss. From the standpoint of word creation the ideal compound is one in which no evidence remains of its compound status. Unless we are etymologists, we do not care to be distracted by the fact that *Hilton* once meant 'hill town.' The loss of accent potential is one phase of the blurring of previously contrastive traits—the reduction of the vowel in *fíre man* becoming *fireman*, the loss of the potential pitch drop in the *white* of *whíte house* when it becomes *Whíte House*,[4] the complete disfigurement of the interior of *Wednesday*, and so on. Compounding is a process of destroying the distinctiveness of formerly separate elements in both meaning and form. As long as it has not gone too far, there is always the possibility of restoring the old accent potential, as in the following attested example:

They have a retáining wáll at the end of their garden.

The normal shape of the compound is *retáining wall*; but the speaker wanted to point out that there was such a thing as a wall there. This would be more difficult with *wildfowl*, as the sense has deviated a bit too much; and it would be practically impossible with *laughingstock*, which is scarcely a form of 'stock' in any contemporary sense.

K. L. Pike (1945: 81) put it best when he said, "The freezing of words into compounds would appear to be a negative characteristic— the loss medially of contour-end potential and rhythm-end potential—rather than a positive one (i.e., rather than the addition of a 'compounding stress' or the like)." He thought it likely that "a graded scale from full freedom of words to tightly bound forms, with various degrees of freezing, would reflect English structure more faithfully than an initial dichotomy into words and phrases, with subsequent subdivision of each."

Accent in Compounds and Phrases

We come back to our original question: if there is a continuum of this sort among compounds, with all degrees of transparency and opaqueness, separation and fusion, freedom to create and fossilization, awareness and unawareness, is there any real dividing line between compounds and phrases? The answer seems to be no, and therefore the scope relationships of the accents are the same in both. If the speaker is exercising a choice when he accents a phrase in a certain way, he may be exercising a choice when he accents a compound in a certain way; more important, if he accents a compound automatically according to a rule or rules, then possibly similar rules are to be found in phrases. What do the two extremes have in common in their accent patterns?

First, accents of power. With such things as *hóle in the head*, *héad in the sand*, *to make énds meet*, *Ódd Couple*, *Róbin Hood*, and the like, we detected a mechanical tendency to backshift the stress. But this is not entirely unrelated to accents of power: backshifting is anticlimactic. The more commonplace the compound "word," the less impact it carries. So there are strong reasons for saying *scárlet féver* and *bláck déath* that do not apply to *gréensickness* or *pínkeye*, even though all four refer to specific diseases and are therefore semantically fused. *Són-in-law* is commonplace by comparison with *attórney-at-láw*. The pressure to backshift is always present, but it is most successful where the pressure is greatest, that is, with expressions that are high in frequency as well as stereotyped in meaning—as happens with *Máster Card* by comparison with *máster cárd*.

Accents of interest cannot be neatly separated from accents of

power, but in the clearer cases the separate influence of the meanings of individual words is evident. Although both expressions name
the same affliction, *Húntington's disease* uses an uninteresting word,
Húntington's choréa an interesting one. *Sólar énergy* speaks primarily
of energy; the *sólar system* speaks primarily of the sun with its satellites. Here is where we come to the most uncertain border between
compounds and phrases. Since the stress does tend to backshift in
compounds, one is tempted to say that all expressions exhibiting the
backshift are by definition compounds. But that has awkward consequences. We would have to say that in

> Come over to mý place!
> Come over to mý apártment!

mý place, unlike *mý apártment*, is a compound. There is a class of
"empty words" (see Bolinger 1986: 120–23) that resemble the generic
second elements in compounds, and indeed the same form may appear under both guises. So we have the fairly obvious compounds *nó
place* ('nowhere'), *cómmonplace*, *wórkplace*, *shówplace*; also expressions
that are midway between phrases and compounds such as *hárd place*
(*between the rock and the hard place*), *éating place* ('restaurant'), *méeting
place, let's gó places* ('make the rounds'); and finally expressions like *mý
place, He búys places* (a real estate speculator), *Don't wréck the place!* (cf.
Don't wréck the hóuse!) in which there is little or no stereotyping but
the low semantic weight of *place* by comparison with the rest of the
phrase leads to the nonaccenting of that second element, whether or
not we can think of an actual *process* of backshifting. These last are
pretty clearly phrases, not compounds. The same spectrum can be
observed with *piece*:

> obvious compounds: tímepiece, másterpiece, éyepiece, fówling
> piece, mántelpiece, áltarpiece
>
> midway: It makes a nice wáll piece, doesn't it?; They played us a
> músical piece (músical number, but músical extravagánza)
>
> phrases: They walked down the róad a piece; Let me trý a piece.

Someone explaining the use of a shoulder-fired rocket-launcher might
say *This is the shóulder piece*, to refer to some part of the device that had
never been called that before; under such circumstances the speaker
is free to coin, within the limits imposed by the more general meaning
of *piece*. At the same time such a piece is apt to have a definite structure in the real world, so that semantically the result approaches a
compound. As far as the prosodic structure is concerned it makes no
difference: *piece* is broad and generic, *shoulder* is specific and contrastive. The more interesting element gets the accent. The same goes

for the partitive use of *piece*, which is normally phrasal: *piece*, like *bit*, *some*, *bite*, *slice*, and other partitives referring to small amounts, represents the "minimum realization" of an action and is accordingly predictable. We do not accent *piece* in *Give me a piece* because if there is to be any giving at all it has to be at least a piece.

In the following pairs we see expressions with "compounding stress" set against expressions using "phrasal stress," the former with uninteresting, the latter with interesting, final nouns. It will be noted that as far as meaning goes, "compounds" and "phrases" occur in both columns, though compounds fall more readily in the first:

kíssing game	kíssing cóusin
wínning streak	wínning éntry
Élm Street	Élm Cóurt
ráiny spell	ráiny spríng
Állen wrench	Phíllips scréwdriver
machíne gun	machíne tóol
stéam engine	stéam locomótive
nérvous system	nérvous Néllie
I chóked him to death	I dróve him to drínk
stóck-breeding	ánimal húsbandry

Interest is about equally divided in *farm management*, which could go either way. (As could one or two others—*machine tool* for instance; there are individual and group preferences.) Lack of interest leading to backshifting need not be inherent: it can result from the submerging of the components in the totality, the loss of separate identity. This is the driving force behind the mechanical backshift described earlier, and it is always present to some degree as formerly "free" expressions are used over and over. In the following,

> At best, dieting should never be undertaken in times of stress. Overweights worried about money, domestic affairs or their jobs should not add the strain of a diet. (*Reader's Digest*, Aug. 1958, p. 109)

even the person who says *You are óverwéight* will shift to *óverweight*— an expression that formerly described is now being used as a mere label. A similar pair:

> She's a séven-year-old.
> She's séven years óld.

The intermingling of automatic backshift with accents of power and accents of interest proves that the same affective and semantic influences observed in phrases must be allowed for in compounds, along a gradient of freedom and fossilization. The question now needs to be turned around, as we noted on p. 220. If freedom loosens even some fairly tight shackles of fossilization, does fossilization reach up to stiffen even some comparatively free combinations with some degree of arthritis? More prosaically, is the speaker precluded by certain rules from allotting accents as freely as power and interest—especially interest—would seem to permit? Ordinarily not every word of an utterance is accented. Is there a grammar that tells us what to accent and what not to accent? One attempt to provide such a grammar is described in the next chapter.

9. Accent in Higher Units

Grammar is important to accent if it can tell us where accents may or may not occur, independently of the general laying on of accents, which, as was shown in Bolinger (1986), follows two broad principles, one of interest and one of power. Accents of power are associated with the assertiveness of an utterance, accents of interest with how the meaning of an individual portion of an utterance hits the speaker (most often, but not always, in relation to its importance to the message, and that in turn most often, but not always, in relation to its informativeness).

The key expression here is "individual portion." What is the scope of *one* accent? We know that it cannot be just a single word because such things as prepositions and articles are usually played down, with the result that a prepositional phrase such as *in béd* or a noun phrase such as *the páper* normally has just one accent.

Segments of lesser extent than that of a full word can be dismissed from our discussion. While there is a "verbiness" that leads to accenting verbs (*exért, dispél, restráin*) and potently active nouns (*distréss, behést, attémpt*) more often on the final syllable than pure chance would decree, and while the favored position of adjectives—in front of nouns—leads (by the "rhythm rule") to accenting first syllables rather than last (*tímid, ábsent, ténder*), these are tendencies that are reflected more in the history of STRESS than in the active role of accent as part of a message.

Deciding what we mean by "individual portion" then compels us to look above the level of the word, which is the typical domain of stress, and below the level of the sentence, which is the typical domain of accents of power. Within that more confined area, what and how much does the grammar favor "putting under" a single accent?

Compounds and Phrases Again

Unfortunately, as we saw in the last chapter, defining an accent domain in this way does not free us from the uncertainties of accent versus stress because the line between "a word" and "a phrase" is not a definite one. Even the so-called "derived" words—those built by the addition of affixes rather than by combining smaller words—offer no security. Take a form such as *non-unidirectional*. It counts as one word because the affixes *non-*, *-uni-*, *-tion-*, and *-al* cannot be used independently. (A rule of thumb for deciding independence is to see whether a word can be inserted between a putative affix and its host: we can't say **uni-the-directional pulse*.)[1] And yet it can support not just one but three accents quite easily: *nón-únidiréctional*. On the other hand, *rhýthm rule* appears to be two words and would not, except in a context of *rhythm rule* versus *rhythm-something-else*, have any accent except the one on *rhythm*. We can call *rhythm rule* a "compound," but that term, as we saw in the last chapter, only names the more or less fossilized extreme of a gradient that reaches at its other extreme toward the full freedom of syntactic phrases. If I write a sociological essay and use the (perhaps totally new) expression *happiness quotient*, have I created a "new word"? I have, if by combining two nouns in that fashion and accenting the first I have created a compound, and if a compound is a word. It all comes down to definition.

To the extent that *háppiness quotient* is a lexical unit, we can say that it is stressed on its first syllable. But if we regard it as a freely formed phrase, then we can say that it has been unified syntactically by being brought under the scope of a single accent. Any native speaker is free to produce similar unifications that are entirely novel (even nonsensical) and that would hardly qualify as lexical items: *bénchmark ratio*, *clóudburst infusion*, *radicalizátion inventory*. Such things are common in technical and pseudotechnical writing and speech:

(1) The [ping-pong balls] prevent heat loss, vapor escape, and fume inhalation.[2]

That the syntax of English permits phrases in which a noun modifies another noun is of course undisputed. Such expressions may run to considerable length when the rule is applied recursively:

(2) Airport Long Term Car Park Courtesy Vehicle Pickup Point.[3]

But whether accent shift—more precisely the DEACCENTING of the following lexeme or lexemes—*creates* some form of information chunking that is then reflected in an accentual scope relationship is another question. It is more likely that a *cultural* conventionalization precedes the linguistic one, that there is some semantic unit already "out there" which is reflected in the noun-noun construction regardless of the position of the accent. In the following,

(3) She has to undergo an órgan tránsplant.
(4) She has to undergo an órgan transplant.

either accentual arrangement is normal, given the medical conventionalization of a particular surgical procedure. We would not say

(5) *She is recovering from a scalpel insertion.

even though the surgeon did insert his scalpel and she did have to recover from it. There is nothing "standard" or sensibly standardizable about inserting a scalpel. (When we accept nonsense phrases such as the *clóudburst infusion* mentioned above, it is because we are willing to imagine that there is such an extant entity even though we are ignorant of it.)

If the referent is already chunked when the noun-noun phrase is used to name it, then it is the noun-noun construction that provides the corresponding linguistic chunking, rather than the accent and its scope relationships. But what is it then that the deaccenting of the terminal element does, and why is it that the majority of such phrases do have the accent on an earlier syllable and are felt to be somehow more unitary by virtue of it?

As new entities take shape in a culture they are most conveniently named by relating them to old entities through some sort of classification. This is the advantage of compounding instead of attaching a name that has no internal structure. There are already pumps of various sorts—suction pumps, bilge pumps, force pumps, sump pumps—so when a new kind of device appears on the scene which is in appearance or in function similar to previously existing pumps it is named accordingly, say *heat pump*. It could be named in a less transparent way, say *calorator*, or in a totally opaque way, say *jovad*; but the compound, with its attached classifier, is the most practical naming device. It follows that such classifiers will be relatively few in number (though by no means few in any absolute sense) and will tend to be the less contrastive member of the compound. There are many kinds of pumps; this one is differentiated by being a héat pump. *Pump* is relatively generic.

We examined such cases in the preceding chapter and found that they involve an accent of interest, with the differential element getting the highlighting. This happens even when the classifier—the second element—is relatively infrequent, so long as it is felt to be the less informative—less interesting—member of the pair. Not much information is lost if we paraphrase (1) like this:

(6) The balls take care of the problems of heat, vapor, and fumes.

—so long as we and our hearer are familiar with the nature of the problems, as we probably would be under the circumstances. Of the three second elements (*loss, escape, inhalation*), *inhalation* is the least likely to be a kind of all-purpose classifier, hence the most likely to receive an accent of its own. It does not matter that the parallelism is broken: we can still say *héat loss, vápor escape, and fúme inhalátion*.

The functional explanation for the accenting (and ultimately the stress) of compounds is thus predictable from what we already know about accents of interest. But there is also a structural—in this case morphological—factor, which is the mechanical tendency to forestress nouns. If we think of a noun as an ACCENT DOMAIN, then we can speak of accent as roughly marking the class of nouns by the placement of accents in nouns of more than one syllable. Baptismal names in English have almost all shifted the accent frontward: *Álbert, Chrístopher, Hélen, Fréderick, Chárlotte, Júliet, Hénry*. Verb-noun pairs are distinguished by this stress position: *pérmit, permít; cóntest, contést; ínsert, insért*. So compound nouns, even though at their source they owe their prosody to the relative interest of their parts, seem particularly appropriate when they imitate other nouns. We note this especially as the word becomes tightly fused, perhaps extended metaphorically, and the parts lose their separate identity: *búttercup, sílverfish, hénbane, shériff*.

Almost all our examples thus far have been two-element compounds, but longer combinations behave similarly. In

(7) She's taking her pípe organ lesson.
(8) She's taking her pípe organ tutórial.

organ is the classifier to *pipe*, and *lesson* and *tutorial* are in turn the classifiers to *pipe organ*; but whereas *lesson* is a common classifier, *tutorial* is an uncommon one. With more use it can undergo (and for some speakers doubtless has already undergone) the same shift as *lesson*. (See Bolinger 1981b: 50–54 for further discussion.)

With compounds and their fusion we are still trapped in morphology, and the discussion up to this point has not described accent so much as stress. The accent on a newly formed compound obeys the principle of greater versus lesser interest, but as the compound is reused (and even at the very beginning if the classifier is a routine one) the possibilities of dual—that is, of essentially SYNTACTIC—accentuation are reduced, and we begin to have fused lexical items that permit the accent in only one position, which is to say that they are now STRESSED at that position. We may still be able to accent either element or both in *fume inhalation*, but *doghouse* is stressed on the first element, which is to say that if it is accented in an utterance there is only one place for the accent to go. Given the fact that words by definition have but one main stress, it is not very revealing to speak of compounds as exemplifying accent domains—it is simply a truism that a word is an accent domain.

Single Domains (Just One Accent)

So the question is, can we find something similar to compounds among syntactic phrases which are not headed for one-word status and therefore can tell us something about the significance of accent where freely syntactic information-chunking is concerned? This distinction has been claimed for expressions of several kinds. The first to be examined here embraces utterances with an early accent such as the following:

(9) Your cóat's on fire!
(10) There's a spárk on your coat!

According to Ladd (1983: 161) and Gussenhoven[4] (henceforth Ladd-Gussenhoven), these two sentences "each form a single information unit, with a single accent. The fact that they can be treated as single information units is due to a variety of poorly understood factors of contextual salience. . . . But *given that fact* [emphasis in original], the location of the accent is structurally specified." The specification is supposed to apply to utterances that are "all new," with nothing given beforehand. Thus (9) would be something out of the blue, or perhaps an answer to *Why are you looking so startled?*, but not an answer to *Something's on fire around here—what is it?* In the latter case we would already know why *on fire* is not accented—it is repeated from the context.

Ladd-Gussenhoven further claims that the explanation in terms of relative interest is inadequate because of the inconsistency in (9) and (10)—how is it possible to express essentially the same meaning with "importance" attached now to the coat and now to the fire? It is better to look for a structural explanation, whereby a single accent is assigned to an Argument (the noun *coat* or *spark*) when it is combined in a single accent domain (hence information chunk) also containing a Predicate (*is on fire*, *is on your coat*).

To say that a single accent can be viewed as the keystone of an integral chunk, with unaccented portions subordinated to it, is a reasonable proposal, though unless the integral chunk can be identified independently of the fact that it has just one accent, the reasoning is circular. Assuming that it can, does it follow that the location of the single accent within the chunk is "structurally specified"? It is supposed to be in (9) and (10) because when an Argument and a Predicate combine, "the Argument is accented" (Ladd, p. 160), and that is what happens: *coat* and *spark* are Arguments and *is on fire* and *is on your coat* are Predicates.

Leave aside for the moment the validity of the explanation offered in this book, that the accent pattern depends on the relative interest of the accented and unaccented items, and consider whether the grammatical rule itself is valid. Given an informational chunk consisting of an Argument and a Predicate (and containing by definition one accent), is it necessary that the accent fall on the Argument?

Consider first the interpretation of "the" accent as referring to "a single main accent" (Ladd, p. 160) with the possibility of other, lesser accents—the latter could conceivably be permitted without dissolving the single accent domain. Take a sequence like

(11) The police raided a flat on Flatbush Street where two drug dealers were holed up. Arrésted were an unidentified youth and his father.

Here *arrested* carries the main accent; *youth* and *father* are Arguments but they are accentually subordinate. If a single information chunk has a single main accent, then this is a single information chunk and it violates the rule.[5] Either the rule is faulty or it requires qualification, perhaps something to do with word order.

Assume now that "the" accent means the *only* accent—an accent domain is not an accent domain if it contains more than one accent, however great the imbalance between them. Consider a situation in which two persons are in bed together; at 2:00 A.M. one wakes up, sniffs, feels the blankets, and says

(12) My Gód! This bed's on fíre!

Here we have one accent, hence one accent domain, but it is the Predicate that is accented. The same speaker, startled out of a sound sleep and without time to gather his thoughts, would more likely say

(13) My Gód! This béd's on fire!

Now it is the Argument that is accented. (We have ruled out the still likelier possibility of "two accent domains," *This béd's on fíre!*) In (12) the bed-location is background, a known location; the speaker is fully aware of where he is and there is no need to call attention to it—the fire is the thing. In (13) the speaker is at first disoriented, and then realizes that it is the bed that is the danger spot. The "known location" of (12) can be illustrated more graphically by naming an environment that does not need to be brought to attention at all, beyond simply mentioning it. Someone in a theater detects smoke and says, still a bit doubtful and not yet panic-stricken,

> (14) I do believe this theater's on fíre!

It would hardly be normal to say

> (15) *I do believe this théater's on fire!

Similarly if we use a catchall term for location, a word that does not call for attention because we are always located *somewhere*, again the Argument need not be accented:

> (16) This place is on fíre!

We would not be apt to say

> (17) *This pláce is on fire!

as required by the rule for accenting Arguments. (In *Thís whóle pláce is on fire!* the Argument gets an accent, but now the subject as a whole has taken on the interest and emphasis of totality.) It would not be incorrect, in fact it would be more usual (in accord with the tendency toward maintaining an initial thematic accent) to accent *place* as well as *fire*,

> (18) This pláce is on fíre!

but the speaker may choose to omit the first accent—and thus create an "accent domain" that violates the rule.

So it appears that with or without accent domains, we are going to have to look at individual accents differentially. What is it that interests the speaker most? In the following,

> (19) I'm not going to buy this thing. The príce is too high.
> (20) I'm not going to buy this thing. The price is outrágeous.

we see 'price' viewed in two different ways. The first is equivalent to

> (21) I'm not going to buy this thing. The príce, you know.

The second adopts the viewpoint that since purchasing is at issue, 'price' is under consideration already. Accenting only *outrageous* dramatizes that word. Examples (9) and (10) need to be approached in the same spirit. In (9) the speaker's attention is on the coat. He might have said

(22) Your cóat! It's on fíre!

The natural primacy of the article of clothing can be seen if we try to reverse the order, using the presentative *there* as in (10):

(23) ?There's a fíre! It's your cóat!

We can also test using the formula *look out for*:

(24) Look out for your coat! It will burn you if you don't get it off!
(25) ?Look out for that fire! It's in your coat!
(26) Look out for that spark! It will set your coat on fire!
(27) ?Look out for your coat! There's a spark on it!

The accents fall exactly where we would predict, knowing what will most interest and excite the speaker. Take a set such as the following, each a casual answer to the question *Whatcha lookin' at?* (the speaker gestures with his head toward the coat, establishing it as potentially known):

(28) Cóat's got a spot on it.
(29) ?Cóat's got a loose thread on it.
(30) Coat's got a spót on it. Here, let me brush it off for you.
(31) Coat's got a loose thréad on it. Here, let me pick it off for you.

In (28) the speaker implies something about the hearer's appearance, to which 'coat' is germane. Spots are common blemishes on clothing, and no accent is needed—mere mention is sufficient. In (29) loose threads are more unusual as blemishes; the likely thing would be to accent both *coat* and *thread*. In (30) nothing is implied about the hearer's appearance (the coat has been gestured to and need not be accented) but the speaker proposes to do something about the spot. The same is true of (31), and would also be true of

(32) Coat's got a búg on it.

with totally unexpected *bug*, though we would be more apt to say, accenting the same word,

(33) There's a búg on your coat.

The determining role of salience—of what catches the attention and interest of the speaker—rather than grammar, can be tested by cross-matching contexts and constructions, to show the essential irrelevance of the latter, along with the whole apparatus of Arguments, Predicates, etc. If someone has said *I thought that secondhand suit was a good buy. Why did you pass it up?* we can imagine these replies:

(34)(a) ?There were ríps in the trousers.
    (b) ?The trousers were rípped.

(35)(a) There were rips in the tróusers.
    (b) The tróusers were ripped.

The salient fact is that something was wrong with the trousers, and 'trousers' thus becomes the focus, regardless of the grammatical construction. There may or may not be subsidiary accents on *rips* and *ripped* in (35); but what makes (35) preferable to (34) is that the primary focus is on what is most salient as an answer to the question: *Why didn't you buy it?—The tróusers were why.* To answer *A ríp was why* would be to bypass what is necessary to orient the hearer. The global fact comes first: *The tróusers were why. They were rípped.* The contrast stands out more starkly if instead of an intrinsically interesting thing such as a *rip* we substitute the less colorful *something wrong with.* The doubtful (34)(a) then becomes totally unacceptable, and (35) can more easily do without any accent except the one on *trousers*:

(36)(a) *There was something wróng with the trousers.
    (b) ?The trousers had something wróng with them.
(37)(a) There was something wrong with the tróusers.
    (b) The tróusers had something wrong with them.

So much for Arguments that are grammatical subjects in their sentences. The Ladd-Gussenhoven rule is also supposed to apply to Arguments that are grammatical OBJECTS when they occur in combination with Conditions, which are such things as complements and adverbials—again it is the Argument that claims the accent. A type that has been discussed in this and in other connections for many years is the following, containing an infinitive complement:

(38) I have órders to leave.
(39) I have órders to léave.

(see Bolinger 1986: 125–26). The speaker in (38) has decided to combine *orders to leave* in a single accent domain. Since by definition this is an "all new" utterance, that is, neither *orders* nor *leave* has been mentioned before, why not say *orders to léave* rather than *órders to leave*? It clearly will not do, because *orders to léave* would impose either the sense of (39) or the sense (ruled out by definition) of already having mentioned *orders.* In short, the Ladd-Gussenhoven rule assigning just one accent, to the Argument, makes the correct prediction for (38) in the intended sense.

Unfortunately it makes the wrong prediction for the form just offered as a possible alternative to (39), namely *orders to léave,* with no accent on *orders.* This is a perfectly natural reply in the following:

(40) Why aren't you staying? —I have orders to léave (= I have órders to léave).

It is just as easy to deaccent the Argument in (40) as to deaccent the Condition in (38). The rule fails, for a simple reason: the accents in both cases are being distributed in terms of relative interest.

To see this we need to ask what the circumstances are under which (38) is most apt to be uttered. A likely situation is the following:

> (41) (Messenger arrives at desk. Functionary asks) Whatcha got there? (Messenger replies) I have some órders to leave.

Under these conditions what counts is the stuff being delivered— orders, not bills nor hot lunches nor summonses. A messenger is *supposed* to leave what he brings. The leaving is relatively uninteresting.

Actually this example is a bad one because of the colorless verb *leave*. It will more often than not be obvious from the nature of the object mentioned that it is something to be *left*. Combinations like *bóoks to read, stóries to tell, a jób to do*, etc., are commonplace (see Bolinger 1986: 125), and lead to an almost stereotyped pattern of accented noun plus unaccented infinitive. The only thing a job is good for is to do it.

So pick a more promising verb, let's say *to notarize*. Our messenger steps into the office of a notary public and says

> (42) I have some pápers to notarize.

Since the notary public's business is to notarize, the verb can be of secondary interest and may pass unaccented. But if the messenger steps into a bank, where various functions are performed but where there is one teller who occasionally accommodates the bank's clients by notarizing, the messenger will almost certainly say

> (43) I have some pápers to nótarize.

The irrelevance of syntactic conditions on accent can be seen in what happens with indefinites and nouns of little intrinsic interest. If in answer to *Why are you so bored?* we hear

> (44) Nothing to dó.

we know where the interest lies and interpret accordingly, even though it is the Condition that carries the accent. And if we hear

> (45) What an odd quéstion to ask!
> (46) What an odd quéstion to ásk!
> (47) What an odd thing to ásk!

we interpret 'question' and 'ask' as the same, and a focus of interest, but *thing* is scarcely more than a slot-filler—it would sound strange to say

(48) ?What an odd thíng to ask.

Some additional oddities with indefinites and uninteresting nouns:

(49) *I have some stúff to report. (OK I have some néws to report.)
(50) *I have a little sómething to give you.
(51) *I have an ítem to discuss with you.
(52) *I have a pérson to see.

The role of pure 'interest' stands out in a pair like the following, in answer to *What are you doing here?*—

(53) I have something impórtant to tell you.
(54) I have something unimportant to téll you.

—the latter spoken with a shrug. To accent just *unimportant* in (54) would be very odd.

The naturalness of the accented Condition in these cases can be seen in the fact that if the accent is shifted the same thing happens as when an accent is shifted from Argument to Predicate: the focus narrows and the interpretation is contrastive (see note 5). If in place of *My móther's calling me* (answering *Why are you in such a hurry?*) we say *My mother's cálling me*, the implication is 'calling rather than something else.' So if the situation calls for *pápers to notarize* and we say *papers to nótarize*, the likely interpretation is contrastive ('notarize, not file away'). And if the situation calls for *less to dó* and we say *léss to do*, the likely interpretation is 'less rather than more.'

Ladd-Gussenhoven offers a semantic explanation for cases like the ones we have just been considering. Comparing the two examples

(55) I even have all these óffprints to file.
(56) He even wanted some Persian cárpets to expériment with.

Ladd-Gussenhoven states (Ladd 1983: 161): "Filing offprints (unlike experimenting on Persian carpets) is a familiar enough activity that the two elements can be combined in a single accent-bearing information chunk. Once that combination has occurred, the fact that the noun is accented rather than the infinitive is a purely structure-dependent consequence of combining them." But as our discussion here leads us to expect, it is not the familiarity of the action but the relative interest of the two components that determines where the accent will fall. The action may be totally unfamiliar without affecting the distribution of accents. Imagine the Rev. Jim Jones standing before his doomed followers and saying

(57) I have some cýanide for you to swallow.

Swallowing cyanide is no more familiar an activity than experimenting on Persian carpets. It is just that as between *cyanide* and *swallow*,
the noun holds the greater interest—*any* form of ingestion (say by in-
jection) would have served as well as swallowing. The experimenting
of (56), on the other hand, is intrinsically interesting.

What has probably led Ladd-Gussenhoven—and others who have
remarked on the apparently inherent accentability of nouns—to suppose that there is a syntactic rule here is that the average noun easily
outweighs the average verb in interest. We do not need a noun as
shocking as *cyanide* to get the same accentual result as in (57):

(58) I have some táblets for you to swallow.
(59) I have some Kóol-Aid for you to drink.

Nouns far outnumber verbs. They are more explicit, and can more
readily stand for the actions that are performed in connection with
them than the actions can stand for the sense of the noun: Kool-Aid
leads to drink more than drink leads to Kool-Aid. The verb, for all its
importance, is *relatively* redundant, and in a scheme of communication that demands a certain economy of emphasis if anything is to
stand out as emphasized at all, the noun has a stronger claim to the
accent. But this is not a "rule." If the Predicate is more interesting
than the Argument, then it gets the accent. Take the two following
answers to the question *Why didn't you just march right in?*—

(60) Sóldiers were standing guard.
(61) People were standing guárd.

—*people* does not deserve, and does not get, the sole accent of the utterance, even though it is the Argument.

All this leads to the pregnant question: Why should constructions
like *I have órders to leave* have been regarded as exceptional in the first
place, and in need of some special provision in a grammar? The answer is that this long and fruitless debate stems from an attempt, in
the remarkable book by Chomsky and Halle (1968), to set up a *syntactic* explanation of a phenomenon that they did not recognize for what
it is: accents of power. We know that the "hat pattern" favors an accent comfortably close to the end, and here the opposite is found. If
you try to predict the end accent by a syntactic rule, you have com-
mitted a fallacy at the outset, and you compound it by confecting a
rule to explain the exception. When for whatever reason of emphasis—including interest—the main accent of an utterance occurs early,
the remaining accents may often be blanked out completely (though
they do not have to be). The case of

(62) Or

     `ders to leave, for Christ's sake.`

in answer to *What have you got there?* is thus the same as

(63) God

     `I wish I didn't have these orders to leave.`

where, incidentally, any distinction between *órders to leave* and *órders to léave* is erased. The "rule" that allows the speaker to play down *to leave* is the same as the one that explains the deaccenting of terminal vocatives, terminal ascriptions, terminal themes, and anything else of secondary interest that comes after the accent that marks the major focus of interest. Note well: focus of INTEREST, not focus of INFORMATION. The grammarian-intonologists have been just as persistent in their advocacy of information structure and truth value as in their advocacy of syntax. Neither is the proper domain of intonation. The irrelevance of information (despite its usual importance as one of the MOTIVES of interest) comes clear when we answer the question, "Why, if something is predictable, is it mentioned at all, instead of being merely deaccented?" In a sentence like

(64) There's not much fóod to eat around here.

the infinitive *to eat* seems to be completely redundant—what other function does food have? But a careful look at the possible contexts will show that (64) and

(65) There's not much fóod around here.

are not the same. If a foraging party had been sent out to scour for food, (65) and not (64) would be a proper explanation for failure; (64) might be said by a complaining teenager: *mentioning* 'eat' expresses the immediate desire. It is even perfectly normal to mention an item that is logically redundant and accent it to boot, if that suits the speaker's purpose. If A says

(66) I don't see John around anywhere—where did he go?

B can reply

(67) I don't know whére he went!

frantically hitting his head as he utters *where*. *Where* carries the main accent in spite of the fact that it has appeared twice in the question, and the "logical" (and calm, and equally correct) response would be

(68) I don't knów where he went.

The point of interest is 'where, oh where?' Or compare the following:

(69) What a lovely síght!
(70) What a lovely síght to see!
(71) What a lovely síght to sée!

We can imagine the speaker standing on Vista Point and sweeping his arms toward the vision as he utters the words *to sée* in (71). The terminal accent both expresses the interest in seeing and adds climax—accents of interest and accents of power are in perfect harmony. The governing fact in these examples is not the logic of predictability in particular or information in general, but the way the speaker feels about what he has in mind. Logic counts, but indirectly.

Climax was abundantly illustrated in Bolinger (1986), but it may help to cite a more striking instance of the phenomenon as it affects the infinitive construction we have just been discussing. In a conversation about wars and inflation one might say any of the following:

(72) I téll you, thése are dífficult tímes to be living through.
(73) I téll you, thése are dífficult tímes to be líving through.
(74) I téll you, thése are dífficult tímes to be líving thróugh.[6]

All potentially have broad focus (no "x rather than y" contrast); each could, in fact, come out of the blue if the form of address is changed slightly. A politician perorates:

(75) My fríends, thése are dífficult tímes to be líving thróugh, and I
     ẃant you to knów what your góvernment is dóing to hélp.

The number of accents on the infinitive phrase responds more to accentuation for power than to accentuation for interest: *tímes to be living through* is deflated, *tímes to be líving thróugh* is climactic. 'Interest' can be backgrounded here because nothing is especially striking: we all live, we do our living in times, and times are always lived through— so one thing is as amenable to highlighting as another.

Though it does not involve an infinitive, the following pair shows opposite extremes of emotive force. Note that 'wanting' is repeated, which justifies but does not compel the deaccenting of *want*. The sentence starts out with *I can think of all sorts of reasons for not wanting a new car*, and continues

(76) . . . but íf you want it . . .
(77) . . . but if you wánt it . . .

76) suggests lack of involvement on the speaker's part both through emphasizing the condition (by suggesting that not-if is more likely)

and through the anticlimax of the early accent. But (77) suggests a high degree of involvement—the speaker is apt to raise his eyebrows and extend his hands palms-up on saying *want*. Putting an accent on that repeated word is not only more forceful but signals a high degree of interest in the other person's wants, to the extent of a symbolic offering of whatever it is (the outflared hands).

Multiple Domains (More Than One Accent)

How does Ladd-Gussenhoven deal with multiple accents? With just one accent, the Ladd-Gussenhoven scheme has involved combinations of "major constituents" (Argument, Predicate, Condition) in which one is subordinated to the other by being combined in a single accent domain, with accent supposedly predictable in terms of which constituents are combined. But the Ladd-Gussenhoven rules also contemplate the more common case of multiple accents (Ladd, p. 159): "For the most part, each major constituent within the focus constitutes a separate accent domain and is therefore accented." An example (p. 160) is

(78) She even studied Classical Chinése at Hárvard.

This sentence "has broad focus"—it "would be appropriate in a discussion of other remarkable biographical facts about the subject— say that she grew up in Brazil, or once shook hands with Helmut Schmidt." Given the broad focus, the rules correctly predict that each major constituent within the sentence will constitute a separate accent domain with its own accent. If either accent is suppressed, the broad focus will give way to a narrow focus. Thus

(79) She even studied Classical Chinése at Harvard.

"could be used in a discussion of things studied at Harvard," while

(80) She even studied Classical Chinese at Hárvard.

"would be appropriate in a context concerned with places where one might study Classical Chinese."

The question now is whether the SYNTACTIC claim expressly stated in the rule stands up, and how it compares with our more flexible pragmatic explanation in terms of what interests the speaker. Is it true that broad focus requires separate accent domains and that when one of the accents disappears the result is a narrowed focus? Suppose we replace *Classical Chinese* with something a little less colorful but without changing the syntax. The speaker starts out with *You think that shaking hands with Helmut Schmidt is all that she has ever done? Why,*

Har
(81) the girl even took courses at
                                    vard; and I →

                                    bus
      la
heard   ter that she had made a career in

                                    iness.

Although each of the two sentences in (81) has only one main accent, the focus has not been narrowed, that is, the first part does not imply something about courses taken elsewhere and the second does not imply other careers than the one in business. In place of *took courses at* one might say *studied at, matriculated at, got a degree from, graduated from*, etc. The main interest is the connection with Harvard and later with business, and the courses, the career, etc. are ancillary and not sufficiently attention-getting to demand an accent. Ladd-Gussenhoven's example is prejudiced by the fact that Classical Chinese, if it is mentioned at all, is of such intrinsic interest that it is almost certain to be accented. This is a matter of words and how exciting they are, not a matter of syntax. Since we *expect* the words *Classical Chinese* to be accented, not accenting them requires a powerful motive, and one of the most powerful motives for not accenting something is that you have already mentioned it; this is exactly the interpretation that Ladd-Gussenhoven puts on (80): "a context concerned with places where one might study Classical Chinese." On the other hand, we have a much weaker expectation of an accent on *taking courses* or *getting a degree* or *matriculating* in an utterance where we are about to mention a prestigious university, and not accenting them does not require prior mention. The speaker has a much wider range of options in not accenting something than the logico-syntactic explanations based on information and accent domains will allow.

Though Ladd-Gussenhoven does not explicitly recognize the *courses at Harvard* type, in which *courses*, unlike *Classical Chinese*, can get by without an accent, it does recognize a parallel case, and offers it (Ladd, p. 169) as something that the accent-for-interest style of analysis cannot account for. The case to be explained is that of the sentences

    (82) I sáw Ron Hárris today.
    (83) I saw Ron Hárris today.

and the strange but accurately noted fact that (82) suggests Ron Harris as "inferrable," whereas (83) presents him as "a completely new discourse entity." Ladd-Gussenhoven's explanation is that "because the informativeness of Ron Harris was as it were weakened, neither predicate nor object could appropriately be subordinated to one another, and the speaker . . . put accents on both constituents in order to emphasize that one of them was contextually inferrable."

In looking for a different (and less information-bound) explanation, we must first ask about the verb *saw*. If (83) were changed to *I ran across Ron Harris today* it is not likely that the verb would be unaccented, which suggests that *see*—at least in one or more of its senses—may belong to a special category of verb, perhaps sometimes unaccented much as the noun *stuff* ought to have been in (49). It is noteworthy that if the speaker merely wanted to bring Ron Harris into the conversation, he could not only omit the accent from *saw*, but omit the subject as well: *Saw Ron Hárris today*. That is not likely to happen with *?Ran across Ron Hárris today*. So it is possible that *see* is being used here less for its lexical meaning than as a presentative verb, rather like an existential *have* or *got*, as in

(84) Anything the matter? — Got a héadache.

If the verb *see* is actually focused on, it is not likely to be deaccented:

(85) Guess who I sáw today. — I'll bite, who? — I sáw Ron Hárris.

In this context *saw* has just been mentioned, which gives the best reason not to accent it; but if it is used at all (the simplest answer would of course be just *Ron Hárris*) it will probably be accented. In fact, in an exchange like

(86) Who did you sée today? — I saw Ron Hárris.

with no accent on *saw*, the answer might suggest 'Well who do you think, stupid? Ron Harris, of course!'

If *saw* is accented in (82) the reason is, then, that the fact of seeing and not merely presenting is of some importance to the speaker. And the fact that Ron Harris seems to be inferrable is due not to the accenting at all, but to the fact that Ron is being identified merely by a proper name, which requires that both speaker and hearer have the identity more or less in mind. (A small child who addresses you, a total stranger, with the question *Where's Susie?* has violated convention by assuming that her friends are known to everyone.) If Ron Harris is not more or less in the upper reaches of consciousness, (82) will take the form of something like

(87) I sáw our old friend Ron Hárris today.

with which the hearer need not have thought of Ron Harris in ages. As for why (83) can get by without the extra identification *our old friend* and still suggest someone well out of mind, it is simply the fact that the speaker has used a presentative construction containing a colorless verb plus the one item that is really of interest. Using the presentative construction suggests that the presentative is *needed*, and that would be the case only if Ron Harris needed to be brought back from some more remote region of memory.

The relative weight of colorless verb and colorful object, as we might expect, can be detected in other situations. If *see* is a possibility, so is *hear*. Compare

(88) Hear the néws? Hoover Dam just burst!

(89) Didja héar the néws? Jodie and Marie are getting hitched.

In (88) the speaker is so overwhelmed with the news that it blanks out both the accent on the verb and the verb's subject. For the question in (88) to be used in (89), the marriage would have to be a shattering event. Try another colorless verb, *to take* in reference to time, responding to the remark *I suppose you carried it off fairly easily*:

(90) It took a whole yéar to accomplish!

(91) It tóok a whóle hóur to accomplish!

To manage the protest in (91) calls for a series of accents—*hour* is too inconsiderable a period of time to overwhelm everything else. The speaker of (90) expresses something akin to awe, and the awe-inspiring element is that formidable period of time, prosodically enhanced by more than just pitch. A similar case is with *do*, likewise colorless. The first speaker refers to the daring of the second in presuming to speak frankly, and asks, *Would you do it to ánybody?* and the second replies,

(92) I'd do it to the Président!

(93) I'd dó it to the máyor!

It is enough just to mention *President* to convey the point of the daring; it is not enough just to mention *mayor*. If a more colorful verb is used, the balance will probably shift:

(94) I'd spéak that way to the Président!

It is appropriate at this point to look at the example that triggered Ladd-Gussenhoven's hypothesis about relative informativeness in the first place. It is the sentence

(95) Trúman díed.

In answer to *What happened?*, and spoken in a context where Truman's health had been a much-discussed news item—in contrast to

(96) Jóhnson died.

which was an unexpected event. Ladd-Gussenhoven's explanation is this (Ladd, p. 168): "Because he had been in the news, Truman was more 'inferrable' . . . than might otherwise have been the case. Consequently, *died* was therefore *relatively stronger* in the sentence and less suitable for subordination in a single domain with *Truman*. In effect, both constituents are accented because one of them is *less* informative than normal."

What this amounts to saying is that 'Truman' is not (semantically) strong enough to impose the "regular" pattern exemplified by (96), whereby the Predicate would be absorbed into a single accent domain with the accented Argument, and this leaves the Predicate too strong, relatively speaking, not to get an accent—and an accent domain—of its own. If this seems a rather tortured way of recognizing that both words, *Truman* and *died*, are entitled, each on its own merits, to receive an accent, that is exactly the case, because it is filtered through the fictitious argument that (96) represents a genuine "rule." To have a pattern such as (95) it is not necessary that *either* element be "more inferrable" than the other, so long as both earn a right to be accented.

Consider a case in which the Argument, unlike the *Truman* of (95), is not inferrable at all. Imagine a divorced mother, who has not spoken to her ex-husband in six months, making a frantic telephone call to him which she initiates with

```
(97) John          killed
          just
      ny
                      ᵗᵒᵐᵉᵇᵒᵈʸ!
```

The mother has to introduce two facts of equal, or nearly equal weight, first that something has affected Johnny and second that there has been a heinous crime. The two are of course related—they are in the same sentence; but their ACCENTUAL relationship is not one of dependency; rather, both are accented for their own sake, and the relative "strength"—speaking now phonetically rather than logically—comes from how the mother reacts to each of the two harrowing facts—she might be maternally more concerned about Johnny, or individually more worried about the police. This conforms to our more general explanation: in both *Truman died* and *Johnny just killed somebody* the relative accenting of Argument and Predicate expresses the speaker's degree of interest. As far as *Truman died* is concerned, since *Truman* is inferrable it need not be accented at all. Degree of accent may reflect diminishing inferrability as the accent is gradiently increased. As for why there should be an accent at all, the answer is that a reminder is needed—Truman is hovering in the background and needs to be brought forward.

As for the accent on *died*, what light does the context shed on the need to accent that word, not because it is more informative than *Truman* but because it is interesting in its own right? The question uppermost in everyone's mind was "Which of the various possibilities regarding Truman's health will be the actual outcome?" In this situation, 'dying' is a member of a restricted set that includes 'improving,' 'being cured,' 'having a relapse,' 'remaining in guarded condition,' etc. From this narrow range of possibilities the speaker selects one: he died. This is a paradigm case of contrastive accent.[7]

The explanation of (96), *Jóhnson died*, is of course Ladd-Gussenhoven's rule that when an Argument and a Predicate are embraced in a single accent domain, the Argument will be accented. Suppose we make the opposite assumption, that it is the relative need for accenting that *puts* the two elements in a single accent domain.[8] Why should *Johnson* be accented and not *died*? In the first place, this is a routine announcement; the speaker is indifferent to the fact of death. It would be hard to imagine Lady Bird Johnson announcing *Lýndon died*, unless perhaps years later or at some other remove from the event. In the second place, *to die* is like *to see* in the sense discussed above—it belongs to an open but still comparatively small class of verbs that "bring on the scene" [+ presentative] or "remove from the scene" [− presentative], and that can more or less readily combine with presentative *there* (see Bolinger 1977b: 90–123):

(98) There was seen a vision of incomparable beauty.
(99) There died many thousands in that battle.
(100) There was lost the last remaining hope.
(101) There arose a storm.
(102) *There reneged several players.
(103) *There suffered many thousands in that battle.

For literal bringing-on-the-scene, compare

(104) That night Chríst was born.
(105) There was born a Sávior.

In presentatives the presentee is what counts, not the manner of presentation. It is not that presentativeness is *needed* for the pattern of accent-nonaccent, only that it supplies a reason for not accenting a verb even when the event is unexpected, provided there is little in the verb to arouse the speaker.

We come now to the most serious flaw in the Ladd-Gussenhoven rules, their neglect of gradient accenting. In the case of Arguments and Predicates—to take one example—the rules imply that along with the accenting of the Argument, the Predicate will be *unaccented*. This leaves us without a solution when we find instances of relative strength in which both Argument and Predicate are accented, though the Argument is the stronger. If we find that the theory of accent domains tells us only about relative strength, whereas accent-for-interest accounts both for relative strength between accents and the gradient strength of each accent, then the latter theory covers a greater range of facts. Imagine that someone coming on the scene is told

(106) Some friend of yours just called for you.

Here we have an Argument, *some friend of yours*, and a Predicate, *just called for you*, which—if all is in a single accent domain—would require that the Argument receive the (main?) accent. The utterance is a normal one with *any* degree of strength in the Predicate from zero up to equivalence with the Argument (even beyond, with proper motivation). Are we to say that this is a single accent domain only when the Predicate has zero strength, or, if we allow the Predicate to have *some* strength, at what point does an additional accent domain put in an appearance? From the standpoint of accents-for-interest it does not matter: the strength will respond to the degree of interest.

It should be noted that there is no question of an inferrable Argument here, such as would supposedly allow the Predicate to be stronger. *Some friend of yours* is unpredictable. The Predicate is stronger (when it is) on the strength of its own intrinsic value.

This suggests an answer to why, in example (95) *Trúman díed*, we are so ready to accept *Truman* as "inferrable." We know of course from our acquaintance with the situation that 'Truman' *was* inferrable, but is there something in the utterance itself, aside from the presence or absence of accent, that cues us to the speaker's intending us to *take* the Argument as inferrable? The answer is yes—the fact that *Truman* is not only a definite but also a proper noun phrase—the case of *Where's Susie?* again. The example *some friend of yours* is not inferrable because it is indefinite. Given a proper noun phrase, if the speaker is to convey the fact that the referent is *not* hovering somewhere in the upper levels of consciousness, he has to raise the ante—as in (97, *Johnny just killed somebody*, in which *Johnny* is boosted in pitch and intensity and given a clear A profile.

Other "Domains"

That there is something resembling accent domains is beyond dispute. And the phenomenon may be quite general—we know that Dutch (Gussenhoven 1983) and German (A. Fuchs 1984) are like English in all important respects. At the outer extreme the hat pattern itself is one such domain, though it is a domain of two accents, the matic and rhematic. At the inner extreme the "word" is typically the domain of a single accent, reflected as stress. But to insert an intermediate layer of structure, an accent domain corresponding to a single information chunk, appears to be superfluous: the phenomena can be accounted for by appealing directly to the accents themselves and the words they are attached to. If such an intermediate layer existed we would expect it to lead to fossilizations with a single accent, of the kind we find with "compounds" like *hóle-in-the-head* and *áppetite suppressant.* Instead, we find items that are clearly unitary which nevertheless preserve more than one accent—the multiple accenting in fact may itself be part of the fossilized pattern:

móney to búrn	áfter áll
múch-to-be-admíred	óut of bóunds
néver-to-be-forgótten	Gód dámn it!
Hów do you dó?	

In addition, there is the whole class of "intermediate compounds" in the shape of B + A contours—again two accents, the B "leaning" on the A as its head (see Bolinger 1986: 280–82). In the following examples (the first accent marks the B, the second the A) we sense a greater closeness with B + A than there would be with A + A:

Démocratic Párty	a fíne thíng
Grégory Péck	nínety-síx
híppity-hóp	Póstmaster Géneral

Does this dismissal of single-accent domains reflecting information chunking and having a grammatically determined locus for the accent mean that nothing can be said about accent in reference to grammatical categories? No, because—among other reasons—when we describe noun phrases such as *tall building, average income, hardy perennial* we are compelled to recognize that the normal thing is to accent the noun no matter how obvious its referent may be from the context and regardless of whether or not the adjective is accented. We will say

(107) The Sears Tower is a tall buílding.

even when we know, and we know our hearer knows, that the Sears Tower is a building. If we say

(108) The Sears Tower is a táll building.

it is not enough that we already know that it is a building; buildings must already have been under discussion. And even though we know that anything can be stuff, we are as apt to say

(109) That's fáscinating stúff.

as to say

(110) That's fáscinating stuff.

This is doubtless to some degree a matter of climax—putting the accent at the end is more powerful. But it also may be for the sake of emphasis on the noun as a noun—an emphasis on reification. If it is possible to accent a word for any one of its semantic components (see Bolinger 1986: 101–4), and if being a noun is pertaining to a class that is semantically motivated (Hopper and Thompson 1985), then accenting *stuff* may have the effect of emphasizing nouniness, of projecting the source of the fascination as something thing-like, manipulable, hence potent in its own right. Reification can be tested in its opposition to action in a case such as

(111) John has been dishonest.
(112) ?John has been a dishonest man.
(113) John is a dishonest man.

The perfect tenses of *be* are biased toward the dynamic sense of that verb, and we tend to interpret (111) and (112) in the direction of 'John has behaved dishonestly.' But that creates a clash in (112), where the noun phrase is biased toward thingness—(113) tells us *what* John is, not how he acts.[9]

At other times the accent of power seems to take over completely:

(114) This is a légal matter. It does not concern you.

(115) This is a légal mátter! I keep telling you! Get it through your head!

It would be strange to accent *matter* in (114), but if we do not accent *matter* in (115) we weaken the utterance as an exclamation.

The closest we can come to a structural-accentual rule for adjective-plus-noun phrases is to say that the noun is "normally" accented, and to point out that if it is not, it tends to suggest a contrastive interpretation:

(116) Why did you punish her? — Because she was such a wícked gírl![10]

If we say

(117) Because she was such a wícked girl!

the likeliest context is one in which girls are under discussion and wicked girls are contrasted with virtuous girls. But as we have seen repeatedly, a contrastive early accent in an utterance with subsequent deaccenting is only one instance of an early accent of interest. If the adjective is one that is intensely interesting for some other reason, and there is a motive for downplaying the noun, then we may get a combination of accented adjective and unaccented noun where no contrast is involved:

```
          I point out                     great
(118) May
                   to you...  with            respect,  that...
```

Forms of respect have not been previously discussed, and *great* is not in contrast. But *great* is intrinsically interesting, and by not accenting *respect* the speaker avoids "hitting" the hearer with a climactic accent.

Here as elsewhere it is hard to draw the line between semantics and grammar. But if a grammatical explanation is valid, it is probably because of the semantics of the grammatical category.

10. Exclamations and Interjections

If exclamations are all things that are exclaimed, then potentially any utterance is an exclamation, because all utterances, regardless of grammatical form, can be spoken as such. But there are certain forms which, while not always exclamatory, lend themselves to being so. Interjections are the typical case, but certain grammatical constructions qualify as well. Interrelationships are close, and all must be studied together, if for no other reason than that no matter how a given expression is used, its meaning tends to remain the same. The 'unexpectedness' of *oh* persists as intonation and context shift it from exclamation to question to discourse particle.

Oomen (1979: 159) cites Quirk et al. (1972: 386) to the effect that "Exclamations are primarily for expressing the speaker's own feelings." It follows, if intonation is basically affective, that the connections between intonation and exclamation must be both broad and deep. Most discussions, unfortunately, concentrate on the syntax, with a once-over-lightly for intonation.

Part of the problem lies with the great variety of intonation that can be used in exclamation. We cannot speak of an "intonation *of* exclamation" even in the rough sense in which we have spoken of the intonation of questions and the intonation of commands, where certain contours truly do predominate. Exclamations draw impartially upon the full repertory of up-down patterns. What characterizes the class is not shape but range: exclamations reach for the extreme—usually higher but sometimes lower. The C profile, despite its 'restraint,' is not uncommon, especially in exclamations of incredulity:

```
You
      d?!
    di
```

(Quality as well as range is a factor here: a low and creaky pitch gives the impression of strangled protest.) A monotone may be exclamatory if it is high enough. One way or another, exclamations are expected to show the voice in some manner "out of control."

In the preceding volume (Bolinger 1986: 298) it was argued that 'surprise' is as ill-defined intonationally as it is emotionally: one can be surprised and happy, surprised and angry, surprised and eager, and so on. Exclamations are manifestations of emotional arousal, and the common locutions that include *to exclaim* bear witness to the variety of particular emotions that can lead to exclaiming:

> "Look!" she exclaimed joyously (delightedly, enthusiastically, ecstatically, incredulously, angrily, in surprise, in alarm, in exasperation, in disgust, in vexation, in awe, in amusement, in consternation, half in tears . . .).

In the broadest sense, exclamations are thus anything at the end of which one would put an exclamation mark. This of course is circular, but it does give a basis for searching out a corpus of examples.

Identification of Types

Unmarked syntax

Exclamation marks are found after utterances that show no structural evidence of being exclamations. One can "exclaim" a statement, a question, or a command:

> I told you I would! he exclaimed.
> I can't! he said.
> Go away! she growled.
> Never! he blurted.
> You told them?! she demanded.

In such utterances intensifiers may point to a difference between exclaiming and merely saying, e.g. *Is it really you!*, *I absolutely can't!*

Beyond such improvised exclamations we find two broad classes that are more or less marked as exclamations. One is syntactic, whether directly exclamatory as in *How tall she is!* or by more or less strong association as in *Isn't it wonderful!* The other is idiomatic and includes the particles *oh*, *ah*, *hm*, etc., and also, indirectly, *well* and *why*, plus an assortment of expostulations and illocutionary stereotypes. All are "effusions," to use Yokoyama's (1986; 90–97) term for noninformational exclamations.

Wh questions

Questions, direct and indirect, are heavily represented. The commonest form of exclamatory syntax is the truncated indirect question.

It may be regarded as the complement of some such underlying verb as *imagine* (*You can't imagine how tall she is!*). The exclamation is thus the equivalent of the wh question minus the interrogative inversion:[1]

> How tall she is!
> What strength he has!
> How little they understand!
> What fortunes they amassed!
> How she fumed!
> What a help they are!

In formal or archaizing contexts the direct form is sometimes found:

> How green was my valley!
> What fortunes did they amass!

As the examples suggest, only *how* (optionally plus intensifiable adjective or adverb) and *what* (plus intensifiable noun or NP) are involved.

An exclamation such as *What a woman (she is)!* has at least three interpretations depending on whether the noun is allied to (1) referential indefinite, (2) nonreferential indefinite, or (3) descriptive:

1. 'Woman' is not a characterization, i.e., it is not predicated of her, but is assumed. The speaker could say in this identical context *What a person she is!* (there is something strange about her qua herself, not qua 'woman'—perhaps she likes raw liver).
2. 'Woman' is predicated as an absolute: 'To what an astonishing degree she fits the category of "woman"!,' 'She is so much a woman!' (The speaker perhaps has a stereotype of women driving carelessly, and she fits it.)
3. 'Woman' is predicated as a degree word: 'How well up on the scale of womanhood she is!,' 'She is so womanly!' (Compare the parallel stereotype of *man*: *What a man he is!* = 'How brave he is!')

Intonation is of little use in distinguishing these senses, though *woman* would tend to be less prominent in (1). This type is well covered in Wierzbicka (1980).

Though degree exclamations are limited to *how* and *what* plus intensifiable, other exclamations in which the interrogative word functions in a nondegree sense allow a wider choice:

> Ooh! What you said!
> God! Where he lives! It's like a pigpen!
> My oh my! When he gets up! It's hardly ever later than 3 A.M.!

Here the interrogative forms are like independent nominals, which can be used in the same way:

Ooh! The things you said!
God! The place he lives! It's like a pigpen!
My oh my! The time he gets up! It's hardly ever later than 3 A.M.!
Heavens! The creature I saw! It was ghastly!

Wierzbicka (1980: 338) offers a semantic deep structure for exclamations of this type, using the examples *This smell!*, *These roses!* Informally, they mean something like 'I am at a loss for words to describe this'; more precisely:

This smell . . . (these roses) . . . =
   thinking of this smell (these roses)
   feeling something because of it [the exclamatory component]
   not wanting to say anything that I can think of
   I say: I want to say more than what I can think of

English has a predicate noun that rather neatly covers the unspoken part of such exclamations, namely, *a caution*, which the *Ninth Collegiate* defines as "one that arouses astonishment or commands attention," exemplifying with *Some shoes you see these days are a caution.* So one may have, in response to *How do you feel about my brother?*,

God, your brother! He's a caution!
Your brother is a caution!

Degree expressions are more frequent as exclamations, for obvious reasons, and even independent nominals can be used to express degree if their meanings are quantifiable, that is, if they are mass or plural count:

Lord, the times I've been there! (how often . . .)
Heavens, the sugar he eats! (how much)

These call for a modification of Wierzbicka's formula:

The times I've been there . . . =
   thinking of the number of those times
   feeling something because of it
   not wanting to mention any amount that I can think of
   I say: I want to mention a larger amount than I can think of

Another common type of wh exclamation—pointed out by Wierzbicka (1980: 316)—is basically a rhetorical question in which the wh word calls for identifying some entity—person, place, time, manner—that is ironically supposed to be rare or nonexistent. They occur as responses, generally to questions, and when the verb is negative the effect is that of a strongly affirmative answer:

Where has Dervla Murphy been? — More to the point, where hasn't she been! (she's been practically everywhere)

The *where* of the answer names a rare or nonexistent place: '(Almost) no-place has she not been.' An example of a response that is not to a question, but simply caps a recital:

> Dervla Murphy has been to Afghanistan, India, Turkey, Peru, Bulgaria, you name it. — Yes, where hasn't she been!

In fact, with the auxiliary verbs (especially when the wh words are *who* and *why*) we have more or less routinized affirmative answers to questions:

> Do you like him? — Who doesn't!
> Are you going to buy it? — Why shouldn't I!
> Like to have a crack at it? — Who wouldn't!

Though Wierzbicka attaches the label "exclamatory negative pseudo-questions," it is not essential that they be negative, only that they reverse polarity. If they are affirmative, the effect is that of a strongly negative response:

> Do you like him? — Who does!
> Are you going to buy it? — Why should I!

Again, the wh word names something rare or nonexistent: *Why should I!* is 'No-reason I should.'

This type of exclamation has a strong tendency to fossilization, as most of the foregoing examples suggest and as we see in the following as well:

Who cares!	What's the use!
Who gives a damn!	How should Í know!
What difference does it make!	Who knows!
What has X got that I	What can I say!
haven't got!	What gives you the right to x!

Still, the pattern is productive, especially if elaborated. Thus though *Who tells!* and *What cán people do!* are not self-contained like the foregoing, they can readily occur:

> Who ever tells a story like that!

> It's impossible to move up, to make a living, to have a family, to protect one's health . . . (In fact,) what cán people do! It's hopeless!

The usual intonation is B + À, given here in expanded form to show the B unambiguously:

Where on earth has

n't she been↓

Who cares! is apt to be B + À, whereas *Who's gonna know!* if intended as an incitement is more apt to be B + Á.

An utterance without explicit negation is not necessarily positive. The word *else*, for example, signifies 'not-this,' and its negation affects the implied polarity of the response:

> Are you going to do the work here? — Where else!
>   (no-place not-this = yes, here)
>
> Are you planning to lift the thing with block and tackle? — How else!

Otherwise, *besides*, and occasionally *but* (*where bút here*) may replace *else*.

The formulaic nature of wh questions used as exclamations is pervasive, and does not always fit some productive pattern:

> What did I tell you! ('I predicted this, and I was right')
> How do you like thát! (general astonishment)
> Lord, how long!
> How cóuld you!
> How dáre you!
> How crazy (dumb, etc.) can you get (be)!
> Where's the beef!
> What next!
> What will they think of next!

Though a variety of intonations are possible, the one that seems most nearly universal for all wh exclamations is B + À. This is in keeping with the demanding nature of the wh: most of these exclamations are challenges. One could add, carrying on with the pretense that they are "true questions," *Come on, tell me! I'm really curious!*

The extent of stereotyping can be seen in two common *what* exclamations that respond to a "foolish question": *What do yóu think!* and *What do you suppóse!* The stereotyping is both accentual and intonational. In the second, the accent must fall on *suppose*, and while in the first it could fall on *think*, that rather spoils it in the intended sense unless *think* is quite high in pitch. The intonation of the second is most apt to be B + Á with uptilted B, and the intonation of the first is almost always B + À, with downtilted B; it can go the other way, but then it is like an ordinary question. With the favored intonation, the *suppose* exclamation is 'indignant surprise that such a question should be asked,' whereas the *think* exclamation is 'disgusted surprise that such a question should be asked.'

Yes-no questions

Not only wh questions, but conducive (agreement-expecting) yes-no questions as well, though fully interrogative in syntax, are highly frequent as exclamations:

> Isn't it wonderful!
> Doesn't he look handsome!
> Won't we have the best time ever!
> Wouldn't you love to try it!

Intensifiables play the same role as before (e.g. *Is it réally you!*). By adding *just* to these examples we create utterances that almost have to be exclamations rather than questions:

> Won't we just have the best time ever!
> Wouldn't you just love to try it!

The strictly modal auxiliaries are found here in their epistemic senses to the extent that they express high probability—we exclaim at what we are sure about, as in

> Can't you just héar the ruckus they're going to raise!
> Mustn't she just búrn with envy!

(the tendency here is to intensify *hear* and *burn* further by increasing the length; the terminal B profile has a tail that levels off or rises only slightly—the rise is concentrated in the verb). We do not exclaim at what is doubtful:

> ?Mightn't they just glow with admiration!

This last example is normal as a question, 'Is it not possible that they would simply glow with admiration?,' but a little odd as an exclamation.

As for nonconducive questions, they may appear as exclamations when they are underlyingly echo questions—they probably started out as repetitions intended to imply 'That is a foolish thing to ask, the answer is so obvious.' A typical introduction is *Boy!* and a typical intercalation (as with *just* above) is *ever*:

> Was she mad!
> (Boy!) Would he (ever) fume!
> Can she (ever) cook! (Í'll say she can!)

Idioms

At the head of the list here are interjections which when used alone are marked in the lexicon as independent exclamations: *Oh!, Ah!, Well!, Hm!, Hah!, Honestly!, Really!, Indeed!, Ay!, Ooh!, Eek!* A number of phrases can be added as well: *I say!, I'll bet!, Says you!, So what!, Come, come!* Many such expressions pass rapidly in and out of fashion. Some instances of profanity have special illocutionary uses (aside from expressing pure astonishment), for example *hell* in a case like

I know he has his faults, but hell!

with *but* at high pitch and *hell* quite low, meaning 'Don't make too big a thing of it.'

Certain interjections, notably *well* and *why*, as in

> Didn't you promise? — W'l yes, but I didn't intend them to take me seriously.
>
> Can't you help me? — Why [waɨ] of course; I was just waiting for you to ask.

are not fundamentally exclamatory, but have exclamatory uses. It is essential to study the entire spectrum of use and meaning.

Intonation of Types

Intonation plays the freest role with unmarked syntax, as we noted. It plays a more circumscribed role with marked syntax, and with the idioms it bonds so tightly that one is tempted at times to posit distinct lexemes on the basis of intonation alone. A quick example is the difference between *Hm!* and *Hm?*

Unmarked syntax

With unmarked syntax, virtually any intonation is possible, freely and independently adding its sense to that of the relatively free and independent lexical material. So we have the 'I did my part (so why didn't he do his?)' of the AC in

```
    gave
I             money!
    him the mon
```

the restraint or placation of the C in

```
I
         him the money!
    gave
```

the perplexed arousal of the B in

```
         him the money!    (and I'm mystified by the way
    gave                    things turned out)
I
```

and so on.

By its nature, the entire syntactic class of imperatives may be treated as exclamatory; the authority to issue a command tends to imply the right to do it emphatically:

Sit down!
Let me see that check!
Don't look now!

Again the various profiles contribute their nuances.

Marked syntax

In marked syntax, intonation is relatively free, but B + A contours are rather heavily favored. The shape B + Á suggests something new—the speaker may be pointing something out as well as exclaiming at it:

```
      fortunate  peo
What
                ple they are ᵢ
```

The shape B + À is more contemplative; the speaker is apt to be remarking something already known to the hearer:

```
      fortunate  peo
What
                ple they are ᵢ
```

With a terminal rise, specifically with a B or C profile, the impression may be one of ineffability—the inconclusiveness of the rise is interpreted as an inability to do the fact justice:

```
What                                      strength he has!
      strength he has!        What  strength he has!
```

The type *What you said!* leans more heavily on intonation. It favors a series of sweeping A profiles on a downward tangent:

```
whaᵗ  yᵒ
       t    u  sᵃ
               iₐ ᵢ
```

If the tangent goes up, as it can, the speaker is not merely surprised but probably scandalized. The most essential part is the sweeping A profile at the last accent; the earlier prominences may be modified for less emphasis. A terminal B profile is possible, but a C is most unlikely (it would require a gestural overlay, e.g. the speaker shakes his head in disapproval).

The *Who doesn't!* and *Who cares!* type favors B + A but with a tendency for B + Á to be preferred when the predicate contains just the auxiliary, whether affirmative or negative, and, though not so strongly,

for B + Á to be preferred otherwise. The reason for the first preference is obvious: *Who doesn't!* and *Who does!* are contrastive; *Who cares!*
is not. For the same reason, a B is normal with the first subtype and a
C with the second; but a B with *Who cares!* is unlikely—it is too much
like an echo question. *Where else!* like *Who doesn't!* is contrastive, and
favors B + Á.

The conducive questions are a little more restricted owing to the
need to avoid ambiguity. A statement can be an exclamation without
ceasing to be a statement, but a conducive question interpreted as an
exclamation is a rhetorical question (*Won't we have the best time ever!* =
We'll have the best time ever!), and should not sound too much as if
it were being asked for information. But "not sounding like a question" depends on so many factors that it is hard to fix a rule, and
about all one can say is that of the intonations that are most frequent
in questions, those with high terminal pitch are less likely as exclamations. So

```
            handsome?
Isn't he
```

with relatively low initial and high terminal pitch is more apt to be a
question—as an exclamation it would be extremely exercised, and
there would be other indications of high involvement; but

```
Isn't he handsome!
```

at mid-pitch and with narrower range is readily exclamatory. This of
course goes counter to the generalization stated above, that exclamations "reach for the extreme"; exclamations of this yes-no type, with
rising intonation, tend not to be particularly "exclamatory."

Falling pitches usually leave no doubt:

```
Won't           best
                     time  ev
    we have the           er|
```

So we are more apt to have

```
Would       love    try
     n't you     to    it!
```

with successive A's than to have the B's in

```
                 try it?
Wouldn't you love to
```

which comes across more as a question, though the gestural accompaniments can make it a perfectly good exclamation.

Intonation is so far from being decisive here that it will do little to tip a question in the direction of exclamations unless other conditions are met, one of which is that there needs to be a tinge of exaggeration in the wording. We can say *How normal (average) he is!*, but regardless of intonation we can hardly make an exclamation of *Isn't he normal (average)*. There is no problem, however, with *Isn't he boring (wise, queer, ugly)*. A heavy rainstorm is not apt to be commented on with *Isn't it raining!* but *Isn't it pouring!* has the requisite degree of hyperbole. Further, the voice qualifiers can make an exclamation out of the most humdrum question: rough voice and extra intensity on *hand-* make an exclamation out of *Isn't he handsome* no matter what the intonation. The same goes for *Isn't it raining* if *raining* is made prosodically hyperbolic (see Bolinger 1972b: 281–92).

Nonconducive questions depend more on intonation to make them exclamatory, and terminal upmotion is less frequent. A common thing is a succession of sweeping A profiles as with *What you said!* above:

$$\begin{array}{llllll} \text{W}^\text{a} & \text{s}^\text{h} & & & & \\ \quad\text{s} & \quad\text{e} & \text{ev} & & \text{m}^\text{a} & \\ & & \quad\text{e}_\text{r} & & \quad\text{d}_! \end{array}$$

(The A profiles approach CA.) Rising and falling tangents to the accents are about equally likely, the former adding to the arousal and perhaps suggesting something unexpected. Though—as McCawley (1973) points out—the falling intonation is typical of nonconducive exclamatory questions (and is probably what sets them off more than any one thing from otherwise identical questions), a rising intonation is possible, and may even be preferred under some conditions. In an exchange like

> Was she mad? — Was she mad? Boy! You've never seen anything
> like it!

we see not only the possibility of the rise (with over-high pitch and overextended length on *mad*),

$$\begin{array}{llll} & & \text{D} & ?! \\ & \text{A} & & \\ \text{M} & & & \end{array}$$
Was she

but also the likely origin of these exclamatory questions. As pointed out above, they are almost certainly echo questions, implying 'How can you ask this?' The speaker pretended to be repeating a question already asked. In the last example we note that the speaker does not say *yes*, but answers the question by repeating it. (On the other hand, if the exchange goes

Was she mad? — Was she mad! She was furious!

there will probably be a high AC profile on *mad* because of counter-balancing it with *furious*—it is a 'yes' by inclusion of *mad* within *furious*.)

A rising intonation (B profiles) may also be used with these noncon-ducive exclamatory questions to express ineffability. There is no re-striction on how high the terminal pitch may go, but it tends to re-main lower than on a genuine question:

```
      those
                   bo
In
   da ys'     y,  was  I  ever  crazy!
```

(The accompanying gesture here is apt to be a slow headshake, sig-nifying the speaker's inability to put his feelings into words.) Elliott (1974: 244) is thus mistaken when he claims that *Boy, does she have beautiful legs!* "with rising intonation is distinctly ill-formed."

This type of exclamation is also highly subject to the emotional backshifting of accent (see Bolinger 1986: 83–84), and here I think a small pocket of univocality can be found. We cannot test with *boy* as the element on which the accent exclusively falls, because that word seems to be limited to exclamations. But *gee* is all right with either ex-clamations or questions, leaving the intonation free to serve as the sole audible cue to the exclamation. So

```
Ge
   e,  does  she  have  beautiful  legs(!) (?)
```

may be either exclamation or question, whereas with emotional backshift

```
Ge
    e,  does  she  have  beautiful  legs!
```

can only be an exclamation.

What gives questions used as exclamations their peculiar power is the element of suspense: by saying *How they ran!*, *Did they run!*, or *Didn't they run!* the speaker suggests his inability to do justice to the facts. But if suspense is the key, we should expect other clause types which are in some way conversationally incomplete (a question, of course, is usually incomplete without an answer) to serve a similar purpose. At least four can be identified in addition to questions.

The first is the unresolved comparative (a *more* without its *than*) or superlative (a *most* without its *that*):

> I've had more trouble with that guy!
> We got into the biggest argument the other day!
> I've seen more people hurt that way!
> She picked up the juiciest bit of scandal at Maude's party!

To resolve these, something like *than* (*that*) *you can imagine* is required. The intonation is most often B + ÁC,

```
          more people hu
I've seen                 r
                          t  that  wayl
```

with the comparative or superlative word taking the accent in the B. But B + ÁC, B + À, and B + Á are also common enough.

The interjection is in the nature of casual comment and is not used for reporting serious matters. This qualifies it for stage humor, as when a doctor is given the line

> I've lost more patients that way!

Without the comparative or superlative, the same intonation may well be used for a serious matter, e.g. *He's lost a lot of patients that way!*

The second is the unresolved negative conditional clause:

> Boy, if she isn't tall!
> Boy, if that isn't just about the worst thing I ever saw!
> Boy, if they haven't messed things up this time!

These probably take their origin from something like one or both of the following:

> Boy, if she isn't tall I'll eat my hat!
> (I'll be) damned if that isn't just about the worst thing I ever saw!

The favored intonation again is B + À:

```
    she isn't
If            ta
                 ll₁
```

This intonation is of course the one that least involves the hearer—although the syntax is suspensive, the intonation is completive—there is little or nothing more to be said. This can be seen in exclamations that are routine—here as elsewhere we encounter a good deal of stereotyping:

```
                isn't my old friend John
Well if it                               Jo
                                           nes!
```

With the B + À there can be no inclination here to add *I'll eat my hat*. It would be unusual to intone this with B + AC. Not so with

```
Bo        she isn't
                          t
   y! If                   a  1!
                            1
```

Now the speaker involves the hearer; he may go on with *Just look at those stilts she has for legs, right?*

Also common is the emotional backshift noted with *gee* above:

```
Bo
   y, if she isn't tall!
```

Or a B + B contour, for added ineffability:

```
                          tall!
   she isn't
If
```

Least likely is B + C.

Third is what might be called the nautical or Country Western imperative. The speaker lets fly with an absurd command usually invoking mayhem on himself and leaving the hearer in suspense as to how to react. The type is usually preceded by *well* (see Chapter 11) and often is followed by a suspensive *if* clause:

Well rock me in the cradle of the deep! If he didn't win after all!

There is much stereotyping here, as can be seen in

Well shiver my timbers!
Well blow me down!

but there is wide latitude for improvisation. Since the command is absurd, the speaker can invent:

Well cross me off and throw me in the round file!
Well take my organs and donate them to charity!

The B + À contour practically rules the roost here.

Fourth are phrases involving *of all*, as in the following:

> Well of all people! I can't tell you how glad I am to see you!

This probably takes its origin from something like

> Of all people you are the last person I expected to see here!

(See p. 310 for "pull-up sentences.") Stereotyping is heavy. This is evident in the example

> Well of all the nerve!

which differs from more typical examples both in form (singular definite noun phrase) and in meaning (no real totality is involved, only the implication 'Person X has a lot of nerve, is very presumptuous'). It is also evident in the fact that generic *people* and *things* are apparently the only nouns aside from *nerve* that may appear in intonationally complete utterances without further elaboration. One can say *Well of all things!* simply as a general expression of surprise. One would not say *?Well of all countries!* though at a stretch a space traveler might be imagined to say *Well of all places!* on waking up at an unexpected but recognizable spot somewhere in the universe. But when qualified by an infinitive, other nouns may be freely used:

> Of all places to visit! Couldn't you find something better than this!
> Of all times to be on a diet!
> Of all books to be reading on a vacation!

And—as with the absurd imperative—one may invent one's own generic nonsense to replace *things*:

> Well of all gripes, groans, and groundhogs!

As usual, the contour B + A prevails, though A + A, AC + A, and C + A are also possible.

Beyond the widely recognized exclamations that use syntactic forms either identical to questions or related to other suspensive expressions such as *if* clauses, it is hard to decide what degree of syntactic or lexical frozenness to require in order to recognize a class of exclamations. Here are two more possibilities:

The first consists of a deictic word (*there, here, that, this*) plus a copular expression plus a degree adjective referring to strangeness plus a noun. The intonation is A + C(+ B) or A + B(+ B). In both cases the terminal rise yields what was referred to earlier as an "observation," which here appears in exclamatory form:

Similarly *That's an unusual necktie!*, *This is a strange coincidence!*, *Here's a startling development!* As exclamations, these express the speaker's surprise and are not merely comments on the situation. Also they tend to broach the subject, and accordingly the simple *That's odd*, with the same intonation, should be included. We note the parallel in

> That's odd! From this angle the landscape seems to be tilting the other way. I wonder why.

> How strange! From this angle . . .

though the intonations (A + C versus B + À) are radically different.

The second class is minimally stereotyped in syntax but maximally in intonation. It consists of negative rhetorical questions using B + C with downtilted B tail, conveying a reproach. If the tail of the B is allowed to remain level or to rise, the interpretation is more easily that of a genuine question. The lowered tension of the B of course merely reflects the fact that the question is already answered:

Can't you ever do anything

rig^{ht!}

Similarly,

> Can't you even budge!
> Isn't it enough that I slave for you every day!
> Can't you understand that I do it just for you!
> Won't she get it through her head that I'm finished with all this!

Syntactically these sentences are identical to the conducive questions already described, the *Won't we have the best time ever!* type. But whereas those exclamatory questions expected a *yes* answer from the interlocutor, these suggest a *no* answer in the mind of the speaker himself, and will elicit an apology, a protest, or silence from the interlocutor. Negative polarity items (*ever* and *anything* in the diagrammed example above) occur here but not in the other type, unless for intensification, as in *Isn't it the best thing that ever happened anywhere!*

Exclamatory Idioms in Detail

It is with the exclamatory idioms that the role of intonation is most critical. Many of the idioms, especially the one-syllable interjections, are of either slight or very diffuse semantic content, which frees the intonation to come through with special impact. Dahbany-Miraglia (1985) has shown how in Judeo Yemeni an entire conversation, with several changes of speakers, can be built out of the one-syllable inter-

jection [hāh/?], by varying the prosody—of course, with a strong as-
sist from the context and from what the speakers already know about
one another's ideas and intentions.

In the companion to this volume it was stated (p. 205), "Visible gesture is never totally excluded from the sound wave." The stances that
our body takes, including the expression of the face, transmit the
messages of those gestures through the changes that are forced upon
the vocal organs. We can "hear" a smile—some recent research has
even shown (Eckert, forthcoming) that certain social groups become
such habitual smilers that they and their opposite numbers, the
scowlers (in Detroit high school parlance, *jocks* versus *burnouts*), begin
to register permanent changes in their vowel sounds—smiling fronts
the sounds and scowling backs them. The transient changes are of
course what interest us here—our ability to detect a smile without
seeing one.

That earlier treatment of gesture neglected one aspect that becomes
important at this point: the facial expressions that in large degree actually *produce* certain sounds that we take as interjections. These are
not gestures that can be "uncoupled" from the sound wave the way
raised eyebrows, for example, are uncoupled from lowered pitch;
here the gesture and the sound (essentially a particular VOWEL sound)
are inseparable. If we make a kissing gesture and a noise in our throat
at the same time, we get something like the interjection *aw*, which itself has meanings related to kissing. If we are bowled over with astonishment, our dropped jaw will result in *ah* if we vocalize at the
same time, and an expression of more controlled surprise will yield
the familiar *oh*. G. W. Turner writes:

> I have heard the theory advanced that New Zealand speech has spread
> vowels because in a new country everyone is expected to approach his neigh-
> bour with a democratic grin. . . . The theory could equally well work in re-
> verse. If Australians tend to use spread-lipped vowels (and they do), they
> perhaps seem matey fellows, and as this begets a friendly response when
> they are abroad, they live up to it, becoming indeed matey. (1973: 63)

It is easy to overstate the primitive origins—probably the sounds
now take precedence over the facial expression in our communicative
intent—but the similarities are too striking to be coincidental. Naturally, like intonation itself, the gestures and the sounds can be socialized and conventionalized in many ways. And there are other
prosodic elements, in addition to intonation, which can be introduced
for special effects—aspiration seems to have a kind of intensifying
effect (as in *Hm?* versus *M-m?* for a question), and the glottal stop is
connected with negation (it is usually spelled with *h*, as in *Oh-oh!* for a
warning). These are returned to below.

'Huh,' 'hunh,' 'hm'

Huh, hunh, hm is our most versatile interjection. It wears the slack face of *uh* to which aspiration is generally added initially. The form without nasalization, *huh*, occurs only when the interjection is very short; only *hunh* and *hm* are (optionally) prolonged. Intonation is comparatively decisive; in fact this interjection might almost be regarded as a mere intonation-carrier. Though it has several conversational uses when it appears alone, its main syntactic use is that of tag in tag questions:

> You like it, hunh?
> It's nice, hunh!

(The latter, with rise-fall, is a comparatively recent development.)

As an exclamation, *hunh* etc. requires an A profile; the terminal fall may have any degree of magnitude, including, for *huh*, a mere downward hook. The falling intonation does not *determine* the status of exclamation. There is also a particular kind of question that may or may not have it, namely a response to a summons: you call me saying *George!* and I reply saying *Hunh!* meaning 'I'm receiving your signal, go ahead'—the nearest paraphrase is *What do you want?* The pitch may go up (B), come down (A), or stay at a relatively high level (B). If *hunh* or *hm* constitutes a reclamatory question ('What did you say?') it seems to require the B profile.

As an exclamation, with its required fall, *hunh* etc. appears to mean something like 'This is a remarkable fact and I continue to wonder about it.' In this respect it differs from *oh*, which omits the wonderment. (Aijmer's remark [1987: 65] that *hm* does not treat prior talk as informative disregards the intonation—extra-high-to-low may be 'super-informative.') So one may say *Oh, of course*, in which the *of course* shows the speaker to be reconciled to the fact, whereas *Hm, of course* is less likely (if it did occur, the speaker would still be wondering about some aspect of the fact—as can be seen in the greater naturalness of the more uncertain *Hm, I guess you're right*).

With a C profile, *hunh* (and *hm* but not *huh*, which is antithetical to the drawl of C) may be either a reclamatory question or, as before, an answer to a summons. As the former, it tends to be incredulous: the interlocutor has said something hard to believe and the interjection is a signal to repeat it for confirmation. The low-pitched accent mitigates the incredulity. As answer to a summons, the C may be to tone down a degree of impatience—the other person has already interrupted more than once to demand attention. An AC may have the same purpose, or may be playfully cordial.[2]

'Oh'

Oh and *ah* are the interjections for which the clearest case can be made for a gestural origin—and probably continuing gestural associations. Both have meanings related to surprise, and between them, in their jaw and lip positions—if we add neutral *uh*—they cover the facial expressions of surprise reproduced in Ekman (1982: 93). Surprise is one of the most consistently recognizable and culturally uniform emotions in its facial manifestations (see Ekman, pp. 101, 139, 149). The rounding of *oh*, which distinguishes it from *ah*, may represent a blend with the kissing gesture produced by mothers in their interaction with infants—one of the typically "exaggerated facial expressions used by caregivers" (Ekman, p. 155). Such a blend would account for two difficulties that beset the analysis of *oh* as an expression of astonishment, the state of pure surprise. Rather than by *Oh!* this should be represented by *Uh!* with high and rapidly rising pitch. This is the medial position in Ekman's diagrams, and the neutral vowel [ʌ] represents no intentional vocalic articulation. The astonishment is conveyed by the wide-open mouth and the rising tension of the pitch curve. Since the vowel is neutral, it fluctuates nonsignificantly, easily verging on [o] or [a]. This is not exceptional—the same thing happens with *uh* as a hesitation sound (see below) and with what might be called the opposite emotion to astonishment, namely pure exhaustion: someone who is worn out drops into a chair and says, with slack jaw and slowly descending pitch,

Uh! I just want to sit for the rest of the week!

—the vowel may wander.

The point is that if the speaker intentionally rounds an [o] or drops the jaw farther to produce an [a], it should be for some purpose. And the fact is that *oh*, as we shall abundantly see, adds a degree of lightness, agreeableness, and *sociability*, with surprise much of the time relegated to the background, just as *ah* adds a degree of "seriousness."

The informal sociability of *oh* explains why in a corpus of 716 examples from recorded conversations in the London-Lund corpus, none at all were found in radio interviews and only three in courtroom proceedings (Aijmer 1987: 81).

If we think of pure surprise not primarily as a symptomatic reaction but as a LINGUISTIC EXPRESSION of astonishment, then we resort not to *Oh!* or *Ah!* but to some such exclamation as *Jesus!*, which can be used in practically all contexts, favorable and unfavorable. Though *oh* is associated with surprise in many languages, in others it is not—the Australian aboriginal languages are an example (Wierzbicka, pers. comm.).

Assuming some primary exclamatory value to *oh* and *ah*, one would expect to find it in cases where the two interjections are discourse-initial and prosodically separated from following conversation. The clearest case is under magnification, so to speak: the [o] and [a] are doubled, with aspiration between. Both express 'surprised discovery,' but there is more—one is self-important, the other is sociable:

> Aha! I knew all along she was up to something!
> Oho! Just look at this handsome lad in his Halloween mask!

A second nonconversational *oh* is encountered with a vocative used to hail someone whose presence has just been noticed. If you are standing on a corner chatting with someone and you catch sight of an acquaintance with whom you want to have a friendly exchange, one way to get him to stop and heed you is to say, with B + Á or with *oh* actually unaccented,

> Oh John! I'd like a word with you!

The *oh* would not do if the acquaintance were moving into range; it pretends surprise at catching sight of the person, but is intended to check an unwanted disappearance. The same is true of the British *Oh, I say!* to flag down someone; also *Oh you there!* (The unfriendliness of plain *You there!* is manifest.) Although the convention of English spelling distinguishes between the interjection and the apostrophe, it seems likely that this vocative *oh* and the *O* of *O ye of little faith!* are ultimately the same.

Turning to *oh* with more verbal context, we look first at a usage which seems only remotely related to 'surprise' and which James (1978) feels should be split off from the *oh* (*oh*₁) we have been considering. This *oh*₂ is encountered with hesitations over choice, e.g. in response to *How many people were at the party?*—

> I saw . . . oh . . . twelve people at the party.

As she points out (James 1972: 243; James 1974), the speaker here looks for the right alternative, makes the best approximation. It contrasts with *uh*, which in

> I saw . . . uh . . . twelve people at the party.

would signify that "the speaker was trying to remember exactly how many people there were, and he would be understood as saying 'exactly twelve.'" But the question is whether this is a valid comparison, given the crucial difference in pitch. The *oh* is higher, and if *uh* is moved up in pitch it assimilates itself to *m-m-m* and its spread (non-labialized) counterparts—a range of sounds all the way from *m-m-m* to *eh*—which readily admit the same 'approximately' as *oh₂*. In fact, *oh₂* brings us back again to a facial gesture, this time protrusion of the lips, especially the lower lip, accompanying a mental search. The eyes are apt to be squinted at the same time, and the mouth can be said to be squinted as well. So we get a kind of close-mouthed *oh-h-h*. It is not even necessary to vocalize: in making that 'approximation' the speaker may purse his lips and blow, and the pursing is also apt to accompany *m-m-m* when so used. The lip protrusion varies in all degrees, which means that *oh₂* can be slackly rounded. This does not happen with *oh₁*: in

> There were oh! so many!

the *oh* is fully articulated and 'surprise' is unmistakable.

So it appears that James is right in favoring a split into *oh₁* and *oh₂* if we recognize that *oh₂* unlike *oh₁* is not a sharply targeted sound but a range of sounds. The distinction is fairly clear even under identical intonational conditions, given the right background. Thus in answer to *How many people showed up at the meeting?* one may have

Oh-h-h maybe a doz
          en or so.

with a high-pitched B plus downtilting tail and a low-pitched A, and in answer to *Do you think I ought to make my complaint officially?* the identical contour occurs in

Oh-h-h I'd be care
          ful about that.

Both *oh*'s are deliberative, but the first is *oh₂*: it can be replaced by *uh-h-h* and is only hesitant, but in the second anything besides *oh* is unlikely and the implication is 'Attention!'—a nuance of surprise, hence *oh₁*. The deliberation is more than mere hesitation; it may serve to avoid giving offense. If the speaker is weighing matters carefully, the hearer is allowed to interpret 'considerateness,' e.g. in

Oh-h-a I think you're
          wrong.

This same contour on *Oh-h-h I think you're right* may be intended to reassure the hearer that he was right after all and need not apologize for his views.

Our interest from here on is just in oh_1, chiefly as a conversational particle. Carlson (1984: 69–75) distinguishes the following variations on 'surprise' as the functions of *oh* in conversation (p. 69):

1. The situation defies all expectation. *Oh* expresses genuine surprise.
2. The situation, despite whatever degree of predictability, diverges from what may be rationally expected.
3. The situation differs from ideal expectations (preferences or desires). *Oh* expresses disappointment.

These categories are suggestive and probably valid as far as they go, but the contribution of *oh* to discourse exploits our inferential mechanisms in far more complex ways. We have already seen the problem with "pure surprise," so we expect more than that even in cases like

> Have you heard about Joe and Marge? — Oh, don't tell me! They're getting divorced?
>
> I feel like keeling over. — Oh, let's rest then. I didn't know the walk was affecting you so.
>
> Their house was broken into last night. — Oh, I wonder why nobody told me!

At the same time that it contributes 'surprise,' the *oh* rules out unfriendly intonations, such as the 'it's up to you' implication of an AC in

```
         rest
let's
          then·
```

or the annoyed B + À with downmoving B tail of

```
I wonder why nobody t
                    o1
                      d
                        me!
```

which would be quite natural after *Hunh!*

Beyond whatever concentration of pure surprise *oh* may carry, we have the things that surprise may imply, and the facets of usage that are organized around those implications. One implication is 'magnitude,' as in the example *There were oh! so many!* We are more apt to be surprised at something large than at something small. So it is logical that *oh* should often suggest enhancement, including emphasis and intensification. Another implication is 'spontaneity.' *Oh* is uttered as (or as if as) an immediate reaction to a stimulus, without prior reflection (though it may itself be deliberative). From this one can infer frankness and sincerity, which in turn associates *oh* with affirmation.

Look first at enhancement. *Oh* is frequent as an intensifier, a typical instance being its collocation with *how, what,* and *so*:

> June's getting divorced. — Oh how awful! When?
>
> It'll cost, but oh what fun we'll have!
>
> The pre-CIA Office of Strategic Services was nicknamed Oh So Secret.

Conventional punctuation puts commas after these *oh*'s, omitted here to suggest the fusion with what follows. There is fusion in the above even with successive A's. Compare the A + A and B + A expressing the most appropriate degree of concern versus lightheartedness in the first two examples above:

```
Oh        aw              Oh what  f
                                    u
    how     ful!                     n  we'll have!
```

In the first, if the speaker were more sincere, the downmotion would occur on the *oh* itself, not following it: *Oh, how awful!*—*oh* then is separately exclamatory, not routinely intensifying. The second example requires no comment, as B + A regularly associates the profiles tightly.

Oh also intensifies large amounts:

> Did you get lots of presents? — Oh tons.
> How much did they invest? — Oh millions.

And it intensifies other intensifiers:

> Was it easy? — Oh very.
> Did he love her? — Oh terribly.
> I wish, oh I do, that she could care for me.

Similarly with covert intensification (scaled adjectives and adverbs):

> Is she good-looking? — Oh beautiful!
> Did it taste OK? — Oh delectable!
> Was it done with care? — Oh meticulously!

Oh intensifier occurs in a pattern with the interrogatives *when, where, why,* and possibly *what,* repeated:

> When oh when shall I see you again?
> Where oh where has my little dog gone?
> Why oh why do they treat me like this?
> What oh what can I believe?

The collocational nature of these—*why-oh-why* rather than *why, oh why*—can be seen in the amount of drama needed to produce something like

> Who, oh who, will help me!

In all these the *oh* may be repeated initially: *oh where oh where.*

Oh also heightens enthusiasm, which is further augmented in the first example below by prolonging the interjection—the speaker affects amazement and inability to do justice to the facts (other voice qualifiers may be added, such as breathy voice):

> How's the weather? — Oh-h-h it's turned out beautiful!
> I've just heard a juicy story. — Oh tell me!
> We've been thinking of taking a cruise this summer. — Oh let's!

There is some degree of stereotyping here—*oh* collocates more or less firmly and in some cases is required as part of the whole exclamation, e.g. although we can say *damn* without *oh*, *fudge* as an exclamation of disappointment or frustration virtually requires *oh*; and *dear* as an exclamation requires *oh* or some other set addition: *oh dear, dear dear, dear me.* Also *oh* can make a large difference in meaning. *Boy!* works equally well with enthusiasm and disappointment (*Boy, it was great!*, *Boy, it was terrible!*), but *oh boy* is mostly limited to enthusiasm—unless further intensified, in which case it again accords with disappointment: *Óh bóy wás ít térrible!*, *Boy oh boy it was terrible!* Similarly, *Oh dear!* is a more forceful expression of dismay than *Dear, dear!* or *Dear me!* as is also *Oh my!* (a "pull-up" expression, probably for *Oh my God!*; see p. 310) or *Oh me oh my!* versus *My, my!*, the latter expressing a somewhat priggish 'disapproval' rather than 'dismay.'

The augmenting value of *oh* in these cases can be seen in the difficulty of combining it with something downgraded:

> I want it oh more than I can say.
> *I want it oh less than one might suppose.

Not all enhancement is positive. One may also emphasize disappointment and annoyance, as was just noted. Carlson cites *Oh, honey, what a shame!* and *Oh, to hell with it Eddie—you know what I mean!* (p. 75). There is a frontier with other interjections (*ah, aw,* [æ]) which enables us to detect that other ingredient of the *o*-face:

> Oh, forget it. I'll tend to things tomorrow.
> Aw, forget it. I'm sick of the whole business.

The first can be good-humored (sociable); the second is not.

Disappointment turns to anguish in

> Oh my dear, my dear! I did the best I could!

The vocative is often repeated, as in *oh where oh where* above:

> (Oh) John oh John! What are we to do!

Except for the *why oh why* type in which *oh* is usually unaccented, the normal intonation contour for these enhancing uses of *oh* is B + À, sometimes B + Á, with *oh* a relatively high-pitched B. For greater emphasis A + A is common enough; we then tend to add commas.

The next derivative of surprise is related to polarity, and is allied to the intensive—there is a good deal of commerce across this frontier, as can be seen in the affirmative use of intensifiers:

> Do you like it? — Yes, indeed (I do).
> It is indeed good.
> Do you like it? — A lot.
> I like it a lot.

So it is only a step from the intensely urging

> We've been thinking of taking a cruise next summer. — Oh let's!

to the affirming

> Shall we take a cruise this summer? — Oh let's!

The sociability component of *oh* is as important as the surprise-spontaneity component, as can be seen in the kind of affirming that it does: it does not assert, it agrees. One cannot answer a question affirmatively with simple *oh*:

> Did she find it? — *Oh.

But one can accept what the other speaker has just said:

> Forget your pills again? Why didn't you take them? — The doctor took me off those pills. — Oh.[3]

(*Oh* has an A profile.) The speaker's impulse to be agreeable rather than to assert comes to the fore in the way *oh* collocates with substitutes for *yes* in the latter's assertive function:

> He paid off the debt did he? — Right. (*Oh right.)
>   True. (*Oh true.)
>   Correct. (*Oh correct.)
>   Affirmative. (*Oh affirmative.)
>   He did. (*Oh he did.)
>   Positively. (?Oh positively.)

Given a B + A contour, *oh* does not collocate well here. But there is no problem when affirmation is by way of reassuring the hearer:

He paid off the debt did he? — (Oh) absolutely.
(Oh) undoubtedly.
(Oh) you bet.
(Oh) assuredly.
(Oh) definitely.
(Oh) certainly.
(Oh) unquestionably.
(Oh) sure.[4]

Compare also

You can manage can you? — (*Oh) I can.
(Oh) easily.

With a change in the prosody, the first set of responses is all right with *oh*, e.g. *Oh, right* with two A profiles and a good separation between them. *Oh* responds to the tag, *right* to the declarative. (Omit the tag and even with separation *Oh, right!* is odd.)

Consent and assent are both forms of agreeing:

We were hoping you might take Nancy to the party. — Oh I will!
I hope you won't insist on more. — Oh I won't!
That's one of her best works. — Oh it is!

If the speaker wanted to disagree here, the corresponding negative responses *Oh I won't, Oh I will*, and *Oh it isn't* would hardly serve. The normal form of rejection would abort the fusion of *oh* with what follows by giving it an A profile and inserting some form of adversative: *Oh but I won't!; Oh you're mistaken, I will!; Oh that's where you're wrong—it isn't!*

The response may be in the form of an opinion that the speaker thinks harmonizes with the hearer's point of view:

What did you think of the party? — Oh I loved it!

with B + À. To disagree using B + À, the speaker might use plain *I hated it!*, but an added *oh* would require separation, most likely in the form of successive A's. But *Oh I hated it!* would be normal enough if it agreed with the supposed viewpoint of the other person:

Wasn't the party terrible! — Oh I hated it! You are so right!

An auxiliary response in question form is better when the speaker agrees:

I plan to take Nancy to the party. — Oh you do? That's great!

I plan to take Nancy to the party. — ?Oh you do? That's not a
good idea.

Plain *You do?* would be better in the latter response. But sociability is
not violated if the speaker is tactful:

I plan to take Nancy to the party. — Oh you do? I wonder if that's
wise.

The same goes for tactful disagreement in nonquestions:

That's one of her best works. — It ís nót!
                        *Oh it ís nót!
                        Oh hardly!
                        Oh pléase!

(*Oh pléase!* is a "pull-up" expression of disagreement, probably stem-
ming from something like *Please don't imagine that I can accept that!*)
Similarly

Are you going to agree to that? — *Oh never! (B + À)
                               Oh, never! (A + À)
                               Oh I don't think so. (B + À or
                               B + C)
                               Oh not at all! (B + À)

Oh becomes an incidental test for the comity of disagreement: we see
here that *not at all* is a fairly polite way of disagreeing.
    Rebukes similarly:

I proposed to her. — ?Oh you blundering idiot!
                      Oh you foolish boy!

The association of *oh* with agreement is a natural extension not only
of sociability but of the fact that unless some credibility is assigned to
what is stated, there is no reason to be surprised:

I couldn't do anything more for them. — Oh I quite understand.
                                    *Oh I don't understand.

But one may be surprised at the saying, and react with an independent, unfused *oh*; here it resembles *yes*:

Johnny came last night. — Yes. That's what they're saying. But I
must tell you, he didn't.

Johnny came last night. — Oh. So that's what they're saying. But I
must tell you, he didn't.

Here the speaker affirms the correctness of the quotation but not of the quoted fact. Similarly if what the other person has said is re-interpreted as an opinion:

> Johnny came last night. — Yes, I know that's what you think. Well, he didn't.

> Johnny came last night. — Oh. You think so do you. Well, he didn't.

If the *oh* of this last set of examples is given a B profile, it becomes a question and then it does hew to the fact, expecting an affirmative response and an explanation (when not rhetorical, as above):

> Ethel turned down the job. — Oh? — Yes, she was already booked up solid.

> I'm not going to do it. — Oh? — No! I've done enough!

In the last example the speaker affirms the original negation.

But the fusibility of *oh* is the best evidence for its association with agreement. At times it appears unaccented, almost like a proclitic:

> This is one of her best works, isn't it? — Oh it ís! I couldn't agree with you more!

—*oh* can be reduced [wɪ'tɪz], with [tɪz] at highest pitch. Similarly *Oh I know*, *Oh I see*, *Oh he did?*, but not with negations like *Oh he didn't*, *Oh I doubt it*, *Oh it isn't*, etc.

This brings us to a seemingly paradoxical stereotype, *Oh no!* (to be distinguished from *Oh, no!* with A + À or A + Á), matching the related affirmative *Oh yes!*, both with B + À and even the possibility of simple A with *oh* carrying the only accent, another case of "emotional backshift" (see above, p. 259). The speaker grants that the fact may be surprising to the other person, excusing his ignorance of it or the need to be reassured about it. The rectification is friendly, which may not be the case with simple *no* (*I'm not*, etc.):

> I hear you're moving away. — Oh no! I'm getting a summer place, but I'd never move away from here permanently.

> I was afraid you weren't going to call. — Oh yes! I would not have neglected that!

Oh no and *oh yes* collocate further in *Oh no it isn't* (*Oh no they don't*, etc.) and *Oh yes it is* (etc.), used in disputation and less abrasive than the same formulas without *oh*. The most frequent contours are A + ÁC with *oh* unaccented and C + B, as in

The latter may give way to A + C + B with the A of *oh* drawled, for a sarcastic effect,

```
o
 h
    yes it  is!
```

The affirmative use of *oh* is corroborated in a richly documented study by Heritage (1984), focusing on the custom of saying *oh* to suggest a change in the speaker's "locally current state of knowledge, information, orientation or awareness" (p. 299), thanks to what the interlocutor has said. The speaker "*oh*-receipts" what the other person has said by certifying that it has led to a change in the speaker's condition (this of course is Carlson's "newness"). The role of agreeableness in this is transparent: no more agreeable response can be made to what we have been told than to give to understand that we have been persuaded by it in some way.[5]

If affirmation is one offshoot of general agreeableness, MITIGATION is another. An *oh* blunts what otherwise might be objectionable. We have already seen evidence of this in cases of tactful disagreement. There is no sharp dividing line.

Among the discourse-initial instances of mitigation we have commands like

> Oh stop bothering me!
> Oh go away, will you!
> Oh just be quiet for a minute!

With *oh*, these reprimands can actually be smiling and playful; without *oh* they may more easily cause offense. We note the same in the implied directive

> Oh that's too much! Half is enough!

addressed to an overgenerous benefactor. The *oh* can be taken as 'pleased surprise'; without it, the utterance might sound like a reproof.

Imprecations similarly. *Oh shit!* is more excusable than *Shit!* A person who says *Oh for Christ's sake!* on receiving an injury is probably less dangerous, more apt to confine himself to *verbal* abuse, than one who says *For Christ's sake!* But if the oath is unmitigatable, then *oh* is out of place with it. We can say *Oh Jesus!*, but probably not **Oh Jesus Christ!*; *Oh hell!* is acceptable, but *Oh hell and damnation!* would signify a weakening of the oath.

As for cases that are not discourse-initial, Carlson calls attention (p. 73) to the "trivializing" effect of *oh*, and cites examples in which the speaker poohpoohs the importance of something—the surprise is that the matter should have come up at all:

What did you see in it? — Oh just the ordinary things.

Y'all just got here! And all the way from England! — Oh, said Henry, this is just one stop on quite an extended tour.

The latter example actually incorporates a boast; it is the same as the more or less stereotyped

Oh that's nothing! Just consider this!

But the speaker may also minimize his own achievement—an instance of real or pretended humility:

What a story you wrote! I could hardly put it down. — Oh it's OK I guess.

Oh is common in expressions of reassurance, mostly using B + C contours with downtilted B:

Oh never mind.　Oh it doesn't matter.
Oh don't worry.　Oh that's all right.
Oh it's nothing.　Oh forget it.

Likewise *oh*—now with an A profile—is common with *sure* used to reassure, contrasting with its absence; e.g. in response to *Isn't the level of radioactive dust pretty high?*—

Oh sure, and what you have to do is wear protective clothing (and then you won't have anything to worry about).

Sure, and what you have to do is wear protective clothing (or you'll have plenty to worry about).

Also common with *sure* and other affirmatives (*yes, fine*) is a high-pitched and usually reduced *oh* that not only contributes its own mitigation but also serves as an intonational foil for the affirmative, which is at a low pitch ("minimizing downskip"; see Bolinger 1986: 222). In answer to *How was it?* one may say, with a tonal ending and a very slight rise (C profile),

oh

fine.

and follow it with *I wás a little disappointed in the trim, but all in all I was satisfied*—the complaint is mitigated.

Whatever the source of the mitigation, there is no mistaking the relative unimportance attached to the misadventure in the first of the following, and the greater importance in the second:

Oh it's bound to come out sooner or later (and we might as well not make a big thing of it).

It's bound to come out sooner or later (and we'd better be prepared for the fallout).

A mitigating *oh* is common with expressions of doubt where the interlocutor's credibility is on the line but the speaker does not want to be "confrontational." *That's impossible!* may be too strong a challenge; *Oh that's impossible!* is easier to take. The typical idiom here is (*Oh*) *I wonder* using a B + À contour. B + C is more likely with the idiom (*Oh*) *I don't know* (downtilting B tail), whose terminal rise seems to invite a question putting the decision up to the hearer:

It was all Mary's fault. — Oh I don't know. Don't you think she did the best she could?

The terminal fall in (*Oh*) *I wonder* (*Oh I'm not so sure*) is a little more compatible with an explanation on the part of the speaker:

It was all Mary's fault. — Oh I wonder. It seems to me she did the best she could.

Less idiomatic expressions go either way, B + À or B + C: *Oh I doubt it, Oh I question that, Oh I'm not so sure about that.*
    Oh is common with cajoling or playful expressions of doubt; the usual intonation is B + À with downtilting B tail:

Oh go on with you!	Oh stuff and nonsense!
Oh come now!	Oh fiddlesticks!
Oh you're kidding!	Oh get out of here!

As we saw earlier, outright denial tends to conflict with *oh*'s propensity for agreement, and in its strongest forms it also conflicts with mitigation. Like certain oaths, *You're a liar* is practically unmitigatable, and **Oh you're a liar!* is an improbable sequence (though *Oh he's a liar!* is possible, as the interlocutor is not being personally challenged, and *Oh you're such a liar!* comes across as almost playful). But milder forms of denial are not incompatible with *oh*, though the intonation usually differs in two ways: first, a terminal fall replaces the rise that is common with mere doubt; second, the *oh* tends to take an A profile. The typical contour is thus A + À:

```
Oh                          Oh
                 ta                        wro
    you're mis                 you're
              ken!                             ngl
```

The lower second A is itself mitigating and makes *oh* more compatible. An A + Á contour is much less likely—the denial is too forceful:

```
             wro
?Oh

   you're    ᵑg!
```

With descending A's on each syllable, even something as potent as *Óh yóu're só wróng!* is possible, spoken more in sorrow than in indignation. The A + À is also possible with the earlier expressions of doubt, turning doubt into something more like denial, with *oh* still mitigating the force of the denial:

```
Oh
      won
   I    deₑᵣ!
```

Oh I don't believe that, *Oh I deny that*, etc. are other candidates. (The first A may be on either *oh* or *I*.)

Finally, the stereotyped *Oh well!* has this same trivializing nuance by contrast with *Ah well!* (see below, p. 282) and with plain *well*:

> Well, Í'm worried, for one. (C, A + C, AC)
> *Oh well, Í'm worried, for one. (B + C, A + C, AC)
> Oh well, Í'm not worried. (B + C, A + C)

The following, from J. D. McClure (pers. comm.), illustrates the trivializing effect of *oh* in a cross-language context:

> In one of the *Asterix* books there's a sequence where Julius Caesar is pontificating about a "glorieux chef," prompting one Roman to ask "De qui parle-t-il?" and another to respond "De lui. Il parle toujours de lui à la troisième personne," whereupon the first speaker says to Caesar "Il est formidable!"—"Qui ça?"—"Ben—vous!"—"Ah! Lui!"—which in the English translation becomes "He's great!"—"Who?"—"Er—you!"—"Oh, him!" Which keeps the main joke, but surely changes the point of the final utterance—"Oh, him!" sounds a lot less laudatory than "Ah! Lui!"

If it appears that *oh* is blowing hot and cold with the same breath—being now an intensifier and now a downtoner—we may observe that surprise can easily stem from opposite assumptions. As a reaction to the *fact* or the appearance of fact, surprise underscores the impact and intensifies. As a reaction to the *saying*, surprise may deny its importance. The two come together in *Oh don't worry*, where the expression as a whole (including the B + C contour usually carried by this expression) mitigates, but *oh* can be said to intensify the mitigation. Lexically the same thing happens with expressions like *much less*, an intensification of the reduction in *less*. How hard it is to distinguish between intensification and mitigation can be seen in a pair of exchanges like

How are you these days, chum? — Not too bad. How's yourself?

How are you these days, chum? — Oh not too bad. I had to have a
disc removed a couple of months ago, but it's OK now.

Both *Not too bad* and *Oh not too bad* are understood to have A + C (the
A is on *not* in the first and on *oh* in the second). The first is a perfunctory response, the second suggests something a little more serious, but does so by mitigation rather than intensification. This can
be seen in the concomitant gesture—the *oh* is apt to be accompanied
by a shrug—'this is of no importance.' But the hearer is cued to
the opposite meaning: 'my friend is just trying to make light of his
affliction.'

In the examples cited in this section, *oh* has been for the most part
accented, but in some cases not. Since an unaccented exclamation is a
contradiction in terms, we have to accept *oh* as a discourse particle on
a par with *well*, *so*, and other "content" words. The mitigating use
makes this particularly clear. In a pair like

```
Oh                          I
       ny                          ny
   I de              Oh    de
           that!                    that!
```

the otherwise more abrasive *I deny that* is toned down in both cases,
but in the first there is still an element of indignant surprise, whereas
in the second the unaccented *oh* has little effect except to mitigate.

This unaccented *oh* is found in the intonational stereotype *Oh yes!*
for 'politely taking exception,' with *oh* a low-pitched proclitic to the A
profile on *yes*. A different *Oh yes!*, with minimizing downskip (to
creak), makes a striking contrast with the stereotype:

```
Oh                       ye

   yes!              Oh    s!
```

We can imagine the respective contexts

Does he really respect them? — Oh yes! No need to worry about that!
Does he really respect them? — Oh yes! And don't you forget it!

The formulaic *Oh yes!* is related to an *Oh, yes!* with A + Á, which
might also be used in the last example, though it would be much
more emphatic. Also, except for the context, it would not be unambiguously 'exception-taking,' for it could serve equally well in a context of enthusiasm:

Did you like it? — Oh, yes! It was wonderful!

To use the unaccented *oh* here might sound as if the first speaker had expected a negative answer and needed to be set straight:

> Did you like it? — Oh yes! What would make you think otherwise?

The formula is commonly used in contexts where the second speaker rectifies the first speaker's ignorance:

```
↑
  didn't know that Jack had been        ted!              ye
                                res                 --  Oh
                             ar                          s!
```

The second speaker carries on with *He was accused of dealing in you-know-what*. An A + Á here might seem like overstating the importance of the event.

Though *Oh yes!* qualifies as a stereotype, this unaccented *oh* is productive and is found with other affirmatives when the speaker feels a need to rectify. In the following, the only accent (A profile) is on *did*:

> I reported the incident to the police. — Oh you did! Was that wise?

As before, an A + Á is also possible here, but the difference is that the A + Á would virtually be required if the speaker is fully approving:

> I reported the incident to the police. — Oh, you did! All the better! Now I don't have to worry about taking care of it myself.

Similarly with *Oh sure!*:

> You do take my word for it, don't you? — Oh sure! But you're forgetting that Clara doesn't trust you like I do. (A or A + Á)

> Want a drink of some of this stuff? — Oh, sure! Wow! I wouldn't miss the chance! (A + Á but not A)

The question is whether the *oh* merely mitigates or remains to some degree exclamatory.

The *oh* is also potentially unaccented with the vocative, as we saw earlier (p. 267). One is tempted to regard this as a springboard for the accent on the name, the *kerwháck!* phenomenon.

Oh yes! is only one of many collocations with *oh*, each, for the most part, with a typical contour. Among those already noted are *oh so, oh how, where oh where, oh boy, oh fudge, oh dear, oh me oh my, oh I don't know*. Among the expostulations there is a consistent difference between the ones that exclaim at something that has already happened and the ones that exclaim at something in progress or to come. The first have their terminal A lowered in pitch (B + À or A + À) for the most part:

Oh, hell (oh fudge, etc.), I left my keys in the house!

The second have the terminal A higher, as a rule:

Oh, heavens! Where have I put my purse!
Oh, look! It's a plane about to crash!

The difference, of course, only reflects the speaker's affective stance. In other words, though the expression may be stereotyped, the intonational association is not arbitrary. Two other cases in which we see this clearly are the stereotypes *Oh nothing!* and *Oh yeah!* The first is a noncommittal reply—the speaker is refusing to divulge more, and this suspensiveness is shown in the terminal rise of B + C:

What are you doing there? — Oh nothing!

The second is the sneering response for 'I don't believe you' with a "stylized" terminal level B profile and unaccented *oh*:

You don't know from nothing. — Oh yeah! And what do yóu know!

'Ah' and still other gestural interjections

The closest relative of *oh* is *ah*, to which James (1972: 243) gives the sense of 'something significant for some reason.' She compares the examples

Oh, you're leaving tomorrow.
Ah, you're leaving tomorrow.

and interprets the second as suggesting perhaps 'That will interfere with our plans' or 'You were about to forget that important fact' (for the latter we can infer a fuller version, *Ah, but you're leaving tomórrow*, with the speaker wagging an admonitory finger to point out the lapse of memory). There is a 'basis' for *ah*—it seems to reach back, and accordingly is odd if used in calling attention to something just appearing on the scene:

Oh look! There's Gladys!
*Ah look! There's Gladys!

We saw earlier that the augmented forms *aha* and *oho* bear out the contrast between *oh* and *ah* (p. 267), and the same is true of the stereotypes *Oh well* and *Ah well*—*Oh well* is comparatively trivial (Aijmer 1987: 71). Both have B + C with terraced monotone:

Ah well, they had not long to live anyway. (Life is ever thus.)
Oh well, we might as well give up for now.

Similarly when the two are combined with cachinnation:

Oh-ho-ho-ho-hó! Nów you want it! Well, I understand.
Ah-ha-ha-ha-há! The laugh is on yóu this time!

The gestural significance of *ah* is hard to identify, but it might be termed the AGHAST face. The deeper, more conclusive implications of *ah* can be seen in situations of pleasure where *oh* and *ah* both occur on A profiles and are accompanied by a sigh, but *oh* tends to have a higher pitch, anticipating renewed excitement:

Ah, that feels good! Now I just wanna die.
Oh, that feels good! Do it some more!

Whatever the original connection, a gestural origin of some sort seems likely given the cross-linguistic evidence for the *oh-ah* distinction.[6]

As the more "serious" of the two, *ah* is never reduced; that is, it is always accented and never proclitic. By the same token it does not fuse in the sort of stereotypes that are so common with *oh*; there is no *Ah dear!* to match *Oh dear!*; no *Ah nothing*, no *Ah yeah*, etc.

If *ah* has a frontier with *oh* on one hand, it has another with the interjection usually spelled *aw*, phonetically [ɔ], which might be called the "sympathy" face, apparently a blend of the kissing gesture and the grieving gesture. (The latter is the opposite of the smile: rather than up, the corners of the mouth are drawn down—the familiar caricature in the comedy-versus-tragedy mask.) *Aw* is much used with children and pet animals:

Aw, poor little thing!
Aw, what did they do to mama's darlin'!

(The adjective *poor* is eminently suited to the kissing gesture and is much used in this transferred sense of 'pitiable.') *Aw* is also extensively found as a protest against what is expected to arouse sympathy, namely disappointment, and then occurs either singly or with a (usually minced) oath:

Aw, couldn't you have waited just a few minutes!
Aw heck, this thing is no good!
Aw shucks, there's not even a postal in today's mail.
Aw the hell with it.
Aw gee, why did they have to go and tease her like that!

(At least some speakers for whom [a] versus [ɔ] has ceased to be phonemically contrastive retain the gestural contrast of the two sounds.) Except for the last example with *gee* (significantly, the most childish of the minced oaths), *ah* could replace *aw*, but the effect then would be more 'disgust' than 'self-pity.' (On the basis of her corpus-based study, Aijmer [pp. 66, 75] claims that an evaluation after *ah* "can be

positive only," e.g. *Ah good*; but we also have *Ah phooey!*) At this opposite frontier, *ah* is leaning toward a gestural interjection that has no
conventional spelling though *ah* may sometimes stand for it: the mid-
low vowel [æ]. It is the 'disgust' face—the upper lip and the nose tend
to be elevated and the lower lip drawn down, the latter perhaps implying a blend with the 'snarl.' It is not much coupled with oaths, but
could easily replace *aw* in the first and fourth examples of the last set.

What we have found is a scale of low and back vowel interjections:
[æ a ɔ o], with meanings associated with the corresponding facial gestures. The degree of conventionalization varies: it is easier to argue
that *oh* is a "real word" than to do the same with the other interjections, and no one would make such a claim for [æ] (the regularity
with which the item is spelled out is a clue to its conventionalized
status); but the connection between shape and meaning is too close
for mere coincidence.

Collocations with oaths and minced oaths tell their own story about
these meanings. If they are compatible they join, otherwise not. So
God, heavens, and *Jesus,* which are as close as one can get to pure surprise, collocate well with *oh* but not with *ah, aw,* nor [æ]. *Gee,* which
with its childish associations downplays importance, does not collocate with *ah* or [æ], but fits the surprised and sympathetic *oh* and *aw*
quite nicely. The all-purpose *shit* is comfortable with the whole set.

The gestural interjections have phonesthematic ties—the 'importance' of *ah,* for example, is consonant with the 'size' implication of
the low vowels. But phonesthemes in general are vaguer and more
often depend on partly accidental clustering in the lexicon—such
phenomena as the 'visual' implications of [gl] in *glitter, glow, gleam,
glisten, gloom,* etc. The gestural interjections are also to be distinguished from vocal segregates such as *ugh* 'disgust,' *sh-h-h* 'be quiet,'
yoo-hoo 'I'm calling you,' which are isolated from syntax.

By their very nature, the significant vowel sounds are not confined
to separate utterance as [æ], *ah, aw,* and *oh,* but are found in combination, especially with aspiration and the glottal stop. We have already
seen *oho* and *aha, hunh* and *hm.* The most interesting connection—
because the sound itself is not part of the system of English phonemes—is with the glottal stop for negativity. It is found in two fairly
distinct clusters of interjections. The first, signifying 'negative admonition' ('Don't do that!,' 'I made a mistake!,' 'Watch out!,' etc.), uses
the full range of significant vowel sounds; the second, signifying 'No,'
uses only [ʌ], nearly always has initial aspiration, and matches an intonationally related set signifying 'Yes' in which the glottal stop is absent. The most familiar spellings for the first set are *oh-oh* and *ah-ah,*
for the second, *hunh-uh* and *hm-m,* and for the matching affirmative,
uh-huh and *m-hm,* the oral forms being with or without nasalization.

The glottal stop, in the forms in which it is used, appears between the two syllables, but it also may occur initially in the 'admonitory' set, yielding, for example, [ʔaʔa] as well as [aʔa]. For additional abruptness and urgency it may even occur at the end, [ʔaʔaʔ], making the interjection a prolonged glottal stop with an instantaneous double release in the middle.

Though only the two spellings *oh-oh* and *ah-ah* are found for the admonitory set, any vowel sound will do (even [iʔi] would be understood as a warning), but [æ], [ʌ], and [ɔ] are more or less conventionalized along with [o] and [a]. The values of the vowels roughly correspond with those already noted for the one-syllable interjections, so we have

> Oh-oh! We did a boo-boo!
> Ah-ah! You mustn't do thát!

where the first is more sympathetic and sociable (*Aw-aw!* could be used as well) and more apt to be used for *self*-criticism, and the second is a more serious warning. As for [æ], the facial gesture is unimportant—what counts here is the greater tension of the vowel, which is reflected in the urgency of the warning: basically [æʔæ] is the same as [aʔa], but [æʔæ] is a stronger demand for compliance. The intonation is also a factor in urgency, and roughly corresponds to expectations, a rise in pitch meaning a stronger demand. Probably nowhere else are the iconic values of the sound system exploited so fully: both vowel height and pitch height are relevant, and the accompanying gestural display may be just as rich. *Oh-oh*, being the most sociable and relaxed, is predictably less likely to have rising pitch.

The most typical intonation in the admonitory set is that of the terraced level, with either a rise or a fall between the two levels, most often a fall. The prevalence of this "stylized intonation" is not surprising, given the likelihood that 'you should know better' (information is redundant) is involved. So we get a repetition of the levels in

```
Oh          Daddy forgot his brief
   oh-h-h!                      case again!
```

But that is only the main trend; actually any intonation is possible, with the familiar meanings associated with the profiles readily detectable. We find the B + C without terminal rise just described, suggesting 'We'd better do something about this,' opposing the B + C *with* terminal rise,

```
Oh                      he
   ohhh!  What have we
                    re!
```

where the speaker has just discovered a glitch and is wondering what to do about it. We find a terminal fall in

Ah

    ^ah !

—a less severe reminder, where the speaker is more confident of being heeded (the second syllable is unaccented), contrasting minimally with

   a

Ah

   h !

where the fall is preceded by a rise (and the second syllable is accented)—the speaker is still confident but the warning is sharper. We have the AC profile with terminal level where, in addition to the alerting nuance that that intonation so often carries, there is also the possibility of adding more syllables:

     ^ah !
   ah
Ah

And we have the bursting-from-restraint of the CA profile, about as stern a warning as can be conveyed by intonation:

       h
Ah ah^h
    h !

The impression that one gets from these possibilities is that around the periphery of the more or less conventionalized interjectional variants, the speaker is operating almost freehand. It is even possible to compose a little tune and not be regarded as eccentric if it does not go too far:

      ah   ah
   ah   ah   ah!
Ah

(the first and last *ah*'s are slightly prolonged).

The length of the two syllables is also open to variation. Both syllables may be prolonged, or just one, especially the second if at a sustained pitch. The speaker in addition may increase suspense by sustaining the stop interval, so that there is an appreciable hesitation between the syllables. These possibilities of course are not absent from the ordinary segmental sounds—one may for instance increase suspense by sustaining the consonant [f] in *What for!* to augment futility—but with the interjections such prosodic antics are not added to segmental morphemes but are at the primary level, along with the intonation and the choice of vowel. They are the very stuff of which interjections are made.

Turning now to the interjections that replace *no* and *yes*, *hunh-uh*, *hm-m*, *uh-huh*, and *m-hm*, we find again the negativity of the glottal stop, which can be traced even in the word *no* itself: [noʔ] is a common variant of [no] along with the variant spelled *nope* (either stop, [p] or [ʔ], contributes to the definitiveness of the negation), but *yep* would rarely if ever be matched by *[yɛʔ].

It was stated above that the vowel for the 'no' interjection is always [ʌ], but—especially in view of *hm-m*—it would be more accurate to say that the vowel here is "neutral," exactly as in the hesitation sound spelled *uh*. That being the case, it can be conditioned by a yawn, a smile, or any other facial gesture, and skewed toward a different vowel. But such changes do not have the significance that they have for the admonitory interjections. Affirmative *uh-huh* has the same neutral vowel and the same conditionings.

The chief difference between the admonitory and the 'no' interjections is the initial [h] that normally occurs in the latter. The medial glottal stop remains the same. The two are linked, however, in the form *uh-uh* without the [h], which is ambiguous when the second syllable is relatively low in pitch but still tonal, and is also ambiguous on an AC profile. If the second syllable falls to creak, *uh-uh* is almost unambiguously 'no.' There is no problem with a B profile on *uh-uh*—it is clearly admonitory, since the 'no' interjection rarely if ever has the B, unlike the corresponding affirmative *uh-huh* and *m-hm*. The lack of B on the 'no' interjection is found even where *no* itself readily takes a B, as in *No, I don't*: *Hunh-uh, I don't* will have something other than B on the interjection, most likely some form of A or perhaps AC (less likely C). Once again, the restriction does not apply to the affirmative: *Uh-huh, I do*, like *Yes, I do* actually favors B, though any of the profiles is possible.

Aside from that minor restriction on the negative, intonation is free in the 'yes-no' interjections: a C is reassuring, an A is confident and conclusive, an AC and even more a CAC is remonstrative, a terraced C is bored, etc., with the familiar values.

More than with the admonition, there is a curious ambivalence about the location of the accent as cued mainly by length. This can be illustrated, on the 'yes' side, by two instances of B profiles, one with accent on the second syllable (which is lengthened for the purpose), the other with accent on the first (likewise lengthened):

```
      h u h·                    huh.
Uh                       Uh-h-h
```

The first might be the kind of 'yes' that a speaker utters at a pause point in a story, expressing keen interest and urging the narrator to continue; the second is somewhat perfunctory. In both, the unaccented syllable is shortened. On the negative side we can cite the most frequent intonation of *hunh-uh*, an A profile with accent on the first syllable and drop on the second to creak, versus an A profile with accent on the second syllable. The two exactly parallel *No sir!* with these two intonations:

```
Nó                  sí          Húnh                    ú
               No                              Hunh
      sir.              r!            uh.                    h!
```

Predictably the second of these is more emphatic. The corresponding affirmatives with their intonations for *Uh-huh* and *Yes sir* are also found, but whereas the first of the two intonations is the commonest for the negative, it is perhaps the least common for the affirmative—in this respect *Úh-huh* and *Yés sir* part company, for

```
Yés

      sir!
```

is commonplace. *Úh-huh* on the same contour sounds perfunctory.

Since the accents have no distinctive value but are there only for their prosodic effect, it is normal for *both* syllables to be accented for greater emphasis. This is easiest to observe when the result is an A + A contour, either A + Á or A + À:

```
      hu              Hunh
Uh                          h
    h    h!                 u  h
                                 h!
```

(*Yes sir!* and *No sir!* again make a good match.)

To summarize: The second syllable is normally accented except in the forms

```
      huh.            Úh            Húnh
Úh-h-h
               huh.                      uh.
```

Elsewhere the first syllable may or may not be accented.

The affective tie between the 'yes-no' interjections and their intonation in part accounts for the prevalence of the simple rise of the B with *uh-huh* and the simple fall of the A for *hunh-uh*. It is difficult to respond ominously with these interjections. Their informality makes for friendly intercourse, and the rise on *uh-huh* comes across as a kind of cheery encouragement, quite unlike a potentially hostile rise on *yes*. The encouraging rise on *uh-huh* enables it to combine with an A profile on *yes*, in either order, in a blend of conclusiveness and openness:

```
Y        huh.              huh,
    uh              Uh          ye
  es,                              s.
```

Similarly a potentially abrupt *no* can be tempered by adding *hunh-uh*, though both with A profiles. The normal conclusiveness of negation discourages the kind of upbeat intonation that is so common with *uh-huh*. The reverse order, *Hunh-uh, no*, is not apt to be used at all.

Aside from this difference in formality and certain collocational differences (*Yes he did!* is not matched by *?Uh-huh he did!*), *uh-huh* and *hunh-uh* can serve just about anywhere that *yes* and *no* can, including acknowledgment of being addressed:

John! — Yes? = John! — Uh-huh?

In addition there is a usage of *uh-huh* not shared by *yes* though still affirmative, where the speaker appears to be answering his own question: the "doctor's soliloquy" familiar in the comedy routine in which the doctor examines the patient and mutters *Uh-húh!* (A profile) knowingly to himself, without disclosing what remarkable discovery he is presumably affirming.

There are probably many more gestural interjections, not so closely tied to the scheme of discourse but still manifesting the relationships to the vowels already touched upon. One, which almost appears to be a phonetic variant of *Hunh!*—with the same aspiration fore and aft but usually without nasalization (see above, pp. 254 and 265)—is *Hah!*, with the vowel [æ]. It expresses scornful disbelief or rejection:

He thought I was going to help him. Hah! I wouldn't lift a finger.

The syllable is short, level, and mid to mid-high in pitch. We see an obvious kinship with the [æ] interjection noted earlier (pp. 284–85), to which it adds a cachinnating [h]. The [æ] vowel has wide-ranging unfavorable connotations in the English lexicon (see Bolinger 1980–81).

Another isolated case is *Pooh!*, using the labiovelar sound [u] which Wescott (1971) associates with derogation and regards as probably a universal. Protruding the lips is one way of "making a face" at someone. The consonant [p] is of course a way of accomplishing that too.

Finally there are the more uncertain cases that have little force in themselves but add to the weight of the evidence. If we want to stop someone who is literally or figuratively going too fast, a good-humored way of doing so is to say *Whoa, there!* with a prolonged [o]. It is not too farfetched to suppose that the sociable [o] makes this less abrasive than *Stop!* or *Hold on!*

Oaths and imprecations

Oaths and imprecations are a miscellany of incomplete phrases which I shall not attempt to catalog but only sample:

> Well bý Gód! They came through after all!
>
> As I live and breathe! She really likes you! (Perhaps on the model of As God is my witness.)
>
> In X's name! (In God's name!, In the name of God!, In the name of all that's holy!)
>
> Dear me! (Perhaps on the model of Dear God!)

All express astonishment, and all favor the same intonation, B + A (B + À unless extremely keyed up), which justifies lumping them together. The same intonation and the same illocutionary intent are found in things as various as *Well I'll be damned!*, *Well what do you know!*, *Well heavens above!*, plus the *Shiver my timbers!* silly commands noted earlier (p. 261) among other productive patterns.

'Astonishment' easily picks up 'protest':

> In heaven's name! Where did you get that ragtag outfit?
> Well how do you like that! She swore at me!

The *by God* example above is marked with accents to indicate that the *by* is given a full level B profile of its own, which *by* does not ordinarily have but picks up here from the prevailing intonation. The example also serves to illustrate another possibility for some of these exclamations, which is to be tagged to what precedes and have no accent at all. The phrase may be intoned

```
Well
     by God!
```

Similar tags are shown in

> I can't find it! — Why don't you lóok for Christ's sake!
>
> I wish somebody would give me some of that dip! — Help yoursélf, for heaven's sake!

These are like exclamatory vocatives:

I'm scared! — Come ón, you idiot! Nobody's going to bite you!

Lexical interjections

To a considerable degree *oh*, *ah*, etc., have been lexicalized—firmed up phonologically and conventionalized in usage—in spite of their likely gestural origin (and persisting Antaean contact with earth). They meet, at the border, with other forms moving in the opposite direction, "real words" that have taken on the functions of discourse particles. This movement represents a continuum. There is no catalog of such particles (except for the unpublished preliminary draft by Östman, 1981), nor are we likely to have one short of an exhaustive analysis of the entire vocabulary of the language, because the potential for conversion is always there. If *boy* and *man* can be converted to signals of enthusiasm toward what is reported, *sir* to a distancing form of address, *bastard* to a pronoun-like epithet (in view of its potential lack of accent), *Jesus* to a sign of surprise, and *she* and *her* to disparaging reference when used where one expects a personal name or title, one suspects tinges of discourse-particleness everywhere. As Yokoyama insists (1986: 149), *"metinformational knowledge is encoded into every utterance"* (her emphasis). So there is no need to apologize for limiting the treatment here to a very few examples. The most important, because of the attention it has received, is *well*, and it is accorded a separate chapter.

Now is a discourse marker basically for change of topic. In this use it is a favorite of the King James Version of the Bible; for example, six of the ten chapters of Ezra are introduced with *now*. The association with the temporal adverb is obvious: the reader or hearer is bidden to set aside what went before and focus on the writer's or speaker's present concern. At a slight remove from this meaning of topic-shift we have the speaker announcing, in effect, 'I'm calling the turn.' Since he is the one who says *now*, he puts himself in command of the situation, and may, at another slight remove, use *now* as a device for not yielding the floor; with some speakers this becomes a habit. Examples:

Now the feast of unleavened bread drew nigh, which is called the Passover. (Luke 22:1)

Now yóu sée hére! I'm not going to tolerate this any longer!

Now you understand that this money is strictly for a rainy day; now don't go asking for it ahead of time; I'm counting on you, now!

The effect of *now* in opening up a new topic can be seen in the contrast with its absence:

> A couple of days later I would have objected.
> Now a couple of days later I would have objected.

The first of these might easily terminate a conversational exchange. With the second, something more is needed; the speaker perhaps goes on to say *By that time the matter had cleared up enough for me to see that it wasn't my fault.* Its effect in "taking command," even hectoring the hearer, is seen in the contrast between

> What do you mean by that?
> Now what do you mean by that!

—the second is more apt to have a descending line from *what* on, a speaker-centered demand. *Now* becomes a sort of assertive intensifier in a case like

> I'm not going to take that any more!
> Now I'm not going to take that any more!

With the latter, the hearer feels more thoroughly "told off."

The usual prosody of *now* is a curious contrast of everything and nothing. It either has the full force of its own A profile with descent to creak, as in the gym coach's

> Now! Everybody watch as I do this next step!

or it is initial or final with no accent at all, as in all the preceding examples except the last, and as in

> Now watch out!
> Watch out, now!

—both with AC profiles, and with *now*, in the second, occupying the rising tail. The same happens with the stereotype *Bye now!*, but in the stereotypes *Well now!* and *Come now!* it is on a falling tail. When it does occur in an interior position it is at a juncture that could be terminal, as in the falling *now* of

> You don't think Í did it, now, do you?

which is ambivalent between the two clauses—it may end the one or start the other.

The exception is with accents of power, which may strike an initial *now* as they strike almost anything:

> Nów yóu sée hére! I won't stand being insulted, get it?

An isolated exception is the B + C contour of

Now, now!

with which a parent quiets a fretful child.

Now thus differs from lexical interjections like *so* and *well*, which may be accented or unaccented in initial position; and it resembles *why*, which is virtually restricted to initial position, unaccented except for an accent of power.

There is a stereotype, *Now then!*, in which *now* is always initial and accented. Where *now* signifies 'make a fresh start,' *now then* signifies something like 'take a fresh look'—at something that has gone before: the *then* is the 'then' of consequence resulting from some intervening consideration that alters the view of things:

> Now then, what was that about there being no corruption in Grant's administration?

—A has maintained that there was none, B has refuted this and now challenges A to take a fresh look and admit the fact. Or the intervening consideration may be the circumstance of someone's having been asked to wait; contact is then resumed with

> Now then, what was it you wanted?

Why is therefore the most subdued of the lexical interjections. When it is produced as an exclamation it is handled in a very special way: a brief phonation is punctuated by a breathy aspiration in the form of a chest pulse (ballistic movement of the diaphragm)—one might spell it *wuh!*, though varying amounts of the [ai] diphthong are apt to be retained. The mood is one of anxious surprise and perplexity, the same as we find with *well* in its reduced *w'l* form when the latter is given the same brief phonation and breathy articulation. It is sometimes hard to tell whether the exclamation is *w'l* or *wuh*. Between exclamatory *why* and what follows, there is a brief pause as the speaker gropes for words: 'This accusation (inference, claim, etc.) is totally unexpected and totally unjustified; I don't see why I should have to deal with it!'

The rest of the time *why* is initial and unaccented, except that in narrative it sometimes occurs medially, as in the following example from Lakoff (1973*a*: 466):

> Now, as soon as the aardvark discovered the anthill, why, he ran home lippity-lop to get his shovel.

She puts this down to "a rhetorical device, meaning something like 'What follows is so obvious as scarcely to need mentioning, I don't know why I bother with this.'" It is appropriate that in the definition the cognate interrogative *why* appears; it implies surprise at the need to bring something up. This is true of explanations,

> If you want to know, why, just ask!

of cases where the answer goes the question one better ('even' is expressed or implied),

> It's just as good, isn't it? — Why, it's (even) better!

of situations that seem unreasonable to the speaker,

> I can't understand what happened to Eddie! Why, just a moment ago he was standing right here!

> It's too heavy for me. — Why, can't you even lift five pounds?

of superfluous invitations,

> It's Johnny, isn't it? And his two friends? (Pause) Why, come in! Don't just stand there!

of realizations of something that the speaker acknowledges should have been obvious to him,

> Didn't the name "Gowers" come up in the conversation? — (Hesitates and strikes forehead) Why yes, come to think of it! And that means . . . !

of consequences that it seems superfluous to point out,

> When they caught sight of my face, why, they practically fainted!

In this last, *why* is almost synonymous with *just* or *simply*: *they just practically fainted.*

The same meaning holds for the exclamation:

> He said I was a four-flusher! Why (wuh!), I never cheated at cards in my life!

Though *why* interrogative and *why* interjection are cognates, there has been a morphemic split that is distinguishable in the speech of those who aspirate the initial consonant in the words *what, where, which*, etc.: the interjection lacks the initial aspiration, even when, as in the last example, it is exclamatory, and in the rare case of a backshifted emotional accent, e.g. *Why you SOB!* with high pitch on *why* and low on *you SOB.*

Really, indeed, and *honestly* can be treated together because they all allude to the truth of what has been said, and they contrast in interesting ways.

Honestly and *really*, but not *indeed*, appear as comments on what the speaker himself has said; they carry an A profile in which the initial syllable has a high pitch:

```
saw            Hon
I                    es
                       tl
    him!              y!
```

All three words may be given B or C profiles as questions and then they query the truth of what has been said:

> Ali came in first. — Really?

This is perhaps more a surprised comment (like *No kidding!*—see below) than a querying-of-truth, which could be better accomplished with *Truly?* In this same context, *Really!* and *Indeed!*, but not *Honestly!*, may be given A profiles without altering their status as exclamatory questions; they only become more skeptical. In fact, *Indeed!* as a one-word response is a condescending question regardless of intonation. (This does not apply to *Indeed I did, I did indeed*, etc.)

There is a more idiosyncratic intonational divergence where *Honestly!* and *Really!* are used to *introduce* a conversational move. When given a rapid fall on, not after, the accented syllable, i.e.

```
H
  o
   n
    estly!
```

the word signifies disapproval (but not reproof—the speaker accepts the possibility that the hearer or others may not disapprove of the behavior) directed at someone who has said or done something that he should have known better than to say or do:

> Honestly, Marie, do you have to leave your room in such a mess?
>
> I know she thinks Ronald is a jerk. But honestly! Was it nice for her to call him one to his face?

The word is doubtless a reduction of something like *Tell me honestly* (and if you are honest you will agree with me, in the last analysis).

Really! may be used in the same way, but, unlike *Honestly!*, it is ambiguous with this intonation and can serve as a disbelieving or extremely restrained question.

The stereotyping of *Honestly!* shows up formally in two ways. First, it may occur alone (verbally speaking) and be understood as an expression of disapproval. This would not be true, for example, of *Sincerely!* Second, the disapproval is generally reinforced with a head-shake. With a nod, *sincerely* may replace *honestly* in the multi-word examples (e.g. *Sincerely, Marie, do you have to leave your room in such a mess?*), but then both *sincerely* and *honestly* (with a nod) are more "open" to an answer from the hearer. There is also in this case less need for downmotion directly on the accented syllable.

As was illustrated in the first example above, an *Honestly!* with this same A profile—and without downmotion on the accented syllable— is used by the speaker to comment on his own sincerity:

> Yes, Jane likes you! Honestly! I wouldn't fool you about a thing like that, would I?

But unlike *really* (*sincerely* is out of the question because in this context it would modify *likes you*, not the performative *I am speaking*), *honestly* is often used when the speaker is pulling the hearer's leg, and then is apt to be said with a twinkle. Fans of the BBC television comedy "No, Honestly!" will remember how well the word fitted the sort of banter for which that program was noted.

As was mentioned above, *indeed* when used alone is a question regardless of intonation.[7] With the A profiles just described, *honestly* used alone is not likely as a question—it needs a heavy overlay of interrogative gesture to be one. *Really*, however, is ambiguous:

> It took me only an hour. — *Honestly? (OK with Profile B)
> It took me only an hour. — Really? (OK with A or B) — Yes.
> It took me only an hour. Honestly! (Really!) (Both A)

Expostulations

Expostulations play variations on the theme of surprise, usually with other attitudes attached: anger, pain, condemnation, disgust, excitement, embarrassment, pleasure, triumph. More or less pure surprise or astonishment is expressed by *Jesus* and its minced forms *gee, gee whiz, gee whillikers*, and numerous other—usually minced— oaths like *mercy, my, heavens, goodness*, archaisms like *zounds, ods bodkins*, etc. *Oops* is surprised acknowledgment of a mistake, *wow* is surprised admiration, *crap* is surprised disgust, *hooray* is surprised triumph, *ouch* is surprised pain, *goody* is surprised pleasure, and so on.

Although there is some room for intonational maneuver, mostly these expressions use contours ending in A in accord with the illocutionary intent. Occasionally a terminal B is found, as may happen with *damn it* or *Jesus Christ* when the speaker intends to go on, e.g.

```
        it!
Damn        Why did I let them talk me into
                                       this!
```

A B is practically guaranteed with *oops*. For obvious reasons there is little likelihood of a C profile.

Illocutionary stereotypes

Illocutionary stereotypes are phrase-length exclamations expressing some attitude toward the situation or its participants, to which intonation typically makes a heavy contribution. A sampling was given
in Bolinger 1986 (Chap. 1), including

(1) Beats me! ('I don't know')

(2) Big deal! ('That is of no importance')

(3) Ho-hum! ('I'm bored with this')

(4) No kidding! ('I'm surprised but willing to believe')

(5) Who wants to know! ('It's none of your business')

(6) Oh, I don't know! ('I'm courteously skeptical about that'; see
above, pp. 277–78, for others with *oh*)

(7) Tell you what! ('I'm about to bring up something I've just thought
of to solve this problem')

(8) I say! ('I respectfully call for your attention')

(9) I'll just bet! ('I don't believe that')

Each of these has a fairly typical contour, in some cases even restricted
as to how the contour is realized. For example, (9) is B + C + A, with
each accent lower than the preceding one; (1) is B + AC, usually but
not necessarily with the second accent higher; (6) is A + B with *oh* and
know carrying the two accents and the tail of the A (*I don't*) quite low.

Others are less tightly constrained in their prosody. A good source
is Wierzbicka (1986), which contains the following:

(10) How dare you!

(11) Go jump in the lake! (similarly Go sit on a tack! Go chase
yourself!)

(12) You x (fool, swine, angel)!

(13) Why can't you (he etc.) understand and be generous!

(14) Why can't you (they etc.) leave me alone!

(15) Leave me alone why can't you!

(16) How many times have I told you (not) to do x!

(17) Why don't you do x!

(18) You know!

(19) Don't tell me x!

All but (18) and (19) would favor a B + À contour with downtilting
B tail, or an A + À, but only with (11) is B + À practically guaranteed.
(With a slight variation, e.g. *I wísh you'd go jump in the láke!* or *Whý*

don't you just go jump in the láke! an A + B would show more exasperation.) With (10) a higher A on *dare* would produce a livelier challenge,
and the same increased liveliness applies to (12) but especially to *You
angel!*, to enhance the positive emotion (a negative one such as *You
fool!* would favor B + À to downplay the insult; B + Á would be exasperated). As for (13)—which really is *Why can't you x* with a wide
range of values for *x*—the choice between B + À and B + Á may hinge
on how much optimism the speaker feels about the hearer's willingness to change his ways. Wierzbicka's (13) and (14) happen, by their
wording, to suggest opposite ends on this scale: (13) is more hopeful,
and if given B + Á it could readily be followed by *Don't you see how
much better that would be? It's not too late! Try it!* But (14) is associated
with repeated pesterings and tends to be little more than a complaint;
if given B + Á rather than B + À, it may be a question (albeit a complaining one) calling for an explanation, as much as a complaint. The
same comment applies to (15), despite Wierzbicka's claim that its
imperative "constitutes an attempt to influence the addressee." That is
a fair statement as applied to (15) with B + Á,

```
            lone
Leave me a
            why can't you!
```

but with B + À,

```
Leave me al
             o
              n
               e
           why can't you!
```

the speaker may have given up hope of influencing anybody, and the
tag expresses his powerlessness—it is more querulous than exigent.
This is not to say that gestural and other concomitants might not
make the latter a genuine plea again, but the falling intonation would
then answer to another purpose than discouragement—the request
is more placating, less keyed up. In one respect, of course, (15) is
unique among the examples in this set in having a low-pitched tag.

As for (16) and (17), the intonation is as free as with any wh question—anything goes. Wierzbicka gives (18) in a fuller form, *Do you
know!*, which is less likely in American English; writers capture the
usual pronunciation with the spelling *Y' know!*, for example,

Y' know, I think he really believes us!

Intonationally (18) is probably B at all times. (*Yóu know*, with AC or
A + C—the two are hard to tell apart—is not a question and has an
entirely different illocutionary force.) There is another expression
closely allied to (18), *Know what?*, as in

Know whát? He really believes us!

also with a B profile, though it might receive a high-pitched C:

Know
     wha^t?

The two differ mainly in that *Know what?* does not expect a comment
from the addressee. (Unless the speaker stops and gives the hearer an
opening for a sarcastic *No, what?*—A + À.) Thus *Y' know, I think he
really believes us!* expects some such response as *Yes, I guess you're
right.* This would be optional after *Know what? He really believes us!*
    The intonation of (19), as in

Don't tell me you two have had another fight!

can be almost anything (though B + A with rising B tail is least likely).

11. 'Well'

The prosody of *well* cannot be studied separately from its syntax, semantics, and usage. *Well* deserves, and has received, more discussion than any of the other interjections, though aside from an occasional acknowledgment that intonation plays a role, few details have been offered.

Interest in *well* rides on the surge of interest in discourse analysis and pragmatics (see Marek 1987, for example), and most of the serious work on it is concerned with such things as turn-taking, game plans, and conversational coherence. Little attention has been paid to what a linguist—as distinguished from a sociolinguist—would regard as the paramount issue: what is the meaning of the word, how does the meaning affect the usage, and how does the usage reveal the meaning? Answers to this compound question involve the prosody as well as the syntax: one of the functions of an accent on a word is to *assert* the meaning of the word, and if *well* is accented we would like to know what is being asserted. Following are some more particular questions that come to mind:

1. Does *well* have a meaning of its own, or is it only a sort of conversational wild card, taking its meaning entirely from the context?

2. If it has a meaning of its own, does that meaning relate to other uses of *well*?

3. Is *well* integral as an interjection, or must we recognize *well*$_1$, *well*$_2$, and perhaps *well*$_n$?

4. To what extent is *well* a free agent? Are there distributional restrictions—collocations, idioms, and the like—and if so, is there a core of meaning preserved in them?

5. Are *well* and the reduced form *w'l* the "same word," or have they diverged in the manner of *an* and *one* or *s'm* and *some*?

Question 1 was raised and answered in the negative in the most recent study of the role of *well* in conversation, Schiffrin (1985), who states (p. 642) that "*well* has no inherent semantic or structural properties . . . its meaning is based solely on its context of occurrence," and later adds (p. 664) that *well* may "occupy turns at talk without encoding any semantic content." Oddly, the latter remark stands directly before the final subtitle of the study, "Why *well*?," a question posed but not answered—I would say unanswerable if, on any properly linguistic as distinguished from truth-functional definition of semantics, one is to discover why *well* is used and not something else. This point is emphasized by Carlson (1984), whose treatment of *well* is closest to the one offered here.[1] Schiffrin's empty *well* is reminiscent of the "transformationally introduced particle" that plagued the treatment of a number of the little words at one stage of transformational-generative grammar.

If we are to place *well* and other words of its class in relation to any sort of field or prototype theory, we must inquire how it relates to other uses of *well*. We may indeed find that the interjection is rarefied to the point where no easy paraphrase comes to mind, but that does not signify a void. The rarefied particle may be only the extreme of a gradient at the other end of which are similar "conversational particles" whose surviving content is obvious: *Wait a minute!* for checking an unwarranted move, *Téll me* (A profile) for opening a ploy that one expects to be decisive, and so on. To resume a conversation that has got off to a flagging start one may say

Well how have you been?
So how have you been?

There is no real 'consequence' in the *so*, but that does not mean that the speaker is not pretending it in a vague and general sense—compare P. Brown and Levinson's (1978) "fake prior agreement." The same goes for *well*. We can never know for certain when, if ever, pretending ceases and the word in question becomes a mere traffic sign. But we cannot know that unless we trace the line of development. To understand *well* as an interjection—including its prosody—we must understand *well* as a word.[2] Schiffrin I think puts the cart before the horse when she says, "It is difficult to imagine an analysis of *well* that does not begin by accounting for its contextual distribution in a corpus of conversation" (p. 642). Studying distribution is a good procedure for discovering meaning, provided something is already known about the meanings of the items distributed; but *accounting for* the distribution of meaningful items presupposes some theory of what the items mean.

Nor is it obvious why even a distributional approach should have as its starting point a corpus of conversation. The range of a corpus is limited to its subject matter. Interjections are particularly sensitive to this if the corpus is polite conversation, since in their full vigor they are apt to be more at home in exchanges that border on the rude. Schiffrin's corpus is unlikely to contain many examples such as the following:

> Well really, Brad, I never expected to find you in the arms of another woman!
>
> Well, which one of you dummies got the bright idea of blocking my driveway?
>
> Well, here goes nothing. (beginning skier about to take off)
>
> Well I never expected it, but it's happened! Donovan's been indicted!
>
> Well look who's here!

These come out of the blue, with little or no obvious relation to prior conversation.

They do relate, however, to "face redress" in the terms discussed by Brown and Levinson, who give full credit to the core meanings of the expressions they cite in accounting for the ways in which they are used to make social interaction possible. Though *well* is not specifically treated (except for a casual reference, p. 172, to Lakoff 1973*a*), it fits their description of "extended usage" as the key both to the politeness function and to eventual changes of form as well as meaning (pp. 264–65).

A reasonable hypothesis is that of Hines (1978 and 1980): *well* is *well*—the interjection is part of a single semantic paradigm, however far-flung and diffuse, or, in local areas, however clumped and formulaic, it may be. And since some parts of the paradigm are easily open to paraphrase, we may start with those.

But first a stab at characterizing the whole field. I would say that *well* represents, in all its uses, some plus on some scale of strength or value. As Hines (1980: 170) puts it, "*Well* apparently has two different senses, one a value or quality sense and the other an amount or quantity." 'Plus value' is the more obvious connotation, given instances like *well-behaved, perform well, feel well*. But 'plus strong,' or intensification, cannot be overlooked: *well-planned* may refer to design, but *well-studied* refers to thoroughness as well as care. Psychologically the two strands seem to be deeply intertwined. We put a high value on strength: *a goodly number, good and hot, for good* ('permanently'), the cognate relation of *value-valor, a man of virtue* and *by virtue of*, etc. Though *well* most often lies on the side of plus-value, plus-strong may occur in a more or less pure state, e.g.

> We couldn't stop them till they were well inside the danger zone.

The predominance of the 'value' sense can be tested by the way *well* collocates as a premodifier of verbs. *Well* is sensitive to linear modification, a phenomenon that can be observed in other more obvious cases:

> The surgeon skillfully applied the scalpel.
> ?The surgeon clumsily applied the scalpel.
> The surgeon applied the scalpel clumsily.
> The surgeon clumsily dropped the scalpel.
> ?The surgeon skillfully dropped the scalpel.

Applying is expected to be skillful, dropping to be clumsy, in this context. Similarly:

> He amicably shook my hand.
> ?He belligerently shook my hand.
> He shook my hand belligerently.

The sense of the premodifier is more apt to be *included in*, and is at least highly consonant with, the sense of the verb; the postmodifier is additive. So with *well* we get

> He well outdid (outmatched, outplayed, outranked) his rivals.
> *He well defeated his rivals.
> It well surpassed the goal.
> ?It well exceeded the goal.
> *It well overshot the target.

Outdo and *surpass* embody favorable judgments of prowess, and they are scalar where strength is concerned, which *defeat* is not; on the other hand, *exceed* is scalar but is not favorable. Similarly:

> It well increases our chances.
> ?It well reduces our chances.
> It well reduces the risk.
> ?It well increases the risk.

Reducing risk is favorable, and that outweighs the minus-strong of *reduce* (which, besides, can be conceptualized as 'powerful reduction'). In a case like

> It well improves our chances.
> *It well betters our chances.
> It well reveals my mood.
> *It well shows my mood.

there are two possible factors. The first is semantic: *improve* and *reveal* are scalar in a sense that *better* and *show* are not. Compare *We gradually improved the condition of our serfs* with ?*We gradually bettered the con-*

dition of our serfs. Better and *show* are more point-action than *improve* and *reveal*. The second factor is phonological: in *It well betters our chances* and *It well shows my mood* there are successive accented syllables (see pp. 224 and 422 for the "rhythm rule"). This may also account for why

> *It well lowers our chances.

is even worse than ?*It well reduces our chances.* As for

> It well portrays my mood.
> *It well betrays my mood.

we have again the plus-value of *portray* and again the more strongly scalar nature of a portrayal. The possible factor of phonology is again present in

> I well understand your objections.
> *I well grasp your objections.

But *grasp*, in addition, is more point-action. Though it is a little awkward to say ?*He gradually understood what I was driving at*, it is at least better to say *He gradually came to understand what I was driving at* than to say ?*He gradually came to grasp what I was driving at*. Further, *understand* is higher in plus-value than is *grasp*, as can be quickly seen in the adjective uses of the participles: *an understanding person* versus *a grasping person*.[3] Past participles[4] similarly. Thus *rid of* is a desirable condition, *deprived of* is not:

> We are well rid of his attentions.
> *We are well deprived of his attentions.

Both plus-value and plus-strength are present in

> She is well out of that relationship.

— *'happily'* and *'thoroughly.'*
    Well is also sensitive to some adjectives. In general this seems to be the case even when the adjective forms part of a compound preposition, as in

> ?It came to a figure well short of what we had expected.
> It came to a figure well under what we had expected.
> ?They pulled well clear of the reefs.
> They pulled well away from the reefs.

Under and *away from* are more scalar than *short of* and *clear of*, as can be seen by attaching a completive modifier: *quite short of, quite clear of*; *quite under, *quite away from*. And in the following,

?Our product is well superior to all the competition.
*Their product is well inferior to the competition.

even though the first is doubtful (a kind of double comparative), it is better than the second.

For some reason, perhaps because of the additional graduating effect of the extra modification, examples such as *He well defeated his rivals and *Our product is well superior to the competition become fully acceptable in the form

> He well and thoroughly defeated his rivals.
> It is well and clearly superior to the competition.

Our general characterization of *well* also covers *well* in compounds and formulas—not exactly a promising source for clues to *well* as an interjection, but evidence nevertheless of the cohesiveness of the paradigm: *farewell, welfare, well off, well to do, welcome, well-behaved* (and other deponents: *well-spoken, well-read), well-meaning, well-intended, well-being, to mean well. Well* resists the comparison in these cases: speakers generally prefer *most well-conceived plan* and *most well-designed figure* to *best-conceived plan, best-designed figure*.

We now turn to cases that give us a more direct clue to the relationship of *well* interjection to the paradigm as a whole.

The first clue is from the most obvious use of *well*, referring to health. *Well* contrasts with *good*:

> I'm feeling well now. (restored to normal health)
> I'm feeling good now. (after a rubdown)
> If I'm well, why don't I féel well?
> If I'm well, why don't I féel good?

The next-to-last example states a paradox, whereas in the last example the *state* of one's internal feelings is supposed to be inferred from the *norm* of one's health. The contrast is a subject for comedy in

> ?I beat him up wéll.
> I beat him up góod.

It is hard to imagine an objective standard for the right degree of rough and tumble; *good* expresses immanent satisfaction.

The second clue comes from the interjection itself as an independent utterance. It is so to speak undiluted. There is no conversation, and the speaker is not necessarily intending to initiate one, only to comment on a potential addressee's behavior (*potential* because the speaker may be speaking to himself or addressing a third party whose behavior is not at issue). Say you come across an acquaintance involved in an intimate scene with a lover, and before backing out and shutting the door you say simply *Well!*, with an A profile on a long and breathy upglide-downglide. The element of surprise is obvious, largely conveyed by the prosody; but *Goodness!* or *Excuse mé!* could convey the same surprise and yet lack the nuance of 'disapproval' that *well* imparts. The speaker has invoked a NORM; the culprits have violated it.[5] At the same time they are not in a position to retort *What business is it of yours?* since the authority is impersonal and they are not being directly challenged. *Well!* in this context is no more accusatory than *Of all things!*, which would mean much the same, and also appeals to a generality "out there." (If the speaker does not CONFRONT, he may be said to ACCEPT, and "acceptance" figures in theories about *well*, as we shall see shortly.)

Well to comment on misbehavior is prone to be repeated. Someone bumping into you and not apologizing merits a *Well, well!* or even a *Well, well, well!* (Though the reproof is not overt and is hard to answer, the target is not entirely without recourse: a bit of faded slang once served the purpose: *How many wells make a river?*) *Well* thus used also tends to be conspiratorial—this follows from its indirectness: if other persons are present, the speaker may embrace them as his audience along with, or instead of, the offender: 'We all know this simply isn't done.' The usual intonational sequence when *well* is repeated is . . . A + A or . . . B + A, with either peak higher.

A third clue comes from further predicative uses of *well*, not this time related to health but roughly in the sense '(It is) fitting.' These are among the best evidence for *well* as 'norm' underlying the interjection:

> It would be well for you to consider this from every angle. (Cf. Well, you'd better consider this from every angle.)
>
> He considered it from every angle and well it was that he did.

The same contrast with *good* is noted as was found in the case of health. *Good* is immanent, *well* is transcendent:

> It would be good to see him.
> It would be well to see him.

While *good* might be used for advice, it includes such things as 'pleasant' and 'satisfying'—immanent sensations. *Well* is advice only; it appeals to the norm—there are requirements "out there" that impose an obligation. The contrast is akin to that between the root and the epistemic senses of the modals, e.g. *need*:

> You don't need to eat that.
> You needn't eat that.

The first may refer to the immanent need for nourishment, the second refers only to the transcendent obligation, imposed by me, by society, or whatever.

Another predicative use occurs in the somewhat formulaic

It's just as well.

Here the speaker takes the longer view: 'Had we looked "out there" in the first place, this is what we might have chosen.'

The same epistemic-transcendent *well* appears in *do well*, commonly modified by an infinitive phrase:

You'll do well to understand that things can't always go your way.
They did well to leave when they did.

Be well advised to is synonymous. The night watchman's ancient cry, once again predicative,

Two o'clock and all's well!

invokes public order—'norm' in the strictest sense.

If this assessment of an epistemic-transcendent *well* is correct, then the two *well*s in

Oh well, I guess we might as well.

are the same, the one contextually implying resignation in face of an unkind norm, the other conformity to it.

The best syntactic evidence that *well* has epistemic ties comes from its use with modals, particularly *may* and *could*. The root meaning of *could* is present in the following, part of a discussion of vacation plans:

We cóuld go to Hawaii. How would you like that? — Super!

But *well* almost forces the epistemic meaning 'It could be that we will go to Hawaii':

We cóuld well go to Hawaii. But who knows?

Similarly *may* and the distinction between 'permission' and epistemic 'possibility':

May I catch the ball? — Yes, you may catch it.
If you throw the ball, will I catch it? — Yes, you may well catch it.

Similarly with *might*, though this is a bit less clear:

We might do that, but I'm not sure just yet what we'll decide.

We might well do that, but of course I can't really say because the decision is not entirely in our hands.

The same epistemic is present with *know*:

You well know that my responsibility stops short of that!

'You can't pretend not to because the objective standard says that you do.' And the range of *know* is expanded to include 'belief' if *can* is added:

> I can well believe (understand, appreciate) those allegations.
> I can well imagine that she would do just that.
> I can well conceive of such a thing happening.

Similarly with epistemic verbs such as *happen*:

> It can well happen (turn out, eventuate, develop, result) that . . .

All these are in the semantic sphere of possibility and credibility. The same concept figures in expressions of obligation, as was noted above: *You would be well advised to.* But in some cases obligation requires the assistance of an intensifier such as *damn* or a minced substitute. Thus we don't say, in response to *He's been thinking of apologizing,*

> *He well better!

but we do say

> He damn well better (ought to, should)!
> He's damn well got (obliged, expected) to.
> He's damn well under obligation to.

   At the periphery of the epistemic arm of the *well* paradigm are emphatic expressions of truth and falsity. Even with *damn*, *well* is unusual in original statements of fact:

> ?They damn well came down with typhoid.

But in reaffirmations of fact, *damn well* is commonplace:

> Did they come down with typhoid? — They damn well did!

Emphatic predictions similarly:

> We'll damn well blast you off the map!

The complex half-formulaic nature of these expressions can be seen in the association of *damn* with *right* and the prosodic interplay. For example, to answer *Did he?* we may say

> You're damn ríght he did!

but not

> *You're ríght he did!

although with a disjuncture the latter is normal:

> You're right. He did.

Another intensifier, *full*, also displays quasi-formulaic restrictions:

> You know full (damn) well that they will reject all this.
> You damn (*full) well know that they will reject all this.

A remaining predicative use of *well* is formulaic but still manifestly connected to the interjection:

> That's all well and good, but consider this . . .
> That's all very well, but consider this . . .
> Very well, but consider this . . .
> Well, OK, but consider this . . .

All well and good and *all very well* fit nicely with the summary of the discourse uses of *well* in Svartvik (1980) under the rubric of "topic shift," but with the special nuance noted—for the interjection—by Lakoff (1973a: 464): "The generalization seems to be that *well* is used in case of an insufficiency in response, either by the respondent himself or by someone else." For example,

> Why didn't you rake the yard? — Well, I mowed it. I didn't have
> time to do any more.

All well and good and *all very well* explicitly attribute the insufficiency to the "someone else." The speaker dismisses what has gone before with a minimum of approval, hinting at irrelevance as well as insufficiency, before going on to the heart of the matter. The same reluctant acquiescence—as much approval as the norm requires but no more—is found in the affirming use of *very well*:

> May I turn in my paper late? — Very well, but it must be done before April 6.

The association of *well* with 'sufficiency (but not much more)' is seen also in the expression *leave well enough alone*.

The next clue is *as well* in the sense of 'also.' As Hines (1980) points out, the additive meaning of *as well* is based on a comparison: *John as well as Jane* signifies 'John to the same extent as Jane' with 'Jane' already valued 'positive.' (This makes it different from *as much as*: *John believes it as much as Jane* does not put a plus sign on 'Jane'—perhaps Jane does not believe it at all.) The comparison implies a common basis by which the new information is "normed." *I shall work and study as well* takes 'work' as given; it is not apt to be said in response to *What are your plans for the summer?* but is a natural response to *Is work all you're going to do next summer?*

The contrast that interests us is between *as well* and *too*. *As well* is more 'in the nature of things,' a sort of epistemic. So there is a shade of contrast between

> Mary hoped to go too.
> Mary hoped to go as well.

which becomes clearer in

> Oh, Daddy, can I go too?
> ?Oh, Daddy, can I go as well?

—*too* more readily embraces the unexpected.[6]

We come now to the interjection itself, and look first at instances that embody a minimum of verbal context, in case the nonverbal situation may give a clearer picture of the meaning.

First are exclamations of surprise. These, like the independent *well* noted earlier to express disapproval, come out of the blue—there is no prior conversation. The speaker reacts to the violation of normal expectations. Though the *well* is initial, it is usually elaborated upon, and some of the elaborations are virtual idioms that cannot do without *well*, for example, certain of the "stop short" or "pull up" sentences, as Jespersen (1928: §2.3₄) calls them:

> *I never! (starred in the relevant sense)
> Well I never!
> ?I'll be!
> Well I'll be![7]

Did you ever? crosscuts intonation in a peculiar way, in that without *well* even on a B profile it can be an exclamation of surprise, whereas with *well*,

$$\text{Well did you } ev^{er?}$$

it is almost certainly an ordinary question tying in with previous conversation (e.g., 'Did you ever go there?'). This is not true of a non-pull-up question such as *Well can you believe it?* With a B + À contour, however,

$$\text{Well } \quad \overset{\text{did you}}{} \quad ev \quad {}^{e}r?$$

either the question or the exclamation interpretation is possible.

Here also belong those hyperbolic expressions of surprise that often incorporate outlandish comparisons and tend to use a B + À contour. Many of them are formulaic and virtually require *well* as part of the formula:

> Well as I live and breathe!
> Well shiver my timbers!
> Well glory be!
> Well of all things!
> Well hallelujah!
> Well what do you know!

Inventive speakers create fanciful comparisons, Country Western style (see p. 261):

> Well dress my carcass and put me in the deep-freeze!

Others are not for generalized exclamation but are used for special purposes, e.g. surprise on encountering a friend after a long absence:

> Well look who's here!
> Well if it isn't my old pal Bill Longworth!

Well in expressions of surprise can be glossed as 'In view of the normal state of affairs, this bowls me over.'

Next are responses to being addressed, and *well* comes as a question. Though potentially a complete utterance in itself, now there is a link with prior communication. It may be wordless. If you lead me to a distant spot and then stand there saying nothing, I may prompt you with a simple *Well?* to remind you that the norm of proper behavior demands an explanation. If vocalized, the prior move is apt to be a vocative, generally a name or title, as in

> Hey, you! — Well?
> Your majesty! — Well?
> Henry! — Well?

The intonation is nearly always rising, though a fall is possible with a heavy overlay of interrogative gesture.

To capture the meaning of *well* here, it can be compared with other acknowledging responses such as *Yes?, Huh?, What?, What is it?, What do you want?, You wanted something?, How can I help you?*, or, again, a name or title—this latter making it possible for the same class of items to serve on both sides of the exchange:

> Madam! — Sir?
> Louise! — Betty?

By comparison with the other responses—except perhaps for those containing *what*—*well* is the most demanding. If repeated, *Well, well?* (B + B), it will not brook a failure to respond; it shows the same impatience as repeated *Yes, yes?*, but its stronger insistence stems from its appeal to the norm, to the hearer's *duty* to respond—an unadorned *Well?* addressed by a waiter to a patron in a restaurant would be insulting. The names and titles are pure acknowledgment, *yes* shows the speaker open to the development of the addresser's message, but *well* invokes the order of things.

Finally, before proceeding to *well* embedded in conversation, we step back to a *well* that has no verbalized preliminaries but nevertheless reaches out to something that has gone before. Imagine a teacher stepping into a classroom, or a tour guide assembling his flock, and saying

> Well, what shall we do today?

Here there is continuity with a norm of activity controlled by the leader. It would be odd to put the question without *well*, because "the speaker is not really beginning from the beginning but already responding to his audience or to his own implicit deliberations" (Carlson 1984: 53). It would be just as odd for a member of the group to put a similar question *with* the word *well*:

> ?Well, what are we going to do today?

The member does not control the application of the norm, and to use this last example might suggest a rude assumption of power: 'You owe it to us to get this show going according to the rules.' Without *well* there is no discourtesy.

Or take a receptionist who greets a party in an anteroom with

> How can I help you?

This is or pretends to be spontaneous, an offer from the heart. But if the same receptionist asks

> Well, how can I help you?

we sense something like 'How can I help you, given the need to tie this in somehow with the business of this office?' It is an action in accord with a protocol.

The "reaching back" effect of *well* can be tested by association with the particle *now*, which signifies a break with the immediate past, as in

> Now if *I* were to do it . . . (breaks away from discussion of how others have done it)

Now what does all this signify? (jumps from preliminary discussion to interpretation)

It might seem that *well now* would be contradictory, but it is not, if *well* reaches back to something that was on the boards some time previously. There is a break with the immediate past but not with the more remote past. Thus one may revert to an earlier conversation by saying

Well, now, where were we?

Or say you have been inspecting boys' shop but stop to chat with a supervisor; then you turn back to your task and say

Well now, how's this lad coming with his magazine rack?

We come now to *well*s embedded in conversation or monolog. These are more difficult to deal with because with interchanges between two or more people the complexities increase—so much more goes on at once.

The "discourse" approach to *well* is exemplified by Lakoff (1973a), Svartvik (1980), Carlson (1984), and Schiffrin (1985). Each of these investigators offers a generalization, which we can examine in turn.

Lakoff's view, as stated above, is that "the generalization seems to be that *well* is used in case of an insufficiency in response, either by the respondent himself or by someone else" (p. 464). Though I believe that this does not quite get to the heart of the matter, there is little doubt that the description fits the majority of instances in which *well* appears in conversation, as in her example 7:

Did you kill your wife? — Well, yes.

This would be said "to imply that there were extenuating circumstances . . .—*yes* is not to be taken as a complete reply giving all the information necessary" (p. 459).

Lakoff's example raises a point that deserves a brief digression, for it affects our later discussion (pp. 325–26). "Sufficiency in response" might seem to be handily met with a simple *yes* or *no*, which are clearly more sufficient than *maybe*, and in fact Schiffrin states unequivocally (p. 646), "When yes-no questions are answered minimally with either *yes* or *no*, the answers are never prefaced by *well*," a claim that is contradicted by the Lakoff example just cited. Even Lakoff falls into the trap of assuming that *Well, no* in that example is not possible unless the speaker felt he was supposed to commit the murder. An exchange like the following is normal enough:

Did you kill your wife? — Well, no. At least I didn't mean to—we were struggling and she fell.

It appears that *yes* and *no* are not the categorically sufficient answers that they are represented to be. Compare also

> Did Yolanda turn those government documents over to the foreign agents? — No, it didn't happen that way. She turned over the papers to them, yes, but she didn't know they were government documents.

But there is another style of affirming and denying that puts "sufficiency" to a more severe test. A really unlikely response in the last example would be

> *She did not; it didn't happen that way. She turned . . .

Using the auxiliary is more categorical, and consequently something like

> Did you kill your wife? — Well, I did (I did not).

involves a more complex set of assumptions—the respondent perhaps feels that he is not being questioned but accused, and answers defiantly: 'Under the circumstances (given the norm) what I did was justified.' Or if the intonation is incredulous, e.g.

```
        you  kill
Did            your
                 wife?
```

where *wife* is non-low and level ('Did you actually kill your wife?'), then *Well, I did* says in effect, 'The burden of the evidence (the norm) is upon me, and I must confess.' In both cases the discourse effect of the response fits Lakoff's principle, because it disappoints the question.

The difficulty of getting examples that are absolutely unacceptable is the best evidence that *well* means something. When that meaning is applied, everything else readjusts itself to cause the meaning to make sense in that setting. And it usually does, often assisted by a change in the prosody.

Carlson summarizes his position thus (p. 94): "*Well* marks acceptance of a dialogue situation, but with a qualification: either the situation is below optimal but has to be accepted anyway, or the game is going to take an important but unobvious turn." The core meaning he adopts is simply the *OED* definition of the interjection, the main part of which is "the speaker accepts a situation." He regards the connection between the meaning of the interjection and the broader meaning of *well* as "etymologically transparent," and points out that "in many languages, 'accept' etymologically equals 'find good'" (p. 27). His "accept a situation" is therefore close to my "invoke a norm."[8]

Schiffrin says much the same, though in more abstract terms: "*Well* anchors a speaker in a system of conversational exchange where the options which a prior referent has opened for upcoming coherence are not fully met" (p. 640), or, in other words, "*Well* shows the speaker's aliveness to the need to accomplish coherence, despite a temporary inability to contribute to the satisfaction of that need in a way fully consonant with the prior discourse" (p. 662). Her example 12 reads

> What does your daughter-in-law call you? — Well that's a sore spot. My older daughter-in-law does call me Mom. My younger daughter-in-law right now is . . .

Schiffrin's focus on her corpus causes her to overlook some of Lakoff's evidence, e.g. the type

> Well, why isn't the garbage out?

in which there is no prior conversation to elicit any response. Here Lakoff extends her principle of insufficiency by allowing it to refer to ACTION as well as utterance (p. 463). Conversationally, that example comes out of the blue. *Well* clearly has its epistemic value. The garbage was *supposed* to be out.

Svartvik summarizes his principle thus (p. 177):

> The common denominator in the uses of *well* in the [London-Lund] corpus seems to be that of shifting topic focus in discourse. It signals that the speaker is going to shift ground, i.e. that he is going to modify one or more assumptions or expectations which have formed the basis of discourse so far. *Well* signals a modification or partial change in the discourse, i.e. it introduces a part of the discourse that has something in common with what went before but also differs from it to some degree.

Wierzbicka (1976: 360) offers the following "rather complex semantic representation":

> "I don't want more time to pass like this
> this is well . . .
> something else has to be said"

The points of contact here with the other analyses are obvious: "I don't want more time to pass like this" = "differing from what goes before"; "this is well" = "acceptance"; "something else has to be said" = "qualified (acceptance)." "Not fully meeting the options of upcoming coherence" and "insufficiency in response" are in the same general area.

All these notions have something in common. They show that *well* is *used* as an agent for smoothing the seams and contradictions in discourse. How does *well* do it? Is this statement of conversational function the only meaning that *well* has, if we take Schiffrin's view, or is *well* used for the purpose because it has a meaning that is appropriately invoked under the circumstances? One way of defining the discourse "particle" *I'll bite* is 'Go ahead and give me the answer.' Another way is simply 'I'll bite,' which opens vistas of other poor fish hooked by trickery, in this case a trick question. If *well* interjection is the "same word" as the other *well*s, it is better to start not with the full orchestra of conversation but with the solo performances where the meaning is more starkly revealed. This approach has brought us to the notion of 'norm,' or, to word it differently, 'conformity,' 'giving due consideration to what it is appropriate to consider,' 'looking to the order of things,' 'There's more here than meets the eye.' Also 'circumspection' and a certain amount of 'deliberation,' since drawing a comparison between present circumstances and the way things naturally are, have been, or ought to be calls for thinking back. The discourse particles with the closest equivalence to *well* are probably *so* and *after all*, the one expressing a consequence and the other a succession.[3] What has gone before is apt to be the established norm, and much of the time either that or the transcendent norm—epistemic *well*—can be appealed to in the same circumstances, even, in the case of *well* and *after all*, combined:

> Why should you enjoy all the benefits of it? — Well (so, after all), who paid for it?

And all three, plus *really* ('reality' is surely akin to 'norm'), are freely used unmodified to express shocked surprise when someone violates the code (see above, pp. 305–6). It is significant that discourse particles invoking what has gone before are so plentiful: *after all, when all's said and done, all things considered, all in all, in the last analysis, when you get right down to it, knowing what we know*.

It is not just the tie with past *conversation* that counts, but the tie with the *past*, as we have already seen with a number of examples. Then, as far as conversation is concerned, *well* comes out of the blue. Suppose a clock fancier is sitting in the clock room and the ticking stops. He may say, with A profile on *well*,

> Well, the clocks have stopped. I wonder what's wrong.

The natural order of things is for the clocks to be ticking. On the other hand, if the clocks are electric and the neighborhood has experienced a number of break-ins leading to the fear that a stopped clock might

indicate someone tampering with the circuits, it would be pretty unusual to put a *well* before

> The clocks have stopped! Look!

The speaker is not interested in making a comparison with a norm but
is interpreting a danger signal. What also makes this odd is the absence of deliberation. Deliberation may—as we saw in the last chapter—be conveyed by *Hm*, and that could substitute in the first clock
example:

> Hm, the clocks have stopped. I wonder what's wrong.

But deliberation alone is not a sufficient condition for *well*—what is
called for is deliberate COMPARISON. In a case like

> Hm, I thought I felt a tremor just now. Did you notice anything?

well would be unusual. There is deliberation, but except in earthquake
country where tremors are routine, there is no norm of tremors to
look back upon. The same applies to conversation. In answer to *How
come you're in such a hurry?* one may say

> The house is on fire!

—no norm and no deliberation; but the response

> Well, my mother's calling me.

is on the mark: the speaker implies 'You know mothers—always demanding.' Another possibility showing the presupposition of a norm
would be

> Well why do you suppose! My mother's calling me!

The collocation of *well* with other interjections can be explained in
terms of compatibility of meaning. Take *For Christ's sake!* This is generally used to protest the outrageous violation of what the speaker feels
is right:

> For Christ's sake, why didn't you say so?

An initial *well* fits here. Similarly *Confound it!* and *Damn it to hell!* The
latter makes an interesting contrast with *Damnation!*, which is not
used to comment on what has gone before but to curse something
that has just hit the scene:

> Damnation! I've just remembered I left my keys at home!

Well can hardly precede. *Damn it to hell!*, however, is at home within
ongoing operations:

(Well) damn it to hell! The handle's come off again!

The difference between the two oaths also shows up in their intonation. *Damnation!* almost always has a terminal fall. *Damn it to hell!* may
readily have a rise if the speaker goes on to explain:

```
                               you
         damn it    hell!  Who told
(Well)            to
                           to butt in!
```

Evaluative exclamations similarly. The speaker reacts with approval
or disapproval to some bit of information. The ones in which the reaction is abrupt and total are less likely with *well*; the ones that are used
when the speaker may still need a little convincing take *well* without
difficulty. Compare *wonderful* and *tremendous* (total approval) with
great and *good* (less than total):

> Great! Didn't I tell you? Isn't that what I predicted all along?
> Good! I never doubted for a minute that things would turn out
> all right!

Wonderful and *tremendous* (also *perfect, terrific*) are somewhat forced in
this context. Also they are less apt to be hedged with a following *but*:

> Great (?tremendous), but aren't you taking a little too much for
> granted?

As the most circumspect of the lot, *great* and *good* may take a preceding *well*, which is unlikely with the others:

> Well great! I always knew you had it in you!
> Well good! A little more and you'll have me convinced too!

On the disapproval side, *too bad* contrasts with *terrible*:

> Well too bad! And do you expect me to shed tears over it?
> *Well terrible (dreadful)! . . .

When the exclamation involves a more or less explicit judgment
there is something to deliberate about, and *well* is normal:

> Well how wonderful!
> Well isn't that tremendous!
> Well that's perfect!
> Well God be thanked!

Well with expletives is not the only sort of collocation that points to
a tie with what is or has been already established. We may also look to
well! combined with other sentence modifiers. It is hard to motivate

combinations like the following, in which the other modifier is oriented away from what is prior or extant:

*well therefore	?well furthermore
*well yet	*well so
?well besides	

These represent something to be added, a conclusion yet to be drawn, an exception yet to be taken, etc. Though *yet* and *nevertheless* are both adversatives and in a sense are synonyms, as in

He promised, yet I believe he is insincere.
He promised, nevertheless I believe he is insincere.

the word *yet* refers to something that has come fresh to mind, whereas *nevertheless* is like *to the contrary notwithstanding*—the counterarguments are already in attention. Hence:

*Well yet I believe he is insincere.
Well nevertheless I believe he is insincere.

As for *well so* it is normal when *so* is anaphoric:

Well so they said.

but not when *so* is a sentence adverb referring to result:

*Well so they did it.

On the other hand, *well, so* causes no problem when *so* refers to something that speaker and hearer are agreed upon as to the facts:

Well, so they did it, so what?

Furthermore is entirely forward-looking, whereas its synonym *on top of that* makes anaphoric reference to what has gone before:

(*Well) furthermore, he called you a liar.
(Well) on top of that, he called you a liar.

There are a goodly number of modifiers that relate to something prior or something extant, which collocate easily with *well*:

well then	well finally
well anyway	well hardly
well really	well of course
well naturally	well even if

These notes on collocations are only a sample from the associative network of *well*, which needs careful study if the point suggested here is to be proved. It is noteworthy that purely additive *and* can precede practically all the expressions mentioned above.

Now what of the claim that *well* necessarily implies an insufficiency or a failure to meet the options opened up by prior discourse? For all that such contexts are propitious for *well*, we find cases like the following:

> See how the kid's standing up to that bully? — Well damned if
> he isn't!

> Marie looks lovely tonight. — Well so she does!

Here the expectations of the prior discourse are met with enthusiasm, and it is the *respondent's* contrary expectations that have to be adjusted to reality. The reaction is SURPRISE. Or:

> Shall we do it? — Well why not! (Well what the hell! Let's!)

The respondent's prior reluctance is adjusted. Or:

> Will you help me? — Well of course!

Now it is the requester's reluctance to ask, which the respondent senses and hastens to put to rest—'It is quite within the norm for you to ask.' The intonation, for greater reassurance, is apt to be[10]

`Well of`

   ^{course} !

Or:

> I told them they had been rash, and I think that I was right. — Well
> absolutely! They had no business doing what they did!

'You were completely within your rights to say so, no need for apologies.' Or, within a single turn of speech,

> You said he would never amount to anything. Well, I couldn't agree
> more.

The two are in accord as to the norm.

In all these cases what we have is emphatic agreement, overcoming real or imagined obstacles. The norm of *well* is invoked as a basis for it. But it can just as easily be invoked for disagreement, and is almost required in the last turn of the following:

> You don't think I can do it, do you! — No, I don't! — *I can!

The most likely choice is *Well, I can!*, but *I can, though*, or *I've just found out that I can* is another possible way of giving a basis for the assertion.

Of course agreement and disagreement may function on more than one level. The following is literally agreement but is a playful pretense at disagreement:

> She's great, isn't she! — Well, you won't get any argument from mé!

The speaker pretends that he has been baited—the question was meant to get a rise. A more straightforward agreement—still with *well*—would be

> She's great, isn't she! — Well she sure is! I've never seen anything like it!

'Let nothing be alleged against her being great, in view of the evidence.'

The point is that whether for agreement or disagreement—or for any of the numerous other cases in which it figures—what gives *well* entry is its meaning.

In fairness to the argument that *well* is some kind of harmonizer of conversational discord, it must be admitted that instances of failure or lack or disagreement outnumber the positive instances and we must ask why. A likely reason is that when one confronts a situation that one can't quite go along with, it is less abrasive to invoke some standard, some more impartial authority, rather than just one's personal feelings or objections.

Given the *meaning* of *well*, one can trace a variety of conversational *uses* consonant with it, some of which were identified earlier as clues to its meaning. As with any instrument, the uses form a continuum (with varying density), along which one can single out various points for exemplification, few or many depending on how finely one cares to discriminate.[11] The list that follows could be doubled, or cut in half; overlapping is unavoidable.

1. Continuity. This is the broad category that corresponds to Schiffrin's "aliveness to the need to accomplish coherence" (p. 662) and Svartvik's "something in common with what went before." The speaker gives the nod to the state of affairs then current, accepting it as background, and goes on to add. The norm is simply what *is*, Carlson's "Nature's alternative" defined (p. 31) as "an objective description of the actual situation." The best examples are from monologs in which the speaker invokes the norm in connection with something he intends to add himself. *Well* creates an expectation:

> I knew something wasn't quite kosher so I decided to wait a little longer. Well, about five o'clock I heard someone knock, and . . .

> She figured she had to fire Janet, who had been with the firm for six years. Well, that was her big mistake. In less than a month . . .

> I was in the shelter, figuring the wind had veered the other way. Well before I knew it all hell broke loose. First the trap door collapsed . . .

If a link to the background is expressly denied, *well* may be odd:

> Well, to return to what we were saying . . .
> ?Well, to change the subject . . .

Though the expectation more often than not leads to expectancy, what is linked up need not be unusual:

> Well you'll never believe what happened next.
> Well what happened next was pure routine.

But *well sir* (in its derived, discourse-particle sense) is *well* specialized for the unusual:

> Well sir you'll never believe what happened next.
> ?Well sir what happened next was pure routine.

Well for continuity is naturally commonplace in dialog. In the following example adapted from Schiffrin (p. 657) the speaker repeats the reference to the background 'cemetery' invoking *well* to create an expectation of further directions to follow:

> Do you know where the cemetery is, where Smithville Inn is?
> — Yes. — Well, when you get to the cemetery you make a right.

Without *well*, making a right might readily be the final move that puts the traveler where he wants to go: *and that's it*. With *well* we expect more, e.g. *Then you go halfway down the block and you're there.* (*Well* serves a rather different function if the words *and that's it* are actually added, yielding *Well, when you get to the cemetery you make a right, and that's it: well* refers to the sufficiency of the response.)

"What went before" can refer to nonverbal context, as in the earlier example of the tour guide greeting the group with *Well, what shall we do today?* If there is strong motivation in the social situation for such a link, not having *well* may be a bit odd and conversely adding *well* when a response usually implies no link may seem even more so. Consider an introduction:

> I'd like you to meet James Jackson. — How do you do?
>
> I'd like you to meet James Jackson. — ?Well how do you do?
>
> I'd like you to meet James Jackson. — ?How do you do? I've been wanting to meet you for ages.
>
> I'd like you to meet James Jackson. — Well how do you do! I've been wanting to meet you for ages!

Much depends, of course, on individual or regional styles; an effusive style, for instance, may assume a link that has not actually been established. In the following, the addition of *well* is compatible with referring to the addressee rather than to some third party in another room; *well* relates speaker and hearer in terms of long-standing acquaintance:

> Look who's here! — Who? — John.
> Well, look who's here! It seems ages! How have you been, John?

Continuity shades into appropriateness. I may say in my own personal desperation,

> What shall I do?

(perhaps adding *Where shall I turn? Who can I trust?*). But if I say

> Well, what shall I do?

I am asking what it is appropriate to do, given the background.

Continuity also shades into continuation. The expectation that *well* sets up demands that the speaker go on to justify invoking the way things are. If I say *How would you lift it?* you may reply

> I'd use a crowbar. How would you?

A preceding *well* would sound a bit odd, since no elaboration of *well* is provided. A suitable context would be

> Well, I'd use a crowbar. It gives better leverage and is less liable to break.

That's how things are with crowbars.

2. Consequences. These may go from a consequence that proves a point,

> They said you couldn't and you did. Well, there you are! You proved them wrong and I'm proud of you!

to a consequence that someone has to suffer:

> You didn't do your homework. Well (then), you shall have no supper.

How slippery the categories are when one deals with interpersonal situations is shown by the fact that this type may be used to express regret (*Well, no supper then, poor child*) or to deliver a reprimand—inviting a separate classification—even more so if *very well* replaces *well*.[12]

3. Concession. The other side of consequence is concession, though in both the function of *well* remains the same: that in view of which the consequence comes about or the concession is made. What the other person has asked or excused himself for is understandable under the circumstances:

> I'm afraid I'm not up to doing the full course today. — Well, just do the best you can.

Sorry I didn't get around to correcting the proofs. — Well, that's OK, I can take care of them myself later.

Aren't you coming along? — Well, I'd rather not, but I guess I'll have to.

Or the speaker simply abandons a position that he finds untenable given the way things are:

I know you'd rather do this differently, but I've tested the procedure and I think this way is best. — Well, you decide.

This last approaches resignation, a more extreme possibility. The last speaker might say just *Well* and throw up his hands. *Ah well* and *oh well* are stereotyped for resignation, using a B + C contour with the barest of terminal rises (see Bolinger 1986: 226–37 for the terraced monotone with "stylized" meanings, and see above, p. 282).

A more positive form of concession is reassurance:

You ask if I'll help you. Well of course! Isn't that what friends are for?

The norm here is explicit: what-friends-are-for.

4. Criticism, disagreement, rejection, challenge: opposition in general. Epistemic *well* makes it easier to attack another's position by putting the onus on an impersonal authority: 'that's the way things are.' So one may reject an unreasonable request:

He asked me to resign. Well I won't, so there.

In the following example from Schiffrin (p. 652) the husband protests the exaggeration of what his wife has just said:

He can usually tell you not only what the piece is, but who it was written by. — Well that's no big deal!

To imply deliberation and perhaps a seemly reluctance to speak out, *well* is often drawled in these negative utterances, and frequently occurs alone, as in this second example from Schiffrin (p. 664), in which Irene and Henry are arguing about a coming election:

No, what this priest said last night he feels a lot of people won't vote. A lot of the Catholic people will *not* come out and vote. — They'll vote. — Well: . . . — Guarantee you they'll vote. — Don't guarantee anything Hen.

Well is often thus used alone in questions that challenge, and then the conversation may degenerate into a contest of *well*s:

Didn't I tell you I had the goods on you? Well? — Well . . . — Well? — Well . . .

In the following,

I wanted to apologize. — Well, it's too late now.

if the speaker omitted *well* it would be as if he were offering practical advice ('there's no use trying'), assuming that the other person has in mind still making a desperate try, instead of merely making a remark about the obvious, the obvious being embodied in *well*. A contradiction such as *That isn't true* is an affront when it gives the lie to what someone else has just said, but

Well, that isn't true.

mitigates the effect by transferring the criticism to a higher authority.

The speaker may go on to explain the norm in explicit terms, adding *You've overlooked the most important point* or *I've seen the original documents* or *A lot has come to light since then.* We may feel that a *well* without such a following explanation is incomplete, even though no added explanation is needed if *well* is omitted. In the following, *why* implies a criticism of what the other has said:

I'm afraid I can't intervene in this. — Why? (long rise-fall)
. . . W'l why? I took care of mý end!
. . . ? W'l why?

The norm is that one has an obligation to do one's share.

Grudging agreement or partial agreement behaves like disagreement. The speaker still finds it useful to share the responsibility with an authority "out there":

Would you be willing to help out? — Well, I guess so.
Do you like it? — Well, sort of.

As before, the norm may be explicated, e.g. for the foregoing with *If I just didn't have so much else to do!* and *It's a little short for my tastes.* Unequivocal agreement contrasts by not associating comfortably with *well*:

Do you like it? — *Well, fully! (*Well, do I!)

But as was noted earlier, if the speaker implies 'It was inappropriate for you even to ask in view of the certainty of my agreement,' or controverts supposed disagreement from some third party, then *well* is again all right:

Do you like it? — Well I should sáy só!

Do you agree? — Well you bet! I never went along with that viewpoint in the first place!

The grudging agreement may be not agreement with an assumed view but agreement to answer. Observe the difference between the unadorned categorical affirmative and an affirmative that is hedged:

> Are you the one they mentioned? — I am. (?Well, I am.)

> Are you the one they mentioned? — Well, I am, if you must know
> (if I have to be frank about it, but keep it a secret, etc.)

A *Well, maybe* of course is noncategorical whereas a ?*Well, definitely* is the opposite. As we noted earlier (pp. 313–14) it is difficult to get a pristinely categorical affirmative or negative because there are so many shades of hedgings, even including a simple *yes*. The word *hardly*, for instance, can agree or disagree and still take *well*:

> He isn't coming, is he?—Well hardly! (agreement)
> He's coming, isn't he?—Well hardly! (disagreement)

Though a speaker may comfortably disagree with the assertion that underlies a question, as in

> Shouldn't John have waited? — (Well,) he shouldn't.

even with *well* it is not good form to disagree categorically (i.e., using the auxiliary) with the assertion itself:

> John should have waited. — *He shouldn't. (?Well, he shouldn't.)

Things change if the speaker disagrees to the point of anger:

> John should have waited. — He shóuld nót!

and *well* hardly fits this degree of certainty. But a hedging makes all things smooth again:

> John should have waited. — Well, no, he shouldn't. (Well, all
> things considered, he shouldn't.)

And the hedging may be prosodic. In the doubtful example ?*Well, he shouldn't*, if *well* is drawled at a low pitch (the drawl is for 'considering the alternatives' and the low pitch is for minimizing the disagreement), it is acceptable.

Criticism is occasionally interpolated within a longer utterance, when a speaker comes to some objection or accusation that needs softening. As the overarching epistemic modifier, *well* always commands initial position except in this instance.[13] *Well* is drawled and is usually at a relatively high pitch—the typical *well* of deliberation, of choosing the right thing to say:

> Didn't you—well—bear down on him a little too hard? I noticed
> him wince.

Self-correction figures as well as correction of others, as in Schiffrin's example (p. 658)

> So we decided since he was living in West Philadelphia, well *both*
> my mother and father, we decided to come out here.

A challenge meets some claim of prowess or whatever—*well* = 'if that's the case'—with a dare to perform; this reverts to 'consequence' —the validity of the claim should compel its substantiation:

> I can do better than any of 'em! — Well, prove it!

> Of course I'm loyal! — Well then you shouldn't mind signing the oath.

> She can eat anything! — Well, let's see her swallow this sowbug.

The challenge may be a threat:

> Who's afraid of yóu? I can lick you anytime. — Well just you wait. I'll show you when I'm in shape again.

Well just you wait, well never you mind, well you mark my word, well we'll see about that, well that remains to be seen, etc. are comparatively firm collocations with *well*. At the bidding of *well*, the powerless speaker commands forces "out there."

5. Extenuation. The speaker insists that in the long view he is not entirely wrong:

> You didn't wash the car! — Well, I put out the garbage. (Wasn't that enough?)

> Where did you hide my watch? —I didn't hide it! — Well, *some-body* did!

If I have kept you waiting for an hour, on arriving I may say to you out of the blue,

> Well, here I am!

This may serve as a wry excuse — in view of conditions, my late arrival is not surprising: here I am, after bucking traffic for an hour. Or it may be self-criticism—knowing the norm for me, you know I will be late: here I am, late as always. The speaker may excuse a failure by making light of the obligation:

> You were ten minutes late. — Well, was it important for me to be right on time?

The usual intonation is B + AC, common in expressions of diffidence ('will what I am saying be accepted?'):

$$\text{Well I}^{\text{put out}}\text{ the}^{\text{gar}}\text{bag}^{\text{e}\bullet}$$

But B + A is normal enough if the response is belligerent:

> You're late! — Well, here I am. (Given conditions, that's as much as you have a right to expect.)

Even so, AC is normal with a defiant question, as in this AC followed with a B tag:

> Well I'm here, ain't I?

6. Topic shift. This is Svartvik's category—the speaker decides to take a different tack and invokes the norm as justification for it:

> Well, to make a long story short (to get down to brass tacks, to be as brief as possible, not to put too fine a point on it) . . .
>
> Well, I hear them calling me so I'd better be off.
>
> Well, you wanted me to take a look at your tax return, so shall we get busy on it?

7. Demands. Whether as command or as question, a demand may be impertinent if unmodified. Suppose I have explained my need for clear passage and you still stand in the way. Even with *please*, as in *Please step aside then*, this may sound a bit abrupt if given a terminal fall; but

> Well, please step aside then.

suggests that the request is normal and reasonable in the light of the prior explanation. *Well?* alone would suffice; the hearer can infer the rest.

If you have been giving me reasons for not associating with someone and I say *How can I avoid him?*, I am asking point-blank for help, but if I say

> Well, how can I avoid him?

I make the request seem reasonable, and you can reply in the same vein—what comes naturally to do under the circumstances ('obviousness'—see below):

> Well, you know, you can cross to the other side of the street, or you can not answer the phone for a couple of days, or you can, well, you know, do lots of things.

An alternative question of the "or not" type is quite demanding, e.g. *Are you coming or aren't you? Well* makes it less so by tying it in with what one has a right to expect given what has gone before:

> Well are you coming or aren't you?

If I feel that you *owe* me an explanation, I may use *well* to demand one. *Well* alludes to the basis for the obligation. The following are from Lakoff (p. 463):

> (1) Well, did Harry capture the aardvark?
> (2) Well, why isn't the garbage out?

(3) Well, didn't it rain yesterday, just like I said it would?

(4) Well, all right, Stanley, *what* have you got in your hand?

The context Lakoff suggests for (1) is a suspenseful story—the narrator has stopped at an exciting point. Another possible context is your failure to give me a timely report about Harry's activities: I demand that you produce one. Or it could be no more than idle conversation—you and I meet some days after we had been discussing Harry's prospects of capturing the aardvark, and I pick up where we left off—this is continuation, not demand. We see how independent the discourse interpretations of epistemic *well* can be. The same is true of (4), which Lakoff interprets to mean that Stanley has been pestering the speaker to be allowed to show his treasure, and the speaker gives permission "just to get the conversation over with." That is concession. But the same utterance can be used if Stanley is trying to conceal something in his hand, and the speaker asserts the parental right to know what it is—a demand. In the latter, but not the former, *hand* is accented.

In response to a request for instructions, a *well* may blunt the abruptness of the order:

> What do you want me to do? — Well, for starters, clean up the mess you've made.

For starters suggests that there are enough things that obviously need attention to make the request for instructions superfluous—the other person should have pitched in without asking. The preceding *well* softens this by invoking the norm as something shared: 'Well, you know, you can see . . .'

8. Prompting. Given the situation, action is called for:

> I think we ought to do something about it, now. — Well, what are we waiting for?

Giving *well* its full form and an accent, the speaker proclaims the norm. With the reduced form

> W'l what are we waiting for?

he assumes the norm, and asks, in effect, why something has not been done about the matter already.

The speaker may prompt himself. This is the case with the example (p. ooo, above) of the beginning skier:

> Well here goes nothing!

The situation covers all the preparations that have been made.

There is a noninterjectional formula using *well* with much the same effect of prompting—(*We*) *might as well*:

> Shall we do it? — Well, let's!
> Shall we do it? — (Well) we might as well.

When the situation is elaborately specified, a sort of anaphoric *well* may be virtually required. Thus in

> Shall we do it? — Do what? — You know! — Well, why not!

To say just *Why not?* here is too abrupt.[14] If there is no such deliberation over the norm, no anaphoric *well* is needed:

> Shall we do it? — Why not!

But if *well* is added here, it still suggests 'a deliberation in view of something presumed to be established.'
    The prompt may be a form of encouragement:

> I can't do it! — Well, give it a try.

The most unadulterated prompting is of course *well* alone, as in

> Do you like him? — Oh, you know, he's . . . [speaker looks vague]
>   — Well?

where *well* asserts a right to know: 'Go on!' The more demanding *Do you?* here would be potentially rude, an attempt to pin the other person down, which can be made explicit in the more elaborate (and more conclusive) *Do you or don't you?* A *well* preceding *Do you?* or *Do you or don't you?* softens the demand.
    As we saw earlier, simple *well* used for prompting may relate to action as well as to speech. If you are supposed to follow me, I may say just *Well?*, without necessarily adding *are you coming?*
    Prompting and demanding are degrees of the same thing. The distinction is mostly contextual and intonational.
    9. Obviousness. This is a nuance of 'consequence.' The hearer is assumed to be able to draw the right conclusion in view of the evidence. *Well* may be used alone, as a question:

> The insurance agent said I needed proof of damage. I showed him the wreckage and said simply, "Well?"

Or it may be an embedded nonquestion. A typical case is the formulaic answer to the silly question:

> Did they suspect he was involved? — Well I should hope so! When they caught him practically red-handed!

This is a cataphoric *well*, so to speak: the circumstances-in-view-of-which come in the following sentence. They can just as easily precede, with a coreferential *after that* to follow:

> They complimented me on this and that, flattered me, slapped me on the back, poked me in the ribs, said, "Oh, you lucky devil!"

> Well, after that there wasn't much I could do but try to sink through the floor.

The frequency with which *well* is coupled to *you know* bears out this aspect of 'norm.'

10. Surprise. It is easy to be shocked at a departure from a norm, whether nonverbal, as in the examples on pages 310–11, or verbal, as in

> Ronald is chasing skirts again. — Well! And him with a wife and six kids!

Added expressions of surprise are commonplace: *Well I'm amazed! Well I can hardly believe it!* Quite a few are stereotyped for the purpose: *what do you know!, for goodness' sake!, if that doesn't beat the band!*

The deliberative component makes itself felt in that the more unpremeditated and spontaneous the exclamation is, the less propitious for *well*. We are not apt to get *Well incredible!*, though *Well how incredible!* is normal enough. *Oh well* is a stereotype, *well oh* an impossibility. Presumably *oh well* originates in a *recovery* from surprise.

Intonation is such a large component of these interpretations that a slight change may displace the surprise of

```
         did
Well he            af
             come   ter all!
```

and substitute the I-told-you-so contradiction of

```
Well he did        af
             come   ter all.
```

occurring in an exchange like

> You said he wasn't going to come, didn't you? — Yes. — Well, he did come after all.

Reversing the intonation would sharpen the contradiction and blunt the surprise.

11. Deliberation. Many of the examples already cited could as well be dropped in this category, since the act of adjusting one's deeds or thoughts to a norm involves a comparison. This can be seen in cases of topic shift in an internal monolog:

> Well, what shall I do next? I guess I'll take care of the bills.

Well comes at the point of indecision, of search for what it is that circumstances call for. Similarly when one must cast about for an answer:

Are you going to jog after lunch or after dinner? — Well, after lunch,
I guess. I usually eat too much for dinner.

Would you say he lost the debate? — Well, yes. At least on points.
But his style was superior.

The norm here is the plausible-reason-for-hesitating.

We have come at the question of *well* from enough directions, I
hope, to have made a case for assigning the word a content, albeit a
content transferred from the locutionary sphere ('relatively good,
relatively strong') to the illocutionary ('matched to a standard or
norm'). I believe that Schiffrin glimpsed this when she adopted the
term REFERENT for what it is that *well* links an utterance to in her
scheme of conversational coherence; but it is not a physical conversational object to which something is subsequently attached—rather it
is an intellectual object *in view of which* a judgment is passed. Coherence is attained not for its own sake but as the result of a regulatory
mechanism that keeps events in line with imperatives. The interjection *well* is an invocation, an appeal to something that transcends the
speaker's immediate interests.

It is time now to take a steadier look at the prosody of *well*. Interjections, by the fact of their diffuse semantic content, take on the coloration of the prosody to such an extent that we are tempted to read in
the intonational meaning as if it were the meaning of the interjection
itself. That was the main reason for the long excursion into the semantics of *well* without particular reference to the nonsegmental garnish.
Criticizing Crystal and Davy (1975), who tried to identify distinct pro-
nunciations of *well* with distinct meanings, Svartvik said, of his own
investigation of *well*: "No such distinct correlations were . . . found
between prosody and meaning. It seems that Crystal and Davy interpret not differences in meaning of *well* but differences in the intonational meaning, which they then attribute to *well* itself" (p. 172).

Svartvik's own figures show some interesting correlations with intonational terminals, the proportion of level tones being considerably
larger, falling tones slightly larger, and rising tones less than the average for terminals in general (pp. 170–71). This gives a rough idea of
the proportion of hesitations (mostly level?), exclamations (mostly
falls?), and questions (mostly rises?), but its main import is that with
well anything goes, intonationally, and we must probably expect the
same autonomy of intonation that we have consistently found in all
other comparisons of this sort.

A better place to start the discussion of the prosody of *well* is with
accent rather than profile, for that is where, if anywhere, the prosody

will have left its mark. Knowing what we know of the development of *why*, we are entitled to wonder if the same kind of morphemic split that distinguishes (for speakers who aspirate *wh-*) *why* interrogative from *w'y* interjection has occurred with *well*. Semantically the *why* paradigm reveals the same underlying unity as the *well* paradigm, yet the interjection branch has developed a distinct reduced form. Is there a similar difference between *well* and *w'l*?

Svartvik notes only the incidence of accent, not that of reduction: in his corpus 44 percent of the instances of *well* were unaccented, 56 percent were accented. It is probably correct to make the division in this way: reduction, when it occurs, is no doubt fully gradient, beginning with loss of accent and extending to the loss of the vowel with only [l] remaining as the vocalic segment. (Or even with further reduction to shwa, as in *W' yes!*) But to test the possibility of a semantic contrast accompanying the process of reduction, it will be easiest to compare full *well* and fully reduced *w'l*.

We have already seen (p. 300) the difference between proclaiming the norm and assuming it. The same contrast may come at a break in the conversation. Suppose a friend drops by and the two of you stand for a moment talking. You may then say

W'l sit down! (We don't want to be on our feet all day!)

Here the friend should have realized already that it was appropriate for him to sit down. But if you say

Well! Sit down! (We have a thousand things to talk about!)

you are *inviting* him to sit down (the norm is hospitality). The same intimation of 'obviousness' on the part of *w'l* can be seen in explanations. If you ask me *Why should you think there's going to be a party?* I may reply

W'l you're all dressed to go out, that's why.

'The reason should be obvious.' With a full *well* in that position, I take credit for my deduction by pointing it out. It appears that accent can have the same foregrounding and backgrounding effect on *well* as with any ordinary content word. With the A profile prescribed for the example (p. 316, above) *Well, the clocks have stopped. I wonder what's wrong*, the speaker proclaims 'Something is out of joint.' It would be impossible to say *W'l the clocks have stopped* in that context; an antecedent like *Why do you think something is wrong?* would be needed as background—the speaker then implying 'Shouldn't it be obvious?'

'Assuming the norm' does not necessarily imply 'obviousness.' It may merely allude without attaching importance. A person casually

reading a newspaper may spot something out of the ordinary and remark, out of the blue,

> W'l look at this!

Without *w'l* the speaker would probably be intending to develop a
point, not just to remark about some departure from the norm. On
the other hand, if at some time in the past you and I have had a difference of opinion and what I spot in the paper proves me right, I may
make preparations to crow about it by saying

^{Well} look at
         ^th_{is}!

with full *well*. I am foregrounding my proofs.

Still, there has been no morphemic split. The full form *well*, without accent, can replace *w'l* without altering the meaning or the presuppositions. The reduced form is just that, a phonological reflex, favored over full (unaccented) *well* as a proclitic before accent, as in

> W'l yóu're no great shakes!
> W'l nów's hardly the time!
> W'l thát's a pretty how-de-do!

and in other instances of pre-onset position, as Svartvik terms it
(p. 170).

Where *w'l* does acquire a certain significance apart from other instances of *well* is in the manifestation of facial gesture. Like other conversational particles—*yes* and *no*, for example, which take on gestural
coloration in forms such as *yep, yeah, yah, nope, noo, naw*—*well* easily
reflects now a pout (*w'l*), now a tensing of the lips as the speaker
weighs alternatives (*weel*), now a relaxation at low pitch for reassurance or minimization (*waal*), etc. A pout is apt to accompany self-
justifications, as in

> W'l you didn't keep your promise!

The gestural [p] of *yep* and *nope*, unreleased as befits a lip closure that
is for 'decisiveness,' can also be found in *welp*, though the phonetic
environment is less propitious for calling attention to it. The gestural
manifestations are additive. We have *well* + pout, not a separate
pouting *w'l*.

Looking at intonational contrasts other than accentual ones, we
find that they too are additive, at least to a degree that permits us to
see the intonational meaning separate from the meaning of *well*. What
stereotypes there are preserve the meanings of their components. For

example, *well* occurs on a C profile where the accented syllable (at the trough) is approached from a falsetto that is no more than a grace note. The effect—and the intonation—is like that of the *But hell!* example cited on page 255—

```
W        he
ell,     didn't really mean that.
```

The wide downskip is 'downplaying.' The low pitch is drawled somewhat, helping to distinguish this C from an A in which the vowel is more at the peak (possibly falsetto here too):

```
We
     things are looking good  af
  11,                            ter all!
```

The autonomy of intonation shows most clearly in the readiness with which it categorizes *well* as to utterance type, conforming in this respect exactly with what happens to a declarative sentence. Give it a B profile and it calls for a continuation:

```
   1?           say
 we1   Why don't you                    (question)
                  something?
```

```
   1,
 we1   maybe                 (incomplete clause)
          so.
```

Give it an A and it suggests termination:

```
              that's
We
  11.  I'm  glad      over.
```

Give it a C and it shows restraint—toning down, say, an imperative:

```
                        u
      why don't you speak
 we1 1,
                    p?
```

A clear downward obtrusion with the C is infrequent because so little else can precede *well*, but an *oh* or an *ah* or a *m-m-m* is possible as ground:

```
M-m-m
          1,  I suppose you're
       well            right.
```

As a question, *well* can use any of the profiles with rising terminal, notably B, C, and AC, and it can use B in any of its shapes, rising, high level, or (very) slightly falling. Profile A is also possible, but needs a heavy overlay of questioning gesture. Lacking any syntactic clue to interrogativeness (as is the case with other particles—*oh, ah, so, hm*), *well* depends on prosodic and gestural clues. All these possibilities, however, are also found in accented *well* used as a preamble to longer utterances. We come to the usual dead end where intonation as a marker of grammar is concerned.

As an independent exclamation, accented *well* is more restricted. One can imagine a person in pain exclaiming *oh!* or *ah!* with a simple rise—the tension goes up but there is no "asking." A similar rise on independent *well* is probably always meant as a question; *well* is too deliberate to get out of control. We may say then that exclamatory *well* is limited to Profile A, or, if *well* is repeated, to contours ending in A.

In such cases of repetition, an unaccented *well* may serve as ground to an accented one, as in the following B + A:

```
       wéll well
W'l              wé
                  ll₁
```

The first and third *wells* are unaccented, and the first, being initial and directly before the accent, optionally reduces. The first is ground to the second and the third is ground to the fourth. In the following A + A, the second *well* is ground to both the first and the third:

```
Wéll        wé
     well   ll₁
```

In the following A, the first and second are ground to the third:

```
            wé
Well well   ll₁
```

Such exclamatory contours of repeated *wells* show the usual gradients of tension and relaxation. A + Á or B + Á, with upward tangent, perhaps suggests that the speaker is heavily impressed. A + À or B + À, with downward tangent, is tempered—the speaker is perhaps disapproving.

Well as preamble is not normally repeated, but in at least one situation—greetings—it may be, and then is most apt to use a B + B̀ contour, spoken slowly:

Well, well if it isn't my old friend Sam Thompson!

(If B + A is used here, we would tend to regard it as an exclamation and punctuate it *Well, well! If it isn't my old friend Sam Thompson!*) Conceivably a repetition with B + C could be used to console or reassure:

Well   that's

   well,   all rig^{ht.}

Most of the time *well* as preamble to locutionary material is unaccented (this excludes utterances like *Wéll, now,* or *Wéll, my friend*), but it may be accented when the speaker proclaims the norm, as in the following response to *Why do you insist on returning the merchandise?*—

Wéll   gó

   it's no   ^od_l

W'l it's no góod would assume the norm. When unaccented—the usual situation—*well* forms part of the ground for a later accent:

W'l   whý   (ground for A on <u>why</u>)
    ?

W'l   (ground for C on <u>may-</u>)
    máy^{be.}

    sóme
W'l   body d^{id.}   (ground for AC on <u>some-</u>)

      bo
W'l   dy   (ground for CAC on <u>some-</u>)
   sóme   di_{d.}

   didn't ^{you?}   (ground for B on <u>did-</u>)
W'l

It may of course attach to other syllables constituting a ground:

            nó
        nó use
W'l it's   _o^{w.}

where *W'l it's* is ground for B on *no* followed by AC on *now*.

The consoling-reassuring *Well, well* above serves to illustrate a final point, the separate contributions of locution and intonation. For all that a given combination may be stereotyped, we have found repeatedly that the two may be studied separately. So a *Well, well* on a B + C contour used to console or reassure is no different from a *Now, now* or a *Come, come*, or (especially) a *There, there* on the same contour for the same purpose. In each case the word makes its contribution: *Well, well* 'in view of the norm, don't worry' (*don't worry* itself uses the same contour); *Come, come* 'bring yourself out of your misapprehension'; *Now, now* 'heed the present (nonthreatening) circumstances'; *There, there* 'distance your troubles.' (The glosses are approximations; 'distancing' is Brown and Levinson's mnemonic for *There, there*.) The intonation, independently, downplays and placates, with its downskip and reverse accent. Svartvik is right in his criticism of Crystal and Davy's attempt to assign meanings to *well* that belong rather to the intonation.

Apart from its intonational variety—but intersecting with it—*well* exhibits some of the variation noted with the gestural interjections *oh*, *ah*, etc. Occasionally it surfaces in eye-dialect spellings such as *w-e-e-l* [wiːl] and *w-a-a-l* [wæːl], the first, with its high second formant running alongside a high pitch, in a situation of intense deliberation, the second, relaxed, in situations of unconcerned deliberation. The phonetic makeup of *well* is not as propitious for this variation as, say, *no*, which has several eye-dialect spellings representing the corresponding gestural intersections: *nah* ([næ] or [na]), *naw*, *noo* [nu]—the latter, often repeated, being a combination with the kissing gesture.

Part IV

INTONATION AND LOGIC

12. Is There an Intonation of "Contrast"?

The expression of contrast, in most discussions of the subject, has been assigned to accentual highlighting, and referred to as CONTRASTIVE STRESS or CONTRASTIVE ACCENT. Whether particular accentual configurations—accent profiles—are involved has been largely overlooked, probably because of the tendency to think of accent in terms of just one profile or pair of profiles—A, or A plus its inconclusive partner AC. Since A is well suited to the expression of contrast, and since contrastivity is the sort of accentual meaning that comes first to mind when one wants to illustrate the notion of accent (*I don't mean x̂, I mean ŷ!*), the two factors have reinforced each other and we have failed to ask whether other profiles may be appropriate and if so what difference they make.

If accentual highlighting is essential to the expression of contrast, one naturally wonders whether the two are skewed or congruent in their relation to each other. Does an accent, in so far as it affects the content of what it falls on (i.e., is not purely an accent of power) always convey a contrast of some kind, and is contrast then just another term for the semantic highlighting that accompanies accentual highlighting? If so, then contrastive accent is the same as accent of interest.

This of course does not preclude some sort of *logical* distinction. Take the utterance

(1) I'm going hóme.

It can respond to the question *Where are you going?* or to the question *Are you going to the office?* The latter involves a CONTRARY: the speaker has in mind a limited number of choices (in this case two), none of which has to be true, of which by affirming one he explicitly denies the other(s). The former involves a CONTRADICTORY: if we assume that he is going, he has to be going either home or somewhere else—one of the alternatives is necessarily true. In that sense there is a

Intonation and Logic

contrast between 'home' and 'elsewhere'; but he is not thinking of
any particular other place. His response entails, but does not explicate, not-going-elsewhere. He is not thinking 'rather than.' Of course,
if he says

> (2) I'm going hóme, and nowhere élse! I'm tired and I want to
> relax.

then the two merge. The distinction is tenuous at best and is not a
likely candidate for any real prosodic differentiation.

At the same time, there is a *psychological* motive for greater involvement where contraries are concerned, because when a speaker feels
called upon to reject one alternative and embrace another, there is a
certain amount of cognitive dissonance, sometimes even a battle of
wills. This is likely to affect the intonational RANGE. It also affects the
choice of profile, A being favored for its assertiveness.

Profile A and the Depth of Fall

Something akin to the viewpoint just expressed is the theme of
Bolinger (1961, 1965), which concludes (1965: 106), "As far as we can
tell from the behavior of pitch, nothing is uniquely contrastive."
Example:

```
                                                Ply
(3) He didn't buy a    rd, he bought a
                    Fo
                                             mouth.
```

```
                                         bo
(4) Just leave him a  ne, and he won't       ther
                   lo                             you.
```

The pitch configuration (A profile, approached from below and with a
drop after) is found on the clearly contrastive ("rather than") *Plymouth*
and the supposedly noncontrastive *bother you*.

Citing this same pair, Couper-Kuhlen (1984: 146–47) claims that
there is an intonational difference, and that the notion of contrastivity
as prosodically marked can therefore be salvaged. She points out the
behavior of the unaccented syllables following the accented one: in (3)
there is a steep drop after *Ply-*; in (4) the drop is gradual. "If there
were a contrastive accent on *bother*," she says, "we would expect

```
        don't                                        bo
(5) I         think
                   he wants         he wants to
                            to    you,
                          help                  ther you."
```

The low-pitched unaccented syllables following the accented one are the key to "type 1" contrastive accent, according to Couper-Kuhlen. For the contrast to be clearly marked, there should be at least two of them (p. 147); if there are fewer—one or none—contrast may still be intended but the phonetic difference is neutralized. Example (3) is such a case, and the same would be true if *Ford* and *Plymouth* exchanged places.

Couper-Kuhlen's claim embodies a correct generalization and an incorrect observation. The correct generalization is that there is indeed a difference between two kinds of drop following an accented syllable. One we have identified with Profile A, which is abrupt, and the other with Profile B, which is gradual and is commutable with a level or a rise. The difference in shape and in function can be seen in

```
          merican Riv                        mer      riv
(6) The A                  is not the only A   i
             er                                  can
                                                   er.
```

with a B on the first *American* and an A on the second. The first is only part of a name, but the second discriminates a meaning.

What Couper-Kuhlen is attempting to do, however, is to tease a further distinction in the shape of the A. To be type-1 contrastive, the second *American* in (6) should have its -*i*- syllable at the same level as -*can*.

And herein lies the incorrect observation, that the shape of *bother* in (4) precludes its being contrastive. Or that giving it the shape of the *bother* in (5) would *make* it contrastive. The fact is that either shape, that of (4) or that of (5), can be used for either purpose, contrastive or noncontrastive. Both are A profiles, and both are appropriate. There are gradient differences: with a steeper and more sudden drop, (5) is more assured and categorical; with a narrower drop, it would remain contrastive but would suggest that the speaker is less in control: there are elements of suspense, impatience, wonderment, or whatever.

The idea that degree of drop plays a crucial role is borrowed from Chafe (1976), from whom Couper-Kuhlen cites the following responses to the question *What happened at the meeting?*:

(7) They elected Álice président.
(8) They elected Hénry tréasurer, and they elected Álice président.

Supposedly the pitch drop on *Alice* in (8) is a deeper fall ("to the baseline"), reflecting its "strictly contrastive" status (CK, p. 146). But suppose in place of (7) we have

(9) They elected a néwcomer président.

Now the shallow drop in the first A profile in (7) goes deeper. Or suppose (7) is said by someone who does not like Alice, and who adds a comment:

> (10) They elected Álice président. So they can do without my donation this year.

Again the drop in the A will tend to go lower. Neither case of lowering has anything to do with contrast in the 'ratherness' sense. In (7) we have a proper name, *Alice*; Alice would not be referred to in this fashion unless she were known to both speaker and hearer, and there is no particular motive for giving her separate attention (we recall Pike's term for A profiles: "contour separation"). That is not the case with *newcomer* in (9), which reports a somewhat unusual fact. (One point of this is that the inventor of prosodic examples should think twice before using proper names with their implication of mutual acquaintance.) Example (10) has its own reason for giving Alice separate attention. And the need for separate attention in (8), with its double contrast, is transparent. Examples (8), (9), and (10) are all linked in this way, by shared need for contour separation, not by shared contrastivity. How easily the deeper drop can be wiped out even when contrastivity is present is seen in

> (11) I suppose that Henry and Alice were both elected to something or other?—Yes, they elected Hénry tréasurer, and they elected Álice président.

The drop in *Henry* and in *Alice* will now tend to be shallower; they have already been mentioned, and there is less need for separate emphasis.

Other Shapes Than Profile A

Couper-Kuhlen recognizes one other contrastive shape, her "phonetic type 2" (pp. 152–55), which corresponds to our Profile AC, namely, (rise)-fall-rise. She is rather more diffident about the strict contrastivity of this type, pointing out that it may be "loosely contrastive or emphatic" (p. 155), and conceding that "the same intonational form may sometimes be used to realize quite different functions" (p. 155).

But what about still other shapes? Especially, what if *any* profile can be used for "ratherness" contrast? Though the highly assertive A is bound to be favored, a little experimentation will reveal that either C or B is perfectly normal in contrastive utterances. Using Couper-Kuhlen's example *There are óther issues in which I would nót back it*, marked for double contrast (p. 150), one can attach C profiles to both accents:

(12) There ^{are}

        oth^{er} issues in which I ^{would}   b^{ack} ^{it.}

                                            not

The difference between C and A here is the difference not between contrastivity and noncontrastivity but between placation and brow-beating; the intonation is playing its universal affective role. As for Profile B, we can imagine an embattled CIA agent saying to his superior,

                             hon   su   I

(13) I would be^{tray} my ^{sa}cred   but

                  o^{r,}   wouldn't →

                      ^re;

              Ag^{ency}!

     betray the

The B on *Agency* is in explicit contrast with the AC on *honor*. Its mood is pleading rather than asserting.

As for AC, its typical manifestation, according to Couper-Kuhlen, is where "the speaker *concedes* that a proposition (or an item in a proposition) is true but *implies* that some other contrasting proposition (or contrasting item) is false," differing from the typical A "in which the speaker *asserts* that a proposition (or an item a proposition) is true and simultaneously *asserts* that a contrasting proposition (or a contrasting item) is false" (pp. 143–44). These can be exemplified by the following modifications of Couper-Kuhlen's examples:

> (14)(a) Why are you out joyriding?—(We're nót.) We're going to Pórtland.
> (b) Why are you going to Bángor?—(We're nót.) We're going to Pórtland.
> (15)(a) Did you water the yárd?—(No, but) I fed the cát.
> (b) Did you feed the dóg?—(No, but) I fed the cát.

(14)(a) and (b) illustrate the assertive type of contrast, (15)(a) and (b) illustrate the concessive; the (a) sentences have "broad focus," the (b) "narrow focus."

Couper-Kuhlen's intonation markings make it clear that (14)(a) and (b) use A profiles and (15)(a) and (b) use AC, and in these contexts the association is natural and spontaneous. But it does not follow that there is any essential or defining connection between the intonation and the contrastive type. In response to *You didn't finish the editing* one may say

```
                   proof
(16) I finished the
                          reading.
```

which is the concessive type, with AC as predicted. But one may also say

```
                di
(17) I certainly
                 id!
```

with the same AC, and it is not concessive but strongly counterassertive. The terminal rise in (16) leaves the statement open to the qualification 'Does that count?,' as Ladd pointed out. The identical rise in (17) is open to a different qualification, perhaps 'if you'll pardon my saying so.' The hearer is on notice that something should be added, and supplies what is needed, by inference (with assistance from the gestural system as a whole, of which the intonation is a fragment). The "concession" that we read in is real enough, but is at a double remove from the fundamental meaning of the intonation. In fact, the concessive meaning can be carried perfectly well by an A profile. Again in response to *You didn't finish the editing* one may say

```
                   proof
(18) I finished the

                          reading.
```

intended to imply, say, that the hearer should know perfectly well that if I had to take time to do the proofreading I wouldn't have enough left to do the editing. And this shows the AFFECTIVE side of Ladd's locutionary 'Does that count?': (16) contains an apologetic whine, appropriate to explaining why one has not done something *else* that was expected; and the same apologetic whine is present in (17), to soften the contradiction. The speaker of (18) is assertive to the point of defiance.

The fundamentally affective meaning of the intonation can be seen even more clearly by examining a type that Couper-Kuhlen regards as out of the question. It involves pairs of lexical opposites, such as *possible* and *impossible* (p. 144): "We can say *it's* ↑ *PÒSsible* (not impossible), but we cannot say *it's PŎSsible* (*but not impossible). This is because if one member of a pair of lexical opposites is true, then the other is necessarily false. There is no room for contingency." The first intonation is A, the second AC; the A answers the question *Is it possible or is it impossible?*, and the AC expresses contingency. Nevertheless, we can readily have, in response to another's having reiterated *It's impossible*, the following counterassertion using three successive AC's:

```
    tel                pos                        lieve
(19) I'm
        ling you, it's      sible, and you'd better be
                                                          it!
```

Here the speaker avoids the assurance of the terminal fall, which might seem rude; the AC avoids closing off debate. With the 'contingency' interpretation, the AC avoids closing off the alternatives. The common element is 'leaving things open.'

Couper-Kuhlen recognizes counterexamples but rationalizes them by acts of faith. One instance is the notion of "overriding." The contrastive form is there, but hidden from view. Take the case of contrastivity in questions. Couper-Kuhlen cites the example

```
                                                then?
(20) Did you object to Parliament entering into it
```

and comments, "Had the speaker made a statement about the addressee's behaviour rather than queried it, we would have expected *you didn't object to parliament entering into it THEN* (so you shouldn't object now). But in actual fact the implicative fall-rise [AC] is overridden by a rise for the yes/no question" (p. 154). The flaw in this argument is that the yes-no question does not require a terminal rise, and if there is no rise to override anything, what happens? The reality is simply that contrastivity does not depend on any particular intonation profile, and if a B profile can be used in a nonquestion like (13) it can be used in a question like (20). As for AC in questions, we know that it is severely restricted (see Bolinger 1986: 322).

Alleged Metaphors and Alleged Mistakes

Another escape hatch is by way of figures of speech: "The contrastive form is simply extended to other semantic content and the result becomes interpretable by analogy" (CK, p. 157). For example, 'The speaker chooses a form which, although not warranted objectively, lets him/her appear to be asserting something and denying its opposite at the same time. S/he thus appears to be particularly forceful and emphatic" (p. 154). Couper-Kuhlen asserts, a bit circularly, that such cases are "not proof of the superfluousness of the contrastive–non-contrastive distinction but a confirmation of its validity" (p. 157). A priori it is just as reasonable to claim that the other functions of the intonation types are central and contrastivity is by extension, as to claim that contrastivity is central and other functions are by extension.

Couper-Kuhlen's position would be strengthened, of course, if there were some preponderance in favor of the contrastive interpretation, perhaps a statistical preponderance (the great majority of instances of a given intonation type being contrastive). But no evidence is offered. Or there might be a preponderance by way of a unidirectional correspondence; say that all instances of semantic contrast require phonetic contrast (even though phonetic contrast may be extended to other uses). This is a claim that Couper-Kuhlen actually makes: "Semantic contrast does not occur without contrastive intonation (except erroneously)" (p. 157). This of course marks contrastivity with Profiles B and C as erroneous. But the claim of "error" is unfounded even within the scope of contrastive intonation as Couper-Kuhlen has defined it. She cites three examples of supposed erroneous use of contrastive intonation. Two of them are indeed errors of a sort (they led to miscommunication), but they are the result not of wrong intonation type but of accenting the wrong word; as far as one can tell, both the contrast and the contrastive intonation are there but have been misaligned.[1] The third example is simply an instance of the broader significance of Profile A, not, as claimed, a misuse of the simple fall where instead there ought to be a fall-rise:

(21)　We $^{\text{have a great deal of free wi}}_{\qquad\qquad\qquad\qquad\qquad\quad 1_{1.}}$

"From the context," Couper-Kuhlen says, "it is clear that free will is being partially but not totally conceded," and therefore the fall-rise is called for (AC on *will*). But suppose we add (22) to (21):

(22)　I ^{grant} You that. But...

The decisive A profile in (21), with its optional repetition in (22), is a way of making a decisive concession, and is in no sense an error.

Even the instances of failed communication do not necessarily involve errors within the system of prosody. They are more likely errors of strategy; the choice is correct, but the speaker has failed to see its consequences. If you say *I suppose John blames me for this* and I reply

(23)　He doe$^{\text{es.}}$　(= He does indee$^{\text{d.}}$)

using a rise to suggest 'Yes, and how am I supposed to react to it?,'
you may interpret my rise as a question, *He does?*, implying surprise
on my part that John should blame you. I may then need to repair my
response:

```
        me          do   ye
(24) I         he
          an,         e
       a              s,   s.
```

Communication has failed, but not through any form of what might
be called prosodic ungrammaticality.

In short, there is little in Couper-Kuhlen's approach to persuade us
that contrastivity of the "ratherness" type is emblematic of Profile AC
and of a certain style of Profile A (with "fall to baseline"). These profiles have affective meanings associated with their shape, and are appropriate for singling out contrastively the components with which
they are associated, but contrastivity is only one of their applications.[2]

I conclude this chapter with a conversation in which one of the
turns—exactly as spoken—may be taken as either contrastive or as
"expanding" (in the sense of Dik et al. 1980: 46). There are three participants. The first asks *How did he raise the money?* The second replies

(25) He sold his hóuse.

and the third chimes in with

(26) He pawned his wife's jéwelry.

to which the second then responds in either of two ways:

(27) No, he sold his hóuse!
(28) That too?!

If he says (27) he interprets the third speaker's (26) as contrastive: 'He
didn't sell his house; rather, he pawned his wife's jewelry.' If he says
(28) he interprets both (25) and (26) as potentially true. Any reason-
ably good A profile will be fine for either sense of (26), with little danger of misunderstanding. For one thing, the contrastive interpretation
will almost certainly be accompanied by a headshake. Intonation is
not rigidly specified, because it does not exist in a vacuum.

13. Accent and Entailment

In Chapter 9 we saw an attempt to deal with accent from the standpoint of "accent domains," constituents of an utterance having a single accent that applies to all its parts and not just to the word or syllable on which it falls. Thus *John shut the dóor* can be an answer to *What happened?*, in which case the accent on *door* belongs to the utterance as a whole; or to the question *What did John do?*, in which case it belongs to *shut the door*; or to *What did John shut?*, in which case the domain of the accent is just *the door*. We notice that in each case the *what* of the question corresponds to the constituent (from full utterance down to just *the door*) to which the accent belongs.

Ordered Entailments

Another way of describing accent domains is by way of logical entailments, as developed by Wilson and Sperber (1979; cited as WS) and Sperber and Wilson (1986; cited as SW). Wilson and Sperber point out (pp. 310–15) that logical entailments offer a clue to an "ordering principle sensitive to stress [= accent]." The following sentence includes ten logical entailments (WS, p. 311; this and subsequent examples from the two works cited have been renumbered to conform to the sequence here):

(1) You've eaten all my apples.
   (a) You've eaten all my apples.
   (b) You've eaten all of someone's apples.
   (c) You've eaten all of something.
   (d) You've eaten something.
   (e) You've done something.
   (f) You've done something to all my apples.
   (g) You've eaten some quantity of my apples.
   (h) You've eaten all of something of mine.
   (i) Someone's eaten all my apples.
   (j) Something's happened.

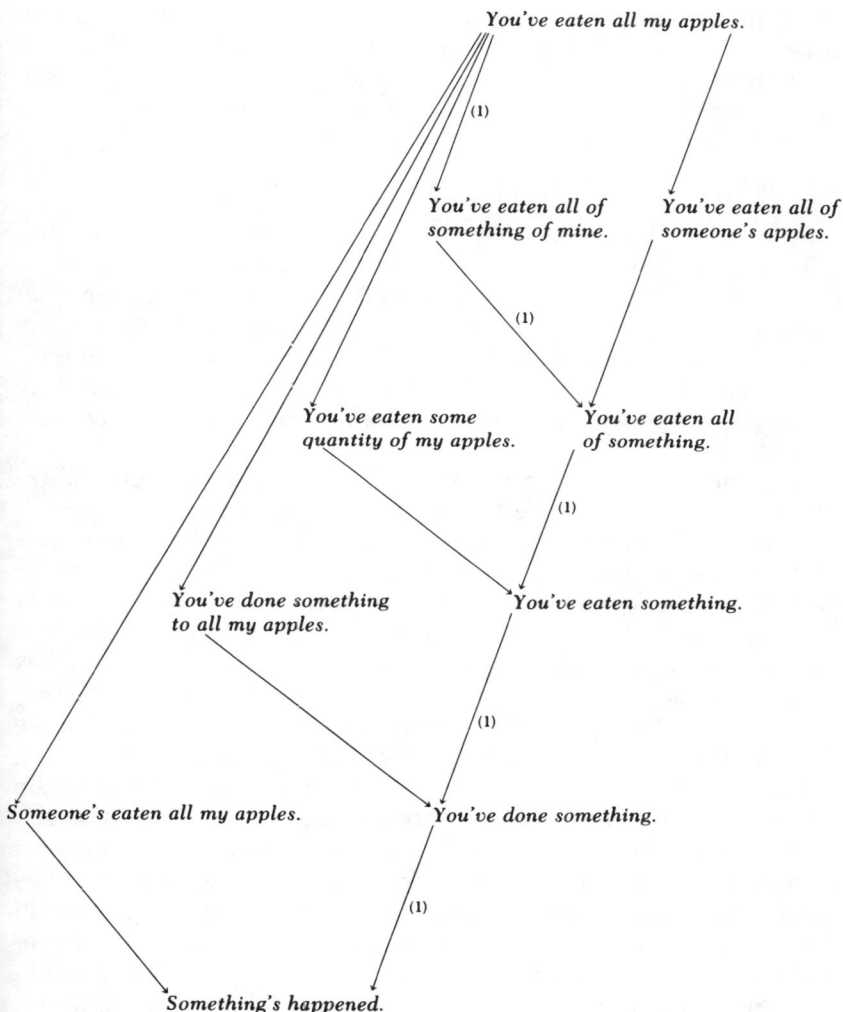

Fig. 2. Ordered entailments. (Reprinted from Wilson and Sperber 1979: 312, with permission of the publisher and the authors.)

In each case (except the first, where the sentence entails itself) a variable with *some-* replaces a constituent of the sentence, e.g. *my* in (b) and *my apples* in (c). There is an ordering in these entailments, which can be diagrammed (WS, p. 312) as shown in Figure 2.

The prosodic claim that Wilson and Sperber make in their work is illustrated by taking a particular path down this diagram. That path constitutes a "focal scale" within the entire "focal range" (consisting of all the grammatically specified entailments, i.e., all of (1a–j). The scale is determined by the location of the accent. So if we follow the path marked by (1), we get h, c, d, e, and j, in that order, with *something* (*someone*) replacing each time a larger grammatical constituent, but all embraced by the single phonological pattern

    (2) You've eaten all my ápples.

This is to say that by locating the accent on *apples* the speaker has offered the hearer that particular focal scale, which happens to be the one favored by the fact that end-accents are normal in English.[1] On that scale, "Any syntactic constituent containing the stressed [= accented] item is a possible focus. Thus in (2) the focus associated with the [accented] item *apples* may be either [*sic*] the N *apples*, the NP *my apples*, the NP *all my apples*, the VP *eaten all my apples*, or the sentence as a whole" (WS, p. 314).

Associated with this is the notion of "foreground" and "background." If the focus is the NP *all my apples* we can substitute a variable for that focus and get *You've eaten something*, which is the background. The foreground is "the proposition or propositions above the background on the focal scale," and this "determines the relevance of the utterance" (WS, p. 315). Commonsensically, if you know that someone has eaten all your apples, you also know that someone has eaten something. The relevance of the foreground supersedes the relevance of the background: knowing that someone has eaten something adds little to knowing that someone has eaten all your apples.

The advantage of such an approach, from the standpoint of the hearer, is that it offers a way of processing efficiently what one hears. Utterances are strung out in time: we hear the first word first, the next word next, and so on. It would make sense for processing to go forward in the same manner—for the first word to raise the question in the hearer's mind "What does the mention of this person in this context signify to me?" and to anticipate that the person was engaged in some activity relevant to me and my interests. The grammar of English justifies our expecting that an NP is going to be followed by a VP. So the hearer hypothesizes 'X did something' and the appearance of *has eaten* as the next item becomes easier to make sense of. *Eaten* stimulates its own hypothesis, 'eaten something,' since *eat* is recognized as a transitive verb, and the mention of *all my apples* confirms it and adds its own relevant information.

The psychological reality of this sequential processing is of considerable importance and will be returned to later, but our main concern is the accentual structure that Sperber and Wilson regard as basic. "When focal stress [= accent] falls on the last word of an utterance, as it does in (2), the set of anticipatory logical hypotheses made during the interpretation process coincides with the focal scale" (SW, p. 209). In other words, no phonological distinction is recognized among the instances of *You've eaten all my ápples* regardless of which constituent (*apples, my apples, all my apples, eaten all my apples,* or *you've eaten all my apples*) is in focus.

The consequences of this can be seen in the example (SW, p. 215)

(3) It rained on Mónday.

which the authors say "has a range of possible foci: 'Monday,' 'on Monday,' and the sentence as a whole. It is thus construable as an answer to the questions *On what day did it rain?*, *When did it rain?*, and *What happened?*"

In the first place, this utterance would not be used at all to respond to a question like *What happened when I was away?* [2] or *Did anything happen while I was away?* With no accent on *rained* and the focal accent on the temporal phrase, the result is either contrastive ('It didn't rain on Tuesday, as you supposed, but on Monday') or it answers the question *When did it rain?* Temporal phrases are not thus exclusively foregrounded. What the speaker could have said to answer *Did anything happen while I was away?* is

```
      rain
(4) It                        (A+AC)
                Mon
      ed on        day.
```

with the principal accent on *rained*. Or the speaker could select the example (SW, p. 215)

(5) On Monday it ráined.

provided she (the feminine is Sperber and Wilson's convention for 'speaker') also put a subsidiary accent on *Monday* (otherwise this answer would have to apply to the question *What happened on Monday?*). We note that the intonation profiles remain the same, but are reversed: the subsidiary is again on *Monday* and the main on *rained*, but the sequence is now AC + A. [3]

One Accent per Phrase?

But the weakness of the prosodic treatment in Sperber and Wilson goes deeper than the failure to take account of melodic prosody. It inherits from its transformational predecessors a hypnotic concentration on one accent per phonological phrase: the focus, main stress, nuclear stress, or whatever. The foreshortening of "accent" to "focal accent" is pervasive in Sperber and Wilson's treatment, as can be seen by the following:

1. The marking of contrastivity. "The distinction between normal and contrastive stress affects the choice of focus. For instance, if (2) is assigned normal sentence stress, with the heaviest stress falling on the noun *apples*, it seems that the hearer is steered towards selection of one of the larger possible constituents as focus: essentially the largest NP, or the VP, or even the S. On the other hand, use of heavy or contrastive stress on *apples* seems to steer the hearer towards selection of one of the *smaller* possible constituents as focus: in this case the noun *apples* or the NP *my apples*" (WS, p. 315).

In the first place, there is no phonological distinction between "normal" and "contrastive" stress (= accent). All we have is a RELATIONSHIP (see Bolinger 1961, 1965). Wilson and Sperber (1979) have not excluded the presence of accents other than the focal one, ("with the heaviest stress falling on the noun *apples*"), but they assign no importance to them, and for all one can tell, such additional accents are present in both the "normal" and the "contrastive" cases. What happens with "contrastive" accent, or what we *hear* as contrastive, is not the phonetic force of that accent (though speakers do tend to make such accents more prominent for affective reasons), but the degree to which it overshadows all others. In a typical contrastive situation there are *no* accents elsewhere, and the contrastive accent dominates the scene by default.

When there are accents elsewhere, there must be a reason, else why would the speaker bother? If the hearer is "steered towards one of the larger constituents" it is not because a "normal" focal accent is given, unless all we mean by that is that other accents are present along with the focal one. Those other accents are what do the steering to the larger constituents, since they are distributed at large.

In this case, accents *before* the focal one are important.

2. A supposed difference between English and French. Given the English (6) and its French equivalent (7),

(6) Yóu must do the washing up.
(7) Il faut que vous fassiez la vaisselle.

Sperber and Wilson (1986) claim that French does not have "utterance-internal contrastive" accent unless the noncontrasted part is an outright echo. That is, it would be limited to an exchange like

(8) He: Il faut que vous fassiez la vaisselle.
    She: Non, il faut que vóus fassiez la vaisselle. (p. 213)

There are two problems with this comparison. First, the French example is doubtful on grounds that have nothing to do with whether French can or cannot have utterance-internal contrastive accent. It is awkward, in the best of circumstances, to highlight a clitic such as *vous* (the echo in [8] forces the issue sufficiently to make it borderline rather than simply unacceptable). If the pronoun is replaced by a substantive, e.g. *Ce matin Paulétte fera la vaisselle*, the result may be utterance-internally contrastive without any echo. (I owe this example to Benoît de Cornulier.) The second problem is that even the English cannot be excused from the "echo" requirement if (6) is to have no prominence whatever after *you*. In a situation where the first speaker is saying, out of the blue, after the meal, *This time you must do the washing up*, and is neither repeating outright nor thinking of some recent discussion of the matter, there will be prominences after that initial blast on *you*:

(9) You

        must ^{do} the ^{wash}ing ^u
                            p.

In this case, accents other than the focal one occur *after* the focus, even when outright contrast (x rather than y) is intended.

3. Topics. According to Sperber and Wilson (1986) sentence topics (= themes) are defined as "generally unstressed [= unaccented] syntactic constituents occurring early in the utterance, whose function in our framework is to give access to encyclopedic information which the speaker regards as crucial to the interpretation process" (p. 216). The latter part of the definition is probably correct. The first part is simply wrong. Whereas topics *may* be unaccented, if they are we can almost be guaranteed some sort of echo, as in

(10) A: What do you think of the new tax laws?
     B: The new tax laws make me sick!

The new tax laws is topic, and as it is recoverable from the immediately preceding context, the speaker is free to put it on a low-pitched monotone, without accent. But it is more likely to carry an accent or two. Otherwise there is usually no point in repeating—the speaker is more apt to substitute a pronoun: *They make me sick!* And when there is no echo, the likelihood of accents is even stronger:

(11) A: Why did your brother hit you?
     B: His excúse was that Í hit hím first.

Far from being regularly unaccented, topics may even be contrastive, as in a case like this response to the question *How does your sister Mary feel about being kissed?*

```
(12) Ma
       ry wouldn't mi
                    nd.
```

—'that's the kind of person she is, unlike other people.'

Where topics more often approach level is when they follow the comment (= rheme), violating Sperber and Wilson's "early in the utterance." The tax question in (10) can be answered

```
          sick
(13) I get
                when I think of the new tax laws.
```

but subsidiary accents can occur even here.

Since topics are by definition nonfocal, we again have utterance material that carries nonfocal accents, this time either before or after the focus.

Sperber and Wilson's "ordered entailments" depend on NESTED variables rather than linear ones. The variables are added one at a time, and each incorporates its predecessor. This makes a neat logical model, but when we ask ourselves what is meant by the "focus being on the entire utterance" we are entitled to wonder why that fact should manifest itself with only one accent, at the end. It would seem that there ought to be as many points of interest as there are things in that utterance that require elucidation, and this makes for a linear model, such as

(14) Somebody's somethinged some quantity of somebody's something.

which would be the entailed background for an utterance like

(15) Yóu've éaten áll mý ápples (you scoundrel, you)!

To insist that the focal accent is not alone is not to deny its privileged status; (15) could be expressed

(16) My ápples! You've éaten áll of them!

There is no need to repeat here the discussions of how accents of power are adjusted to accents of interest (see Bolinger 1986: 88). What concerns us now is the multiple points of interest that are encountered in most ordinary utterances—even, occasionally, multiple foci with interest equally shared as in the example (see Bolinger 1986: 294)

(17) An
```
        as                        Ma
            teroid  just landed on      rs
                                          !
```

—to say nothing of the cases of pure power where there is a complete separation between accent and focus, as in the threat

(18) Get

your carcass out of here!

in which everything after *get* can be reduced to a virtual whisper.

Extra Accents and "Relevance"

If Sperber and Wilson had only realized it, they had in their grasp a strong confirmation of their main theoretical point, and they let it slip because of the dead hand of transformational prosody. For their guiding principle of "relevance," the key factors are the "contextual effects" of the perceptions and inferences of which the hearer is beneficiary,[4] plus the ease of processing the assumptions that the hearer makes. If our conception of "interest" is correct, it is very close to Sperber and Wilson's "relevance for the hearer," and extra accents to point up what is most relevant would be the best prosodic contribution the speaker could make toward ease of processing. So if we take an utterance such as (19), in response to *What is the problem, then, where regulating the field is concerned?*

(19) Certain deviant hypotheses defy formulation.

the likelihood is that every word will carry an accent, simply because every one is interesting by reason of expected effects on the cognitive world of the hearer. Focus on the utterance demands focus on all of its lexical items, which, as semantic contentives, are far stronger candidates for emphasis than the abstract category of any grammatical constituent. To have a single accent, on *formulation*, would be normal only if part or all of the stuff were already on the boards and could be expected to have few or no contextual effects. In testing accent it is critical to separate banal examples from interesting ones. Just the first word of (19) is enough to suggest what is wrong with cases that are a flat desert until one arrives at the nuclear accent. *Certain* is a determiner, like *the* and *a*; but unlike *the* it does not imply that its noun referent is already known (or, if cataphoric, is to be explained forthwith), and unlike *a* it does not suggest something indifferent or trivial. Instead, the hearer is invited to look around for the identity and to narrow the field. The majority of Sperber and Wilson's examples have, as subjects, either pronouns or proper nouns, both of which imply *familiarity* to speaker and hearer. Sperber and Wilson are interested in contextual effects of varying degrees of strength; it is important for their position to realize that those degrees are reflected directly (though not without modification by other factors) in the strength of the accents.

The groundwork for what I am calling *familiarity* has already been done by Sperber and Wilson in their truly excellent discussion of mutual knowledge and mutual manifestness (SW, pp. 38–46). They point out that for their position, "background information is information that contributes only indirectly to relevance, by reducing the processing effort required; it need be neither given nor presupposed. Foreground information is information that is relevant in its own right by having contextual effects; it need not be new" (p. 217). These overlapping realms imply a scale of need-to-highlight. Communicators may assume familiarity without assuming that what they assume to be familiar to the interlocutor is also given or presupposed at the moment of speaking. They may also assume that something is striking enough to produce contextual effects in their hearers without assuming that it is assumed to be new. In all this we have the theory of mutual manifestness whereby "'manifest' is weaker than 'known' or 'assumed,' a notion . . . which does not suffer from the same psychological implausibility as 'mutual knowledge' or 'mutual assumptions'" (p. 41). What is mutually manifest comes by way of shared physical and cognitive environments, with all degrees of overlap.

So it is quite consonant with Sperber and Wilson's general position that two responses to the question *What are your plans for the evening?* such as

(20) I'm having a date with a friend.
(21) I'm reading some Shakespeare with a friend.

are apt to show differences that have nothing to do with the fact that *friend* will probably be accented in both. People have dates all the time. The questioner may already know that the respondent frequently goes out on dates. Friends are people that one is apt to have dates with, so that just mentioning 'friends' can encapsulate the likelihood of a date without emphasizing the word *date*. The upshot is that (20) can be produced with a single accent, on *friend*. The circumstances do not require that dates or having dates or having this particular date or this person's being involved need have been mentioned by the respondent or thought of by the questioner beforehand. Quite the opposite is true of the second response. Unless the interlocutors are on intimate enough terms for the questioner to know that the respondent makes a practice of reading Shakespeare with a friend, assuming that that is actually the case, the content of the utterance is unfamiliar enough to arouse the speaker (subjectively) or to cue him (objectively) to a need for explicitness, and for the hearer to require some help in processing it. This is evident merely at the phonetic level: the hearer needs extra help in hearing clearly what is relatively unexpected. The result is that both *reading* and *Shakespeare* will be accented. The differences are made more dramatic if the responses are put in the opposite order. It is normal to say

```
         friend
(22) A

             and I are having a date.
```

with terminal flat monotone, whereas

```
         friend
(23) ?A

             and I are reading some Shakespeare.
```

would be quite unusual. In (22) we are *allowed* to have extra accents after the main one (so long as the speaker wishes to put in the extra effort, the hearer has no cause to complain), but in (23) we are virtually *forced* to say, with added accents,

```
         friend
(24) A
                         read          Shakes
         and I are       ing some
                                          peare.
```

And here you can take your pick of what you want to regard as "focus"—*friend* or *Shakespeare*. Unless the speaker implies something like 'Just imagine that!,' in which case *Shakespeare* could have the higher pitch, the highest pitch will go on *friend*, the center of interest in this case. Accent cannot be isolated from intonation where focus is concerned.

With some adjustments, all this could be fitted into Sperber and Wilson's major treatment without disruption. A theory of relevance-to-the-person is expansive enough to embrace it.

The Psychological Reality of Left-to-Right Processing

The one-accent-per-utterance position is essential to Sperber and Wilson's notion of ordered entailments and focal scales, and if more than one accent must be accounted for, the scale breaks down, because it depends on the hearer's ability to pick out the focal accent in the course of processing item by item from left to right (from before to after). Here is how they describe the process, using the two examples (SW, p. 215)

>   (25) On Monday it ráined.
>   (26) On Mónday it rained.

By the time the hearer of (25) has processed the words 'On Monday,' he knows that there is some question about what happened on Monday which the speaker thinks is relevant to him. In other words, the effect of fronting the unstressed [= unaccented] constituent 'On Monday' is to force it into the background. By the same token, by the time the hearer of (26) has processed the words 'On Monday,' he should know that they give the answer to some question which he should at this point be able to access for himself.

This would be true if in (25) *Monday* were truly unaccented—that is, a flat monotone at reduced energy with no pitch variation—in which case 'Monday' would have been mentioned in the immediately preceding context. But 'background' has to be more inclusive than this— the speaker can surely have in mind that there is something about Monday's happenings that will be relevant to the hearer, without the stipulation that that something be the hearer's own immediately preceding utterance. And in that case (and potentially even with the actual repetition) there will be an accent on *Monday*.

The problem that the hearer now confronts is how to identify the accent on *Monday*. With strict left-to-right processing there is no way for him to judge whether that accent is subsidiary, in which case the description of (25) correctly applies (except for the "unstressed" part), or is focal, in which case the intended utterance is (26). It is true that if the accent on *Monday* is quite reduced there is a greater expectation that a more potent accent will follow, but that is not guaranteed—the speaker may have decided to be more subdued overall.

So it appears that the kind of left-to-right processing atomism that may or may not be appropriate for syntax will not do at all for prosody. Before the prosodic pattern of an utterance can be identified it must be scanned in its entirety. In particular, the relative height of accents is so crucial that earlier ones cannot be judged without reference to later ones. This applies to intonation terminals as well: something as important as whether an utterance is a question or a statement may, if a question is marked by pitch alone, have to be left in the balance till the last accented syllable. It is surely more efficient to remit an entire utterance to echoic memory than to have to work through and correct initial assumptions that are subject to this degree of error.[5]

The Importance of Words

Against Sperber and Wilson's view that accents belong to syntactic constituents we have set the view that accents are part of the richness of words. What kept Sperber and Wilson from seeing this, even though it is congenial to their theory of encyclopedic memory, was apparently the impoverishment of the lexicon under which so much recent linguistic theorizing has labored. Truth-functions have deprived it of semantics and reductionism has left it a heap of disassembled parts.[6] Disregard for words pervades Sperber and Wilson's work, and is not limited to the prosody. It shows up in the overlooking of entries, in the insistence on computation when none is necessary, and in the virtually orthographic setups used to illustrate disambiguation. I give an example of each.

To illustrate "concepts . . . which are not lexicalised and which therefore have an empty lexical entry" (SW, p. 92), Sperber and Wilson identify "the general concept lexicalised as 'the military' or 'the armed forces'" for which the counterpart term embracing 'soldier/ sailor/airman' is lacking. Not only does such a term exist, it even has its gender distinction: *serviceman, servicewoman.*

Sperber and Wilson assert that the utterance *This room is a pigsty* "is not an explicature" (= does not communicate its logical form), as it would be if the speaker expected the hearer "to start looking around for pigs" (SW, p. 225). "The only obvious explicature" of this utterance is *The speaker is saying that this room is a pigsty*, not *This room is filthy*. Given the fact that any current dictionary of English has to give 'filthy place' or words to that effect as one of the definitions of *pigsty* or *pigpen*, there is no need to compute a meaning by way of the original metaphor. In fact, *This room is a pigpen*, *This room is filthy*, *This room is a mess*, and *This room is a disgrace* have been repeated so many thousands of times that they are retrievable whole.

The disambiguation of the sentence *I saw that gasoline can explode* is treated as if only the spelling counted. The hearer will find "the complementiser interpretation [of *that*] . . . less effort-consuming" and therefore prefer it (SW, p. 187). But since the complementizer has shwa and the demonstrative *that* has [æ], in addition to the fact that a verb such as *see* plus *that* with shwa is grammatically formulaic, plus the fact that *can*, too, will have a telltale shwa, there is no ambiguity to compel any such calculation.

What Segment Owns the Focal Accent?

Whatever one may say about other accents, there is still the question of whether the FOCAL accent is the property of some individual word (or its meaning) or of some grammatical constituent larger than the word.

There is of course no either-or answer, if for no other reason than that of the indefinite boundaries of lexical entries. Flexional forms are not accented on their inflexions, and a "free" element that serves the same function will not necessarily be accented either, and the upshot is that some syntactic segments are treated as a unit and given a single accent:

(27) Where did you go?—Hóme(ward).
(28) Where did you go?—To the óffice.

Granted this much (with of course the reservation that the function words *can* be accented in their own right), we can restate the alternatives: does the accent belong more to the word or more to the larger constituent?

Since we have seen that in all cases there may be subsidiary accents before or after the main one, it must be conceded that the subsidiary ones, at least, belong where they fall, and to the larger constituent only indirectly. (Though "where they fall" conceivably applies to some segment larger than a word.) That leaves the question of where the main accent belongs, which is the problem addressed by ordered entailments and Sperber and Wilson's theory of left-to-right processing, as well as Gussenhoven's "accent domains." Can we make a case for that accent belonging to its word more than to the larger constituent—that is, that its position is determined by the particular significance of that word within the whole, more than by other factors?

On one thing there is no dispute: every complete utterance has at least one accent. That accent was identified as "rhematic" (Bolinger 1986: 49); it is associated with what the utterance is *about*. The other pole of the opposition, the thematic accent, though it may be just as prominent as the rhematic one, is optional, because themes so often represent assumptions already shared by the interlocutors. So the issue is further refined: is the position of the rhematic accent determined by some principle of lastness, or by the nature and meaning of a given word and the special contribution that that word makes to the whole?

We must not make the mistake of denying a principle of lastness. There is such a principle, but it belongs in a description of accents of power: the great majority of major accents occur at or near the end, because speakers want to convince their hearers, and end position is the position with greatest impact, with the strongest implication of earnestness. And that fact is exploited by maneuvering important words into that position. But it does not have a direct bearing on the relevance of the individual word, and can be eliminated from our comparisons by carefully selecting an example to which it does not necessarily apply—an example in which the speaker is free to place the rhematic accent in any one of several positions without implying an echo or a repetition. In a case like

> (29) You ought to be ashámed of yourself!—Yóu ought to be ashamed of yóurself!

the unaccented material between the accents in the response is repeated. What we are looking for is something that can come out of the blue, requiring no more familiarity than a generally shared cognitive environment on the part of the interlocutors.

Try a mini-conversation like this, where the question poses the theme and the entire response is the rheme:

> (30) A: What is wrong with this society?
> B: The average American expects too much of people.

A has set the stage so that everything in B's response is easily accessible by B. 'This society' embraces 'the average American'; 'something wrong with' suggests something out of alignment, only a short step from 'too much'; and 'people' are always around. So everything here is a possible candidate for no accent at all, and we are free to put the main accent according to the point that we want to make, uncluttered by other accents. The rhematic accent can fall in any one of five positions:

> (31)(a) The average American expécts too much of people.
> (b) The average American expects tóo much of people.
> (c) The average American expects too múch of people.
> (d) The average American expects too much óf people.
> (e) The average American expects too much of péople.

In Sperber and Wilson's terms, any one of these answers, and not just the one with the accent on *people*, may "focus" on the utterance as a whole—that is, may answer the question *What happens?*, *What gives?*, *What's the situation?*, etc. What then, aside from the power aspects, controls its falling in one place rather than another?

The answer is in what the word contributes to the point that the speaker wants to make. That point can be extracted, placed first, and then commented upon with the accent at the designated place. Responses (a)–(e) then look like this:

(32) (a) (What's wrong with this society is) óptimism. The average American expécts too much of people.

(b) Always going to extrémes. The average American expects tóo much of people.

(c) Not knowing when enough is enóugh. The average American expects too múch of people.

(d) Miscalculating what you can gét. The average American expects too much óf people. ('of' = 'out of')

(e) We're only húman. The average American expects too much of (mere) péople.

What's wrong with our society is our (over-)optimism, our demandingness, our exploitativeness, and our frailty. The speaker is free to emphasize any one of these as the main point, or any two, or three, or all together, and in any combination. All are "relevant" by virtue of the speaker's intent and all are codifiable in the language. There are power differences in the position of the accent and in the number of accents, but that is a separate matter.

Of the two competitors, the word asserts a stronger claim to the accent than does any larger constituent. In a way it almost seems as if the whole debate were set on a false premise, that something has to be accented in order to count and that if a VP, say, lacked an accent it would somehow not be there. If we utter something at all it is as much a part of the substance of what we say as when we accent it. The accent is designed—as the term *focus* originally meant—to highlight some *part* of the utterance as particularly significant. If other parts are significant, more accents are added. There is a kind of absurdity in the notion of focus on some larger constituent, especially "focus on the sentence as a whole." If we floodlight the side of a barn, that hardly amounts to focusing on anything. It may be that when we say *The average American expects too múch of people* we are also interested in averages, in Americans, in expecting, and in people; but what we are *focusing* on is a muchness. To wring another meaning from *focus* is to distort the immediacy of what the speaker does when he puts an accent on something.

What we highlight in greater or lesser degree is what we feel most intensely about, as embodied in our lexical code; and that feeling is governed, at least in part, by—what else?—Sperber and Wilson's principle of relevance.

14. Accent and Denial

In a section of his article "Focus, Mode, and the Nucleus," Gussen-hoven (1983: 406–11) broaches the question of "mode" in relation to the placement of accent. Mode has two values, [+ counterassertive] and [− counterassertive]. A [+ counterassertive] utterance is one with which the speaker "tries to prevent the addressee from adding an incorrect Variable to the Background," that is, from misinforming what is already pertinent shared knowledge with some incorrect fact that is not part of that knowledge. A [− counterassertive] utterance is simply the unmarked value, that is, anything else.

Examples of [+ counterassertive] are

(1) The HOUSE is on fire. — The house ISn't on fire!
(2) The hóuse isn't on FIRE. — The hóuse ís TOO on fire!

Examples of [− counterassertive]:

(3) Are you planning to VISit them? — Our CAR is out of commission.

(4) They prefer not to be TOLD. — There's no need TO tell them.

(The acute is used for non-main, and capitals for main, accents.)

Where the fun starts is the point at which the plus and minus values of [counterassertive] meet. Counterassertion involves denial, by definition. But certain [− counterassertive] utterances also deny. Gussenhoven exemplifies with

(5) What OTHer artistes [besides Patty Grey] have been in your car? — Patty Grey was never IN my car.

in which the speaker denies the false premise that Patty Grey had been there. The same relationship holds when countering the presuppositions in wh questions in general, e.g.

(6) Why was Patty Grey in your CAR? — Patty Grey was never IN my car.

The term that Gussenhoven adopts (p. 406) for this sort of [− counterassertive] utterance is *counterpresuppositional*, following Dik et al. (1980: 51). Gussenhoven's interpretation of the term seems to differ from that of Dik, however,[1] and had best be judged on its own merits. An example of what he regards as counterpresuppositional is the following:

> (7) (Stop squirting WAter all over the house. I TOLD you.) The house isn't ON fire!

Instead of diverting an incorrect Variable from the Background, the speaker here "is concerned to 'debug' his addressee's Background" (p. 406). In (1) an assertion is countered; in (7) a false assumption is rectified.

Direct and Indirect Denial

A [− counterassertive] "polarity" sentence is thus an INDIRECT DENIAL, contrasting with the direct denial of the [+ counterassertive]. Here is a pair, adapted from Gussenhoven's example 114 (p. 412), in which the "counters" are identical but the first is direct and the second indirect:

> (8) You tóok the gárbage out when I told you NOT to. — I DIDn't take the garbage out!
>
> (9) Whý did you take the garbage out when I told you NOT to? — I DIDn't take the garbage out!

This pair shows that there is no necessary "surface" distinction between the two kinds of denial. The presupposition in a wh question may be fairly close to an assertion, and the same is true of a factive verb:

> (10) It's tóo bád you took the GARbage out. — I DIDn't take the garbage out!

As Gussenhoven describes the situation, the two homonymous responses in (8) and (9) are presumably the result of coincidence. In a direct denial the accent "goes to the operator," which in (8) is *did* (separately on *not* is an alternative possibility),[2] whereas in an indirect denial it goes "to the last verb phrase element but one, or to the rightmost preposition or *to* particle, if present" (p. 411). Examples (9) and (10) illustrate the "last verb phrase element but one" possibility, which here again is *didn't*; examples (5) and (7) illustrate the prepositional possibility, and the following illustrates *to*:

> (11) After you búy it, what will you DO with it? — I have no móney TO buy it!

The possibilities are actually wider than Gussenhoven's formulation allows. A direct denial may go to the main verb:

(12) You didn't do what I TOLD you. — I DID what you told me! Every BIT of it!

This is almost preferable to *did do* because of the repetition in the latter. Similarly *have* as a main verb, at least in some dialects:

(13) She says you have the time to DO it. — Unfortunately I HAVEn't the time.

Likewise in dialects that use *never* as a simple negative particle:

(14) She sáys you bróke her CHIna. — I never BROKE her china, and I don't care WHAT she says!

In keeping with the later position of the accent this is a more truculent retort than *I DIDn't break her china*. Though ungrammatical, "foreigner English" does the same:

(15) I no BROKE her china!

This is common enough in infant speech.
    The accent may even fall on a later element, as in

(16) I díd exACTly what you told me! Every bit of it!

or in

(17) You didn't leave me the KEYS. — I léft them right there on your DESK!

and even just *I léft you the KEYS!* is a possible response, despite the repetition—or rather because of the repetition as a means to make the response more threatening: it can be accompanied by an ominous shaking of a finger.[3]

Relevance of Direct and Indirect to Accent

If the formal restrictions are not quite as depicted, we have the right to wonder whether the contrast of direct and indirect denial is actually the key to whatever differences in accentuation there may be. Even in manifestly direct denial we have the possibility of a climactic shift of accent:

(18) A: By this time John will have been studying for at least an HOUR.
    B: You're misTAken. John WON'T have been studying.
        John won't HAVE been studying!
        John won't have BEEN studying!!

And supposed cases of indirect denial are also suspect. Looking at (7) again, we detect an element that does not exclude direct denial, namely *I told you*. Does *repeating* a denial have something to do with the shift of accent? Make the repetition explicit:

> (19) The HOUSE is on fire. — The house ISn't on fire. — Ha, HA! What's that SMOKE coming out of the basement? The house IS on fire! — I'll téll you aGAIN, the house isn't ON fire! That smóke is stéam from the CLOTHES-drier!

If the interlocutor were to persist still, the speaker's next round might be to say

> (20) I've TOLD you and I've TOLD you, the house isn't on FIRE!

There is thus a gradation of stronger and stronger denials:

> (21) The house ISn't on fire.
> The house isn't ON fire.
> The house isn't on FIRE.

As a last resort, the speaker may accent everything:

> (22) The HOUSE IS NOT ON FIRE!

The reader may test the orderliness of this buildup by trying to reverse the sequence: to say *The house ISn't on fire* as the last rather than the first response is insipid. The power function of accenting *on* can be seen when the speaker directly denies his own previous assertion:

> (23) The HOUSE is on fire. — You're NUTS. The house ISn't on fire . . . NO, WAIT, WAIT! It's really ON fire! WOW! You were RIGHT!

We shall presently be concerned with the semantic value of such elements as *on*. It can be discerned here in the partial synonymy between 'It's really ON fire!' and 'It's really GOing!'—the *on* refers to process, i.e., to something *ongoing*.

I believe that this manifestation of CLIMAX is what underlies the phenomena that have been attributed to [± counterassertion], and that the role of such logico-semantic concepts is not immediate but contributory.

What we need at this point is an array of examples similar to (7) in the accenting of the preposition but with the import of direct denial:

> (24) The rival firms are now under CONtract. — NO, they're not UNder contract. They will probably NEVer be.

> (25) Our próblems are out of the WAY. — NO, they're not OUT of the way yet. There's a LOT still to do.

(26) The bóok is by Elías KAHR. — NO, the book isn't BY that author. It's by a compárative NEWcomer.

(27) Librárian, pléase let me have the BOOK. That lády is thróugh with her READing. — She's not THROUGH with her reading. Pléase be PAtient.

With these possibilities before us, it does not seem too strange that one might give the same direct denial in the *house* example, especially if the deixis is sharpened with a demonstrative and the intonation, after a rising *no*, is uniformly falling—the speaker has given careful thought to the matter and intends to go on with an explanation: In response to *That HOUSE is on fire!* he says

```
         o, that house isn't
(28) No                       o
                              N
                                fire.   It ⟶
      looks
just
         that way in the  set ting  su
                                      n.
```

The speaker's reflectiveness is also evidenced in the fact that whereas *No it ISn't on fire* can be spoken without a prosodic break after *no*, (28) requires the break—the speaker is formulating his thoughts. The same pattern serves when the speaker blunts the emphasis by apologizing:

(29) That HOUSE is on fire. — Bégging your PARdon, that house isn't ON fire.

or by pretending that the fact is new to him, the emphasis being due to 'surprise':

(30) The HOUSE is on fire. — Oddly eNOUGH, the house isn't ON fire.

The advantage conferred in these cases is that of being emphatic without being rude. To emphasize the negative, e.g.

(31) Our próblems are out of the WAY. — NO, they're NOT out of the way.

(32) She's thróugh with her READing. — She ISn't through with her reading.

is pretty close to calling the addressee a liar, and the speaker's strategy is to move away from contradicting him and toward setting him straight about the facts.[4] Any segment of the facts is a potential for his diversionary emphasis. In (26) the speaker introduces the anaphoric term *author*, which is a factual interpretation of the writer's name and a good alternative candidate for the accent:

(33) NO, the bóok isn't by that AUthor.

To do the same with the name of the author would be normal but would again risk offense: parroting is dangerous.

This gives us a clue to the effectiveness of indirect denial. It enables the speaker to introduce material for accenting, and leave it up to the hearer to infer the connection: cf.

(34) We had a gréat tíme at Láke PLAcid, dídn't we? — You were DRUNK the whole time.

Since the material has to be related to what is being denied, the speaker must limit himself to what the hearer will infer to be connected—in other words, Background. So in a case like

(35) That HOUSE is on fire. — That house is ábsolutely FIREproof.

the hearer has an easy task: since x is the case, y is not the case, y being the allegedly mistaken assertion *That HOUSE is on fire*. An answer like the one in

(36) This HOUSE is on fire. — This house *manifestly doesn't have* the *propensity to catch on fire*.

provides eight locations at which just a single accent suffices, or the speaker may accent any combination. The indirect denial yields, of course, 'Since the house manifestly doesn't have the propensity to catch on fire, it isn't on fire.'

In some cases the indirection is so slight that the denial is virtually direct; in fact, it may represent indirection as a courtesy device, as in the following:

(37) The HOUSE is on fire. — (a) The house CAN'T be on fire!
                              (b) The house can't BE on fire!

If the house can't be on fire, it isn't on fire. The factual is inferred from the potential. (The [a] response is understood here in its literal sense, not as expressing doubt as to the veracity of the speaker's own judgment—a sense to which *can it?* would be a natural addition.) But what is of prosodic interest is the separation of *be* from the auxiliary, and the resulting possibility of accenting it and so accenting the element of stativeness. A similar separation can be managed with the future of probability:

(38) Right about NOW, John will be in his GARden. — Right about nów John WON'T be in his garden.

(39) Right about NOW, John will be in his GARden. — At thís time
of day John won't BE in his garden.

—direct denial in the first, indirect in the second, which is roughly
equivalent to

(40) At thís time of day it isn't John's *custom* to *be* in his garden.

This again offers two positions for accent, either or both of which may
be used. Given the denial of the consuetudinal aspect of the verb or of
the literal word *custom* itself, the hearer can infer that the stative aspect is also denied. Example (38) has the same possibility—*will be*
stative, *won't be* consuetudinal, but the homophony in the two senses
of *won't* makes it difficult to see.

Validity of the Distinction

It is obvious from these examples that at their point of closest contact it is difficult to maintain the logical distinction between direct and
indirect denial. Pragmatically, if a person states something to be true,
he usually does so because he has come to the supposition that it *is*
true, and supposition can harden into presupposition. That is one
reason why indirect denial so handily uses extra emphasis: the interlocutor may be doggedly holding to a hardened position, and the
speaker becomes impatient. Logically, too, the distinction is tenuous
because given the consequent relationship 'Since x is the case, y is not
the case,' one can substitute the second variable for the first and come
out with a truism for direct denial: 'Since y-is-not-the-case is the case,
y is not the case.' The presence of *but* also suggests that the speaker is
objecting not directly to the interlocutor's utterance but to something
that lies back of it (nearly all of Gussenhoven's examples of indirect
denial either have or can be equipped with *but*):

(41) The HOUSE is on fire. — But we've góne through the place
róom by ROOM. The house (obviously) *isn't on fire.*

The speaker could stop at *ROOM*, and the response would be indirect; but he goes on to make the direct denial himself, but still with a
choice of three locations—or any combination thereof—for the accent. The equivalent of *but* may come via intonation:

42) The HOUSE   FIRE!
              isn't on

—'how could you suppose such a thing?'[5] Just the difference between an A and a CA profile may accomplish this. In response to *With all those péople around you múst have seen SOMEone!* the CA

(43) There
                n't
              anybody
      WAS   there!

has the effect of a protest, just as with (42), and the most obvious reason for the protest is an unreasonable assumption on the part of the interlocutor. A *but* may easily be added. Less so with the A profile

(44) There
            WAS
           n't anybody there.

unless *simply* is added (But there símply WASn't anybody there!), which again—now verbalized—contains the element of impatience. And this again is true of (44) if *WAS* is prolonged. Any kind of prosodic adornment that suggests arousal tends to carry the implication that the interlocutor has taken an unreasonable position.

The possibility of a presupposition at the very outset is particularly clear with negative assertions, which may well be universally presuppositional anyway.[6] We note that a *but* comes more naturally in countering a negative assertion than in countering an affirmative one:

(45) Mr. SMITH, you have MONey. — Mr. JONES, I DON'T have money.

(46) Mr. SMITH, you don't have MONey. — But Mr. JONES, I DO have money.

As far as I can tell, any assertion may thus be treated as presuppositional, and the distinction between direct and indirect denial vanishes. At the point where an interlocutor asks a question (*I smell smoke. Is the house on fire?*) it is possible for the speaker to prevent the addition of false information to the Background, but once an assertion has been made, the speaker may view it as simply wrong and deny it with the least display of arousal, or as wrongheaded, with various prosodic means to convey dissatisfaction.

The uncertain border between direct and indirect denial can also be found in expressions lacking explicit negation, as in

(47) The HOUSE is on fire. — That's WRONG (= I deNY that the house is on fire).

(48) The HOUSE is on fire. — You're WRONG.

—(48) is indirect (since you are wrong in what you say, what you say is wrong) but pragmatically direct. Similarly

(49) The HOUSE is on fire. — You're CRAzy!

Since you are crazy to say this, this is crazy, i.e., false. It appears a bit farfetched to claim an allusion to Background here, specifically the assumption on the part of the hearer, 'I am sane'; it seems rather to be a straightforward denial, with a reaction to wrongheadedness.

Contributing to the uncertainty of the border is the fact that indirect denials are constantly being adopted for direct denial, i.e., for the minimal condition of 'since y-is-not-the-case is the case, y is not the case.' *You're crazy* probably belongs here, as do many stereotypical expressions that either deny generally, as in these responses to *The jury acquitted him*:

(50) Like hell they acquitted him!
(51) The jury acquitted your grandmother!
(52) That's rich!
(53) You're talking through your hat!
(54) In a pig's eye they did!

or deny by some formula associated semantically with the assertion to be countered:

(55) The machíne will FLY. — Like a léad balLOON.

(56) My pócket knife will do the TRICK. — Your pócket knife wouldn't cút hot BUTter.

A test for true consequent relationship—hence indirect denial—is whether the utterance can be paraphrased somehow with *because*. To respond to *The HOUSE is on fire* with

(57) That is not the case, because you are wrong.

is simply redundant. In fact adjectives such as *wrong* prove the indistinctness of the border between direct and indirect in the ease with which the personal becomes impersonal and the impersonal becomes personal. *Wrong*, like *mistaken*, is a FACT modifier, yet we permit both to serve as predicate (not as attributive!—*a wrong person) of a [+ human] subject. *That's wrong* and *That's mistaken* give way to *You're wrong* and *You're mistaken*. *Crazy* moves in the other direction: *You're crazy* alternates with *That's crazy*.

True consequence, with *because*, can be illustrated with a modification of (6):

(58) It is not the case that any artiste in addition to Patty Grey has been in my car, because Patty Grey herself has never been in my car.

Other forms of denial are incorporated in subtle fashion, increasing the variety of ways in which speakers can deny directly. Among these are polarity items, some of them impinging on the central forms of negation. For example,

> (59) Mr. SMITH, you have MONey. — Mr. JONES, I HAVE no money.

No is a quantifier, and though it is spoken sotto voce here and the response is pragmatically a straightforward counterassertion, the consequent relation is still discernible: 'since what I have is zero money, I don't have money.' The speaker could have said

> (60) Mr. JONES, I have NO money.

and the role of the quantifier would become clearer, and more so in

> (61) Mr. JONES, I don't have a CENT.
> (62) Mr. JONES, I don't have a pénny to my NAME.[7]

The overlap between direct and indirect denial is a discourse phenomenon as well as a logical one. The speaker may communicate on two levels at once, denying both directly and indirectly. In response to *John sees lots of bullfights* one may say

> (63) NO, John's never BEEN to Spain. OR Mexico.

The initial *no* is a direct denial, the rest is indirect: the Background includes 'bullfights are confined to Spain and Mexico.' In place of *no*, the speaker may simply produce a headshake, simultaneous with the rest of the utterance.

Direct and Indirect Affirmation

It would be surprising, given the ubiquity of inference in discourse, if affirmation did not show the same direct and indirect choices as denial. So we have direct affirmation:

> (64) John TALKS a lot. — He DOES talk a lot, dóesn't he?

and indirect—(65) is again in response to *John sees a lot of bullfights*:

$$(65) \ \text{We}^{1} \text{,} \ \text{John goes to Spain } \text{every} \ {}_{\text{A}}\text{R.}^{\text{YE}}$$

'therefore you are right, he must see a lot of bullfights.'

The Power Function

The power function of indirect denial—arousal (mostly impatience), whether restrained or not—has already been pointed out. Take the stereotypes using quantifiers. Semantically they provide an a fortiori comment: negate the least and you negate everything above it—in fact, *least* can be so employed:

> (66) Mr. SMITH, you'll be glád you inVESted in this enterprise. — Mr. JONES, I've *never had* the *least* (the *slight*est) in*tention of investing in* it.

And prosodically they provide extra syllables for accenting. In (66) any one or any combination of the italicized syllables may be accented, with *least* being favored.

It is the scalar nature of *least*, *slightest*, and other superlatives that makes the a fortiori comment possible. It follows that a preposition such as *near* can be used in the same way, e.g. in the response to *John climbed the Sears Tower*:

> (67) John *never has been in Chicago*.

Again, any combination may be accented, but if *near* replaces *in* it will attract the most prominent accent. Similarly other scaled expressions:

> (68) I'm SURE you'll like our PROduce. — I wóuldn't feed it to a DOG.

In all these cases 'even' or 'so much as' is implied.

More elaborate indirect denials afford an array of accentables—for instance, subordinate clauses:

> (69) *If* the *house were on fire* you'd see SMOKE.

Any of the italicized words may carry the main accent of the clause. In (69) there is a sort of encapsulation of direct denial in indirect: the *were* is counterfactual, and is also the likeliest candidate for the main accent.

Accents on "Unimportant" Words

A final side issue needs to be disposed of, namely the apparent oddity in the accenting—often the exclusive accenting—of the "little" words, not just in indirect denial, but generally. Accustomed to thinking of prepositions, relatives, conjunctions, and the like as mere function words, we are reluctant to grant them the same accentability as the so-called content words. But looked at carefully, their semantic contribution is seen to be substantial enough to warrant accenting it, for its own sake as well as for power. The preposition *near* in (67) would carry the a fortiori import of the utterance. *In* carries at least the locative sense, and compares with *there* in *John's never been THERE*. Similarly *been* carries the locative sense of *be* (as in *Has the postman been?*), and *has* embraces the entirety of John's past actions: each separate point in the past is denied, and that cancels the point at which the climb might have been made. Provided they make a semantic contribution, the function words serve as well as any others. This enables the speaker to choose as many x's as desired and place them in accentually strategic positions. When the utterance is a global negation, he may focus on any part of it that can semantically result in an overall denial—in a string of $(x_1 x_2 \ldots x_n)$ a negative on any interior member, e.g. $(x_1 \sim x_2 \ldots x_n)$, results in a negation of the whole $\sim (x_1 x_2 \ldots x_n)$. The accent picks out the item to be negated, just as it does with privative *only* in *He ónly goes there on THURSday*.

When a function word does not make a contribution to the meaning of the whole, it is less apt to be accented. There are a good many instances of almost purely mechanical governance of prepositions, where the meaning of the preposition is irrelevant or sometimes even contradictory, and the accent tends to shun these cases. The following is a conversation between a fast-food operator and a supplier. The supplier asks *How much ground beef are you going to need?* and the operator replies

(70) OH, we're not IN the hamburger business now.
(71) OH, we're OUT of the hamburger business now.
(72) *OH, we're out OF the hamburger business now.
(73) OH, we're FINished with the hamburger business now.
(74) *OH, we're finished WITH the hamburger business now.
(75) OH, we're not WITH the hamburger business now.
(76) OH, we're long gone FROM the hamburger business now.

In (72), *of* makes no discernible semantic contribution, and the obvious sense of *with*, 'association,' does not apply to the 'separation' sense of *finished with* in (74), though it fits quite nicely in (75). And a comparison of (74) and (76) shows that the problem does not lie in the grammar of the particle, since *from* does well enough—it signifies the 'dissociation' that fits the context. The most colorless preposition is *of*, but it may be relevant, as in

(77) I like REgency novels. I thínk I'll check out *Góne with the WIND*.
— But *Góne with the Wínd* isn't OF that period.

On the other hand, accentability of these words is a relative matter, responding not only to their meaning but also, as we have repeatedly noted, to the emotive pressure. If in the hamburger examples the question is changed to *Why can't you sell me a hamburger, dammit?*, responses (72) and (74) can well be

> (78) Because we're out OF the hamburger business now!
> (79) Because we're finished WITH the hamburger business now!

And this points to function words as the most effective basis for accents of power, for the pure surprise value of having an accent in an unexpected place: the hearer infers that some special force must apply to put it there. To a certain extent, then, such accents represent DISTORTIONS, and if the phenomenon is a general one we should be able to find instances that do not involve function words. Looking at (70)–(76) we realize that some of the phrases involve expressions that have been to a degree lexicalized: *out of, finished with, gone from* (*out of* gets its own separate entry in many dictionaries). When the accent moves—for example from *out* to *of* in *out of*—one can say that there is a distortion *within* a lexical item. The same shift—especially but not exclusively rightward—is fairly commonplace in longer words whose rhythmic pattern facilitates it. We can thus build climax into Gussenhoven's example (p. 414), containing responses to the question *Have you seen Brídeshead ReVISited?*:

> (80) I don't WATCH television.
> (81) I dón't watch TELevision.
> (82) I dón't watch teleVISion!

The first response denies the relevant action, the second the relevant object while at the same time adding some pressure, and the third does the same with more pressure. Maximum pressure would be found in

> (83) I DON'T WATCH TELeVISion!

Distortion in the opposite direction—leftward—is less frequent, but is found in cases of anticlimax: the impact comes at the beginning, commanding the hearer's attention, but then is played down. Hearing something like

> (84) AGgravation is not something we have to put up with.

with *AG-* high and everything else at a low terminal level, we sense the conciliatory tone, absent in

> (85) Aggravátion is not something we have to put UP with.

This same example illustrates climactic distortion—*put up with* is a lexical item carrying lexical stress on *up*, but the main accent can fall on *put* or on *with*, or it can remain on *up* and be heightened, with maximum climax involving accent on *with* plus other accents as desired. (See Bolinger 1985: 86–90 for more examples of distortion.)

Accent on function words is a larger subject than direct or indirect denial. *Do* is an affirmation-carrier generally:

> (86) You DO understand, I hope.

and the same, in a restricted way, is true of *to*:

> (87) I prefér TO do it rather than NOT to do it.

but this arises from the semantic value of *to*, as can be seen by substituting other elements:

> (88) My préference is FOR doing it rather than NOT doing it.
> (89) I'm more inclíned TOWARD doing it than NOT doing it.

and also by the difficulty of using *to* when this 'favoring of the action, leading toward the action' is missing or reversed:

> (90) Why don't you DO it? —?Because I'm forbídden TO do it.
> (91) Why don't you do it? — Because I'm prohíbited FROM doing it.

Accent on a particle may signal an anaphoric relationship, as in

> (92) If there were anything around here TO eat, I'd be háving a squáre méal ríght NOW.

which is the same sort of backwards coreference as in

> (93) If there were anything around here FOR him, I'd be gíving something to Jóhn ríght NOW.

And accent on a preposition may support a deixis ad oculos, as in

> (94) It's not MUCH, but you're WELcome to it.
> (95) It's not MUCH, but you're wélcome TO it.

—the latter is apt to be accompanied by a gesture pointing to the object in question.

And so on. Indirect denial is only the most interesting breeding ground, because of the way it exploits the possibilities.

Various influences converge on the strategy of indirect denial, enhancing its effectiveness. First, the contradiction is not direct, which allows the speaker to insinuate disagreement without insult. Second, the indirection forces the hearer to figure out the consequent relationship for himself; if he complains about the nondelivery of the mail and is reminded that it is Sunday, he can be made to look foolish. Third, the indirection provides an array of accent positions, enabling the speaker to fine-tune his emphasis (or, less teleologically, enabling various shades of arousal to shine through). Fourth, among those accentable items one often finds or may insert some 'least' condition which when denied makes the statement a fortiori all the stronger. And fifth—perhaps tied in with the accentability of 'least' things—an accent displaced onto a small word or an odd syllable suggests that normal accent has been overpowered and this adds to the impact.

15. An Intonation of Factuality?

We have examined the role of intonation as a definer of, or as defined by, various features of grammar, and have found that almost invariably the relationship is not defining but contributory. There is no "intonation of" grammatical types, but the self-contained meanings of intonational patterns contribute to intersectional meanings that depend on much more than intonation.

Is it possible to overstate this role as well, to see intonation as not merely contributing to a *probable* intersectional meaning but as helping to make such a meaning precise and exceptionless? Do intonational feature A and, say, grammatical feature B add up to exactly logical or informational meaning C, or does vagueness pursue us wherever we go? Of course, assuming full knowledge of the circumstances, a given instance may well have to mean what it means (though to lay claim to full knowledge is to pretend omniscience); the real problem has to do with the utterance and its identifiable and enumerable trappings as a linguistic object, a part of the code, independent of the circumstances of use.

Factuality and Counterfactuality

A made-to-order example is the treatment of "factuality" in Oakeshott-Taylor (1984). Oakeshott-Taylor sees the problem of intonation and grammar with admirable clarity. He rejects the "supposed 'grammatical' functions of intonation" in the phenomena he describes and criticizes the failure to "mention the *contribution* of intonation to the data" (p. 20; I supply emphasis). In his own view, intonation "in some cases . . . is as essential an aspect of sentence structure as syntax" (p. 20). But essentiality is perhaps too strong a claim. Intonation in Oakeshott-Taylor's treatment is made to appear part of a conspiracy to get a fix on a certain meaning, when its role may actually be more limited and diffuse, more in keeping with affect and attitude than with transmitting a certain kind of information. The information does get transmitted, thanks to circumstances of discourse, but one may wonder if the intonation does less on the informational side, and more on the affective, than at first appears.

A more immediate question is whether factuality is a valid linguistic category. The term is reminiscent of the many attempts to impose truth-functional logic on language. What a logician sees as a unitary phenomenon is not necessarily embodied as such in the language.

The point that Oakeshott-Taylor deals with has been dealt with before, by the analysts whom he credits but additionally by Bailey (1983: 16) and Nash and Mulac (1980), most explicitly by the latter. Oakeshott-Taylor's key sentences, in his notation, are

> (1) I `*thought* he was ,married.
> (2) I thought he was `*married*.

responding to *This is John's wife* and *This is John's fiancée* respectively. The contours can be shown as

```
I                                                      mar
  thought                         I  thought he was
        he was  mar^rie^d.                             ri_ed.
```

The lack of accent on *married* in (1) can be seen in the fact that the trough can occur on unaccented *it* in *I `suspected ,it* (after which one can add *He's married!*) or on *so* in *I `thought ,so, he's `married!*; in other words, an AC contour with accent on *thought* rather than an A + C or A + B with additional accent on *married*. 'He was married' is semantically repeated material and unaccented. Anticipating a bit—a question of grammatical tense is involved—the entire fall-rise can occur on the single word *figures* in

```
(3) It  fig              mar
           ures!  He's
                        ri_ed!
```

Example (1) is an instance of 'factuality,' (2) is one of 'counterfactuality.' An example such as

> (4) I think John's married.

is an instance of nonfactuality, which is not under consideration. The speaker "merely reports the contents" of his thoughts.[1]

Intonation does have a lot to do with the interpretations we give to (1) and (2), but to discover how much, we need to look at what each of the factors contributes, including the nonintonational ones, and, in the process, not fall victim to the tendency noted by Nash and Mulac (1980: 239), to prefer imposing "definite, albeit contradictory, interpretations, rather than to recognize inherent ambiguity."

First we need to look a little more carefully at how close the tie is between the intonations and the interpretations. For Nash and Mulac, it is not absolute, but scaled. In (1), the accent in the AC profile is downmoving. Make it upmoving and (1) becomes about evenly balanced between factuality and counterfactuality, given, of course, the appropriate contexts. In response to Ada's *Why did you keep insisting that John had a wife?*, Delia may reply

(5) I ^{thought} he was _{mar}r^{ied.}

which is apologetically counterfactual.

At the same time, a counterfactual interpretation can also be applied to the downmoving intonation in (1) though with a striking difference in affect, which can be appreciated if we add some follow-up words. For counterfactuality with (5), Delia can appropriately add *How could I have gone so wrong!* But Delia could also use (1) and add *It's no fault of mine if everybody misinformed me!* In other words, (5) is sincerely apologetic, (1) in the counterfactual interpretation is self-excusing, potentially churlish. If now we can say that (1) in the factual interpretation is self-congratulatory, the *self* part gives us a clue to a commonality of meaning to be looked at later. The speaker is in control.

There is probably no way, intonationally, to rule out the counterfactual interpretation, with or without an accent elsewhere than on the main verb. Oakeshott-Taylor's (2) has an accented *married* and is counterfactual, but (1), with unaccented *married*, can also be counterfactual, as we have seen. With A, B, C, or CA, the counterfactual interpretation comes through, though with different mood effects, for example the B

(6) I ^{thought he was married.}

is virtually protesting in its appeal: 'This was my best effort, I'm blameless if I was wrong.' The factual interpretation is also possible: the speaker is crowing with delight—she might add

(7) And ^{lo} _{ok!} I was ^{ri} _{ght!}

On the other hand, the factual interpretation becomes more difficult when there is a dominant accent elsewhere than on the main verb. As I have written (2), there is a B on *thought*, but the A on *married*, as in B + A contours in general, is dominant, and to get a factual interpretation on that example one must build in other presuppositions. Imagine that Ada says *This is John's wife*, and Delia replies *Well, sure; I thought he was married* (or *I did think he was married*, or *I grant you that I thought he was married*), using the intonation of (2) (an AC in place of the A on *married* helps this interpretation), and adds *But I thought he was keeping it a secret*. This provides a justification for the accent on *married*: merely having the legal document contrasted with being up-front about it. Other presuppositions lead to a similar result. If Delia assumes that Ada is springing her remark *This is John's wife* as a surprise move to prove that Delia's assumptions are wrong, Delia may assert her real assumptions in the form

(8) I re^{s,} thought he was mar ri e d.

(with rising tail on the B profile), adding *You're not telling me anything I didn't know*. The irritation shows up in a terminal accent of power, though the speaker could just as well have used the more restrained profile in (2). For whatever reason, a dominant accent on *married* does not eliminate the possibility of a factual interpretation. Nevertheless, we still need to explain why on first impression an unaccented *married* is so conducive to a factual interpretation.[2]

Conformatory and Confirmatory

What is it that makes the intonation of (1) more conducive to a factual interpretation and that of (2) less conducive? To put the intonation in its proper relationship with other factors that may lead to the same result, we need to ask what the speaker is doing when he utters (1). "Expressing factuality" is too broad; that can also be done with *I know he's married* or with the unembedded *He's married*, given the appropriate intonational and gestural accompaniment. What the speaker is expressing, as Oakeshott-Taylor points out, is a relation between "the state of affairs described in the complement" and "the real state of affairs, as this is perceived by the speaker or by the subject of the matrix verb" (p. 7). The two are supposed to conform. But this is also true of *I thought he was married and this proves it*, regardless of intonation. More than a conforming relation is implied; there is also a CON-FIRMING one. It is not necessary to add *and this proves it*; the main verb plus its complement plus the intonation will suffice, given a proper context. Confirmation implies a preconception of the state of affairs to which the "real" state can be matched. This is why the main verb is so apt to be past, even though the utterance is "clearly embedded in present time" (p. 2). So the speaker, or the person for whom the speaker is speaking, is enjoying a small triumph: 'I (or he, or they) told you (the rest of the world, etc.) so!'

This suggests why the intonation of (1) is prototypical of confirmatory utterances. The pronounced descent from a relatively high pitch reflects speaker-in-control; we have seen it in other connections, e.g. commands and uncontestable assertions (see pp. 146–47), in the self-excusing tone of (1) when given a counterfactual interpretation, and here it is the means by which the speaker congratulates himself. An alternative possibility is to go down all the way:

(9) I
    th
      o
       u
        ght
            he was married.

But that might seem rude; it is better to leave the conclusion 'open' (to further comment, to your taking exception, or to suggest understatement), hence the terminal rise. The most important feature of the contour, however, is the absence of an accent (or the presence of a secondary accent) on the complement, which marks it as relatively unexciting. This is most readily interpreted as 'unexciting because we already know it,' which in turn equates the complement with something that has already been said or implied. There is no accent on *married* because interlocutors who know 'wife' are already tuned in to 'married.'

The factuality of Oakeshott-Taylor's examples is thus a complex of factors, a complex that can be manipulated. First, everything may remain the same except that there is no confirmation. In response to *Meet all my friends* one may say

(10) I 'know you're ‚popular. But you don't have to rub it in.

Here the complement is factual, conforming to the perceived state of affairs ('You have lots of friends'), but there is no preconception to serve as a motive for self-congratulation when it is confirmed.

Second, the complement may be factual and confirmatory without the favored intonation. If Steve is overheard to say *I saw Evelyn sneak into Claude's bedroom last night*, Rick may say to Jeff,[3]

(11) I ^{kne}w ^{it!}   They're ^{mar}_{ried!}   (Are _{n't} _{they?)}

The unaccented *it* is the implied repetition of the actual state of affairs, even though the speaker finds it necessary to explain his confirmatory burst. The same intonation can be used on *What did I tell you!*, in which *what* is the anaphoric element. That the same true-life factuality is involved can be seen by matching (11) to an utterance using *thought* and the favored intonation:

(12) I ^{thou}_{ght} _{so}^{o·}   He   finally   ^{ma}_{rried}   her.   (Did _{n't} _{he?)}

There is of course a mood difference: (11) is outgoing, (12) is introspective.

Third, if the factuality or counterfactuality is LEXICALLY determined, anything goes; the intonation will not alter the situation. The most interesting case is that of DISCONFIRMATION, with puzzlement at being wrong replacing satisfaction at being right. Except for the possible presence of an additional accent, the intonation can remain as in (1); the crucial difference is in the particular information verb that we choose or the modification that we place on it. The prototypical verb is *swear* in the shape *could (would) have sworn*, and the most likely preamble is not *yes* but *hm*:

(13) Hm! I could have 'sworn he was ,single!
(14) Hm! It seemed so 'obvious he was ,single!
(15) Hm! I had no 'idea he was ,married!

These are counterfactual and have the same pitch configuration as (1) though the contour is different, A + C or A + B rather than AC, given the added (and contrasting) accent on *single* and *married*. But the intonation of (2), with no change in contours, can be used as well. Though the lexical cues in (13)–(15) are pretty definite, some expressions are ambiguous, e.g. *to be sure*, given a context. So we can have the factual

(16) Yes, I was 'sure he was ,married. (AC)

but also the counterfactual

(17) The police couldn't find any sign of a break-in. — Hm! I was (so) 'sure I saw someone prowling ,around! (A + B)

On the other side, there are certain interesting factuality stereotypes, the nicest example being *as much*, which serves as a confir-

matory anaphor. Like the full complements already cited, it favors a
nonpresent verb:

> (18) I 'thought as ,much.
> (19) I've always 'thought as ,much.
> (20) ?I 'think as ,much.

It comes closer to being a confirmatory stereotype than does *so*, which
can replace it in (20): *I think so*. *As much* is accordingly more stable in
its association with factuality, whereas *so* is more sensitive to changes
of intonation. With a fall on *thought*, as in (12), we have the confidence that is more apt to be associated with factuality; but with a rise
on *thought*,

(21) I $^{th^{ough^t}}$
$so^{o\cdot}$

there is a stronger likelihood of 'but I was wrong.' *I thought as much*,
even with this intonation, would probably not be taken counter-
factually, but there would be a mood difference: *and you see?* makes a
more likely sequel than *and I was right*.

Further, *as much* comes close to being stereotyped with the most-
used verbs in confirmatory utterances: *I thought, I expected, He told me*,
less likely *I hoped, I learned, I knew*, etc. Accordingly, the speaker can
use any intonation consonant with the fact that *as much* is anaphoric
and therefore not apt to be accented—if there is an accent, it will be
one of power. So in response to *This is John's wife*, one may say, emphasizing each word separately, and with a glaring expression, to imply 'See how right I was!,'

(22) I thought as ^{mu} He's mar
$c_{h!}$ $r^{i}e_{d!}$

Or a simple rise can be used, or a rise-fall-rise, or, of course, the
favored (18).

As much is not alone in this function. *Just as I thought* is also confirmatory in its own right, with *just as* now the anaphoric element (and
with *thought* getting the entire movement of the AC if that profile is
chosen). We also have the zero anaphor of the deleted verb, which
can be compared to the anaphoric *it* of (11) above. Example of *it*:

> (23) A: This is John's wife.
> B: Yes, I 'figured he'd ,do it.
> A: Do what?
> B: Get married, of course!

In place of *Yes, I figured he'd do it* we can have the form with zero anaphor, *Yes, I figured he would,* followed by *Would what?* etc. And there is no problem with accenting *do* or *would*; unlike *as much*, there is a certain amount of semantic content to support the accent:

```
              figured he wo
(24) ye^s, I                u
                             l_d.
```

Beyond items that are more or less stereotyped anaphorically, we have a limitless horizon for confecting coreferential complements, containing as many interesting and accentable items as we like. So in addition to the possible response

(25) Yes, I `figured he'd make a ‚fool of himself.

('make a fool of himself' = 'get married') with the intonation of (1), or its near cousin with an accent on *fool*,

```
         fig
(26) ye^s, I                    fool
            ured he'd make a        of himse^lf.
```

we can also say

```
                                  fool
(27) ye^s,                  to make a
           I had him figured          of himse^lf.
```

with the main accent in the complement, and a tone suitable to the implication 'Just see how we mortals are'; the speaker shakes his head sagely. Even though 'get married' implicates 'make a fool of himself,' the latter as complement can carry a major accent if it is interesting enough.

A Congeries of Cues

Many other factors besides accent and intonation are a help or a hindrance to factual interpretations. It will suffice to mention two of those brought forward by Oakeshott-Taylor.

First is the tense of the main verb, which, according to Oakeshott-Taylor, has to be nonpresent. We have seen why it is *apt* to be so: a confirmatory relationship implies some past assumption that is now verified (Nash and Mulac speak of "verifiability"). But we have already seen, with *it figures*, that the verb may be present. The current metaphor *it computes* is the same. Other expressions may be implicated by something in the past that is not necessarily explicitly stated:

(28) So I'm `not so ‚dumb! (I `thought he was ‚married.)

Second is the effect of particular main verbs. For instance, Oakeshott-Taylor claims that *wonder whether* "can readily take a factual but not a counterfactual complement" (p. 13). The truth is that not only are both possible but they readily use the same intonation. In response to *John hasn't apologized for his behavior yet* we may have either of the following, the first factual, the second counterfactual:

(29) I was 'wondering whether he was going to ,forget it.
(30) I was 'wondering whether he was going to ,remember it.

What makes *wonder* peculiar is that its complement is underlyingly a question, answerable by either yes or no, and *remember* and *forget* are a yes-no pair. The modals are also supposed to have their effect—*needn't have*, for instance, "only allows the counterfactual interpretation" (p. 14), yet we find both possibilities in

(31) A: I see John wasn't worried at all.
     B: Well, he 'needn't have ,been. There was no danger.
(32) A: John was terribly worried.
     B: Well, he 'needn't have ,been. There was no danger.

—with the same intonation in both; (31) asks, in effect, 'Why should he have been?'

What we seem to have left from these side visits is that factuality is a congeries of loosely related phenomena without a prototypical core, each of which leaves open an INFERENCE of factuality or its opposite, but—except for the complements of verbs that are lexicalized for factuality (the nonemotive factives, plus verbs of assertion such as *have concluded that, have decided that, can tell you that, assure you that*, etc.)—is not a linguistic device for SIGNALING factuality. However firm it may be in logic, factuality in language is not a Rock of Gibraltar, nor even a low island, but a Sargasso Sea. The discourse factors that bear on it are so various that one has little sense of controlling them as a class.

But certain of these enclaves have an intrinsic interest and invite a more thorough investigation. Unlike factuality in general, confirmation of the *I 'thought he was ,married* sort represents a commonplace activity, that of crowing over being right. There are lexicalizations some of which show the characteristic terminal rise which may well justify regarding the intonation as conventionalized too, e.g. *it figures, as I thought, true to form*, though the convention covers more than factuality, in view of *nothing new, same old story, as you were*, and other expressions of routineness.

An Intonation of Factuality?

Theme and Rheme

Instead of coming at the intonation of (1) from the standpoint of factuality, we can sort out the data better in the more general terms of the thematic organization of the utterance. That is essentially what we have in (1): 'John's having a wife' ('being married') is the theme carried over from the prior remark *This is John's wife*, 'I thought' is the rheme added to it, the theme is postposed, and one of the typical intonations of postposed themes comes as a result. (See Bolinger 1986: 72.) The situation is the same as with

(33) A: What do you think of Henry?
   B1: I `hate ,Henry.
   B2: 'Henry I `hate.

where *Henry* is theme and, when postposed in B1, has its typical terminal rise (or can simply lie flat).

With confirmatory utterances we are not apt to have literal repetitions, but neither are they necessary here:

(34) B1: I `hate people like ,him.

What is essential is the EQUIVALENCE (the coreferentiality, the entailment relations) in the theme, which in Brazil-Coulthard[4] terms favors the "referring tone," the terminal rise, that we find in the intonation of postposed themes.
Applying this to our confirmatory utterances we get things like

(35) A: John slapped Mary.
   B1: Yes, I needed no `convincing that he's a ,boor.
   B2: Yes, that he's a 'boor I needed no `convincing.

Given the freedom in (35) to respond with either B1 or B2, why do we not have the same freedom in (1)? What prevents us from responding to *This is John's wife* with

(36) B2: *That he was 'married I `thought.

placing the rheme in its normal position at the end? Apparently this reflects the semantics of *think* and certain allied verbs when they constitute the rheme. They are so routine that they are odd when given the climactic accent and counterbalanced against their seemingly more important complements. In reverse order the problem does not arise: I `thought they were ,married takes the accent away from the complement; it is played down, and *thought* is able to outvie it. In the regular order, (36), with theme first, the complement being up front makes a bid for an accent, forcing *thought* to take an incongruously heavier one. This can be remedied in one of two ways. Either the theme can be given in the shape of some anaphoric and therefore obviously "given" an unimportant form, as in

(37) Just as I $_{tho}$ $_{ugh}t$!   It $_{fig}$ $_{ures}$!

where anaphoric *just as* and *it* are weak themes and rhematic *thought* and *figures* easily outweigh them, or the main verb can be strengthened to justify putting it last in spite of the relatively heavy complement:

(38) That he was ^{married} I had a ^{pretty} damn $_{good}$ $_{hunch.}$

which, inverted, gives us (1) again:

(39) I had a ^{pretty} damn $_{good}$ $_{hunch}$ he was $^{married.}$

or, in Oakeshott-Taylor's notation,

    (40) I had a ˈpretty damn ˈgood ˈhunch he was ˌmarried.

What about the counterfactuals? Within a theme-rheme frame of reference, the confirmatory counterfactuals are instances of the rheme in its normal position, at the end:

    (41) (I didn't think they were ˌmarried.) I thought they were ˈdivorced.

but can also reverse theme and rheme:

    (42) ˈDivorced (is what) I thought they were.

with the greater likelihood of a low-pitched ending but still the possibility of a terminal rise, depending on the mood.

As for counterfactuals that are not confirmatory, they can have the identical intonation that is favored for factuals, provided the theme-rheme relevance is kept:

    (43) It's news to ˈme that they're ˌmarried!
    (44) I can't ˈbelieve that they're ˌmarried!

Though the theme-rheme analysis offers a broader view of the phenomena, I believe it is still too restricted as far as intonation goes, and that we should see the playing down of the complement as one more instance of 'nothing new, nothing interesting here,' and the addition of the terminal rise (not essential, as we saw) as not-being-too-positive, which is socially desirable when one is vaunting one's foresight or shrewdness—the same mitigation can be extended by a tag question,

(45) I 'told you he was ‚married, `didn't I!

or expressed as an outright rhetorical question:

(46) Didn't I 'tell you he was married!

And if the speaker wishes to be just as reserved about his counter-factual even when it contains a named and contrastive alternative, he may use the same pitch configuration as in (1) (but with the added accent as in examples 13–15):

(47) And I 'thought he was ‚divorced! Silly me!

The speaker implies 'Can you imagine that!,' and perhaps laughs at his own stupidity.

16. A Practical Case: Broadcast Prosody

It starts at 6:00 A.M., or at any other point from which you care to measure, and continues through the day: the parade of newscasters, commentators, talk show hosts, and all others who speak with the aid of a script or a teleprompter instead of directly from the heart, with their intermittent placing of the wrong emphasis here and the unintended inflection there, mostly innocuous but sometimes misleading and all too often distracting. Ginny Casella from Chicago describes the *Jackson caravan* headed for the Democratic convention and immediately follows it with *Jackson supporters will be joining the CARavan* as if the second mention of *caravan* were entirely new, instead of the more suitable (but less exciting) *will be JOINing the caravan*. That's at 6:04. At 6:06 a local announcer reports the aftermath of a multimillion-dollar fire at a Safeway warehouse: *Safeway officials and union leaders met through the day YESterday*, falsely playing down what should count as an intensifier, *through the day*. Casella's mistake was to confront that big word *caravan* at the end of a phrase and automatically give it a big bang; the other speaker's was the opposite—*through the day* was inconspicuously back from the end, and lost out to the relatively unimportant *yesterday*.

When speakers organize and express their own thoughts, it usually takes an extraordinary amount of noise in the system for a normal stress to be distorted by an accent of power. It does happen, of course. A fifteen-year-old says *I was not imiTAting you, I was just looking at you*, carried away by her protest at being unjustly accused of imitation. The author of these lines advises against buying a prescription in Britain *because there is no reFUND*. A Harvard dean points to the *rules and regulations governing teaching fellowSHIPS*. These may count as mispronunciations (certainly they disregard the "normal" lexical stresses), but they reflect the way the speaker feels about the meaning of the utterance.

True lapses occur in unguided as well as guided speech and writing. The unguided lapse is usually the result of a scrambled command to tongue or fingers: the mind orders "Do so-and-so" and it is done, but to the wrong thing or in the wrong place. You mean to write *When are you going to take golf up again?* and you discover that you have written *When are you going to talk*: the order was something like "Produce a monosyllable with a silent *l*," and *take* gets it instead of *golf*; this is aided, of course, by the fact that there *is* such a word—and a highly frequent one—as *talk*. San Francisco's popular radio doctor, Dean Edell, announces *the story of a woman who took the bull by her own horns*, misplacing the command to "Intensify something." A county official reports that the transmission in his car was erratically *slowing up, speeding down—slowing down, speeding up*, in which the command "Make a contrast" is foiled, at first, by the fact that the same event can be described as *slowing up* and *slowing down*. Automatisms are the culprit. We can monitor our performance only up to a point without becoming tongue-tied, and when some subsidiary action is delegated to a routine, the routine itself takes over and sometimes produces a monstrosity.

With guided speech, above all with reading aloud from written notes, the misapplied orders may be on a larger scale. A small-scale instance would be the misreading of a single word, as when Ronald Reagan in a speech delivered in China in April of 1984 came up with *issues that should neither be glossed over nor dented* [chuckle]—*denied, I should have said*. The large-scale lapses are the result of a peculiar ability that practiced readers have, which is to utter a complete account in a way that is quite intelligible to a listener but without internalizing, or remembering, any part of it. The conscious brain seems to be decoupled. Naturally, under such circumstances, a lot can go wrong, especially with the prosody, which depends on our "meaning" what we say. (Since unguided speech is rarely automatic to this degree, it is less often marred by prosodic errors.) A radio announcer is always somewhere between close monitoring and no monitoring at all of what his script calls for. The less monitoring, the more artificial the spontaneity of the accents and intonations. The free-wheeling part of the brain makes its best guess, which is to accent a word if it looks big and important, to accent practically *every* word if that will make sure that nothing is missed, to shift the stress in compounds if they are not recognized as such (the compound rule of stress *before* the end is anticlimactic), and to build almost every sentence toward a climax at the end. The result is an excess of fist-pounding, doubtless useful to keep drowsy motorists awake on the road but otherwise rather wearisome to listen to for long. What goes by the board is the delicate shading of "communicative dynamism" as the Prague linguists call it.

Some examples from broadcasts, mostly San Francisco stations:

> The 1984 season taught [Sparky] Anderson a few THINGS. (KQED-FM, Aug. 19, 1987, 1:57 P.M. Should be *TAUGHT Anderson a few things—things* is an empty word.)

> Some restrictions apPLY. (KCBS, Dec. 17, 1986, 9:25 A.M. There is nothing that a restriction can do but apply; one could as easily say just *There are some restrictions*.)

> [Restrict their election reporting] until all the polls are closed in the COUNtry. (KCBS, Mar. 4, 1984, 7:20 A.M. The accented *country* is shifted to get the accent at the end, making it suggest 'rural polls'; should be *all the polls in the COUNtry are closed*, with lowered voice at the end.)

> It [the bales of hay] is a gift from [farmers in the South], who drove MANy of the rigs. (KCBS, July 14, 1988, 8:02 P.M. The half-conscious mind spots *many* as some form of hyperbole, but that is irrelevant in this context, which calls for *who DROVE many of the rigs*; the relevant fact is that they themselves did the driving.)

> It might stop the victim from proseCUting the . . . (NBC News, Channel 4, Los Angeles, Jan. 25, 1987, 5:48 P.M. Overemphasis on an important word to the point of mispronouncing it.)

> . . . traffic backed up . . . to about the railroad TRACKS. (KCBS, May 3, 1983, 7:25 A.M. Disregard of the compounding rule for the sake of climax.)

> A lightning-CAUSED fire was declared under control. (KQED-FM, July 18, 1988, 6:03 A.M. Same comment.)

To get an idea of how pervasive this dubious prosody is, I recorded a randomly selected 45-minute segment of newscast from KQED-FM, the leading PBS radio station in the San Francisco area. A PBS station is ideal because there are fewer interruptions than with commercial stations (commercials are interesting, but have their own special rhetoric), though my casual observation is that a wobbly intonation is just as common in one medium as in the other. (For a similar look at a commercial station, see Bolinger 1982.) Following is the log plus commentary. (Numbers following the speaker identifications indicate positions on the tape, 0–620 by counter.)

Prosodic Log, San Francisco Radio KQED-FM,
July 12, 1988, 10:15–11:00 A.M.

Speaker JD, 21
    . . . must publicly admit the country's role IN that tragedy . . .

Speaker BD, 39, 63

A new forum for arms-conTROL talks is being prepared.

Western stalling in this exceedingly complex area seems to have opened the way for appealing PUBlic proposals from the Soviet Union.

Speaker U, 87, 90

The winds will be westerly up to THIRty miles per hour.

Michael Dukakis expected to announce his choice . . .

Speaker CC, 102

. . . a vice presidential RUNning MATE.

Speaker HB, 118, 139

That flight is NOT supposed to take place without one more test FIRing of the shuttle booster rocket.

They don't believe this INcident [profile A] will force them to CHANGE [profile AC] their flight schedule.

Speaker RH, 157, 160, 173, 202

But man-made instruments have LANded only on THREE extraterrestrial OBjects . . .

It looks like a giant boulder . . . trapped in orbit less than six THOUSAND miles from the Martian surface.

Soviet space experts HAVE HINTED [B + Á contour] at a manned mission to Mars.

Just a couple of YEARS [peak pitch] ago they were still debating exactly what instruments to put on their spacecraft.

Speaker MS, 237

The problem is what to do if Congress needs FUture cuts in the Medicare BUDget . . .

Speaker DA, 288

Alameda County supervisors have approved a grant for a number of different community organizations this morning; but the supervisors BALKED at sending a check to ONE [peak pitch] of them.

Speaker U, 370, 376

The internationally renowned faculty . . . will perform a PROgram of baroque chamber music.

. . . depicting the contributions of Edison [no break] Tesla, and Marconi.

Speaker NT, 400

. . . having served as assistant attorney general in the Ford administration and before that as one of the U.S. atTORneys in Pennsylvania.

Speaker AG, 438, 458

Kuwait's crown prince . . . FLEW to Washington aboard the jumbo jet.

Officials argue the Gulf states are likely to offer military cooperation if the U.S. is providing the weapons, and they say that [demonstrative] cooperation is better if the COUNtries are using compatible systems.

Speaker CW (BBC), 480

The method of atTACK suggests . . . ['attack' already introduced]

Speaker U, 483, 503

. . . and is to HOLD [AC profile] an emergency CABinet MEETing.

SIMple HARmonies [peak pitch] recall brighter, sweeter days.

Speaker JB, 563
  He can disqualify a group entirely if the material is not sentimental enough
  or if it strays from SIMple CHORD [peak pitch] patterns.

I have included one obvious lapse as a token of the error-prone nature of all such pressure-driven speech: U's (376) pronunciation of *Edison Tesla* as if *Edison* were Tesla's first name. Also included is U's (90)
expected without the finite *is*, to illustrate newscasterese as a distinct
style: the same breeziness that leads to prosodic excess also decrees
that the humble auxiliary shall be abandoned, making every third sentence a headline.

We first note JD (21) with its highlighting of the preposition *in*
rather than *role*, a mannerism of contemporary speech that lends
perkiness without any semantic commitment.

Next come BD (39), CC (102), HB (118), and U (483), with their mispronounced compounds *arms conTROL*, *RUNning MATE*, *test FIRing*,
and *CABinet MEETing*. Rightshifting the accent in such words is sometimes justified, but in the context of broadcasting it is another form of
pulling out all the stops.

BD (63) seems to have been simply garbled—is *appealing* an adjective or a verb?

Next are U (87) and RH (160). A newscaster—especially one who
reports weather and raceway speeds—must grow pretty sick of even
mentioning *miles*, to say nothing of emphasizing it. But the listener is
less concerned with the broadcaster's state of mind and more with the
fact that *miles* still contrasts with *leagues*, *furlongs*, *light years*, and *par-
secs*, and needs the accent.

Next are HB (139), RH (157, 202), DA (288), U (370), NT (400), AG
(438), U (483, 503), and JB (563). In spite of the small size of our
sample, the frequency of this practice of false emphasis is the clearest
sign of how newscasterese goes wrong. The speaker overreaches in
his eagerness to spellbind the hearer, putting the highest peak on
something relatively unimportant. U's (483) merely existential *HOLD*
is treated as if it were literally 'cling to,' and his *HARmonies* (503) suggests that harmony is something surprising in a discussion of music.
JB's (563) *CHORD patterns* sounds as if they were being distinguished
from *meLODic* or *RHYTHmic* patterns, and DA's (288) *ONE* sounds
as if it were in contrast with *MORE*. (The hearer does not necessarily
draw such nonsensical inferences, but the material for them is there
and imposes an extra effort.) AG's (438) *FLEW* suggests that flying to
Washington was quite extraordinary, just as RH's (157) *LANded* treats
the outcome of something long planned as if it were an unexpected
event, and just as U's (370) *PROgram* hints that a program is an un-

usual way to present a performance. Similarly HB's (139) *CHANGE* assigns a high value to a routine act where schedules are concerned and NT's (400) *atTORney* overlooks the fact that attorneys have already been mentioned. HB's (139) *INcident* and RH's (157, 202) *OBjects* and *YEARS* highlight words that are inherently unimportant. It is not that these particular words do not deserve an accent; the excess lies in their being given the supreme effulgence within their contexts. The parallel case is that of words that deserve no accent at all. (We may or may not wish to include prepositions and the second element of compounds in this generalization.) MS's (237) accenting of *BUDget* is superfluous—that budget is precisely the already-presented topic; the only new idea here is the *FUture* of *FUture cuts*. CW's (480) *atTACK* is also old stuff within its context. Similarly AG's (458) *COUNtries*, which merely duplicates the earlier *Gulf states*; no accent is needed, and if one is assigned it should at least be at low pitch. No particular classification fits RH's (173) *HAVE HINTED* with its skyward peak on *hinted*, as if the speaker were disclosing something highly conspiratorial.

Maybe all this should be excused simply as the ingredients of a professional style. But for the constant listener it would be restful if occasionally the newscasters and their associates would just COOL IT. A daily exercise in taming the wild accents and toning down the ends of sentences might help.

APPENDIXES

Appendix A.
Accent in Answers to Questions

In this section we consider an attempt to give a grammatical explanation for a certain kind of distribution of accents. In answers to questions, according to Gussenhoven (1983: 408–9), the distribution of accents depends in part on whether the question is yes-no or wh. Answers to wh questions put the accent "on the requested bit of information," as in

> (1) Who was born in Paris in nineteen-forty-síx? — Jóhn (was born in Paris in 1946).

But yes-no questions are said to behave differently. Since the focus is on 'yes' or 'no,' one would expect the accent to fall on that part of the answer which normally carries the affirmation or negation. Negative yes-no answers fulfill this expectation:

> (2) Is he the gárdener? — No, he ísn't the gardener.

but affirmative yes-no answers allegedly more often have the same accent pattern as the question. So, while (3) is possible,

> (3) Is he the gárdener? — Yes, he ís the gardener.

(4) is more likely:

> (4) Is he the gárdener? — Yes, he's the gárdener.

Is the claim true? In particular, can one generalize from copular sentences such as (2)–(4)? In the following, the distribution of accents differs from that of the question and yet the answer is at least as "natural" as when the distribution is the same:

> (5) Do you like Máry? — Yes, I líke Mary.
>
> (6) Did they shóot the prísoners? — Yes, they shót the prisoners.
>
> (7) Did you léarn the lésson? — Yes, I léarned the lesson.

(8) Did she spénd the móney? — Yes, she spént the money.

(9) Do you knów the réason? — Yes, I knów the reason.

(10) Did they líquidate their stócks? — Yes, they líquidated their stocks.

(11) Can you shów me whý? — Yes, I can shów you why.

To keep the same accent distribution in these answers as in their corresponding questions could well give a disagreeable impression of sarcastic parroting. But there would be a more serious drawback. The surprise value of the complements is low. Mary is a person much talked about. Prisoners may well be slated for execution. Lessons are regularly learned. But in a case like

(12) Did he ópen a háberdashery? — Yes, he ópened a háberdashery.

if we say

(13) Yes, he ópened a haberdashery.

it is as if we said 'Yes, he really did open a haberdashery'; the surprise value of the actual opening has to be that strong to outweigh the otherwise more unexpected *haberdashery*. But *haberdashery* is not so highly charged as to yield a B + Á contour on the reply in (12). The word is, after all, repeated, and needs to be toned down somewhat— the likeliest contour is B + À:

(14) Ye^{s,} ^{opened a} hab
      he   erdashery.

The B + Á contour would suggest 'He opened even a haberdashery.'

Gussenhoven's inclination to regard (4) as somehow exceptional is based in part on the fact that even though *gardener* is repeated from the question, it nevertheless is apt to carry the accent. But with (12) we see how elastic our response to the "interest" of something may be—repetition militates against it, but the sheer "wow" value of the item in question can override that, even if only to the extent of a B + À, with lowered pitch on that item.

The same choices are available in (15)–(18), again with B + À in the first of the two answers, and A in the second (the À of the B + À has been zeroed out); (17)–(18) are normally end-stressed idioms:

(15) Did they stárt a revolútion? —
Yes, they stárted a revolútion.
Yes, they stárted a revolution.

(16) Did they réap the cónsequences? —
    Yes, they réaped the cónsequences.
    Yes, they réaped the consequences.
(17) Did he thrów a fít? —
    Yes, he thréw a fít.
    Yes, he thréw a fit.
(18) Did she máke a mistáke? —
    Yes, she máde a mistáke.
    Yes, she máde a mistake.

This last response would suggest 'Yes, she really did make a mistake.'

(By comparing the two kinds of answers we are not assuming that either one would be the best choice in a live conversation. A much more usual response would be *Yes, they did, Yes, she is,* etc.)

It is obvious that no simple grammatical rule of accent assignment will account for the positioning of the accent in these cases. The speaker must sense the relative weighting of the items at every step. Suppose we take the case of a "focus domain" in which the predicate noun phrase picks up the accent, as in

(19) Éverything went wrong. — Let me guess: it was Jóhn's fault.

By Gussenhoven's account, if this is converted to a question the answer should have the same focus domain as the question:

(20) Was it Jóhn's fault? — Yes, it was Jóhn's fault.

—with an A contour. This is normal enough, but a B + À is just as normal:

(21) Was it Jóhn's fault? — Yes, it was Jóhn's fáult.

—and now, instead of differing by one *fewer* accent than in the question, the answer differs by one *more*. Yet the principle remains the same: the questioner in (21) is interested in determining *who*, namely John; the respondent is just as much interested in carrying out an act of blaming. In addition, the accent on *fault* is climactic, so it serves a double purpose.

Now suppose we substitute *doing* for *fault*. The equivalent of (20) is fine:

(22) Was it Jóhn's doing? — Yes, it was Jóhn's doing.

But the equivalent of (21) is a bit odd: *doing* is less explicitly guilt-imposing than *fault* (with the accent on *doing* one is tempted to read in some special sense of *do*), and we are about as likely to pick the auxiliary for the accent:

(23) Yes, it wás John's doing.

There remains one aspect of the problem as Gussenhoven posed it that needs a separate look. It is certainly true that (2) with its accent on *isn't* is more likely than (3) with its accent on *is*. The reason lies in the nature of yes-no questions. It is generally assumed that they are grammatically neutral as regards expecting an affirmative or a negative answer. (Pragmatically they can be tipped one way or the other, of course—by context, intonation, etc.) That being the case, an accent on *is* or *isn't* should be equally likely, and there would be no reason for a difference between (2) and (3). The fact is, however, that yes-no questions are usually guesses about the state of affairs, and we guess what is likely to be true, not, as a rule, what is likely to be false. Even grammatically there is a bias in favor of affirmative answers. If that were not the case, answers like the following would be incomprehensible:

(24) Did your investment pay off? — Certainly (absolutely, true, 100%, nearly, almost, barely).

Such adverbial or nominal answers are predicated on making the affirmative choice. The same goes for

(25) Is this the way to Elm Street? — That's right. Just take . . .

(It is true that there are a couple of negative adverbs, *hardly* and *scarcely*, that may be used similarly, but the affirmative ones are vastly more numerous.) Conclusion: a negative *isn't* is going to have a lot more shock value than an affirmative *is*.[1]

Example (3) proves the case in yet another way. The response *Yes, he ís the gardener*, in one interpretation, takes the question *Is he the gárdener?* as an item of positive information: 'By golly you're right! He ís the gardener! I hadn't realized it before!'

Gussenhoven notes a further supposed oddity in sentences where there is but one accent, on the subject: namely, that the answer will introduce a new accent, on the predicate. His example:

(26) Are the volcánoes dormant? — Yes, the volcánoes are dórmant.

But this too depends on how interesting the predicate is. In the following,

(27) The rally lasted only an hour. — How come? Did the políce come in? — Yes, that's what happened, the políce came in. Full force.

the predicate is merely presentative, and *came ín*, while possible, is no more likely. Similarly

(28) Get a move on. — Why? Is bréakfast ready? — Uh-huh, bréakfast's ready.

Here *réady* would be equally likely. But in

(29) Uf! Move over! — Why, is my bréath bad? — Yes, that's the
   problem, your bréath's bad. And you'd better do something
   about it.

the speaker may have good reason for soft-pedaling *bad*.

How little it takes to tip the balance can be seen in the case of a
parallel construction:

(30) Time to go to bed. Are the líghts out? — Yes, the líghts are out,
   the dóors are locked, and the wíndows are shut.

The contrasting items are more interesting than their complements,
which are pegged to them anyway—lights are thought of in terms of
on or off, doors in terms of being locked or unlocked, and windows in
terms of being open or shut. Now suppose we rearrange and get

(31) The líghts are out, the wíndows are shut, and the dóors are
   locked.

This is normal enough, but let's assume that the speaker thinks of
door-locking in terms of security—in fact, if *secure* replaces *locked*
there would be a stronger tendency to say

                dóors are se
(32) and the   cúre.

Locked, as a synonym of *secure*, could get the same treatment, which is
also promoted by the tendency to climax: it is a "stronger" utterance
with the main accent on the last syllable. And this is furthered by an
additional tendency to explicit topicalization of the last item in a series like this: 'And as for the dóors, they are lócked.'

We have not dealt directly with Gussenhoven's example (26). A
context can be set up to permit the opposite weighting:

(33) It's deathly quiet around here. I wonder why. Are the volcánoes dormant (do you suppose)?—Yes, by golly! That's the explanation! The volcánoes are dormant!

Here we see the justification for adding *that's what happened* in (27),
that's the problem in (29), and *That's the explanation* in (33). The accents
could remain exactly as they are without those insertions, but what the
insertions do is objectify one of the two purposes that the question-
answer series is assumed by the hearer to serve. If he is interested in

the condition of the volcanoes, the extra accent on *dormant* is in order. If he is interested in the unnatural quiet, then (unless he wants to split his reply in two and say *Yes! The volcánoes! They're dórmant!*, in which case both words are accented) the accent on *dormant* will be suppressed, because what he is saying is in effect 'It's the volcánoes' fault,' 'The volcánoes are responsible'—and if *dormant* were fully accented, the accent there would, by virtue of its final position, overshadow the one on volcanoes and destroy the attribution of responsibility. Similarly (27) says in effect 'The políce are what happened' and (29) says 'Your bréath is the problem.' In each case the accent falls on the item of greatest interest.

It is likely that Gussenhoven had something else in mind with his (26), more on the order of

(34) How's Hawaii these days? Are the volcánoes dormant?

Now the question is approximately equivalent to *Tell me about the volcánoes*. The speaker has collapsed two questions into one: 'What about the volcánoes—are they dórmant?'; and in the process he has suppressed the second accent which would otherwise be dominant by virtue of position. That is, an appreciably lighter accent on *volcanoes* than on *dormant* would suggest that 'volcanoes' were being discussed already, when in fact they are being brought on the scene. There is no such inhibition in the answer: 'volcanoes' have been mentioned and may accordingly be given the nondominant accent, and the respondent is free to address the second half of the compound question and put the extra accent on *dormant*.

Consider next the type of yes-no question that expresses a request. We'll first put this in indirect form so as to get a display of A profiles, whose accents are easier to identify:

(35) She ásked him to wríte her a recommendátion and he wróte her a recommendation (he wróte her one).

If we say *he wróte her a recommendátion*, the hearer will infer that the recommendation is somehow different from the recommendation. The sentence is either nonsense, or—with a boost to the word—*recommendation* repeated could mean 'a whopper of a recommendation.' It is not a normal sequel to the request. Accordingly in the *direct* discourse answer to *Will you write me a recommendation?*

```
              I'll  ʷrí
         s,             te
(36) Ye
                    you a recommenda tion.
```

recommendation probably has the same status as in (35), that is, unaccented, just as *one* would be on the same profile. This would make (36) an instance of AC rather than A + C. (The terminal rise—that is, the choice of either AC or A + C—can be justified by the speaker's intent to go on, say with *Be glad to!*)

More important than the AC versus A + C ambiguity is the fact that with the accent—if any—at a low pitch, the repeated material is played down. Is this true in a *relative* sense, with successive A profiles (rather than AC or A + C), which are presumably the shape that Gussenhoven was working with? What we find is that it is not necessary to go all the way to complete deaccenting in order to achieve deemphasis on repeated material. If we strip away the *yes* from Gussenhoven's yes-no answers, the difference stands out starkly. The answers are to the question *Is he the gardener?*:

(37) He's the   gar
         gar   (38)*He's the
            dener.   dener.

The effect of (38) is the same as that of *recommendátion* if substituted in (35): 'gardener is different from gardener.' Prefixing *yes* to (38) cancels that interpretation, forcing the hearer to a different one, perhaps 'Yes, he's the gardener, but what you didn't suspect is that he is also the murderer.' On the other hand, if the item is intrinsically interesting, forced interpretations are not necessary. Both of the following,

(39) Is it stránge? — Yes, it's stránge.
(40) Is he a gíant? — Yes, he's a gíant.

may readily have the higher A of (38); this is less likely with

(41) Is it sád? — Yes, it's sád.
(42) Is he a dwárf? — Yes, he's a dwárf.

Compare also

(43) Did she go to New Yórk? — Yes, she went to New Yórk.
(44) Did she go hóme? — Yes, she went hóme.

York may readily take the higher A; *home* is less apt to.

We thus have a cline, from a high A in *Yes, he's a gíant*, to a lower A in *Yes, she went hóme*, to total deaccenting in *Yes, I líke Mary*. There may be something of a rule in (37) and (38): "Fully specified answers to yes-no questions when expressed without *yes* and with A profiles will have an A preceded by a higher pitch." [2] Otherwise the choice is subject to various influences.

Appendix B. Tagged Imperatives

The text refers (p. 154) to an early attempt to derive the imperative transformationally from a question tagged with *will*. Though questions and commands are unquestionably related, the formal derivation was judged to be unworkable. A later attempt, Sadock (1970), was similarly flawed, as demonstrated by Bouton (1982). Bouton himself offers a solution, the first to give intonation a central position in defining the features of tagged imperatives. This Appendix is a review of his analysis.

After a detailed examination of the possibilities of tagging, limited to *will, would, can,* and *could,* Bouton offers his conclusions in a table, reproduced here (Table 2) in slightly modified form for easier reference. Cells 1–3 are for intonation, with three terminal "contours": 3 + is high rise, 2 + is low rise, and 31 is fall. Cells 4–6 are for stem polarity, e.g. *Sit down, Don't sit down.* (The stem is the imperative proper without the tag.) Cells 7–9 show where *can* is possible as opposed to *will.* Cells 10–12 are for the freedom of the tag to vary in polarity independently of the stem, e.g. *Sit down, will you?* and *Sit down, won't you?*, both possible with a 3 + on the tag, but allegedly impossible elsewhere. Cells 13–15 are for the possibility of *would* and *could* instead of *will* and *can,* supposedly found with a 3 + ending but not elsewhere. Cells 16–18 are self-explanatory. Cells 19–21 refer to the possibility of a tag such as the one in *Open the door, will someone please?* Cells 22–27 are for sentences like *You take care of it, will you?* and *Someone hand me the paper, will you?* in which the stem as well as the tag has an explicit subject. These interlocking features are supposed to account for the full array of tagged imperatives.

Bouton's merit is not only to have brought intonation into the picture but to have shown that a variety of other factors are relevant to the description of tagged imperatives. But the analysis falls short in two respects. First, the plusses and minuses in the table are approximate and not all-or-none; recognizing that something is not arbitrarily

Table 2. Effect of Stem Polarity and Tag Intonation on the Imperative-Plus-Tag Construction

	1 — 3+		2 — 2+		3 — 31	
Tag intonation						
Stem polarity	4 Pos.	Neg.	5 Pos.	Neg.	6 Pos.	Neg.
Possible auxiliary: Will	7 +	+	8 +	+	9 +	+
Can	+	−	−	−	−	−
Tag polarity free (not controlled by polarity of stem)	10 +	−	11 −	−	12 −	−
Past tense (*would, could*) possible in tag	13 +	+	14 −	−	15 −	−
Can be followed by *please*	16 +	+	17 +	+	18 +	+
Indef. tag possible	19 +	−	20 +	−	21 −	−
Tag still possible when stem has explicit subject — Def. stem	22 +	+	23 +	−	24 +	+
Indef. stem	25 +	+	26 +	−	27 +	+

SOURCE: Bouton 1982, p. 36. (With permission of the publisher.)

so but only likely to be so compels us to ask why, and that takes us beyond a mere tabulation of features. Second, many more factors than those listed affect the acceptability of tagged imperatives. In particular, limiting the tags to just the central four cramps the vision. Chapter 6 showed the enormous and unlimited variety of tags that may occur with imperatives, in all degrees of fusion with the stem. To the extent that stem and tag are relatively independent of each other— and they are more independent than is the case with questions—the problem of describing their coupling is the problem of accounting for any other *pair* of closely related and juxtaposed sentences. Grammars have been written, more or less successfully, for individual sentences. Predicting when two sentences will appear side by side, and accounting for what happens when they do, is another level of complexity.

Consider first the supposed restrictions on *can* in the cells 7–9.

"*Can* is restricted to 3 + tags on a positive stem" (p. 38). Yet one finds things like

    (1) Just don't fight back, can't you this once?

What this provides is a context in which the negative can be viewed as an injunction to take some positive step involving the hearer's ability to perform. One could also say here

    (2) Just don't fight back, can you maybe just this once?

'Refrain from fighting back.' It would be obviously absurd to say

    (3) *Don't let me catch you here again, can't you?

in which no positive step is enjoined. By testing in this fashion we discover that the problem lies with the semantics of *can*. Unlike the three other central auxiliaries (*could, will, would*) *can* has stronger leanings toward root as against epistemic meanings. This shows up in a variety of oddities, including

    (4) ?If you can, don't fight back.

where *could, will,* and *would* fit nicely. What (1) and (2) above provide is a more energetic context which is able to accommodate the root meaning of *can*.

Examples (1) and (2) also discredit the restriction on intonation, since, contrary to both cell 7 and cell 8, they can take either a 3 + or a 2 + terminal, with the same affective difference that we have observed elsewhere: the low rise is a kind of despairing entreaty, the high rise expresses irritated frustration. There is also the possibility of B + C,

(5) cán't you this

              ónce?

with a fall to a tonal ending, expressing the resignation of a request that has become routine. (Other B shapes are also possible.)

As for positive stems in cell 8, again the restrictions on *can* with 2 + do not apply—for example,

    (6) Hand me the small one, could you²⁺—it's right over there.
    (7) Just have a little more consideration, can't you?²⁺

The pitch on *could you* in (6) needs no rise at all, or only a slight rise. Without rise it represents the tightest intonational amalgam with the stem, a mere continuation of the fall on the imperative proper, and semantically it is offhand: the speaker is targeted on the next thing he is about to say (*it's right over there*). Here we see how local conditions, and not some grammatical superstructure, determine the intonation. As for (7), the slight rise suggests petulance: I am resigned to your being an inconsiderate person.

Looking at cell 9, with its 31 terminal and decisive fall, we come closer to a true restriction, though not quite in the form contemplated by Bouton. As we discovered with questions (pp. 118–20) and their imperative analogs (p. 163), there is a problem when a same-polarity tag is given an A (31) profile:

```
        like                        do
    do                                  will
(8) ?You                    (9) *Sit  w
    it                                n,
        you?                            you?
```

The effect of the 31—when the stem also has a 31—is to drive a wedge between stem and tag: they are relatively independent of each other, and (8) results in the nonsense of *You like it. Do you? With reversal of polarity the separation does not result in a contradiction: You like it. Don't you? Separate or not, the reverse polarity gives a conducive question: the speaker thinks he already knows the answer.

So given a degree of blending with questions, an A + A contour with reverse polarity gets by. Bouton's example (32a) is

> (10) Don't tell Pete about this mess we got ourselves into, will you?[31]

and one with the opposite reversal would be

> (11) Help him to make up his mind, won't you?[31]

The blend is with the following, respectively:

> (12) You won't tell Pete about this mess we got ourselves into, will you?[31]
>
> (13) You'll help him to make up his mind, won't you?[31]

If the related question is not suitable as a directive, then there is no blending and both question and imperative are odd with A + A:

> (14) ?You'll sit down, won't you?[31] (queried in the relevant sense)
> (15) *Sit down, won't you?[31]

The difficulties with can in cell 9 are the same as in cell 8, but given a full stop and wide separation, we can have

> (16) Just don't fight back. Can't you this once!

—hardly a tag, however.

Though cell 9 permits will with a negative stem, as in (10), Bouton identifies a semantic distinction between the 31 there and a possible 3+: "On a tag appended to a negative stem, the 3+ contour indicates that the speaker is referring to some action that is going on at the moment, and that he wants the addressee to stop doing whatever it is. . . . The 3+ tag cannot be used on a negative stem unless this is the meaning intended" (p. 30); otherwise a 31 is appropriate. This was referred to in the text (see above, p. 162), and it embodies an insight that is partially correct. In a case like

    (17) Don't step on my toes, will you?$^{3+}$

'ongoing activity' is pretty strongly implied. But the claim is easily falsified if one tries to generalize it. In (18), the action is not going on at the moment but is habitual. It is in response to *What's wrong nów? What do you want me to do?*—

    (18) Just don't complain all the time, will you?$^{3+}$ I get bored as hell
        with your moodiness.

The speaker's irritation leads to the 3+. The excitement of a piece of gossip can affect the intonation of

    (19) Don't breathe a word of this, will you!$^{3+}$

And the earnestness of the warning can affect that of

    (20) Never insult him again, will you?$^{3+}$ Promise?$^{3+}$ Promise?$^{3+}$

Bouton's claim is true to the extent that if the action is going on at the moment, stopping it is apt to involve more urgency. Emotive pressure, not grammar, controls the intonation.

    Cells 10–12 establish the claim that only with a positive stem and a 3+ terminal on the tag is the tag free to be either positive or negative, e.g.

    (21) Try a little harder next time, will you?$^{3+}$
    (22) Try a little harder next time, won't you?$^{3+}$

The restriction to positive stems is almost true, at least as far as *will* is concerned; the greater detachability of *can* opens the door a crack:

    (23) Can't you just not be so insistent?
    (24) Just don't be so insistent, can't you?$^{3+}$

The difficulty with *will* is illustrated by example (9)—the tag cannot be "either" positive or negative if it cannot be positive, and we saw there the problem with same-polarity tags and A+A contours (by definition having a 31 tag). But though a 31 may be next to impossible, it does not follow that the tag has to be a 3+. There is no reason why a dispirited (21) or (22) could not end with 2 +, or, for that matter, with a terminal level that makes it a tail to the A profile of the stem.

Cells 13–15 give us to understand that the past tense of the tag is possible only with a 3 +. It is true that *could* and *would* usually make a strong plea, and for that reason are apt to take 3 +. But it is not hard to motivate other intonations, for example, in response to *Sorry, I have no information on when he's arriving,* one may have

(25) Well, then, tell me what time he's leaving, could you?

with the low-pitched level on *could you* that marks it as a tail to the A on *leaving*. The speaker regards this as a CONCLUDING request—he has failed in his first inquiry and now makes a last attempt, using the intonation of finality. Either *could* or *would* may appear here. As for cell 15, it is approximately correct, though with a positive stem an instance such as

(26) Help

                                  would

    us

       out just this on

                 ^{c}e,   you, please?

is possible—a case of an A profile on the tag to reinforce the plea. *Would* may be given extra intensity and length, and a pleading head-shake, frown, and sidewise lip-pursing (kissing gesture) are likely accompaniments. For greater emphasis, a speaker may protract the tag with a series of A profiles (31 "contours"), as in the following, spoken by an exasperated theater-goer:

(27) Tá   ó   thá há wóu   yó plé

     ^{k}e ^{f}f   t   t ^{l}d   u ^{a}s$_{e\,|}$

—accents of power building to a climax.

Cells 16–18 are by way of showing that *please* may be appended to all types of imperative. (Of course, in doing this we ensure that the imperative will be a *plea* of some sort, and not, as in *Go to hell,* an objurgation.) But what is most interesting about *please* is its capacity to free up otherwise doubtful cases, making them interpretable as genuine pleas (cf. pp. 158–59, above). Example (26) without *please* would hardly be normal. The *please* acts on the A-profile tag itself. It is not a reagent for some preexistent selection rule, but turns the tag into a deeply felt entreaty.

The effect of *please* as well as other factors on intonational possibilities can be seen in an intonational test that Bouton proposes (p. 30), with which the reader is invited to "discover the boundary between these two contours" (3 + and 2 +): "Slowly reduce the amount of the rise in the intonation pattern of the tag [3 +]. When the positive tag becomes ungrammatical, we have moved from the 3 + pattern to the 2 +." This claim is particularly interesting because its effect would be to divide a gradient into two distinct ranges—an all-or-none contrast reflecting a phonemic status for the two patterns. Since this is something that has been consistently questioned in the present volume and its predecessor, it calls for careful examination.

Bouton's example (33a),

(28) Be quiet now, will you?$^{3+}$ $^{(*2+)}$

nicely illustrates the distractor that almost makes his generalization seem true. With a 2 + (or, better, we should say just a relatively low rise), this is a common intonation that *challenges* in question form— the *will* is taken in the literal sense of willfulness:

(29) Call me a liar, will you!$^{2+}$ Take that!

'that' being a punch in the nose. Even though the wording of Bouton's example is not what one expects in a challenge, the truculence of the challenge carries over and spoils the intended plea for quiet. That the trouble is just this sort of ambiguity can be seen by adding *please*,

(30) Be quiet now, will you please?$^{2+}$

which, disambiguated, is no longer "ungrammatical" but simply low-key. It can also be disambiguated gesturally—if the speaker uses a low voice and holds a finger to his lips, the possibility of 'challenge' is again eliminated; the 2 + is quite appropriate to a hushed request.

Bouton's second example is (his 33a)

(31) Come see us before you leave, will you?$^{3+}$

To the extent that this is meant as a cordial invitation, it virtually has to show a degree of warmth, which 2 + hardly supplies, but adding *please* would again eliminate the problem—the 2 + could have some other motivation than lack of warmth.

To illustrate the opposite end of the supposed contrast between 3 + and 2 +, where 2 + is "grammatical" and 3 + is not, Bouton appeals to tag questions "used imperatively" (p. 30), e.g. his (34b):

(32) You won't bounce that ball, will you?$^{2+}$ $^{(*3+)}$

used in the sense of *Don't bounce that ball, will you?* (which would be acceptable with either 2 + or 3 +). Again, the supposedly forbidden intonation, in this case 3 +, is perfectly normal, as can be seen by its compatibility (and disambiguating potential) with other directive signals. One is the postposition of unaccented *now*:

(33) You won't bounce that ball, will you now?[3+]
(34) You won't bounce that báll now, will you?[3+]

Another is the inclusion of threatening gestures: scowl and finger-wagging, with no change in the sentence itself. The lower pitch is more apt to be encountered in a threatening context, the higher in a cajoling one, but both are normal as implied commands.

Cells 19–21 coordinate indefinite tags (tags using an indefinite pronoun subject such as *someone* rather than one of the personal pronouns) with stem polarity and tag intonation. The claim is that tags are possible only with positive stems and rising terminals (either 2 + or 3 +).[1] Bouton's examples (40a, b) illustrate:

(35) Pick up that target over there, will someone?[3+]
(36) Put the chairs back before you leave, will everyone?[3+]

As for the exclusion of 3 + and 2 + when the stem is negative, the problem seems to be a confusion between commands and questions, since when a disambiguating *now* (unaccented) is added, the command comes across acceptably, more easily with 2 + than with 3 +:

(37) Don't rush ín, now, will anyone?[2+]

And as for the exclusion of 31, all it takes as a counterexample—at least when the stem is positive—is some motivation for an accent on the tag subject, e.g. a situation in which a bus has been mired down and the driver is trying to get some—*any*—of his reluctant passengers to put their shoulders to the wheel:

(38) Give it a push, now, won't sómeone[31] back there please!

The cajoling negative tag is appropriate, but a more demanding positive tag, *will sómeone*, is almost equally so.

The upshot is that only one minus remains in cells 19–21, the one corresponding to a 31 tag on a negative stem in cell 21. Even that permits a plus, provided the negative stem enjoins a positive act or effort. An instructor at the end of a self-expression course might say

(39) Don't be
        $_{sh}$
      y   an
        now, will   y$_{one}$!

and add *You'll disgrace me as an instructor if you do!*[2]

Cells 22–27 cover the possibilities of tagging when the imperative has an explicit subject, whether definite or indefinite. Except for negative stems followed by a low-rising tag, all combinations are alleged to be possible. And even for the forbidden 2 +, Bouton implies (p. 34) that some speakers accept the type

(40) Don't anyone leave before I say to, will you?[2+]

I suspect that those who reject this would accept it if it started with *Please*, which makes the comparatively brusque stem more compatible with the pleading *will you?* This puts a plus in the negative column for indefinite stems (cell 26). What about definite (cell 23)? Bouton stars his (46a),

(41) Don't you leave before I say to, will you?[2+]

which probably needs an overlay of threatening gesture to remove the asterisk. The plea in the *will you* is again too cajoling for the brusque stem. But if the brusqueness is playful, as easily happens among friends bantering in an affectionate way, then compatibility is restored:

(42) Don't you forget to write, now, will you?[2+] I'm counting on those letters.

Similarly the use of *go and* which can playfully impute intentionality:

(43) Don't you go and lose it, now, will you?[2+] I'd hate to have to buy another one.

In one sense the discussion of "*you* as grammatical subject" is irrelevant. What counts is *you* as VOCATIVE. Whatever its position, but particularly when displaced to a salient spot, a *you* trespasses on the privacy of the interlocutor and makes a command more stringent:

(44) Don't say that.
(45) Don't you say that.
(46) ?Don't dare say that.
(47) Don't you dare say that.
(48) You come here this minute!
(49) Come here, you!

A *will you?* is hardly possible with any but the first of these. But if the *you* is contrastive, there is no problem:

(50) Don't yóu say that, will you, John? I can't control what the others say, but I can plead with you for a little consideration.

Conclusion: There is nothing to prevent the tagging of imperatives with explicit subjects, regardless of indefiniteness, so long as the speaker does not combine incompatible moods (which his communicative competence would normally prevent him from doing anyway; it is mostly grammarians, probing their psyches for examples, who get their signals mixed).

Bouton calls attention to a restriction that he omits from the table, the supposedly obligatory "definitization" of the tag subject when a tag is attached to a stem with an explicit subject. More than that, only *you* is supposed to serve as the subject thus definitized. Bouton cites (his 35a, b, c)

(51) Everyone go home now, will you?
(52) Someone shut the door, will you?
(53) Don't anyone say anything about this to Mike, will you?

These, of course, are normal enough. But the fact that in questions, comparable tags allow agreement in number and person and are not restricted to *you*, e.g. Bouton's (38a, b)

(54) Someone bought himself a new car, didn't he?
(55) No one here had their radio on all night, did they?

leads him to suppose that, in the case of imperative tags, there must be "an *ad hoc* restriction to limit the form of the tag subject in this context" (p. 32).

But is it truly ad hoc? If we take Bouton's rather strained example (37),

(56) Someone cut themselves a piece of cake, will you?

and transform the indirect object,

(57) ?Someone cut a piece of cake for themselves, will you?

the result is even more forced (probably because of the proximity of the nonconcordant pronouns), and becomes still worse if the indirect object is postposed:

(58) *Someone cut a piece of cake, will you, for themselves?

but not if the indirect object agrees:

(59) Someone cut a piece of cake, will you, for yourselves?

This suggests that there is more than an ad hoc reason for "definitizing," and doing so with *you*, as one moves to the right. Once an entity has been mentioned, subsequent mentions are definite to the extent that they invoke something already referred to. And the speaker is more apt to zero in on a particular 'you' after having first addressed a plurality.

But all we can say is "more apt." The tendency to be definite is gradient. If the speaker, say, is in a hurry to get to an appointment and is obliged to leave companions behind who will be responsible for securing things, he may say

(60) Someone shut the door, will they? I've got to get out of here fast.

The *will they?* is an offhand toss as the speaker takes his leave; he is not focusing, nor making as if to focus, on anyone in particular. There is no eye contact. Alternatively the speaker may take advantage of the relative indefiniteness of *they*[3] to carry on with an indefinite form of address:

> (61) Somebody answer the last question, will they, so we can all go home? Anybody? Anybody?

That much is pragmatically determined. The tag subject does not have to be *you* when there is an explicit subject in the stem. But does it even have to be definite? Is there in fact "a very common rule in English that makes subsequent reference to any noun phrase antecedent [+ definite]" (p. 32)? If there is, it does not apply to the basic indefinite pronoun *one* in tagged questions:

> (62) One should be cautious in these matters, shouldn't one?

And if the speaker wishes, as a way of needling someone, to throw a mantle of indirection around an obvious reference to a culprit, he may say

> (63) Somebody not doing what somebody's teacher says is going to earn somebody a big fat F.

To which we can add

> (64) A body has to do what a body has to do. That's the way the world goes.

Bouton's article contains valuable observations, but the facts are gradient, better described in terms of markedness or prototype theory than categorically.

REFERENCE MATTER

Notes

Introduction

1. What might have been a little harder to predict was that the same results were obtained for the *green house* versus *greenhouse* type of contrast, which might seem to be purely linguistic. But as we see in Chapter 8, the choices here are anything but clear. The pattern *gréen + house* is of course the normal one for the horticultural sense, but it is also the normal one for 'house that's green' in a conversation like

You live around here?—Yes, I live in the green house.

if the situation is a normal city street and 'house' does not have to be distinguished from 'apartment.' The subjects in the test may well have been confused.

Chapter 1

1. Stevick (1967) reports that in some medieval manuscripts the spaces within compounds or between words were adjusted for length—wider for longer, narrower for shorter.

2. As reported in the *Los Angeles Times*, Sept. 24, 1978, part 1, p. 13. For a popular account see Marjory Roberts, "No language but a cry," *Psychology Today*, June 1987, pp. 57–58.

3. Fernald and Simon (1984) cite an experimental study (Papoušek and Papoušek 1981) which found that mothers "commonly use low, falling pitch contours when soothing a distressed infant." With "highly aroused infants, the low frequency tones were found to be more effective." By "low, falling" here the authors surely mean sustained and saliently low, that is, with low-pitched accents, not merely low terminals.

4. A possible difference between British and American English in the fall-rise makes the British style especially ambiguous for an American. With the—more American?—shape

She   m i g h t   have   m e•   told

rather than the British (at least according to the markings)

She
  might
           have   told me.

there is (for the American) virtually no ambiguity—this has to be epistemic. The *told* at the trough is unaccented, making the profile unambiguously AC. But the British rise on *told* makes the contour potentially A + B (or AC + B with sandhi), and *told* can be more readily heard as accented; this is conducive to the root-modal interpretation, where *told* is new to context.

5. The British designation actually covers the low-pitched variants of three profiles, A, C, and B. But it does not matter here, since in all three cases the speaker pushes the main accent down.

6. What is probably this same contrast was enshrined not as a difference between the sexes but as a difference between languages, by linguists concerned with comparing English and Spanish. Taking the range of pitches produced by Spanish male speakers, and observing that it could be handled by recognizing just three levels, these linguists assumed that their observation applied not to men but to Spanish as a whole, which therefore, with only three levels, supposedly contrasted with English and its required four levels (and its more active feminism!). The "level analysis" of course is not the one followed here. See Stockwell and Bowen (1965: 23–25).

Chapter 2

1. For further comparisons and references see Bolinger (1964) and Bolinger (1978).

2. For more discussion of varieties of English see Pellowe and Jones (1978).

3. See also Odé (1986: 420–21), Types A and B.

4. It is hard to tell from Odé's description of her Type D whether these cases are all of a kind or are perhaps divided between our C and a low-pitched AC. Since both are "held down," the similarities are obvious, and the differences are probably due to different criteria for classification rather than to differences in the intonational systems of the two languages.

5. I owe this reference to Isamu Abe.

Chapter 3

1. See also Brazil, Coulthard, and Johns (1980: 98–99), Lindsey (1981), Siertsema (1962: 390), Fox (1982: 100), Schubiger (1958: 90), Thorsen (1983: 209), and Cutler and Isard (1980: 264).

2. Even at those levels there are problems in trying to match prosodic with syntactic structure. Selkirk (1980: 19) posits a separate phonological phrase for the category *subject*, and points out that whereas Liberman and Prince (1977) would have to say that *Marcel proved* would have "a prosodic structure identical to that of" *Márcel Próust*, altered from *Marcél Próust* by the rhythm rule, for her analysis the subject category resists this shift, leaving the original

pattern intact. Thus in the utterance *That's one of the theorems that Marcel proved* we find *Marcél próved*. But this context confers a certain semantic importance on Marcel as the responsible actor, one of the forces opposing isochrony (Bolinger 1986: 70). If we set up the context so as to have both the subject and the predicate under previous consideration, and take a name that has been anglicized for more years than *Marcel* has, the backshift can easily occur:

> If she couldn't go home, where could Cláudette gó?
> I'll only say that where Cláudette wént is none of your business.

3. *American Scholar* 33 (1964): 518.
4. *New Yorker*, Feb. 7, 1948, p. 32.
5. *Reader's Digest*, Sept. 1960, p. 97.
6. *American Scholar* 25 (1956): 467.
7. Somerset Maugham, quoted in *American Speech* 24 (1948): 133.
8. Of a class of nine advanced students at the University of Colorado, October 1960, only one said the title correctly.
9. *Modern Language Forum* 35 (1950): 55.
10. The notion of "imitation" was suggested in private correspondence by Isamu Abe in 1956. The example he cites is *Is that one of your jobs? Coming in contact with people?* The problem of imitation is related to that of intonational scope, such as we find in quotations, e.g.

"Are you coming?" she asked.

where the ascription carries out the final rise. But in the latter case there *has* to be a rise on the final statement, *she asked*. If it fell, the question that is being quoted would have had a terminal fall in the original. (See Bolinger 1946.)
11. The example is definitely A + B, not AC. If it were AC, the equivalent without the vocative would not be the shape that *What were you doing there?* has but would take a terminal rise on *there*, a much more demanding question (though it would be normal as an echo question).
12. For the notion of ghost sentence see Bolinger (1981*a*).

Chapter 4

1. For large-scale—sentence and larger—divisions marked prosodically, see Chafe (1980) and Lehiste and Wang (1976).
2. From H. Key (1961): 148–49.
3. It is registered to a slight degree by the phonotactics. For example, a word ending in a /t/ does not aspirate the /t/ in American English. This makes *bite apes* audibly distinct from *buy tapes*, where the /t/ is aspirated. There are other oddments of clues as well, such as the fact that the sound [ŋ] usually occurs at the end of a word (and almost always at the end of a morpheme, as in *ringing*; exception, *gingham*).
4. *Official Register of Harvard University*, vol. 60, no. 22 (Sept. 5, 1963), p. 36.
5. *Columbia Journalism Review*, Jan.-Feb. 1981, p. 9.

6. This discussion is not meant to imply that the number sequence in question might not be totally disambiguated by other phonological means. For example, if *twenty* is reduced to [twēi], the interpretation will be *27th St.*, since the house number would be almost necessarily unreduced.

7. See Modini (1982).

8. KGO, San Francisco, May 9, 1981, 3:00 P.M.

9. See Haiman (1983). See also Greenbaum and Meyer (1982), for discussion of ellipsis and some observations on prosody.

10. To point up the contrasts, compare

    a hardy and a fearless soul
    ?a hardy and a fearless dog
    a happy and a prosperous man
    ?a happy and a prosperous merchant

Also, a sensitivity to euphony shows in our reluctance to use the combination *and an*:

    an elegant, masterly style
    an elegant and a masterly style
    a masterly, elegant style
    ?a masterly and an elegant style

11. *Is is* was first noted in print, to the best of my knowledge, by Norman Shapiro (1979). See also Bolinger (1987*b*).

12. Heard on KCBS, San Francisco, Jan. 10, 1976, 9:50 P.M.

Chapter 5

1. In Norwegian, "there is no special tone for questions" (Haugen and Joos 1952: 61). In Finnish "there is no special interrogative intonation" (Iivonen 1978: 52). The same appears to be true of Estonian (Vende 1971: 17–20). For French, Faure (1973) found, among various subjects whom he tested, an all-or-none distinction between merely inconclusive ("progredient") terminals and interrogative ones (yes-no questions without syntactic cues). But were these subjects perhaps striking a pose? If told to "make a question," did they feel prompted to produce a "real question" with all the trimmings? The result would not necessarily be the same as might occur in a conversation where degrees of curiosity and indifference could vary up and down the scale. A study of Ontario French (Maury and Wren 1973) found no difference in configuration between inconclusive and interrogative terminals. The same conclusion for Parisian French was reached by Grundstrom (1973)—no obligatory distinction is needed between interrogative and declarative.

2. Example from E. Fuchs (1935: 4–5).

3. As suggested by Prof. Wierzbicka (pers. comm.). See also Wierzbicka (1986).

4. Correlations between grammar and intonation depend on what "grammar" is defined to cover. It has been claimed by Scherer et al. (1984) that there

is a connection between intonation and the grammatical feature of MARKED-NESS, which is a refined way of saying that there are exceptions to all rules: the form that follows the rule is unmarked, the exception is marked. The unmarked meaning of *doghouse* is 'house for a dog'; the marked meaning is 'disfavor,' as in *He was in the doghouse.* It seems reasonable to say (and we can assume) that the unmarked intonation for yes-no questions is rising, while the marked intonation is falling. The reverse is true of wh questions.

Now if we find that something about intonational meaning is tied neither to yes-no questions nor to wh questions directly but to unmarked questions whether yes-no or wh, and similarly for marked questions, then we have evidence for a tie with grammar. A given meaning cannot be extracted from intonation alone nor from question type alone, but rather from their interaction with markedness.

Scherer et al. tested this idea in a series of experiments in which subjects were asked to assess questions in terms of the following affective-semantic labels: polite, impatient, reproachful, doubtful, friendly, unsure, relaxed, understanding, and aggressive. It turned out that when certain of these were combined, specifically "plus" on the 'friendly' and 'understanding' scales and "minus" on the 'reproachful' and 'aggressive' scales, subjects responded fairly consistently. Call this combination "evaluative." Yes-no questions were judged "high" on the evaluative scale when they rose, "low" when they fell; wh questions were the reverse. In other words, unmarked intonations received high scores and marked ones were low. It appears that high evaluation does not attach to a rising intonation or to a falling one, nor to a wh question or a yes-no question, but to a grammatical feature interacting with both.

Stripped of mystification surrounding the concept of markedness, what does it mean to say that a rising intonation is sometimes high-evaluative and sometimes low, hence inherently neither? One interpretation is that evaluation is the wrong label to use for intonational meaning. It may, in fact, not be an emotional primitive at all, but a highly complex semantic entity itself dependent on the interaction of other simpler semantic entities among which are primitive ones that do attach directly to intonation. The latter would covary with sentence types, context, etc. to produce what we label *evaluation* with its subdivisions of friendly, relaxed, etc.

Suppose, for example, that the subjects had been asked to judge the questions in terms of the labels *demanding* and *inquisitive.* It is not too farfetched to imagine that the falling intonations as such, whether on yes-no or wh questions, would have picked up the 'demanding' label, and the rising ones the 'inquisitive.'

Scherer et al.'s view is that intonational contours do not have meanings of their own but only through configurational relationships with other variables. The position of this book is the opposite, that intonational contours have meanings of a more primitive sort than the ones tested in this case, and that the latter are epiphenomenal or configurational at a higher level. Affective labels of this more primitive (but not necessarily rock-bottom) sort include incurious-surprised, excited-subdued, interested-indifferent, knowing-suspensive, intent-withdrawn, serious-smiling, settled-unsettled, upbeat-downbeat, satisfied-unsatisfied. Interacting with other variables these more or less primitive classes can be matched with secondary ones: depending on what else goes into the pot, 'subdued' can be either 'bored' (which is bad) or 'reserved' (which may be good).

For the present case, take 'settled-unsettled' and apply it to questions. If the intonation is presented pure (as with the carrier sound *m-m*), it is fairly certain that the fall will be associated with 'settled' and the rise with 'unsettled.' And if the 'settled' intonation is applied to a wh question it will probably be accorded most of those plus-evaluative labels, simply because a wh question already begs a presupposition: the speaker who asks *When are they coming?* is settled as to the fact that they are coming. Not so with the speaker who asks *Are they coming?*, who, if he uses a fall, is apt to be taken as settled when he should not be.

It is necessary to choose labels that are appropriate to the medium being tested. There is nothing in intonation to suggest that the parameter of 'friendly' is appropriate in any way at a basic level; there is much to suggest that 'settled' is appropriate. (Voice quality is a different matter: gruffness at high intensity may well be taken as 'unfriendly.') What these experiments do prove is that the emotive labels that have so often been used in the past need to be viewed with skepticism. "Anger" and "enthusiasm" are both manifested intonationally as "arousal." See Bolinger 1986: 247–50.

5. For the interrogativeness of *wonder*, compare its use in tags, e.g. *Do they like it I wonder?*, and as an ascription, more or less equivalent to *ask: John wondered if they liked it and I assured him they did.*

6. Some of the rises may of course have been manifestations of C or AC rather than B, but B was undoubtedly in the majority.

7. "What's My Line," Mar. 13, 1960.

8. Two book-length studies of English tag questions, Houck (1984) and Nässlin (1984), give considerable attention to intonation.

9. For the extremely complex possibilities of tagging alternative questions and wh questions, see Bolinger (1957), pp. 115, 117, 120, 123, 125–30, 133–34, 139, 140, 143.

10. A speaker quoting himself will transform *eh* to the regular form:

You like him, eh? — What did you say? — I said you like him do you?

11. There is the usual ambiguity between A + C and AC. The AC could be used in the context of (104) on *You like him* alone, without the tag. So the tag is either a C added to an A, or, with AC, either an unaccented tail or an AC + C with tonal sandhi. See Bolinger 1986: 316–17.

12. If they are one in surface structure and in mutual qualification, are they underlyingly two? Nässlin (1984: 16) adopts the two-in-one analysis and diagrams as shown in the accompanying figure (reprinted with permission of the publisher).

13. As a response used independently—i.e., not tagged—an AC is possible, especially for British speakers, e.g. in a conversation such as

I don't intend to take that part. — Don't you?

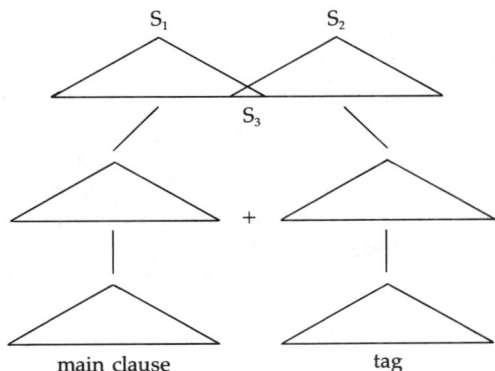

Fig. to note 12

This type of response is dubbed "newsmark" by conversation analysts. See Heritage (1984: 340–44).

14. If the pitch drop is delayed until *-y*, leaving the syllable *-ar-* at the peak, the result is B + A + C with a climactic mispronunciation—the full but unstressed syllable *-ar-* receives the A.

15. In testing an example like (136) one must be careful to avoid any rise in pitch on *do*, since it will bias the result toward conducive reversal.

16. Apheresis is the process by which initial unaccented material is dropped when it is immediately followed by a main accent (especially when, as in [138], the unaccented material—*is it*—is at low pitch, given the likely B profile, hence doubly indistinct). Other examples: *Gotcha!* for *I got you!*; *Race you to the corner* for *I'll race you to the corner*; *'Fraid so* for *I'm afraid so*. That apheresis is the explanation we can infer from the fact that the deletion does not occur systematically for all intonations but only for those in which the elided element is entirely overshadowed by the following accent. So an A + À with reversed polarity is normal with the deletion,

```
Lost
        did
           n't
    it
              they?
```

but a C + B or a C + A is less so, since the C of the stem is apt to put the stem subject *they* at a high pitch:

```
        did
*Lost  it   n't
              they?
```

17. Other verbs than *be* are marginal: *?Tired did they get? ? Silly did she act? ?Worn out did they seem?*

18. There is a curious restriction on irregular past participles such as *broken*, mainly affecting stems that have pronoun subjects. They "sound wrong."

Compare:

> *She taken it has she?
> *He done it already had he?
> *You broken it again have you?

This surely reflects our reaction to substandard uses of the irregular past participles: in *He done it already had he?* the *had* comes too late to mend the impression of *He done it*. Regular past participles get by because they sound like the regular past tense and the perfect tag is close enough in meaning not to create a conflict even when the hearer makes a preliminary judgment of "past tense" when he hears the verb:

> They left already have they?
> She sold it has she?

19. Their existence also raises the possibility of a two-step derivation for Int. The first step is a deletion from *Are you going?* to produce *Going?* The second step is the addition of the tag. This bypasses the somewhat doubtful type represented by (138). A third possible derivation is by a movement transformation that simply shifts the auxiliary and subject to the end: *Are you going?* → *Going are you?* This is unlikely for two reasons. First, it would equate a main auxiliary with a tag. Second, the subject in the stem can be a noun, which would not permit such a transfer: *Did your brother lose it?* → *Lose it did your brother?*

20. Even in "normal order," with the "main verb" first, the content of the grammatically subordinate clause may be what is responded to:

> You say he's coming? — Yes he is.

(*Yes I do* of course is possible here.) How formulaic *suppose* is can be seen in its independent use as a weak affirmative:

> Is he coming? — I suppose.

21. This is perhaps a case of homonymic conflict: with a simple AC, *He's coming / to be sure* is too readily taken for *He's coming to be sure*.

Chapter 6

1. The reader is urged, in testing these examples, to try more than one intonation on the tag—especially, if in doubt, to try the low flat monotone that attaches the tag as an intonational tail to the stem. In the text example *Take the best, why shouldn't you?* it would be a mistake to give *why shouldn't you?* an A profile as that would break up the combination and produce *Take the best. Why shouldn't you?* Tagging requires an intonational tail here.

2. This example shows that even with the tags using just auxiliary verb and pronoun, the tag may be syntactically independent of the verb in the stem: there is no *May I let me help you?* Stem verbs other than *let* are possible but not common:

Remind me to give you a hand, may I?
Invite me to come to your party, may I?

Tagging a grammatically subordinate verb in the stem is of course regularly found in questions with tentations like *suppose, think, figure, reckon*:

I suppose you knew that, didn't you? (*don't I?)

3. In this section particularly, and in most of the others generally, the tags are instances of what Ross (1975) calls "slifting." Among his examples (p. 242) are

I want you to tell me when dinner will be ready → When will dinner be ready, I want you to tell me.

Can you tell me who Sam is pitching to next? → Who is Sam pitching to next, can you tell me?

Ross's study also contains valuable observations on *please*.
4. See Andersen (1978), and compare the following advice from fitness expert Jack LaLanne (Owen Spann program, San Francisco radio KGO, rebroadcast Oct. 24, 1982, 9:30 A.M.):

The only way [to keep healthy] is to don't [avoid exercise].

5. On San Francisco radio KCBS, Nov. 11, 1986, 6:00 A.M. My impression is that a generation ago *all right* used in this way was mostly for coaxing children, and that is still a major use (one does not compel a child, one negotiates). I suspect that *OK* in this same context would be less fused, which is to be expected, as it is the innovating expression.

Chapter 7

1. Frances Trollope, *Domestic Manners of the Americans* (London: Whittaker, Treacher, and Co., 1832), p. 89.
2. Robert Colby, *Murder Times Five* (Greenwich, Conn.: Fawcett, 1972), p. 122.
3. This is particularly evident in collocation with *just*:

*Just in case you strike gold, let me know.
Just in case you strike gold, you'd better take precautions.

Oddly, *in that case* is not affected and can be purely conditional: *What if I strike gold? — In that case (if that happens) let me know.*
4. See Fox (1984) for British.
5. Bill Walker, *The Case of Barbara Graham* (New York: Ballantine, 1961), p. 53.
6. This example was suggested by Judy Gilbert.
7. And rarely zero: *Did you send word (that) I was to come?*
8. Among other complications is that not all simplexes have corresponding clefts. Adjectives, for example, are sometimes barred from *it* clefts in Standard English:

Mary wasn't beautiful, what she was was pretty.
*Mary wasn't beautiful, it was pretty that she was.

9. These are counterexamples to the claim by Gilbert Rappaport reported by Thompson (1983), according to which clauses of this type either themselves have a clause-final falling intonation or are preceded by a clause having such a terminal fall. See Bolinger (1977*a*).

Chapter 8

1. For an adjective plus noun combination to become a fore-stressed compound requires stronger fusion as a rule. Any box for cash can be a *cásh box*, almost any box for tools can be a *tóolbox*; but not just any box that is strong can be a *stróngbox*, and a *hótbox* is not a box in the ordinary sense at all.

2. In Bolinger (1986: 56–57) this tendency was associated with the notion of "thematic accent," typically located at the beginning of the utterance. In *The móckingbirds were sínging* the theme is *mockingbirds*, and the leftward push of the thematic accent favors initial stress on that word, as on any noun serving as theme—which is a favorite role for nouns and therefore a reason for the backshifting of stress *on* nouns (just as the rightward push of the RHEMATIC accent creates a tendency for verbs to have stress at the opposite end). Words tend to pick up their stress patterns by imitating the favored accent patterns of whole utterances: "There is a strong tendency for utterance phenomena to narrow their domain to the word unit" (Hyman 1978: 454).

3. *The Life and Adventures of Jonathan Jefferson Whitlaw* (London: Richard Bentley, 1836), 1: 325.

4. Loss of this potential, and loss in general, is of course characteristic of all routinized speech. A speaker was heard to say *Were you ever in O. Henry's house?*, with the given-name initial pronounced exactly as if it were the O of *O'Henry*. Asked how he would say *Have you ever been in R. Long's house?* the same speaker gave a clear A profile to the initial letter *R*. Frequent mention of *O. Henry* has made a "compound" of the two-part name. The same happens with the routine formulas *No, thank you* → *No thank you* and *No, I'm sorry, I (haven't)* → *No, I'm sorry I (haven't)*—the latter e.g. in answer to *Have you heard about it?*

Chapter 9

1. Except for intensifying infixes of the *fandamntastic* type. See Bolinger 1986: 86.

2. Legend under photo, *Palo Alto Times*, Dec. 16, 1976, p. 6.

3. Sign at Gatwick Airport, London, reported by Norman A. Heap, in *Verbatim* 8 (1981) 2: 18.

4. The citations are from, and the comments here are on, Ladd's (1983) review of Gussenhoven (1983). For a further development of this debate, see Gussenhoven et al. (1987).

5. If *arrested* is played down in such a way that *youth* and *father* are more prominent, then we get the "narrow focus" that Ladd assigns in such cases:

'It wasn't the two well-known dealers who were arrested, but this pair of unknowns.' Actually the construction is not appropriate, because we would probably want to convey the latter sense with something like *But the ones arrested were . . .*

6. The possibilities are even broader, though (72)–(74) are about as far as one can go with intonation alone. If we say

> (a) Thése are dífficult times to be living through.

with no accent after *difficult*, or

> (b) Thése are difficult times to be living through.

with only the accent on *these*, one needs, in order to avoid narrow focus, additional qualifiers on top of the final accent: extra length on the accented syllable and—especially in (b)—a slow and deliberate shaking of the head, with an air of making a sage observation.

7. Schmerling (1976: 90–93) commits the same error in criticizing Bolinger (1972*a*): "Bolinger's theory would appear to suggest . . . that the mention of Truman in the relevant context should have suggested 'death' and, therefore, that *died* . . . should not be stressed." The fact is that the mention of Truman in the relevant context suggests the contrastive set, not any particular member of it. It would be irrelevant to argue that we all have to die sometime and therefore 'death' should have been more strongly suggested. It could of course be, but that would be reflected in the relative height of the accents, e.g.

```
(a)  Tru                                          di
           di                      (b)  Tru
       man                                   man

              ed.                                          ed.
```

with (a) for greater expectation of death, (b) for possible recovery. (See Bolinger 1977*c*.)

8. This deprives the Ladd-Gussenhoven rule of content except in so far as one might still say "nouns are more apt to be accented than verbs."

9. The noun phrase is compatible with the dynamic interpretation if it is some form of epithet: an accusation of misbehavior is stronger if expressed with an epithetical noun or noun phrase if one is available (e.g. *bad boy, fool*) than when expressed with an adjective (*bad, foolish*): *John has been a bad boy!; John has been a fool!*

10. Whether *girl* is semantically redundant is debatable. One's being a wicked girl is not necessarily the same as a girl's being wicked.

Chapter 10

1. For discussions of the syntax of "questions used as exclamations" see Elliott (1974), Oomen (1979), and Wierzbicka (1980).

2. For *hm, sh, phew,* etc. see Martin (1977: 160–64).

3. Carlson claims (1984: 70) that *oh* registers merely the newness of the information, not the fact that the speaker agrees. Yet the *oh* of this example,

while compatible with a following *I see, I understand*, or *That explains it then*, is hardly compatible with *That's impossible*, given successive A's (as shown by the punctuation, *Oh. That's impossible*). Qualified, as in *Oh, that's impossible*, under a single contour, the disagreeing response is normal. The point here is that an INDEPENDENT *oh*, with no interrogative intonation or gesture, tends to affirm.

4. As I have phrased the question, it embodies both content and appeal-from-speaker (question proper), in the dual form of the overall question: the content is expressed in *He paid off the debt* and the appeal in *did he?*, the two together forming a same-polarity tag question. If the content were not thus split off, so to speak, not all the answers in the first set would be equally appropriate. This would happen with an ordinary yes-no question:

Did he pay off the debt? — ?True (?right, ?correct).

but not with a question in declarative form:

He paid off the debt? — True (right, correct).

In the second set the speaker is responding to the appeal of the *did he?* Carlson would claim in this instance that adding *oh* suggests surprise that the question should have been asked: 'You didn't really need to ask'—hence the reassurance.

5. Unfortunately, further comment on the Heritage study has to be largely negative. Too much reliance is placed on a corpus (the author realizes the limitations, but neglects to point out any specific insufficiencies), and—most important to us here—makes only occasional reference to intonation. The upshot is a series of claims for which counterexamples are too easy to find:

(a) "It may further be suggested that 'oh' receipts, in proposing a questioner's now-informed status, also implicate the questioner's acceptance of an answer as fact" (p. 339). This would exclude *oh fiddlesticks, oh pooh, oh that can't be true*, etc.

(b) " 'Oh' is scarcely ever . . . associated with further turn components that assert prior knowledge of 'oh'-receipted information" (p. 305). The author strengthens this (n. 9) with examples in which *some* prior knowledge is asserted, but in every case mingled with something new or newly remembered. But there is no problem in prefacing an assertion of *complete* prior knowledge with *oh*:

```
       I
            tha
Oh   know
                at!
```

The prefacing of *oh* makes the rejection less abrasive, and the gestures tend to conform: without *oh* the utterance would more easily be an eye-contact challenge; with it, the speaker is more apt to avert his gaze.

(c) "Whereas 'oh you did?' appears effectively equivalent in sequential terms to 'oh did you?' a parallel equivalence does not hold between 'you did?' and 'did you?' Whereas 'you did?' may project disagreement . . . 'did you?'

does not project the possibility of upcoming disagreement" (p. 343). It is true that the lower degree of curiosity of *you did?* is more apt to convey skepticism or even sarcasm, but this is qualified not only by *oh*, as Heritage notes, but also by intonation. In fact, the qualification by *oh* is probably itself at least partly intonational, in that the surprise value of *oh* encourages a B profile or a higher-rising B if a B is already in the works. Without *oh*, the simple expedient of using a high B will reverse the negativity of *you did?* And *did you?* can be similarly reversed. A deep-throated C on *did* in *did you?* may convey ironic denial, and the same occurs with an A profile if *did you?* is tagged with *now*:

```
Did

    you now!
```

Further, if *Oh you did?* is tagged with either *eh* or *did you* (*Oh you did did you?*) and given an AC profile, the result is easily an expression of disbelief:

```
       di
Oh you  ᵢdˀ   I'll just
                    b
                     eₜ
                        you did!
```

(d) "Whereas 'oh' is routinely used to receipt information, its sequential role is essentially backward-looking. Specifically, the particle does not invite or request further information" (p. 311). Again, whether it looks backward and ratifies a receipt, or forward and expects more to come, is entirely a matter of intonation. The ratification does not need *oh*—a mere *m-m-m* on an A profile will receipt the information. The same *m-m-m* on a B profile is not nearly as good as *oh* to elicit further clarification, which appears to make *oh* more forward- than backward-looking. In fact, we find that one of the chief differences between *oh* and *ah* is the latter's backward look. The meaning of *oh* cannot be grasped independently of its contrast with its closest relatives among the vowel interjections, *ah* and *aw*. If *ah* had been considered, its possibilities for "information receipt" would have been seen to rival those of *oh*.

It appears that a barrier we thought for a time had been leveled is back in place: the data people are neglecting theory and the theory people are neglecting data. Heritage takes a timid step toward a theory of the meaning of *oh* when he refers to it (p. 337) as "deeply implicated in the behaviors of 'coming to see something.'" Aijmer faithfully reproduces intonation but then sometimes fails to distinguish its separate contribution to some potentially stable meaning of *oh*. All marriages are chancy, but discourse analysts need to court theories of meaning with more élan.

6. This same *oh–ah* or *oho–aha* contrast is found in Chinese (Xiao-nan Chen, pers. comm.), most dialects of Finnish (Lauri Carlson and Jan-Ola Östman, pers. comm.), Spanish, and Hungarian. The situation is similar in Swedish (Alvar Goës, pers. comm.), where subjects in an informal test strongly favored *ah* and *aha* for the Swedish equivalent of *Aha! I caught you that time, didn't I!* (Britt-Louise Gunnarsson, pers. comm.).

7. A possible exception to this generalization is an *Indeed!* used as a sober, thoughtful assent to an opinion expressed by the interlocutor. The meaning is 'How true!,' and the speaker seems to address an unseen audience as much as his interlocutor. The eyes are apt to be averted, voice qualifiers are likely to be present (a sigh if a C profile is used, a low-pitched half-growl and a drawled tail if A), and there is apt to be a slow nod (if C) or a headshake (if A) as well.

Chapter 11

1. Hines (1978) makes the same point regarding Lakoff (1973*a*), and in Hines (1979) she argues for a unitary treatment of *well* and *good*.

2. Carlson accepts this fully and justifies the positing of a single abstract meaning with "quite informative conversational inferences" based on it. The task of defining a semantic content to the best of one's ability imposes another obligation that the linguist does not share with the sociolinguist, the invention of negative data. Discourse analysts may *find* deviance and feel constrained to explain it, but the kinds of deviance that bring to light the precise contrasts that one requires for clear definition are a rarity, and one is compelled to invent. Definition is like map-making: we want to be able to say not only that a given point is part of the U.S.—anywhere in mid-America will qualify—but also to say that it is not part of Canada, and for that we need to mark the border. One cannot discover a rule or a meaning without studying the consequences of misuse or violation. In spite of the occasional abuse of starred forms, we cannot do without them, and they are rarely to be found in a corpus.

3. It is true that *grasping* veers off here into a totally different semantic field, but it is the basic sense of the verb that allows the deviation.

4. I do not refer to compounds, such as *well-appointed, well-expressed, well-delineated*, etc., though these still obey the general semantics of *well*: we do not say **well-betrayed, *well-diminished*.

5. *Really!* is more or less synonymous here, with the same intonation, and the two may be combined, as in the first example on p. 302. I speculate: 'given the reality of things' is close to 'given the norm of things'; but *well* is stronger.

6. The most recent generation of English-speakers may be losing any sense of *as well* except that of plain addition, in view of the widespread tendency nowadays to replace *and* with *as well* as correlative of *both*:

> Margi [a language] . . . makes extensive use of both labialization as
> well as rounding.

7. The prosody of these sentences is adjusted to the hat pattern template (see Bolinger 1986: 46–50) by preserving the original terminal accent and attaching it to the final word. Thus the full form of *Well I'll be!* is *Well I'll be damned*, with the main accent on *damned* and ordinarily no accent at all on *be*; but it becomes *Well Í'll bé!*

8. He does not, however, note the transcendent versus immanent senses of *well* and *good*, which have been appealed to here in order to show the close

tie between the interjection and other epistemic uses. *Very good* and *very well* are cited, p. 27, only in terms of their "near equivalence."

9. It is no coincidence that *so* and *well* are most often translated to Spanish with *pues, pos* 'post-, after.'

10. The shape B + Á rather than B + À, i.e.

Well of ^{co} $^u{}_{r}{}_{s}{}_{e}$ ↓

would suggest 'How could you think otherwise?'

11. Carlson lists the following (in a hierarchical arrangement that I do not reproduce here): defective questions, defective answers, conversational maxims and other interests compromised, rejoinders (called *replies*), arguments, corrections, comments, exclamations, topic suggestions, dialog openings, transitions, closing, turn-internal cases.

12. Actually *very well* is not the same overall as *well*, but belongs rather with *all right*, *OK*, and, peripherally, *fine*, though it expresses a more severe judgment. Like *OK* etc. it can combine with *well*:

Well OK, you shall have no supper.
Well very well, you shall have no supper.

All these expressions of literal approval can be used in this situation—the outcome is undesirable, but the speaker ironically gives the nod to the circumstances: 'That's fine, you've made your bed, now you can lie in it.'

13. Also in the stereotypes *Oh well* and *Ah well*, and after the hesitation sound *m-m-m* and *well* itself, i.e., a repeated *well*.

14. There are gestural substitutes that would permit the speaker to omit *well*. He can pause, look inquiringly at the interlocutor, change his expression to one of 'knowing' with perhaps a truncated nod, then shrug the shoulders and flare hands out, before saying *Why not?* None of this, of course, is in slow motion, as the description seems to imply.

Chapter 12

1. One can even question the judgment of misalignment. One of Couper-Kuhlen's alleged errors is the following: "It's amazing that the people who are NOW saying that parliament has no part in it where were you when the original aBORtion bill was being put which was . . . legalizing abortion on a large scale." The speaker "gets no reaction from his feminist contendant until his meaning becomes clear" (p. 155)—he should have accented *original* rather than *abortion*. But was he guilty of a linguistic mistake, or of a mistake in judgment? *Original*, with its implication of 'then,' is a clearer counterpoise to *now*; but if the speaker thinks of the abortion bill when it occurred as an *event*, then that event had a time, which was 'then.' Calendars are marked by the historization of nouns: *post–Civil War, after Pearl Harbor, between breakfast and lunch*. A word can be accented for *any* aspect of its meaning, with other features in abeyance.

2. For example, what do we have when a contradictory takes the shape of a counterassertion?—

Why didn't you write the letter? — I wróte it!

which can be paraphrased 'Why, rather than write the letter, did you not write it? — I didn't not-write the letter, rather, I wrote it!' The deep fall that Couper-Kuhlen describes for contrast is clearly in order here—for the affective reason that I maintain applies regularly: the speaker is making an assertion that will not brook rejection. In a sense, every affirmation (denial) is a repudiation of its corresponding denial (affirmation), and contrast is universal. Alternative questions pose the same dilemma for a clear distinction between contraries and contradictories:

Is it moving or standing still?
Is it moving or not?

Chapter 13

1. Sperber and Wilson consistently use capitals to denote accent, and capitalize the entire word, e.g. *APPLES*, rather than the accented syllable, *APples*. This is in keeping with their notion of accents falling on grammatical rather than phonological constituents. It implies that no attention is given to accents of power, which in many cases need to be marked on syllables, as for example in

She admíts it's the best compromíse that could be hammered óut.
  (Radio broadcast, 1985)

where the stress has significantly shifted in *compromise*.
2. I change the wording to make it clear that the "focus is on the sentence as a whole." The plain *What happened?* is ambiguous. It could occur in an exchange like

A: No, she didn't take first place.
B: What happened?
C: She came in thírd.

3. These examples are particularly unfortunate because they come right at the spot where Sperber and Wilson dismiss Halliday's notions of theme and rheme in the following terms: "While the theme-rheme distinction may be a valuable way of highlighting these intuitions, it has no place in the technical descriptive vocabulary of either linguistics or pragmatics" (SW, p. 216). By placing all their prosodic bets on accent, Sperber and Wilson miss what has been pointed out before in these pages, that AC profiles are quite regularly associated with themes, in whichever order, and a linguistic treatment of intonation must surely recognize this fact.
4. Having contextual effects = "enlarging mutual cognitive environments" (SW, p. 193).
5. This does not apply, of course, to syntactic or lexical best guesses early

in the game. Someone hearing just *a stitch* may we l be justified in laying out the full scenario of *A stitch in time saves nine*. This s like best-guessing items that are not clearly heard—best guesses do not have to be revised so often that there is much loss in relying upon them. To some extent this can be done with prosody too, but the risks are greater. Sperber and Wilson allow (p. 141) for a "specialized short-term memory" in which information about the physical environment may be "very briefly retained," and transferred as needed "to the general short-term conceptual memory store." I would say that for prosody there is a related echoic memory, providing for verbal and intonational afterimages to be consulted immediately.

6. Sperber and Wilson specifically state (p. 107) their atomistic view of memory storage where "information" is concerned: "We assume, as do most current models of memory, that information is broken down as far as possible into smaller units before being stored in memory, so that a conjoined assumption, for example, is not stored as a unit but is broken down into its constituent conjuncts, which may end up in different encyclopedic entries. Any organism interested in improving its overall representation of the world must therefore be interested in recovering as many synthetic implications as possible from any set of assumptions it is currently processing, before the set is dismantled for separate storage." Whether "information" here includes information about the lexicon is not clear, but if "current models of memory" is meant to picture the lexicon as a set of small units into which everything higher is dismantled before being tucked away, then the models are in conflict with much recent work on automatic language and holistic storage. Shopping separately for turnips, onions, beef chunks, and spices represents one form of efficiency; buying a complete prepackaged frozen stew represents another.

Chapter 14

1. For Dik et al. (1980: 51), *counterassertive* and *counterpresuppositional* are not proposed as companion terms, but rather *counterassertive* is rejected in favor of *counterpresuppositional*. A presupposition is what the speaker has in mind whether conveying it directly or obliquely. Counterpresuppositions thus include counterassertions: "The essential factor would thus seem to be, not what the other has just said, but what the speaker assumes about the pragmatic information of the other at the moment of speaking. The constructions involved are thus 'Counter-presuppositional' rather than 'Counter-asserted.'" This accords more closely with the conclusions arrived at here.

2. More than a possibility with *am not*, owing to the lack of *amn't*.

3. Gussenhoven presumably excludes these from his rule because they are not instances of "polarity focus," that is, focus as manifested by accent on some part of the verb phrase including *not*. From the standpoint of indirect denial, and also by comparison with Gussenhoven's own greater liberality in assigning accents in [−counterassertive] utterances, this is unjustified.

4. There are of course other ways of blunting a contradiction. One is to appear to concede the speaker's knowledge by adding *you know* on a rising terminal (*really* has the same effect):

```
              IS
   O,     house
NO   the        n't on fire, you know.
```

5. Gussenhoven correctly assigns this to selection from rather than addition to Background: the hearer is supposed to know already. But I attribute the intonation not to a logical notion of 'selection from Background' but to an affective *plea* for acceptance. See Bolinger (1987a: 125).

6. See Givón (1979: 93–116).

7. Both (61) and (62) involve polarity expressions. We do not, for instance, say

> Mr. SMITH, you dón't have MONey. — Mr. JONES, *I háve a CENT (*I háve a pénny to my NAME).

but we can say

> Mr. SMITH, you dón't have MONey. — Mr. JONES, SEE, I have a PENny!

Other instances of polarity items include

> Jóhn is a LINguist. — Jóhn doesn't know BEANS about linguistics.
> She sáys you bróke her CHIna. — I dídn't do a THING to her china.

The latter is reminiscent of French *rien*, and is clearly related to

> I dídn't do ANything to her china!
> I did nóthing whatsoEVer to her china!

and these merge with other polarity items that are more of the inference-demanding sort and are therefore up on the indirect denial side of the gradient:

> I dídn't so much as TOUCH her china.
> I wóuldn't STOOP to háve anything to DO with her china!

Chapter 15

1. But this can hardly be an accurate formulation. To report the contents of one's own thoughts one would say something like *I am thinking to myself 'John's married.'* It is true, of course, that *I think John's married* means "I do not know what the real state of affairs is" (pp. 1–2), but it is hardly true that I am giving "no indication of whether I believe 'John is married' conforms with the real state of affairs" (p. 1).

2. If an accent falls on the complement (*married*, in the example) but is not the dominant accent, there is less of a problem for the factual interpretation. Take the A + AC in the following response to *This is John's wife*:

```
I
 thought
             mar   d.
                 i e
    he was    r
```

The speaker feels that 'married' is interesting, probably because it is not entirely redundant—it would be consistent for him to add *though I might have hesitated between wife and ex-wife; married* accordingly gets a secondary accent without necessarily destroying the factual interpretation. The response is appropriate to either *This is John's wife*, in which case it is factual, or to *This is John's fiancée*, in which case it is counterfactual. The latter could be reworded *And I thought he was married—how stupid can one be?* And in the latter case the accent on *married* is logically the major accent despite its lower pitch. In other words, this utterance is ambiguous as between major and minor accents.

3. This proves that *know* in the past tense is not necessarily a factive verb, especially with this rising intonation. Here it is equivalent to *just know*, a hyperbolic way of expressing strong conviction (*I just know he's going to do that! I can feel it in my bones!*), and that expression could be used here with the same intonation: *I just knew it!* Gesture, too, can render *know* nonfactive. The *I knew it* of the example can be pronounced on a uniformly falling contour (with delayed release and increased volume on *knew*) if the speaker wears an expression of pleased surprise. The same even holds for *I `knew they were ,married!,* as in (1), the intonation that most concerns us. It would not be appropriate for the interlocutor to ask *How did you know it?*, as would be the case with truly factive uses of the verb *know*.

4. See Brazil, Coulthard, and Johns (1980), pp. 14–16.

Appendix A

1. The fact that we say *ísn't* alongside *is nót*, i.e., that we can emphasize the part that is not in contrast, proves that in limited ways Gussenhoven's concept of "focus domain" is valid. *Isn't* has ceased to be a phonologically analyzable form, and the accent strikes it as a whole.

2. If the answer has a nominal rather than a pronominal subject, the requirement of the B + À contour is all the more striking. Again, the answer is to *Is John the gárdener?*

```
(a) John's the                    (b) *John's
              gar                              the  gar
                 dener.                            dener.


          gardener is                          gar
(c) The                           (d) *The            Jo
                  Jo                      dener is
                    hn.                              hn.


           gar                               gar
(e) *John's the                   (f) *John's
                dener.                     the
                                              dener.


                    Jo                               Jo
          gardener is                        gar
(g) *The                          (h) *The   dener is
                   hn.                               hn.
```

The terminal A without a higher-pitched preceding B is in some sense contrastive. (Put a *yes* or a *you're right* in front, and all these answers become possible.)

What the above seems to illustrate is the status of one of the nouns as theme, and the presentation of the theme as the main item of interest (hence the higher pitch). The question is ambiguous from the standpoint of theme. The respondent can treat it as 'You want to know about John (what he does)?' or as 'You want to know about the gardener (who it is)?'—(a) answers the first and (c) the second, both using the same intonation to give prominence to the chosen theme:

> You want to know about Jóhn, he's the gàrdener.
> You want to know about the gárdener, it's Jòhn.

The initial B profile reflects the fact that the theme has already been introduced in the question. If that is not the case, that is, if the theme is being newly introduced or newly reintroduced, the dynamics of relative height remain the same but the speaker may give the theme an A profile. Take the following series, in response to *Let's check on the agenda, item by item*:

> OK. The léaves have been cómposted, as you ordered. Also the trées have been deep-wátered. Next, the hútches have been scrúbbed. Last, the fértilizer has all been púrchased and laid bý.

The themes are *leaves, trees, hutches,* and *fertilizer,* all higher-pitched than their predicates *composted, deep-watered, scrubbed,* and *purchased and laid by,* whether the contour is B + À or A + À. (Reverse the heights and the themes become something probably already under discussion.) It is not a question of grammatical subject or of nouns as such, but of theme and rheme: the first sentence could be *The boys have composted the leaves, as you ordered,* with *leaves* still higher than either *boys* or *composted,* because the speaker is saying in effect 'As to the leaves, as to the trees,' etc., and this active sentence, with the accents as noted, could be inserted in that otherwise passive context. It would be possible also, in fact quite easy, to add items of which only the thematic word itself is accented, e.g. *The fértilizer's been applied,* with no accent on *applied,* since that is what is usually done with fertilizer.

The common factor in all this is the relative WEIGHTING of the accents, with higher-to-lower as likely as higher-to-zero. This is the generalization that Gussenhoven seems to have been trying to capture in his "focus domains," but he overstated the higher-to-zero relationship, neglecting the higher-to-lower. What the above examples show is that the last accented syllable of the tone group is not necessarily the "nucleus" if by nucleus we mean the most prominent accent.

Appendix B

1. I assume that Bouton's example (40c) is a misprint—it should be starred, since a later example, his (44f), *Don't come early tomorrow, will anyone?*,[31] is so marked, and since the corresponding cell for 31 in the table, cell 21, has only minus signs.

2. As Bouton points out (p. 34), the indefinite subject may appear in simple (= tagless) imperatives too. But he errs in claiming that imperatives like

> Go down to the office and tell them that we are ready.

"are always interpreted as having *definite* subjects," in view of

> Would you like someone on my staff to take them a message? — Yes,
>   go down to the office and tell them that we are ready, if he will.

Just as a *you* subject is inferred in the situations in which a *you* is appropriate, so a *someone* subject is inferred in *this* situation; the number of *you* situations is overwhelmingly large, but that does not imbue the *verb* with any particular subject—it is still the bare infinitive form, open to inferences from the context (see Bolinger 1977b: 179). An intended *someone* subject, in the simplest case, surfaces as a vocative tag in

> Speak up, someone!

where the vocative is usually sotto voce, but may be highlighted:

> Speak up, hey, sómebody here! I can't stand this holding back
>   forever!

3. When is a pronoun "definite"? *They* is part of the paradigm of personal pronouns in English, but it has indefinite as well as definite uses:

> They say it's going to rain.
> I wish they'd pass a law prohibiting that.
> What are they doing in Milwaukee these days?

Is exhaustiveness of the reference a criterion, so that in

> Both of you take hold of this end and either of you the other, will
>   you, and we can heave it on board.

both of you is definite and *either of you* is indefinite? If so, what is the *you* of the tag? And what about

> Step this way, will all of you please?

where *all of you* is the periphrastic second-person plural, and just as "definite" as *you all* or *youse*? We are as much in need, pragmatically, of recognizing "referentially definite" versus "referentially indefinite" among the so-called definite pronouns as among the indefinite ones. What counts pragmatically is whether the speaker intends to be definite.

References Cited

Abe, Isamu. 1955. Intonational patterns of English and Japanese. *Word* 11: 386–98.

———. 1979. Melodic patterns of street cries. *Humanities Review* (Tokyo Institute of Technology) no. 3: 19–26.

Abramson, Arthur S., and Katyanee Svastikula. 1983. Intersections of tone and intonation in Thai. *Haskins Laboratories Status Report on Speech Research*, Apr.-Sept., pp. 143–54.

Aijmer, Karin. 1987. *Oh* and *ah* in English conversation. In Willem Meijs, ed., *Corpus Linguistics and Beyond: Proceedings of the Seventh International Conference on English Language Research on Computerized Corpora*, pp. 61–86. Amsterdam: Rodopi.

Allen, George. 1983. Some suprasegmental contours in French two-year-old children's speech. *Phonetica* 40: 269–92.

Allen, George, Sarah Hawkins, and Margaret R. Morris. 1977. Development of nuclear accent marking in children's phrases. *American Association of Phonetic Sciences Bulletin*, December, p. 7.

Andersen, Elaine S. 1978. "Will you don't snore, please?" Directions in young children's role-play speech. *Papers and Reports on Child Language Development* (Stanford University) 15: 140–50.

Arndt, Walter. 1960. "Modal particles" in Russian and German. *Word* 16: 323–36.

Bailey, Charles-James N. 1983. A concise but comprehensive approach to intonation for learners of English. *Arbeiten aus Anglistik und Amerikanistik* 8: 3–27.

Barbizet, J., M. Lederer, M. Pergnier, and D. Seleskovitch. 1979. Vouloir-dire, intonation et structures des phrases. *Folia Linguistica* 13: 237–45.

Bolinger, Dwight. 1945. The minimizing downskip. *American Speech* 20: 40–44.

———. 1946. The intonation of quoted questions. *Quarterly Journal of Speech* 32: 197–202.

———. 1948. The intonation of accosting questions. *English Studies* 29: 109–14.

———. 1957. *Interrogative Structures of American English*. Publication of the American Dialect Society no. 28. University, Ala.: University of Alabama Press.

———. 1961. Contrastive accent and contrastive stress. *Language* 37: 83–96. Reprinted in Bolinger 1965, pp. 101–17.

———. 1964. Intonation as a universal. In Horace G. Lunt, ed., *Proceedings of the Ninth International Congress of Linguists, Cambridge, Mass.*, 1962, pp. 833–48. The Hague: Mouton.

———. 1965. *Forms of English*. Edited by Isamu Abe and Tetsuya Kanekiyo. Cambridge, Mass.: Harvard University Press.

———. 1972a. Accent is predictable (if you're a mind-reader). *Language* 48: 633–44.

———. 1972b. *Degree Words*. The Hague: Mouton.

———, ed. 1972c. *Intonation: Selected Readings*. Harmondsworth, Eng.: Penguin.

———. 1977a. Another glance at main clause phenomena. *Language* 53: 511–19.

———. 1977b. *Meaning and Form*. London: Longman.

———. 1977c. Review of Schmerling 1976. *The Finite String* (*American Journal of Computational Linguistics*) 14, no. 5: 2–24.

———. 1977d. Transitivity and spatiality: the passive of prepositional verbs. In Adam Makkai, Valerie Makkai, and Luigi Heilmann, eds., *Linguistics at the Crossroads*, pp. 57–78. Padua: Liviana Editrice; Lake Bluff, Ill.: Jupiter Press.

———. 1978. Intonation across languages. In Joseph H. Greenberg, ed., *Universals of Human Language*, vol. 2, *Phonology*, pp. 471–524. Stanford, Calif.: Stanford University Press.

———. 1980–81. An uncouth preposition. *Boletín de Filología* (Universidad de Chile) 31: 625–32.

———. 1981a. Consonance, dissonance, and grammaticality: the case of *wanna. Language and Communication* 1: 189–206.

———. 1981b. *Two Kinds of Vowels, Two Kinds of Rhythm*. Bloomington: Indiana University Linguistics Club.

———. 1982. The network tone of voice. *Journal of Broadcasting* 26: 725–28.

———. 1984. Intonational signals of subordination. In Claudia Brugman and Monica Macaulay, eds., *Proceedings of the Tenth Annual Meeting of the Berkeley Linguistics Society, Feb. 17–20, 1984*, pp. 401–14. Berkeley, Calif.: Berkeley Linguistics Society.

———. 1985. Two views of accent. *Journal of Linguistics* 21: 79–123. Reprinted in Gussenhoven et al. 1987, pp. 51–105.

———. 1986. *Intonation and Its Parts: Melody in Spoken English*. Stanford, Calif.: Stanford University Press.

———. 1987a. More views on "Two views of accent." In Gussenhoven et al. 1987, pp. 124–46.

———. 1987b. The remarkable double *is. English Today*, January, pp. 39–40.

Bouton, Lawrence F. 1982. Stem polarity and tag intonation in the derivation of the imperative tag. In Robinson Schneider, Kevin Tuite, and Robert Chametzky, eds., *Papers from the Parasession on Nondeclaratives*, pp. 23–42. Chicago: Chicago Linguistic Society.

Brazil, David, Malcolm Coulthard, and Catherine Johns. 1980. *Discourse Intonation and Language Teaching.* London: Longman.

Brend, Ruth M. 1975. Male-female intonation patterns in American English. In Barrie Thorne and Nancy Henley, eds., *Language and Sex: Difference and Dominance,* pp. 84–87. Rowley, Mass.: Newbury House.

Brown, Gillian, Karen L. Currie, and Joanne Kenworthy. 1980. *Questions of Intonation.* London: Croom Helm.

Brown, Penelope, and Stephen Levinson. 1978. Universals in language usage: politeness phenomena. In Esther N. Goody, ed., *Questions and Politeness: Strategies in Social Interaction,* pp. 56–324. Cambridge, Eng.: Cambridge University Press.

Browne, Wayles, and Anuška Nakić. 1975. The intonation of questions in Serbo-Croatian and English. In Rudolf Filipović, ed., *Contrastive Analysis of English and Serbo-Croatian,* vol. 1, pp. 172–79. Zagreb: Faculty of Philosophy, University of Zagreb.

Camarata, Stephen. 1988. Iconicity in semantics: a case of suprasegmental marking in the acquisition of the English plural. Paper at Child Language Research Forum, Stanford University, Apr. 10.

Carlson, Lauri. 1984. *'Well' in Dialogue Games: A Discourse Analysis of the Interjection 'Well' in Idealized Conversation.* Amsterdam: Benjamins.

Chafe, Wallace. 1976. Givenness, contrastiveness, definiteness, subjects, topics, and points of view. In Charles N. Li, ed., *Subject and Topic,* pp. 25–55. New York: Academic Press.

———. 1980. The deployment of consciousness in the production of a narrative. In Wallace Chafe, ed., *The Pear Stories: Cognitive, Cultural, and Linguistic Aspects of Narrative Production.* Norwood, N.J.: Ablex.

Ching, Marvin K. L. 1982. The question intonation in assertions. *American Speech* 57: 95–107.

Chisholm, William S., Jr., and Louis T. Milic. 1974. *The English Language: Form and Use.* New York: McKay.

Chomsky, Noam, and Morris Halle. 1968. *The Sound Pattern of English.* New York: Harper and Row.

Classe, André. 1939. *The Rhythm of English Prose.* Oxford: Blackwell.

Clumeck, Harold. 1977. Topics in the acquisition of Mandarin phonology: a case study. *Papers and Reports on Child Language Development* (Stanford University) 14: 37–73.

Cohen, Antonie. 1972. Some observations on the pitch of questions. In Albert Valdman, ed., *Papers in Linguistics and Phonetics to the Memory of Pierre Delattre,* pp. 97–103. The Hague: Mouton.

Cooper, William E., and John M. Sorensen. 1981. *Fundamental Frequency in Sentence Production.* Berlin: Springer-Verlag.

Couper-Kuhlen, Elizabeth. 1984. A new look at contrastive intonation. In Richard J. Watts and Urs Weidmann, eds., *Modes of Interpretation: Essays Presented to Ernst Leisi,* pp. 137–58. Tübingen: Gunter Narr Verlag.

Coustenoble, Hélène N., and Lilias E. Armstrong. 1934. *Studies in French Intonation.* Cambridge, Eng.: Heffer.

Cruttenden, Alan. 1974. An experiment involving comprehension of intonation of children from 7 to 10. *Journal of Child Language* 1: 221–32.

————. 1981. Falls and rises: meanings and universals. *Journal of Linguistics* 17: 77–91.

————. 1982. How long does intonation acquisition take? *Papers and Reports on Child Language Development* (Stanford University) 21: 112–18. (Material cited is from an earlier, unpublished draft of this paper.)

————. 1985. Intonation comprehension in ten-year-olds. *Journal of Child Language* 12: 643–61.

Crystal, David, and D. Davy. 1975. *Advanced Conversational English*. London: Longman.

Cutler, Anne, and S. D. Isard. 1980. The production of prosody. In B. Butterworth, ed., *Language Production*, pp. 245–69. London: Academic Press.

Cutler, Anne, and D. R. Ladd, eds. 1983. *Prosody: Models and Measurements*. Berlin: Springer-Verlag.

Cutler, Anne, and David Swinney. 1987. Prosody and the development of comprehension. *Journal of Child Language* 14: 145–67.

Dahbany-Miraglia, Dina. 1985. How to address your spouse in Judeo Yemeni. Unpublished paper.

Daneš, František. 1960. Sentence intonation from a functional point of view. *Word* 16: 34–54.

Dascălu, Laurenția. 1971. Some remarks on enumerative intonation in Romanian. *Revue Roumaine de Linguistique* 16: 401–10.

————. 1974. On the "parenthetical" intonation in Romanian. *Revue Roumaine de Linguistique* 19: 231–48.

————. 1975. What are you asking about? (on the intonation of emphasis in "yes-no" questions). *Revue Roumaine de Linguistique* 20: 477–80.

————. 1979. On the intonation of questions in Romanian: the rising pattern. *Revue Roumaine de Linguistique* 24: 35–44.

————. 1980. A "reminding" wh-question and its intonation in Romanian. *Revue Roumaine de Linguistique* 25: 123–28.

de Pijper, Jan Roelof. 1983. *Modelling British English Intonation*. Dordrecht: Foris.

D'Eugenio, Antonio. 1976. The intonation systems of Italian and English. *Rassegna Italiana di Linguistica Applicata* 8, no. 1: 57–85.

Dik, Simon, et al. 1980. On the typology of focus phenomena. *GLOT* (*Leids Taalkundig Bulletin*) 3, nos. 3, 4: 41–74.

Eckert, Penelope. Forthcoming. Social polarization and the choice of linguistic variants. In Penelope Eckert, ed., *New Ways of Analyzing Sound Change*. New York: Academic Press.

Edelsky, Carole. 1979. Question intonation and sex roles. *Language in Society* 8: 15–32.

Ekman, Paul. 1979. About brows: emotional and conversational signals. In M. von Cranach, K. Foppa, W. Lepenies, and D. Ploog, eds., *Human Ethology*, pp. 169–249. Cambridge, Eng.: Cambridge University Press.

————, ed. 1982. *Emotion in the Human Face*, 2d ed. Cambridge, Eng.: Cambridge University Press.

Elliott, Dale E. 1974. Toward a grammar of exclamations. *Foundations of Language* 11: 231–46.

Emeneau, M. B. 1956. India as a linguistic area. *Language* 32: 2–16.

Emmory, Karen. 1984. The intonation system of Toba Batak. In Paul Schachter, ed., *UCLA Occasional Papers in Linguistics* 5: 37–58. Los Angeles: University of California.

Faure, Georges. 1973. La description phonologique des systèmes prosodiques. In Grundstrom and Léon 1973, pp. 1–16.

Fernald, Anne. 1984. The perceptual and affective salience of mothers' speech to infants. In L. Feagans, C. Garvey, and R. Golinkoff, eds., *The Origins and Growth of Communication*, pp. 5–29. Norwood, N.J.: Ablex.

Fernald, Anne, and Thomas Simon. 1984. Expanded intonation contours in mothers' speech to newborns. *Developmental Psychology* 20: 104–13.

Foldvik, Arne Kjell. 1981. Voice quality in Norwegian dialects. In Thorstein Fretheim, ed., *Nordic Prosody II: Papers from a Symposium*, pp. 228–32. Lund: Tapir.

Fónagy, Ivan. 1969. Métaphores d'intonation et changements d'intonation. *Bulletin de la Société de Linguistique de Paris* 64, no. 1: 22–42.

————. 1971–72. Le signe conventionnel motivé. *La Linguistique* 7: 55–80.

————. 1982. Prolégomènes a une caractérologie vocale. In *Voix: carrefour de la personnalité: Communications du Congrès Scientifique, Bordeaux, Oct. 15–17, 1981*, pp. 75–95. Paris: Commission de l'Information.

Fox, Anthony. 1982. Remarks on intonation and "Ausrahmung" in German. *Journal of Linguistics* 18: 89–106.

————. 1984. Subordinating and co-ordinating intonation structures in the articulation of discourse. In Gibbon and Richter 1984, pp. 120–33.

Fretheim, Thorstein. 1984. What is accent and what is stress in East Norwegian sentence prosody? Unpublished paper.

Fries, C. C. 1964. On the intonation of yes-no questions in English. In David Abercrombie et al., eds., *In Honour of Daniel Jones: Papers Contributed on the Occasion of His Eightieth Birthday*, pp. 242–54. London: Longman.

Fuchs, Anna. 1984. "Deaccenting" and "default accent." In Gibbon and Richter 1984, pp. 134–64.

Fuchs, Eugen. 1935. *Zur Intonation des englisches Fragesatzes*. Bonn: H. Ludwig.

Galligan, Roslyn. 1987. Intonation with single words: purposive and grammatical use. *Journal of Child Language* 14: 1–21.

Gårding, Eva. 1984. Chinese and Swedish in a generative model of intonation. In Claes-Christian Elert et al., eds., *Nordic Prosody III, Papers from a Symposium*, pp. 79–91. Stockholm: Almqvist and Wiksell.

————. 1985. Constancy and variation in Standard Chinese tonal patterns. *Lund University Department of Linguistics Working Papers* 28: 19–51.

Gårding, Eva, Zhāng Jiālù, and Jan-Olof Svantesson. 1983. A generative model for tone and intonation in Standard Chinese. *Lund University Department of Linguistics Working Papers* 25: 53–65.

Geluykens, Ronald. 1987. Intonation and speech act type: an experimental approach to rising intonation in queclaratives. *Journal of Pragmatics* 11: 483–94.

Gibbon, Dafydd. 1981. A new look at intonation syntax and semantics. In Allan James and Paul Westney, eds., *New Linguistic Impulses in Foreign Language Teaching*, pp. 71–98. Tübingen: Gunter Narr Verlag.

Gibbon, Dafydd, and Helmut Richter, eds. 1984. *Intonation, Accent, and Rhythm: Studies in Discourse Phonology*. Berlin: De Gruyter.

Givón, Talmy. 1979. *On Understanding Grammar*. New York: Academic Press.

Glasgow, George M. 1952. A semantic index of vocal pitch. *Speech Monographs* 19: 64–68.

Greenbaum, Sidney, and Charles F. Meyer. 1982. Ellipsis and coordination: norms and preferences. *Language and Communication* 2: 137–49.

Grundstrom, Allan. 1973. L'intonation des questions en français standard. In Grundstrom and Léon 1973, pp. 19–50.

Grundstrom, Allan, and Pierre R. Léon, eds. 1973. *Interrogation et intonation en français standard et en français canadien*. Montreal: Didier.

Gumperz, John J. 1982. *Discourse Strategies*. Cambridge, Eng.: Cambridge University Press.

Gumperz, John J., T. C. Jupp, and Celia Roberts. 1979. Crosstalk, text to accompany BBC film. Southall, Middlesex: National Centre for Industrial Language Training.

Gussenhoven, Carlos. 1983. Focus, mode and the nucleus. *Journal of Linguistics* 19: 377–417. Reprinted in Gussenhoven et al. 1987, pp. 1–50.

———. 1985. Two views of accent: a reply. *Journal of Linguistics* 21: 125–38. Reprinted in Gussenhoven et al. 1987, pp. 108–23.

Gussenhoven, Carlos, Dwight Bolinger, and C. E. Keijsper. 1987. *On Accent*. Bloomington: Indiana University Linguistics Club.

Hadding, Kerstin, and M. Studdert-Kennedy. 1964. An experimental study of some intonation contours. *Phonetica* 11: 175–85.

Haiman, John. 1983. Iconic and economic motivation. *Language* 59: 781–819.

Hall, Edwin T., Jr. 1955. The anthropology of manners. *Scientific American*, April, pp. 84–90.

't Hart, J. 1984. A phonetic approach to intonation: from pitch contours to intonation patterns. In Gibbon and Richter 1984, pp. 193–202.

Haugen, Einar, and Martin Joos. 1952. Tone and intonation in East Norwegian. *Acta Philologica Scandinavica* 22: 41–64.

Heritage, John. 1984. A change-of-state token and aspects of its sequential placement. In J. Maxwell Atkinson and John Heritage, eds., *Structures of Social Action: Studies in Conversation Analysis*, pp. 299–345. Cambridge, Eng.: Cambridge University Press.

Hermann, Eduard. 1942. Probleme der Frage. Nachrichten von der Akademie der Wissenschaften in Göttingen. *Philologisch-Historische Klasse*, nos. 3, 4.

Hines, Carole P. 1978. Well . . . In Michel Paradis, ed., *The Fourth LACUS Forum 1977*, pp. 308–18. Columbia, S.C.: Hornbeam.

———. 1979. Lexical integrity: *good, great,* and *well*. In Wolfgang Wölck and Paul L. Garvin, eds., *The Fifth LACUS Forum 1978*, pp. 134–41. Columbia, S.C.: Hornbeam.

———. 1980. *As well* and *as well as*. In William C. McCormack and Herbert J. Izzo, eds., *The Sixth LACUS Forum 1979*, pp. 170–76. Columbia, S.C.: Hornbeam.

448   *References Cited*

Hopper, Paul J., and Sandra A. Thompson. 1985. The iconicity of the universal categories "noun" and "verb." In John Haiman, ed., *Iconicity in Syntax*, pp. 151–83. Amsterdam and Philadelphia: Benjamins.

Houck, Noël. 1984. The pragmatics of tag questions: a model for epistemic speaker-hearer acts. Ph.D. dissertation, University of Southern California.

Hyman, Larry. 1978. Word demarcation. In Joseph Greenberg, ed., *Universals of Human Language*, vol. 2, *Phonology*, pp. 443–70. Stanford, Calif.: Stanford University Press.

Iannucci, David, and David Dodd. 1980. The development of some aspects of quantifier negation in children. *Papers and Reports on Child Language Development* (Stanford University) 19: 88–94.

Iivonen, Antti. 1978. Is there interrogative intonation in Finnish? In Eva Gårding, Gösta Bruce, and Robert Bannert, eds., *Nordic Prosody: Papers from a Symposium*, pp. 43–53. Lund: Department of Linguistics, Lund University.

James, Deborah. 1972. Some aspects of the syntax and semantics of interjections. In P. Peranteau, J. N. Levi, and G. C. Phares, eds., *Papers from the 8th Regional Meeting of the Chicago Linguistic Society*, pp. 242–51. Chicago: Chicago Linguistic Society.

———. 1974. *The Syntax and Semantics of Some English Interjections*. Ph.D. dissertation, University of Michigan, 1973. University of Michigan Papers in Linguistics no. 1.

———. 1978. The use of *oh, ah, say,* and *well* in relation to a number of grammatical phenomena. *Papers in Linguistics* (Edmonton, Can., and Carbondale, Ill.) 11, no. 3–4: 517–35.

Jarman, Eric, and Alan Cruttenden. 1976. Belfast intonation and the myth of the fall. *Journal of the International Phonetic Association* 6, no. 1: 4–12.

Jassem, Wiktor, and Dafydd Gibbon. 1980. Re-defining English accent and stress. *Journal of the International Phonetic Association* 10, nos. 1–2: 2–16.

Jespersen, Otto. 1928. *A Modern English Grammar on Historical Principles*. Part III: *Syntax*, vol. 2. London: Allen and Unwin.

Jones, Daniel. 1956. *An Outline of English Phonetics*. New York: Dutton.

Katz, Jerrold, and Paul Postal. 1964. *An Integrated Theory of Linguistic Descriptions*. Cambridge, Mass.: MIT Press.

Keijsper, C. E. 1983. Comparing Dutch and Russian pitch contours. *Russian Linguistics* 7: 101–54.

Kenworthy, Joanne. 1978. The intonation of questions in one variety of Scottish English. *Lingua* 44: 267–82.

Key, Harold. 1961. Phonotactics of Cayuvava. *International Journal of American Linguistics* 27: 143–50.

Key, Mary Ritchie. 1975. *Male/Female Language*. Metuchen, N.J.: Scarecrow Press.

Klein-Andreu, Flora, ed. 1983. *Discourse Perspectives on Syntax*. New York: Academic Press.

Knowles, Gerald. 1984. Variable strategies in intonation. In Gibbon and Richter 1984, pp. 226–42.

Kontra, Miklós, and Mária Gósy. 1987. Interference in intonation: notes on Hungarian Americans. In Ilah Fleming, ed., *The Thirteenth LACUS Forum 1986*, pp. 136–45. Columbia, S.C.: Hornbeam.

Kuiper, Koenraad, and Douglas Haggo. 1984. Livestock auctions, oral poetry, and ordinary language. *Language in Society* 13: 205–34.

Kvavik, Karen. 1974. An analysis of sentence-initial and final intonational data in two Spanish dialects. *Journal of Phonetics* 2: 351–61.

———. 1976. Research and pedagogical materials on Spanish intonation: a re-examination. *Hispania* 59: 406–17.

———. 1984. On Spanish fall-rise intonations. In Donald F. Solá, ed., *Language in the Americas, Proceedings of the Ninth PILEI Symposium, Ithaca, N.Y.,* pp. 167–87. Ithaca, N.Y.: Language Policy Research Program, Latin American Studies Program, Cornell University.

———. 1988. Is there a Spanish imperative intonation? In Robert M. Hammond and Melvyn C. Resnick, eds., *Studies in Caribbean Spanish Dialectology.* Washington, D.C.: Georgetown University Press.

Ladd, D. R. 1980. *The Structure of Intonational Meaning.* Bloomington: Indiana University Press.

———. 1983. *Even*, focus, and normal stress. *Journal of Semantics* 2: 157–70.

Lakoff, Robin. 1973a. Questionable answers and answerable questions. In Braj B. Kachru et al., eds., *Issues in Linguistics: Papers in Honor of Henry and Renée Kahane*, pp. 453–67. Urbana: University of Illinois Press.

———. 1973b. Language and woman's place. *Language in Society* 2: 45–79.

Leed, Richard L. 1965. A contrastive analysis of Russian and English intonation contours. *Slavic and East European Journal* 9: 62–75.

Lehiste, Ilse, and William S.-Y. Wang. 1976. Perception of sentence boundaries with and without semantic information. In Wolfgang U. Dressler and Oskar E. Pfeiffer, eds., *Phonologica 1967, Akten der dritten Internationalen Phonologie-Tagung.* Vienna.

Liberman, Mark, and A. Prince. 1977. On stress and linguistic rhythm. *Linguistic Inquiry* 8: 249–336.

Lieberman, Philip. 1967. *Intonation, Perception, and Language.* MIT research monograph no. 38. Cambridge, Mass.: MIT Press.

Lindau, Mona. 1984. Testing a model for Hausa intonation. *Lund University Department of Linguistics Working Papers* 27: 145–63.

Lindsey, Geoffrey. 1981. Intonation and pragmatics. *Journal of the International Phonetic Association* 11, no. 1: 2–21.

Loi Corvetto, Ines. 1982. L'intonazione nell'arabo siriano. *Lingua e Stile* 17: 371–93.

———. 1983. Saggio di Fonologia dell'arabo siriano. *Annali della Facoltà di Magistero, Università di Cagliari,* Quaderno n. 21.

Macafee, Caroline. 1983. *Glasgow.* Amsterdam and Philadelphia: Benjamins.

Malone, Kemp. 1926. Pitch patterns in English. *Studies in Philology* 23: 371–79.

Marchand, Hans. 1969. *The Categories and Types of Present-day English Word Formation.* Munich: C. H. Beck.

Marek, Bogusław. 1987. *The Pragmatics of Intonation.* Lublin: Redakcja Wydawnictw KUL.

Martin, Howard Rodney. 1977. *The Prosodic and Paralinguistic Analysis of Dramatic Speech: A Practical System.* Natural Language Studies no. 24. Ann Arbor: Phonetics Laboratory, University of Michigan.

Maury, Nicole, and Phyllis Wren. 1973. L'interrogation mélodique en français canadien de l'Ontario. In Grundstrom and Léon 1973, pp. 101–22.

McCawley, Noriko A. 1973. Boy! Is syntax easy! In Claudia Corum, T. Cedric Smith-Stark, and Ann Weiser, eds., *Papers from the Ninth Regional Meeting of the Chicago Linguistic Society*, pp. 369–77. Chicago: Chicago Linguistic Society.

McClure, J. D. 1980. Western Scottish intonation: a preliminary study. In Waugh and van Schooneveld 1980, pp. 201–17.

McConnell-Ginet, Sally. 1983. Intonation in a man's world. In Barrie Thorne, Cheris Kramarae, and Nancy Henley, eds., *Language, Gender, and Society*, pp. 70–88. Rowley, Mass.: Newbury House.

McCormack, William C. 1984. Intonation and foreigner talk. In Robert A. Hall, Jr., ed., *The Eleventh LACUS Forum 1984*, pp. 101–12. Columbia, S.C.: Hornbeam.

Miller, W. R., and S. Ervin. 1964. The development of grammar in child language. In Ursula Bellugi and Roger Brown, eds., *The Acquisition of Language*. Monographs of the Society for Research in Child Development no. 29. Chicago: University of Chicago Press.

Modini, Paul. 1982. Semantic-syntactic disparity. In Paul Modini, *Syntactic Questions from a Functional Perspective*. Published by the author, GPO Box 2510, Sydney NSW 2001, Australia.

Morton, Eugene S. 1986. Sound symbolism and its role in non-human vertebrate communication. Paper at Sound Symbolism Symposium, University of California, Berkeley, Jan. 16–18.

Nash, Rose, and Anthony Mulac. 1980. The intonation of verifiability. In Waugh and van Schooneveld 1980, pp. 219–41.

Nässlin, Siv. 1984. *The English Tag Question: A Study of Sentences Containing Tags of the Type 'isn't it?,' 'is it?'* Stockholm: Almqvist and Wiksell.

Navarro, Tomás. 1944. *Manual de entonación española*. New York: Hispanic Institute in the U.S.

Nemni, Monique. 1981. L'Identification de l'incise par l'intonation. In Pierre Léon and Mario Rossi, eds., *Problèmes de prosodie*, vol. 2, *Expérimentations, modèles et fonctions*, pp. 103–11. Ottawa: Didier.

Nosek, Jiří. 1973. Parenthesis in modern colloquial English. *Prague Studies in English* 15: 99–116.

Oakeshott-Taylor, John. 1984. Factuality and intonation. *Journal of Linguistics* 20: 1–21.

Odé, Cecilia. 1986. Towards a perceptual analysis of Russian intonation. In A. A. Barentsen, B. N. Groen, and R. Sprenger, eds., *Dutch Studies in Russian Linguistics*, pp. 395–442. Amsterdam: Rodopi.

Ohala, John J. 1983. Cross-language use of pitch: an ethological view. *Phonetica* 40: 1–18.

———. 1984. An ethological perspective on common cross-language utilization of Fo of voice. *Phonetica* 41: 1–16.

Olsen, Carroll L. 1975. *Grave* vs. *agudo* in two dialects of Spanish: a study in voice register and intonation. *Journal of the International Phonetic Association* 5: 84–91.

Oomen, Ursula. 1979. Structural properties of English exclamatory sentences. *Folia Linguistica* 13, no. 1, 2: 159–74.

Östman, Jan-Ola. 1981 (completed 1986). Pragmatics as implicitness: An analysis of question particles in Solf Swedish, with implications for the study of passive clauses and the language of persuasion. Ph.D. dissertation, University of California, Berkeley.

Papoušek, M., and H. Papoušek. 1981. Musical elements in the infant's vocalizations: their significance for communication, cognition, and creativity. In L. Lipsin, ed., *Advances in Infancy Research*, vol. 1, pp. 163–224. New Brunswick, N.J.: Ablex.

Pellowe, John, and Val Jones. 1978. On intonational variability in Tyneside speech. In Peter Trudgill, ed., *Sociolinguistic Patterns in British English*, pp. 101–21. London: Edward Arnold.

Penfield, Joyce. 1984. Prosodic patterns: some hypotheses and findings from fieldwork. In Jacob Ornstein-Galicia, ed., *Form and Function in Chicano English*, pp. 49–59. Rowley, Mass.: Newbury House.

Petecka, Janina. 1985. A study of question intonation in Polish. *Lund University Department of Linguistics Working Papers* 28: 151–73.

Pike, K. L. 1945. *The Intonation of American English*. Ann Arbor: University of Michigan Press.

Pye, Clifton. 1983. Mayan telegraphese: intonational determinants of inflectional development in Quiché Mayan. *Language* 59: 583–604.

Quirk, Randolph, Sidney Greenbaum, Geoffrey Leech, and Jan Svartvik. 1972. *A Grammar of Contemporary English*. New York and London: Seminar Press.

Ross, J. R. 1975. Where to do things with words. In Peter Cole and Jerry L. Morgan, eds., *Syntax and Semantics*, vol. 3, *Speech Acts*, pp. 233–56. New York: Academic Press.

Sachs, Jacqueline. 1975. Cues to the identification of sex in children's speech. In Barrie Thorne and Nancy Henley, eds., *Language and Sex: Difference and Dominance*, pp. 152–71. Rowley, Mass.: Newbury House.

Sadock, J. M. 1970. Whimperatives. In Jerrold M. Sadock and Anthony L. Vanek, eds., *Studies Presented to Robert B. Lees by His Students*, pp. 223–35. Edmonton: Linguistics Research, Inc.

Samarin, William. 1952. Intonation in tone languages. *African Studies* 11, no. 1: 80–82.

Scherer, Klaus R., D. R. Ladd, and Kim E. A. Silverman. 1984. Vocal cues to speaker affect: testing two models. *Journal of the Acoustical Society of America* 76: 1346–56.

Schiff, Naomi B., and Ira M. Ventry. 1976. Communication problems in hearing children of deaf parents. *Journal of Speech and Hearing Disorders* 41: 348–58.

Schiffrin, Deborah. 1985. Conversational coherence: the role of *well*. *Language* 61: 640–67.

Schmerling, Susan. 1976. *Aspects of English Sentence Stress*. Austin: University of Texas Press.

Schubiger, Maria. 1958. *English Intonation, Its Form and Function*. Tübingen: Max Niemeyer.

———. 1959. The expanded form of the verb and intonation. *English Studies* 40, no. 4: 1–6.

———. 1965. English intonation and German modal particles. *Phonetica* 12: 66–84. Reprinted in Bolinger 1972c, pp. 175–93.

———. 1980. English intonation and German modal particles II: a comparative study. In Waugh and van Schooneveld 1980, pp. 279–98.

Séguinot, Candace. 1979. The intonation of yes-no questions. In Pierre Léon and Philippe Martin, eds., *Toronto English*, pp. 129–41. Ottawa: Didier.

Selkirk, Elisabeth O. 1980. *On Prosodic Structure and Its Relation to Syntactic Structure*. Bloomington: Indiana University Linguistics Club.

Shakhbagova, D. A. 1982. *Varieties of English Pronunciation*. Moscow: Višča Skola.

Shapiro, Barbara E., and Martha Danly. 1985. The role of the right hemisphere in the control of speech prosody in propositional and affective contexts. *Brain and Language* 25: 19–36.

Shapiro, Norman R. 1979. Is is is. *Verbatim* 6, no. 2: 12.

Shen, Xiao-nan. 1986. Tone, stress, and intonation in Mandarin Chinese. Ph.D. dissertation, University of California, Berkeley.

Siertsema, Bertha. 1962. Timbre, pitch and intonation. *Lingua* 11: 388–98.

Silva-Corvalán, Carmen. 1983. On the interaction of word order and intonation: some OV constructions in Spanish. In Klein-Andreu, 1983, pp. 117–40.

Sperber, Dan, and Deirdre Wilson. 1986. *Relevance: Communication and Cognition*. Cambridge, Mass.: Harvard University Press.

Stenström, Anna-Brita. 1984. Questions and responses in English conversation. *Lund Studies in English 68*. Lund: CWK Gleerup.

Stevick, Robert D. 1967. Scribal notation of prosodic features in *The Parker Chronicle*. *Journal of English Linguistics* 1: 57–66.

Stockwell, Robert P., and J. Donald Bowen. 1965. *The Sounds of English and Spanish*. Chicago: University of Chicago Press.

Studdert-Kennedy, Michael. 1983. Review of H. W. Dechert and M. Raupach, eds., *Temporal Variables in Speech: Studies in Honour of Frieda Goldman-Eisler* (The Hague: Mouton, 1980). In Haskins Laboratories Status Report on Speech Research SR-74/75, pp. 201–7.

Šustikova, T. V. 1970. K voprosu ob intanacii russkoj razgovornoj reči. *Russkaja razgovornaja reč*, Saratov, pp. 47–55.

Svartvik, Jan. 1980. Well in conversation. In Sidney Greenbaum, Geoffrey Leech, and Jan Svartvik, eds., *Studies in English Linguistics for Randolph Quirk*, pp. 167–77. London: Longman.

Svensson, Jan. 1976. Reportindicators and other parentheticals. In Fred Karlsson, ed., *Papers from the Third Scandinavian Conference of Linguistics*, pp. 369–80. Turku: Text Linguistics Research Group, Academy of Finland.

Sweet, Henry. 1898. *A New English Grammar, Logical and Historical*. Part III: Syntax. Oxford: Clarendon Press.

Tannen, Deborah. 1984. *Conversational Style: Analyzing Talk Among Friends*. Norwood, N.J.: Ablex.

Tarone, Elaine E. 1973. Aspects of English in Black speech. *American Speech* 48: 29–36.

't Hart, *see under* Hart

Thompson, Sandra T. 1983. Grammar and discourse: the English detached participial clause. In Klein-Andreu 1983, pp. 43–65.

Thorsen, Nina. 1983. Standard Danish sentence intonation—phonetic data and their representation. *Folia Linguistica* 17: 187–220.

Turner, G. W. 1973. *Stylistics*. Harmondsworth, Eng.: Penguin.

Ultan, Russell. 1969. Some general characteristics of interrogative systems. *Working Papers in Language Universals* (Stanford University) 1: 41–63.

Vaissière, Jacqueline. 1983. Language dependent prosodic features. In Cutler and Ladd 1983, pp. 53–66.

Varga, László. 1975. *A Contrastive Analysis of English and Hungarian Sentence Prosody*. Budapest: Linguistics Institute of the Hungarian Academy of Sciences and Center for Applied Linguistics.

———. 1983. Hungarian sentence prosody: an outline. *Folia Linguistica* 17: 117–51.

———. 1988. The stylized fall in Hungarian. Unpublished paper.

Vende, K. 1971. Perception of tonal contours of questions: gradual or categorical? Paper at Seventh International Congress on Acoustics, Budapest (no. 19 C6 in *Proceedings*).

Watanabe, Kazuyuki. 1977. Is the early drop the norm for British English? *Bulletin of the Phonetic Society of Japan* 155: 7–9.

———. 1978. Comparison of British and American intonation patterns in broadcasting. In Masao Inishi, ed., *Study of Sounds*, vol. 18, pp. 183–92. Tokyo: Phonetic Society of Japan.

Waugh, Linda, and C. H. van Schooneveld. 1980. *The Melody of Language*. Baltimore, Md.: University Park Press.

Weeks, Thelma. 1982. Intonation as an early marker of meaning. In Mary Ritchie Key, ed., *Nonverbal Communication Today: Current Research*, pp. 157–68. Berlin: Mouton.

Weintraub, Sandra, Marsel Mesulam, and Laura Kramer. 1981. Disturbances in prosody: a right-hemisphere contribution to language. *Archives of Neurology* 38: 742–44.

Wescott, Roger W. 1971. Labio-velarity and derogation in English: a study in phonosemic correlation. *American Speech* 46: 123–37. Reprinted in Roger W. Wescott, *Sound and Sense: Linguistic Essays on Phonosemic Subjects*, pp. 362–77. Lake Bluff, Ill.: Jupiter Press, 1980.

Wieman, Leslie. 1975. The stress pattern of early child language. Ph.D. dissertation, University of Washington. Eric document 111 201.

Wierzbicka, Anna. 1976. Particles and linguistic relativity. *International Review of Slavic Linguistics* 1: 327–68.

———. 1980. *Lingua Mentalis*. New York: Academic Press.

———. 1986. A semantic metalanguage for the description and comparison of illocutionary meanings. *Journal of Pragmatics* 10: 67–107.

Wilson, Deirdre, and Dan Sperber. 1979. Ordered entailments: an alternative to presuppositional theories. In C.-K. Oh and D. Dineen, eds., *Syntax and Semantics*, vol. 11, *Presuppositions*, pp. 299–323. New York: Academic Press.

Yokoyama, Olga T. 1986. *Discourse and Word Order*. Amsterdam: Benjamins.

Ziv, Yael. 1985. Remarks on parentheticals and functional grammar. In A. M. Bolkestein, C. de Groot, and J. L. Mackenzie, eds., *Syntax and Pragmatics in Functional Grammar*, series 1, pp. 181–213. Providence, R.I.: Foris Publications.

Index of Profiles and Contours

(Last Two Profiles Only)

General Index

In this index an "f" after a number indicates a separate reference on the next page, and an "ff" indicates separate references on the next two pages. A continuous discussion over two or more pages is indicated by a span of page numbers, e.g., "pp. 57–58." Passim is used for a cluster of references in close but not consecutive sequence.

can, 15, 308; tag, 154–58 passim, 160, 169, 408–12. See also *could*
Canadians, 39
can't, 15; tag, 164, 410, 412
Carlson, Lauri, 269, 271, 276–77, 301, 312–15, 321, 431, 433–35
case: *in case*, 177; *in that case*, 429
Casella, Ginny, 392
cataphoric: *well* for, 330–31
categorical, 161–62, 343
cause: vs. motive, 199
caution, 251
Cayuvava, 82
certain, 357
Chafe, Wallace, 343, 423
challenge, 414; *well* for, 324, 327
Chicano, 48
Chinese, 3, 12, 49–50, 61, 433
Ching, Marvin, 38
Chisholm, William S., Jr., 191
Chomsky, Noam, 235
Christ (exclamation), 276, 290, 296
Christmas tree: accent on, 218
Classe, André, 68
classifier, 227
clause, subordinate (dependent), 70–71, 74, 171–200, 203–9
clearly, 90–91
cleft sentence, 28, 116, 140, 163, 203–5, 429–30
climax, 74, 214, 216, 237, 246–47, 288, 367–68, 377–79, 392–97, 403, 405, 413
Clumeck, Harold, 12
coaxing, 131. See also appeal
cognitive verb: as tag, 156, 164
Cohen, Antonie, 105
coherence: *well* for, 332
cohesion: between stem and tag, 130–32, 154–55
coinage of words, 215
Colby, Robert, 429
collocation, 201, 219; *oh* in, 271, 281; oaths with, 284; *well* in, 319, 327
come: *come again?*, 138; *come come!*, 254, 338; *come now!*, 292
comma, 83f, 90–95 passim, 184, 191, 193–94, 200, 270, 272
command, 50, 62, 81, 98–100, 113, 138, 144, 146, 150–58 passim. See also directive; imperative
comment, 190–91. See also rheme
communicative dynamism, 394
comparative degree: in exclamations, 260

compound, 95, 215–28, 394, 396; freezing of, 220; intermediate, 245, 430
concession, 177, 345–46, 348; *well* for, 323–24, 329
conciliation, 377
concord: in negation, 160
condescension, 159, 295
Condition, 232–34
condition that, on, 177
conditional clause, 153, 172–82; as imperative tag, 157; like question, 157, 172–73, 182; position of, 180; as exclamation, 260
conduciveness: reverse polarity for, 116, 124–25, 131–32, 163, 168, 170, 257, 263, 411, 427
confirmation, 101–2, 383–87
conformatory, 383
congratulation, self-, 382, 384, 388
conjunction, see subordinator
consequence, 175, 180, 373–74, 378–79; *well* for, 323, 327
constituency, 96–97
constituent: immediate, 85, 95, 186; discontinuous, 95; major, 238; nested, 352, 354, 361–62, 364
construction: compounds with, 219
consuetudinal, 317, 412
content word, 71, 74
contextual effects, 357–58, 436
continuation: Profile B for, 335
continuity: *well* for, 321–23
contradiction: contradiction contour, 135; *well* for, 325, 331
contradictory, see contrary
contrary: vs. contradictory, 341–42
contrastive, 217, 234, 243, 246–47, 257, 341–49, 354, 391, 436, 440
contribution: vs. *contributory*, accent on, 216
control, 145–46, 150, 384. See also speaker dominance
convention, 1, 20, 28, 37, 64, 106, 226, 264, 284, 286. See also arbitrariness
coordination: of adjectives, 200–201; intonation of, 207
coreference, 387, 389. See also anaphoric
Cornulier, Benoît de, 355
corpus, 301–2, 432, 434
could, 307; in tag, 408, 410, 413
Coulthard, Malcolm, 389, 422, 439
count: vs. mass, 251
counterassertion, 346–47, 365–66, 368, 374, 437

Ekman, Paul, 13, 266
Elliott, Dale E., 431
ellipsis, 92–96, 118, 123–27, 424
else 'otherwise,' 184
Emeneau, M. B., 216
Emmory, Karen, 60
emotion, 64, 68, 241, 283, 293, 298, 412, 426. See also curiosity
empty words, 217, 221, 241
English: American, 4; Modern vs. Old, 10; Southern U.S., 24, 37–38, 46; British and American, 28–32, 64, 136, 421; vs. other languages, 40; Northern U.S., 62; Black, 173
entailment, 350–64
enthusiasm, 426
entreaty, 159, 410
epistemic, 17, 254, 306–8, 310, 315–16, 326, 329, 410, 422, 434–35. See also future of probability
Ervin, S., 14
Estonian, 424
euphony, 424
evaluation, 425–26
even, 43, 73, 177–79, 375
ever: in exclamations, 254, 257
exasperation, 298
exception-taking: *oh* for, 280–81
excitement, 412
exclamation, 144, 248–99; unmarked by syntax, 249, 255–56; marked by syntax, 249–63 passim; degree expression as, 250; question as, 295–96; *well* with, 311
expectation: *well* for, 321–23
expostulation, 296
extenuation: *well* for, 327–28
extraposition, 163. See also fronting
eyebrows, 13, 73, 102, 130, 156, 174, 182f
eyes: contact, 418, 432; aversion of, 434
Ezra (Bible), 291

face redress, 302
facial expression, 264, 266, 283–89 passim, 338, 413, 439; *well* with, 334
factuality, 380–91
fall, terminal, 33f, 50, 206, 278, 286, 347, 425, 430
falling-rising, 57
falsetto, 22–24, 106, 174, 178, 335
familiarity, 94, 147–48, 198, 234–35, 358, 363. See also old stuff
fandamntastic, 430
fault: accent on, 403

Faure, Georges, 424
feedback, conversational, 38, 50
Fernald, Anne, 11, 14, 20, 24, 421
Fifth Column, 215
figure (verb), 387; *it figures*, 381, 388, 390
finality, 60, 81, 102–3, 153, 183, 207–8, 287, 289, 335, 413; semantic completeness, 52. See also settled-unsettled
finger: gesture with, 414f
Finnish, 424, 433
flagpole (compound), 216
focus, 49, 67, 203, 232–40 passim, 351–60, 364, 403, 439; broad, 237f, 345, 354, 356, 363; narrow, 238, 345, 354, 430–31; "polarity focus," 437. See also under accent
Foldvik, Arne Kjell, 22
Fónagy, Ivan, 23, 28, 64
football scores, 17–18
for X to, 199
foreground, 352, 358
foregrounding, 333–34. See also salience
forestress, see backshift
formality, 289
formula, verbal, 147, 159–61, 176, 253, 280–81, 308–9, 311, 373. See also idiom; routine; stereotype
forsooth, 127
fossilization, 220, 222–23, 252
Fox, Anthony, 207, 422, 429
frame sentence, 185–92 passim
French, 14, 78, 206, 354–55, 424
frequency code, 1
Fretheim, Thorstein, 27
Fries, C. C., 105
from, 376–77
fronting, 186, 189; emotive, 48
Frost, Robert, 69
Fuchs, Anna, 244
Fuchs, Eugen, 111–12, 424
fudge (exclamation), 271
full well, 309
function word, 70, 74, 89
furthermore, 319
fusion, 119, 121, 129, 165–67, 187, 200–201, 215, 218, 220, 227–28; 409, 430; *oh* with, 270, 273–75, 283; *well* with, 305, 334. See also nexus
future of probability, 370–71

Galligan, Roslyn, 13, 18–20
gangrene: accent in, 214
gapping, 95

peremptory, 164
perfect tense, 246
performative, 296
permission, 151, 158, 307
perplexity, 293
perseveration, 76–79, 106, 114, 207–9
person (empty word), 85
persuasion, 161–69
Petecka, Janina, 51
Petterson, Thore, 42
petulance, 411
phew, 431
phonestheme, 284, 289
phooey, 284
phrase: stress on, 215–18, 222; vs. compound, 220, 225–28
piece (empty word), 221–22
pied piping, 109
pigsty, 361
Pike, K. L., 220, 344
pitch, fundamental, 27; demarcative, 81–97 passim; high, in questions, 103. See also height
placation, 345
place (empty word), 221, 230
plateau, 36
platitude, 80
pleading, 345, 413–14, 438. See also appeal
please, 150f, 155, 157–60, 167ff, 274, 328, 413–14, 416, 429
point action, 304
polarity, 272; in tag questions, 116–23, 131–32; reversal of, 251–53, 411, 427; polarity expressions, 263, 438; in tagged imperatives, 408–18. See also conduciveness; intensive
Polish, 50–51
pooh, 289
poor: in exclamations, 283
possibility, 308
possible, 346–47
Postal, Paul, 154
potential for accent, 214f, 219
pout, 334
power, accent of, 55, 57, 213f, 220–24, 235, 237, 246, 292–93, 341, 356–57, 362–63, 368, 375, 383, 392–95, 413, 436
pragmatics, 68, 144, 300; pragmatic meaning, 74–75; of discourse, 78; vs. grammar, 79
Prague School, 394
predicate: subject and, 96–97
Predicate, 228–38 passim, 242–44

prepositional phrase, 91; fronting with wh, 109; accent on preposition, 366, 368, 376, 378
presentative, 240–41, 243, 404
presupposition, 204, 358, 365–66, 371–72, 383, 426
Prince, A., 422
probability, 370–71
processing: left-to-right, 352, 359–60, 362; ease of, 357–58
proclaiming: accent for, 333–34, 337
profanity, 254–55, 290–91; *oh* with, 276
prompting: *well* for, 329–30
pronouncement, 146–47
proper name, 240, 244, 344
protest, 290
prototype, 157–58, 418
pseudocleft, 96, 203
pues (Spanish), 435
pull-up expression, 262, 271, 274, 310
pump: (compounds with), 226
punctuation, 10, 69–70, 92, 106, 184, 215
purposive act: with *because*, 199
Pye, Clifton, 18

quantifier, 375
que, qu' (French), 78
querulousness, 298
question, 39–40, 49, 98–143; declarative as, 50; original, 51, 102; in Arabic, 53; vs. command, 57, 152f, 159, 162–63, 179; rhetorical, 101, 251, 257, 263, 391; like condition, 172–73; clues to, 176–77; as parenthesis, 188; like series, 206; defiant, 328; vs. suspensive, 424. See also under adverbial
—accosting, 108, 135
—alternative, 40, 59, 113–16, 137, 205–6, 328
—complementary, 40, 57, 112–13, 136f, 179
—ditto, 133, 136–37
—echo, 47, 51, 101, 133–36, 138, 142–43, 254, 257f, 423
—quoted, 133, 140–43; as echo, 142
—reclamatory, 33, 37, 50, 107, 110–11, 138–40, 169; tagged, 116; restricted, 138; general, 138, 265
—reflex, 133–36
—reminder, 47, 140
—reprise, 40, 60, 133–43
—wh, 33, 40, 105–12, 165, 298, 365f, 401; A + C with, 23: in Anglo-Irish, 37; terminal fall with, 47, 51; AC with, 51;